CW00546756

Laurence Fleming is hin children of the Raj'. He is an artist, landscape designer and author of *The English Garden*, *Old English Villages*, *Roberto Burle Marx: A Portrait* and *The Entokil Man: The Life of Harold Maxwell-Lefroy* as well as several novels. He lives in St Leonard's-on-Sea, East Sussex.

Mark Tully is also a last child of the Raj, and returned to India as a journalist. He was the BBC's Indian Bureau Chief for over 20 years. He still lives in New Delhi, and was knighted in 2002.

Last Children of the Raj

To
All the Memsahibs
and to
Jean Fleming and Patience Tully
in particular

Last Children *of the* Raj

British Childhoods in India

VOLUME 2: 1939–1950

Compiled by
Laurence Fleming

Introduction by
Mark Tully

Dexter Haven Publishing
LONDON

Paperback edition first published 2016 by
Dexter Haven Publishing
Curtain House
134–146 Curtain Road
London
EC2A 3AR

Original hardback edition first published 2004 by Radcliffe Press Ltd

ISBNs   Volume 1: 978-1-903660-20-1
        Volume 2: 978-1-903660-21-8

A full CIP record for this book is available from the British Library

Typeset in Caslon by Dexter Haven Associates Ltd, London
Printed and bound in Sweden by ScandBook

Contents

Acknowledgments

This book owes its existence to the generosity of:

Mrs Janet Axelrad, Miss Jessica Baker, Mr Philip Banham, Mrs Jane Barclay, Mr Marcus Barclay, Mrs Patricia Bartoszewicz, Mme Paul Beauvais, Mr James Benthall, Mr Patrick Berthoud, Professor John Blandy, Mr Bob Bragg, Captain Peter Broadbent, Mr Barry Bryson, Mrs Ernest Campbell, Mrs Sheila Carmichael, Mrs Noel Cash, Mrs Joan Carter, Mr Bill Charles, Mr Leonard Crosfield, Mrs Ann Davies, Miss Ruth Dear, Mrs Shirley Donald, Mrs Patrick Evans, Lady Egremont, Mr Dan Ferris, Mrs Philip Fielden, Mrs Marion Forward, Mrs William Fleming, Mr Adrian Frith, Mr Patrick Gibson, Mrs John Haddon, Mrs Valerie Harrison, Mrs Andrew Hastings, Mrs E.M. Hedley, Mr Robin Herbert, Mrs John Heyworth, Mrs Betty Higgins, Mrs Sonya Hilton, Miss Gloria Hollins, Mr and Mrs Thomas Inglis, Miss Elizabeth Ireland, Miss Lavender Jamieson, Mr John Judge, Dr Desmond Kelly, Mr and Mrs John Langley, Dr Jonathan Lawley, Mr Jeremy and Miss Jane Lemmon, Mrs Hugh Leslie, Mr John Lethbridge, Mrs Sheila Litt, Mrs Jane Lloyd, Mrs Dorothy Lowes, Mrs W.P.G. Maclachlan, Mr Robin Mallinson, Mr Robert Matthews, Mrs Betsy McCutcheon, Mrs Christopher McDowall, Mr Michael Muller, Mr Malcolm Murphy, Mrs Barbara Norton-Amor, Mme Maurice Nosley, Mr Ian O'Leary, Mr Tony Orchard, Mr John Pakenham-Walsh, Mr Blake Pinnell, Mrs Maeve Reid, Lady Rix, Mrs Lynette Sherwood, Mrs Russell Smallwood, Mr and Mrs John Smith, Mr Paddy Smith, Mr Graham Spencer, Mr Patrick Stevenage, Mr David Thom, Mrs Lorna Thomson, Mrs Yoma Ullman, Mr Francis Valentine, Mrs Janet Valentine, Miss Hilary Virgo, Mrs Ruth Walker, Mrs Margaret White, Mrs Auriol Young and two anonymous donors.

The extracts from *A Memoir of a Childhood in India* by Yoma Crosfield Ullman appear with her permission. Extracts from *The Way It Was* by John Langley appear with his permission. Extracts by Laurence Fleming from *Harrow on the Hooghly* by John Lethbridge appear with his permission. Extracts from *A Railway Family in India* by Patrick Hugh Stevenage appear with his permission. The picture of the *Stratheden* on page 57 appears by courtesy of the Peninsular & Oriental Steam Navigation Company.

Our warmest thanks are due to Susan Lynn for all her valuable help in the early stages of this project.

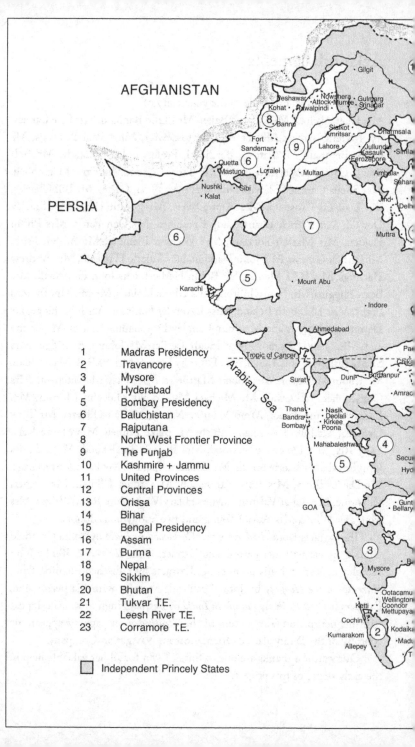

1   Madras Presidency
2   Travancore
3   Mysore
4   Hyderabad
5   Bombay Presidency
6   Baluchistan
7   Rajputana
8   North West Frontier Province
9   The Punjab
10   Kashmire + Jammu
11   United Provinces
12   Central Provinces
13   Orissa
14   Bihar
15   Bengal Presidency
16   Assam
17   Burma
18   Nepal
19   Sikkim
20   Bhutan
21   Tukvar T.E.
22   Leesh River T.E.
23   Corramore T.E.

Independent Princely States

The Indian Empire 1936

500 Miles

T I B E T

CHINA

River Brahmaputra

ver Indus

anges
ndari Glacier
orie
aini Tal
athgodam

Pasighat

Sadiya · Chapua
· Dibrugarh · Ledo
Digboi

⑲
Yatung
⑳

ly

⑱

now·
wnpore·

Gangtok
Darjeeling
Kalimpong

Myitikina

⑳

⑯

Gauhati · Dimapur

Kohima

Allahabad ·
Mirzapur·

⑭

⑮

Saidpur
Darbhanga
Patna·

Shillong

Bhamo

Parbatipur

Haflong

·Katha

Dhanbad

Goalundo

·Aijal

Imphal

·Tamu

Lashio

·Schwebo ·Lashio

⑫

· Kamptee

· Hazaribagh

Asansol

Kanchrapara
Barrackpore
· Dum Dum
· Calcutta

Faridpur

·Tiddim

·Chandpur

Chittagong

Monywa

Maymyo
Mandalay

Akyab

⑰

Tropic of Cancer

Taunggyi Loilem
· Kalaw

⑬

Puri
Gopalpur

Bay of Bengal

Yenangyaung ·
Toungoo ·
·Prome

River Godavari

· River Kistna

Pegu

· Moulmein

Rangoon
Syriam

River Irrawaddy

Madras

ddalore

kuppam
ambur

ANDAMAN
ISLANDS

0

NICOBAR
ISLANDS

YLON

SUMATRA

above A group of children at St Andrew's Colonial Homes, Kalimpong, now Dr Graham's Homes, with Dr Graham himself on the right. About 1930.

left A small space in the midst of South Park Street Cemetery, into which the surviving plaques and broken tombs from the French Cemetery were moved on its closure in 1979. Carried out by BACSA with sponsorship from the Total petrol company.

'We Few, We Happy Few…'

Mark Tully

The first definition of Anglo-Indian in the *Oxford Dictionary* I have kept from my school-days is not Eurasian, it is 'Of British birth but living or having lived for a long time in India'. According to that definition almost all of us last children of the Raj were born Anglo-Indians, in that our parents lived for a long time in India. Often we came from families like my mother's with relatives in India for several generations. Our families were apparently a separate and significant group, otherwise we wouldn't have found a place in the dictionary. The only other Anglos in my dictionary are Americans and French. So what was so special and so significant about our families?

Perhaps we were considered special because of India's position in the Empire and in the imperial imagination, including the imagination of Queen Victoria. India was, as everyone knows, described as the jewel in the crown. Victoria declared herself Empress of India. India only shared with Ireland the grandeur of a Viceroy; other members of the Empire were governed by holders of titles more remote from the crown. Our families maintained the British presence in that very special country. They were fiercely proud of their Britishness, and determined to retain their identity and culture. In Calcutta, where I was born, they ensured that we children knew from the earliest days that we were not Indian. I remember our British nanny, when she caught me learning to count in Hindustani from the driver, hitting me across the head and saying, 'That's not your language, that's the servants' language.' Her sole responsibility seemed to be ensuring that we did not get too close to the servants, and that we only played with other British children. Of course nothing was watertight. My grandfather used to undermine my nanny by teaching us nursery rhymes in Hindustani.

Both Nanny and Grandpa came back to me at the BBC appointments board I faced after applying for my first job in India. When the board suggested I must know an Indian language, all I could say was, 'I can say "Little Miss Muffet" and "Humpty Dumpty" in Hindustani.' To my amazement, instead of being rejected as someone with a misspent childhood and a misplaced sense of humour, I got the job.

Of course not every child of the Raj had a nanny as strict as mine. As a general rule you could say that the further parents were away from the big metropolitan cities and sizeable European communities the more likely it was that their children would pick up an Indian language. Rudyard Kipling was an exception to that rule. Although he was a young child in Bombay, he and his sister spent so much time with their *ayah* and bearer that they had to be reminded to speak in English when they came into the dining room to eat with their parents. But even a man as sympathetic to India and Indians as Lockwood Kipling deposited his son in Britain at the age of five-and-a-half. Children of my generation were spared that fate by the shortage of transport during World War II, but we were sent off to appropriately anglicised boarding schools in the hills at a similar age.

The authorities did not encourage Britons to think of themselves as belonging to India, but as above it. It was believed that we needed to convince Indians we were a different race, that our culture was superior, if our claim to the right to rule was to be accepted. This was why settling in India was discouraged. According to the tradition of Anglo-India, a man would spend his working life in India but was expected to retire 'back home' to demonstrate where he really belonged. 'Staying on' was not encouraged. This policy bore fruit during the negotiations for independence. There were no settler communities like those which caused such difficulties in Kenya and Rhodesia when it came to negotiating their independence.

The separateness of the British in India fitted in with Indian culture. To Indians we became another caste, and, in accordance with that complicated system, we developed our castes within our caste. I was born into the *boxwallah*, or businessman, caste, not by any means the Brahmins of British India. Within that caste there were sub-castes, with a recognised pecking-order. I remember my father often used to say that a Calcutta businessman who had risen to a distinguished position still had a chip on his shoulder because 'he'd come out in retail'. That was considered an inferior caste among *boxwallahs*.

But although our parents lived as a separate race, they were Anglo-Indians, in that they were touched by India. No one who lives in India for any length of time can remain unaffected by it. In fact it is, I believe, the very power of India's syncretic culture, its long history of absorbing other cultures, that made the British fear for their separate identity, fear that they too would be absorbed, if they did not erect barriers to protect themselves and their children, did not disapprove of those who 'stayed on' after retirement, and despise those who 'went native'. For me, and I am sure for many other children of the Raj, that strategy was not entirely successful. The very first day that I returned to India twenty years after leaving as a child the scent of the winter flowers in my hotel garden, the smoke from the *malis'*

Birthday party in a private garden, Tollygunge, January 1941. William Grice, Jane's brother, far left. Katharine Tully at front, Prudence Tully next but one to her, Mark Tully looking away.

cow-dung stoves, the pungent aroma of the food they were cooking, suddenly brought back my childhood. Those years in India seemed to race through my mind like an electric train. From that moment I knew that I had come home. Perhaps more understandably, when Kipling's sister Trix was taken away from India it was, she said, 'like a double death, like an avalanche that had swept away everything happy and familiar'. Trix belonged to India as well as Britain, she was Anglo-Indian as defined in my dictionary, and so I believe are we, the last children of the Raj.

left The Victoria Memorial in Calcutta. Designed by Sir William Emerson, it was built on the site of the old gaol and was opened by the Prince of Wales in 1921. (Ann Prowse)

below The old pontoon bridge over the Hooghly at Howrah. It was made in Scotland in the 1880s and towed out to India. It was still the only bridge in 1941. (Ann Prowse)

Glossary

almira	wardrobe
amah	Burmese nanny
anna	Indian coin, 16 to a rupee
armsuth	dried mango pulp
ashram	place of religious retreat
avatar	incarnation
ayah	Indian nanny
ayngyi, anghi	Burmese woman's blouse, jacket
babu	Indian clerk
babul	a tree, *Acacia arabica*
bagh	garden
baksheesh	gratuity, tip
balloowallah	owner of dancing bears
bandicoot	kind of large rat
bandobast	any kind of arrangement
baniyas	traders or shopkeepers
barfi, burfi	kind of sweet
basha	hut of woven bamboo
basti, bustee	village
begum	wife or mother of a Maharajah
bhil	marsh
bhiljeewallah	electrician
bhindi	okra, ladies' fingers
bhisti	water-carrier
bhotiya	Buddhist farmer, originally Tibetan
bhutta	maize
bidi, biri	small, pungent cigarette
bistra	bedding-roll
bobbachee, bovachee, bochi	cook
boda	bullock calf, bait for tigers
boxwallah	travelling tradesman; European in commerce
bulbul	brightly coloured bird
bungi	labourers' yokes for carrying loads
burkha	tent-like covering for Muslim women

burra . . . . senior, large
butties, hart butties . . . . hurricane lamps
cantonment . . . . urban area occupied only by military and Police
cha, gurram cha . . . . tea, hot tea
chapatti . . . . unleavened bread
chaprassi . . . . office messenger, peon
charpoy . . . . string bed on wooden frame
chatti . . . . earthenware water pot
chenar . . . . the Oriental Plane, *Platanus orientalis*
chibbutra, chabuttra . . . . raised platform in the garden
chikor . . . . small partridge
chini . . . . sugar
chinkara . . . . four-horned antelope
chokra . . . . boy or youngster
chota . . . . small
chota hazri . . . . early morning tea
chota peg . . . . small whisky
chowkidar . . . . night watchman
chuckla . . . . cobbler, shoemaker
chula . . . . kind of brazier
chula purdah . . . . Muslim seclusion for wives
chummery . . . . house shared by two or more bachelors
chunna . . . . kind of pea
coolie . . . . porter or workman, labourer
curriga, nay curriga . . . . can do, can not do
cutcha . . . . inferior
dah . . . . small sword, Burmese
dahl . . . . lentil sauce or soup
dak . . . . post
dandi . . . . litter carried on shoulders
deodar . . . . a tree, *Cedrus deodara*
dhirzi, durzi . . . . itinerant tailor
dhobi . . . . washerman, laundryman
dhooli, doli, doolie . . . . shoulder-borne litter; fly-proof cage
dhoti . . . . single-strip garment worn by Hindu men,
                                            with one end pulled through the legs to form
                                            'trousers'

dhurrie, dhurry . . . . cotton rug
Diwali. . . . . Hindi Festival of Lights
doodwallah . . . . milkman
Durbar . . . . Jubilee, Coronation, Wedding celebration of Kings, Maharajahs
durwan . . . . night watchman, messenger
fakir . . . . Hindu holy man, ascetic
feringhees . . . . strangers, foreigners, 'from beyond the pale'
gharry . . . . horse-drawn carriage
ghat. . . . . step, as down to a river; also steep hillside, as in Eastern or Western Ghats
ghee . . . . clarified butter
ghur . . . . raw molasses syrup
ghusal-khana . . . . bathroom
godowns . . . . store rooms
gooli, goolie . . . . a ball
goolie dunda. . . . . a game, tip-cat
gulab jaman . . . . kind of pudding
gully-gully man. . . . . conjuror coming on board at Port Said
gunny . . . . jute
hajji. . . . . one who had made the pilgrimage to Mecca
havildar. . . . . NCO in Indian Army
hookahs . . . . Indian pipes
howdah. . . . . canopied seat on elephant's back
hulwa . . . . kind of sweet
jamadar, jemadar. . . . . sweeper; also NCO in Indian Army
jampani. . . . . 'dandi' carrier
jellabee . . . . kind of sweet
jheel, gheel . . . . reedy lakes, marshes
jutewallahs . . . . Europeans in the jute trade, frequently Scottish
kabaddi. . . . . a game, similar to Tom Tiddler's Ground
kalassi . . . . boatman
kansama, khansama . . . . cook
karezes . . . . underground wells, joined
kebabwallah . . . . seller of kebabs
khabari . . . . thief

khana, khanna. . . . . dinner, food in general; also a room
khitmagar . . . . butler
kukri . . . . Gurkha fighting knife
kul-kul . . . . kind of sweet
langur . . . . kind of monkey
lascars . . . . Indian crew on India-bound liners
lathi . . . . long, heavy baton, metal-tipped
layhee . . . . flour-and-water paste
lotha . . . . clay water pot
ludoo . . . . kind of sweet
lungyi, longgyi . . . . long 'skirt' worn by Burmese men
machan . . . . wooden observation platform at a tiger
                                    shoot
mahout . . . . elephant rider
maidan . . . . park or large meadow, open space
maither . . . . sweeper
makan . . . . butter
mali . . . . gardener
mangowallahs . . . . seller, sometimes grower, of mangoes
marg . . . . garden
masalchi, malchi . . . . washer up
mehterani . . . . sweeper
mela . . . . festival, celebration, party
moochie . . . . leather worker, cobbler
moonshi, munshi . . . . clerk, writer, teacher, esp. of language
muleteers . . . . mule riders, owners
mullah . . . . Islamic priest
murghi, moorghi . . . . chicken
mynah . . . . a bird that could be trained to speak
naan . . . . kind of bread
nappy, nappit . . . . barber
nawabs . . . . lords
neem . . . . a tree, *Melia indica*
neilghai, nilgai . . . . kind of deer
ngapi . . . . dried fish, Burmese
nimbu pani . . . . fresh lime juice and water
nullah . . . . ditch or stream

numdah . . . . small white Kashmiri rug

pan, pahn . . . . betel-leaves chewed as a stimulant

pandal. . . . . flower arch of welcome

pani. . . . . water

paniwallah . . . . water-carrier, washer-up

parata . . . . kind of bread

peon . . . . office messenger

pice. . . . . Indian coins, 4 to an anna

pinjamwallah . . . . one who renewed stuffing in pillows and
                                   mattresses

poongyi. . . . . Burmese Buddhist priest, monk

popadams . . . . crisp pancakes

puggri, puggaree . . . . cloth bound turban

puja. . . . . Hindu festival

pukka . . . . superior

punkah . . . . ceiling fan

punkahwallah . . . . punkah operator

purdah . . . . lit. curtain, Muslim seclusion of women

pwe. . . . . Burmese celebration, festival, party

rajahs . . . . lords, titled landowners

roti . . . . bread

sadhu . . . . Hindu holy man

sahib-log. . . . . principally: the British in India

sari . . . . Indian woman's garment, one long strip
                                   cunningly arranged

shamiyana, shamayana . . . . . very large tent

Sherpa . . . . race from high Himalayas, principally Nepal

shikar . . . . hunt, usually for tiger

shikara . . . . long, elegant Kashmiri boat

shola. . . . . woodland, large copse

sirdar. . . . . in charge of porters, travel arrangements

subadhar . . . . NCO in Indian Army

suttee . . . . burning of Hindu widows

syce. . . . . groom

tamasha. . . . . any kind of party

tatti, chatti . . . . matting or slatted blinds against the sun

thaka, tikki, tikka, gharry . . . small horse-drawn carriage

thana. . . . . Police station
tonga. . . . . small horse-drawn carriages
tongawallah . . . . tonga driver
topee. . . . . pith helmet worn by all Europeans
towdu . . . . rice husks, rice chaff
tum tum . . . . horse-drawn trap
tussore. . . . . kind of silk
waler. . . . . kind of horse
wallum . . . . a boat
Yuvaraj . . . . heir to a Maharajah
zebus. . . . . Indian cattle

I

1939

1 September	Germany invades Poland
29 September	Russia and Germany divide Poland
30 November	Russia invades Finland

At a quarter past eleven on the morning of Sunday 3 September 1939, the Prime Minister, Mr Neville Chamberlain, broadcast to the nation:

I am speaking to you from the Cabinet Room at Ten Downing Street. This morning the British Ambassador in Berlin handed the German Government a final note stating that, unless we heard from them by 11 o'clock that they were prepared at once to withdraw their troops from Poland, a state of war would exist between us. I have to tell you now that no such undertaking has been received and that consequently this country is at war with Germany.

You can imagine what a bitter blow it is to me that all my long struggle to win peace has failed. Yet I cannot believe that there is anything more, or anything different, that I could have done and that would have been more successful. Up to the very last, it would have been quite possible to have arranged a peaceful and honourable settlement between Germany and Poland. But Hitler would not have it. He had evidently made up his mind to attack Poland whatever happened and, although he now says he put forward reasonable proposals which were rejected by the Poles, that is not a true statement. The proposals were never shown to the Poles nor to us. And though they were announced in the German broadcast on Thursday night, Hitler did not wait to hear comments on them, but ordered his troops to cross the Polish frontier the next morning. His actions show convincingly that there is no chance of expecting that this man will ever give up his practice of using force to gain his will. He can only be stopped by force and we, and France, are today, in fulfilment of our obligations, going to the aid of Poland, who is so bravely resisting this wicked and unprovoked attack upon her people.

We have a clear conscience. We have done all that any country could do to establish peace, and a situation in which no word given by Germany's ruler could be trusted, and no people or country could feel itself safe, had become intolerable. And now that we have resolved to finish it, I know that you will all play your part with calmness and courage. At such a moment as this the assurances of support which we have received from the Empire are a source of profound encouragement to us.

When I have finished speaking, certain detailed announcements will be made on behalf of the Government. Give these your close attention. The Government have made plans under which it will be possible to carry on the work of the nation in the days of stress and strain that may be ahead. But these plans need your help. You may be taking your part in the fighting services, or as a volunteer in one of the branches of Civil Defence. If so you will report for duty in accordance with the instructions you receive. You may be engaged in work essential to the prosecution of war, or the maintenance of the life of the people in factories, in transport, in public utility concerns, or in the supply of other necessaries of life. If so, it is of vital importance that you should carry on with your jobs.

Now may God bless you all and may He defend the right. For it is evil things that we shall be fighting against, brute force, bad faith, injustice, oppression and persecution. And against them I am certain that the right will prevail.

JOHN BLANDY

My mother came home for the summer holidays of 1939, and I can still remember going to Church on the Sunday morning that war was declared. The next few days were hectic: we motored up and down to London to get passages and passports. I can remember the sky being filled with barrage balloons as we queued up in Petty France and there were gangs digging slit trenches in Hyde Park.

On 12 September we had a splendid lunch in the Grill Room at the Regent Palace Hotel: I wanted water, and the waiter asked 'Chateau la pompe?' Then we took a taxi to Tilbury, where we got on the old *Modasa*. I can still remember unpacking our things in our cabin. The voyage began rather disappointingly: we waited somewhere in the Thames estuary for our convoy to collect, but when we finally set off it was a very impressive fleet of about 40 merchant vessels and cargo boats. We stopped first at Gibraltar, a little sobered by hearing the news of the sinking of the *Victorious*. We were allowed ashore, and spent a happy afternoon shopping while the ship took on coal. I can remember how delighted my sister Helen was with the Chinese silk dressing gown that was bought for her.

From Gibraltar we called in at Malta and were taken round the sights and shown the huge gasometers on the skyline, which we were told were dummies, the real thing being safely underground. (This was, alas, not the case.) After Malta came the Suez Canal, and by this time even the children were playing mah jong to while away the boredom. The ship was still making a 'peacetime' voyage, and every now and again there would be a gala dinner with crackers and specially printed menu cards. The only difference was the blackout, which made below-decks very stuffy at night, so we slept on deck, woken only by the gang of sailors holy-stoning the deck who did not at all mind slyly watering a sleeping 12-year-old. We stopped of course at Port Said to buy the wrong sort of *topee* at Simon Artz and watch the *gully-gully* man do magic with chickens. There was another stop at Suez for coal, where we went ashore for a brief visit. A few days later we called in at Aden and bought a mah jong set and had coffee, and were taken to see the revolting manatee preserved in formaldehyde and advertised as a mermaid.

The next port of call was Cochin, but we did not go ashore: I can still remember its amazing greenness. We did stop at Colombo, where the ship stayed for three days, and we were taken to lunch at

Mount Lavinia and bought wooden elephants. Next stop Madras: I can remember swimming in a Club's swimming pool and going round a museum, but little else. Finally, after the six-week voyage, we came into the Bay of Bengal and before long the sea had turned yellow ochre with the silt from the Hooghly, and in the distance there appeared a tiny white pilot launch. To our delight, one of its few passengers was my father, whom we had not seen for two years. He had a very prickly moustache.

By the time we reached Calcutta it was dark and we were all tired. The next morning we went shopping for necessary clothes, and I can still remember the coming-back feeling as I saw the violent sunshine and smelt the long-forgotten smells: there is something about the first cranial nerve which makes it trigger memory. My very old friend, Habib, my father's bearer, had tears in his eyes: me too.

One of the delights of this period were the trips we made to interesting things that were going on. For example we all went round the Ordnance Depot, where we saw *topees* being constructed and watched ropes being tested to destruction. Once, we all went over the new Howrah Bridge, then under construction: there was a visit to a jute factory, and a tour round the Statesman printing works.

Perhaps of even more educational value were the days we spent at the Saturday Club, where there was swimming and the library: I read endlessly. My parents were never bothered with what I was reading, and I read indiscriminately: Edgar Wallace and Conan Doyle slipped down between Sacheverell Sitwell and Edgar Allan Poe. The only books I never read were those that were strongly recommended, a habit which, I fear, has remained. Among my companions in the Saturday Club swimming pool were the two sons of the French Ambassador. One day they failed to turn up. Later on we learned that the entire family had been interned: he had followed the Vichy Line and was regarded as a security risk. Ironically, it was my father's decision to have him put away.

Calcutta in those days, for a small boy with a bicycle, was safe and clean. I could lean my bike up against the wall of Hogg's Bazaar and mooch about, knowing it would be there on my return. I suspect this is not the case today. My parents were quite happy for me to cycle anywhere I wanted to go.

NICOLE WALBY

We had no roots in India – my father went out in 1937 with my mother and young sister, and my younger brother and I were left in England with Grandfather and an aunt.

Our most exciting journey was the trip out to India in 1939. My French mother had come home with my four-year-old sister for the summer holidays which we spent in France. War threats were rumbling, and when my French relations started losing the male staff to the Maginot Line, they insisted my mother return to England and rejoin my father in India. September saw the War declared, and in December we boarded the P&O *Stratheden*. It was felt that being a powerful ship, and faster than a submarine, we could sail on our own, zig-zagging to Gibraltar – my mother had met a sea captain on board who was going to join his ship in the Far East. He insisted we be trained for an emergency, and would wake us up at odd hours to see how quickly we could put on our life jackets and whether we knew exactly where our boat station was.

Port Said was the first revelation. As we arrived, a Sheikh on a magnificent white horse galloped alongside the ship on a strip of land leading to the port. I'm of the generation when Sheikhs on white horses were incredibly romantic, and to actually *see* one was breathtaking. We reached Bombay in January, and it had been a perfect voyage – constant sunshine, a vast swimming pool, excellent library, lots of friends – I hardly saw my family.

The next revelation was Bombay: the hordes of people, the calls of the street sellers, the different smells of spices and smoke and the colour – oh, the colour! I loved all these things immediately – then the vast train to carry us to Calcutta and days of journeying, gazing at the huge expanse of India: its glorious sunset, its elegant, slow-moving people and slow, steady buffaloes, seemingly relaxed, and a far cry from the rat-race.

Whilst my mother had been away, the flat in Calcutta had been let and my father had moved to the factory several miles down the Hooghly, past the jute mills etc. With our unexpected arrival, and until the our flat was free, we also moved to the factory – the compound contained several bungalows and tennis courts etc., and ran alongside the Hooghly. The paint factory itself lay beside the one and only road leading from Calcutta.

I'm glad we had this short time here, as not only did our tennis improve, but it was fascinating watching the funerals. First the cremation on high piles of wood, and then the ashes and flowers floating down the river.

The family home was in Ballygunge, Circular Road; we had a cook, a sweeper of a lower caste, who also looked after the dogs and was a delightful and very good-looking man, a houseman and houseboy. My mother would see the cook in the morning and plan the day's meals – she was very firm that lettuce etc. should only be washed in water, not 'pinky' (permanganate), and felt that a little local dirt immunised one! None of us were ever ill.

A house in Ballygunge, Calcutta, thought to have been a boarding school for girls at The New School. (Barbara Dixon)

Calcutta, though sprawling and crowded, was a warm-hearted place. I cycled everywhere on my own with no fear. One of my favourite spots was the covered market, where salesmen sat cross-legged at waist height off the ground, in tiny shops cheek-by-jowl with the next and crowded with their wares. I was with my mother once buying material, and she was bargaining for an end piece. The salesman suddenly said, 'Let's toss for it', which they did, and my mother won, and had it for free, much to his amusement and that of the other vendors around!

PADDY SMITH

My grandparents came out to India in 1938 to spend the cool-weather months with us. Apparently the understanding was that I would return with them to Britain in order to enter Cabin Hill, the preparatory school for Campbell College in Northern Ireland.

However, my parents, in view of the worsening situation in Europe, decided to keep me in India and send me to school in Darjeeling. So I spent one year at the Loreto Convent where they took boys of pre-prep school age, five to seven years old, and I have memories of being very well looked after by the Sisters and the Mother Superior. I believe that Mother Teresa was there in my time there, but unfortunately I cannot recall meeting her. She would have been in her last year, I think.

I entered the preparatory, or junior school, at St Paul's School in Darjeeling in 1939, a decision I was very grateful for then, and have been ever since. St Paul's had been founded in 1845 to provide, with other such schools, an English public-school education in India. The school was originally situated in Calcutta, but in 1864 moved to its splendid site on a hilltop overlooking Darjeeling and facing the magnificent Kanchenjunga massif.

Life at St Paul's was austere – in keeping with the English tradition of such schools. We were woken at 6.30 a.m. each morning by a gong, and started the day with a mad rush to bathe, change into day clothes (scratchy flannel shorts and itchy woollen jerseys), then *chota hazri* – a cup of tea and a biscuit – then PT in the icy morning air, chapel and then a proper breakfast before the routine of the day's lessons was begun. Prep was not a feature of junior school routine, and after the evening meal our time was our own, to play, relax or indulge in one's hobbies until bedtime.

The three terms in the eight-and-a-half-month year were Easter, Monsoon and Michaelmas. The end of the Easter term was marked by a short holiday, but the end of the monsoon term was followed by a longer break. As boys were not allowed home during the school year, only those whose parents were able to visit Darjeeling were allowed *exeat* from the school. However, those left at the school had a very pleasant interlude from schoolwork as the staff organised camps for the Cubs and Scouts, treks across the mountains to Sandakphu to view the Everest peaks more closely, and generally created an informal, relaxed atmosphere over the holiday period.

The parent of a friend of mine, John O'Brien, owned a tea garden, the Goomtee, near Kurseong, a few thousand feet below us. It was a delightful place, and warranted the description of 'garden'. I can still vividly recall the heady scent of the tea leaves in the drying rooms of the factory. I spent several of these short holidays at Goomtee and sometimes part of the cool-weather three-and-a-half-month holiday there as well.

In retrospect, I am amazed how quickly small boys can adapt themselves to a change in their routine. At home, in varying degrees, we enjoyed the very privileged life of a *chota-sahib* in India. We lived in large, comfortable homes, were waited on hand and foot by servants and had acres of ground to play in and all the facilities of one's father's Club at one's disposal – swimming, tennis, and, for the older boys, shooting duck by the local *jheels*, or lakes.

St Paul's put things in perspective in very short order. It did not matter who or what your father was. One jolly well had to muck in, and we soon realised that this was as it ought to be. This quickly engendered a lasting camaraderie and an intense pride in, and loyalty to, the school.

There were of course the not-so-good days. I recall the acute home-sickness we all suffered at the beginning of the long school year. Many of us took a little time to adjust to the change in altitude and suffered from various complaints – the most common being 'Darjeeling tummy', with its attendant risk of incurring the Matron's displeasure if one had a 'mishap' in consequence. A few of us, myself included, suffered from severe nosebleeds from time to time until we adjusted to the change in altitude.

JAMES BENTHALL

When war started, my father took lease of a house in Darjeeling, which became our real home until the end of 1944. Darjeeling is a sprawling town, spread along a long ridge, with the main town at about 6500 feet altitude. From the ridge, one looks down precipitous hillsides to the Teesta and Rangeet rivers several thousand feet below. Some of the more accessible slopes are covered by tea gardens, with their tea bushes neatly laid out. Beyond the rivers, one sees range upon range of foothills climbing up to the great mountains of

1944: The Kanchenjunga Range, with the town of Darjeeling in the foreground, the red spire of the popular Mount Everest Hotel bottom right. (Sheila Wright-Neville)

the Himalayas, with Kanchenjunga always dominant and drawing the eye when not covered by cloud. At the time, one could only get to Darjeeling from Calcutta by an overnight journey to Siliguri at the foot of the hills, followed by either a long and twisty car ride, climbing all the time, which children very often found sick-making, or the much slower approach by the famous Darjeeling Himalayan Railway, or 'toy train'. All the cars stopped in Darjeeling below the Chowrasta, and it was said that there were only two cars allowed on the other roads – the Governor's and the ambulance. I never saw either. Transport in the town was either by pony (small and scruffy), which could be hired then, as now, where the Calcutta Road left the Chowrasta, or by rickshaw. Darjeeling rickshaws were extraordinary, and needed to be. They were very smart, with good leather seats, and heavy-duty hoods for wet weather. They had very superior wheels, and a two-man push/pull bar in front and behind. They were manned by four Tibetans, who managed to carry two people up the very steep hills, and controlled their descent. The *rickshawwallahs* had a reputation for gambling, drinking and fighting. They were all controlled by a formidable Tibetan lady known to all as Annie, and their base was just below the Planters' Club. On arrival in Darjeeling by train or car, the trunks and suitcases were loaded on to the backs of hill women, who had a strap round their forehead and the bottom of the trunk. They then set off up the hill at a pace which was hard to match, even without a load. There was a story, which may have been apocryphal, that one woman carried a piano up the hill on her back! Everyone who was not unwell got used to walking.

Our home was Marjoree Villa, which was on the narrow ridge road running from the Chowrasta (a focal point, town square, parade ground, and meeting place) up to Jalapahar, where there was a military establishment. Going up beyond our house one first came to Terpsithia, where there was a junior school of sorts, and then, round a couple of bends, one came to The New School. Further on again was the famous St Paul's School, one of the great boys' schools of India. Then the Army barracks before the road eventually meets up with what used to be called the Calcutta Road, and then Ghoom, the highest point on the little Darjeeling Himalayan Railway.

Marjoree Villa was a semi-detached house with two living rooms downstairs and two bedrooms upstairs. In addition, there was a single-storey bedroom at one side of the house, with its own bathroom, and across a path and linked by a roof was another quite separate bedroom and bathroom (this was only rarely used, and we called it the Bus). The whole house had a corrugated iron roof, which made the most wonderful noise, especially in the single-storey rooms, in the monsoon rain, and even more thunderous when it hailed. The house was set a little above the road, with a small garden in front and a little more round the side by the Bus. Between the garden and the road was a fence with orange flowered *Abutilon* bushes. By the drive up to the house was a sort of rockery with *Rhododendron arboreum* trees at the top, with orchids growing on their branches. Stretching behind the Bus, and screening us from neighbours, was a long clump of dwarf bamboo. By the house were all scarlet *Pelagoniums*. Behind the house, the slopes of the ridge were largely rough, although partly cultivated in small terraces for maize and other crops. Here also the slopes were very steep. For some reason which I don't recall, at one time we had a donkey that lived on the slopes behind the house, until one day it slipped, and broke its neck on the Calcutta Road below. There was a pipeline carrying water from Ghoom to Darjeeling all along this slope, with a rough path more or less following the pipeline. On the road in front of the house again, there were two tracks zig-zagging down to lower levels, one from perhaps 50–100 yards down towards Darjeeling, and the other perhaps 30–40 yards up. At each junction there was a *pan* shop, not only selling *pan* but also tea, and all the usual roadside stall-holders' goods. Among these was *ghur*, a kind of lump molasses made from a palm. Occasionally we used to pluck up courage to buy some *ghur*, which was a great treat.

Darjeeling at that time was a safe place for small English children to roam. There were hazards. Among these were the storm drains. These were fearsome concrete affairs, running straight down the precipitous slopes for hundreds and hundreds, and perhaps thousands of feet, wide enough to accept a small child and foaming with water in the monsoon. It was sternly drummed into us that small children were often swept to their deaths in these, and I remember always treating them with great respect.

We used to wander, aged eight to ten, round the bazaar on our own, or with a friend, watching gold and silver workers hammering their metals, or *kukri*-makers demonstrating their knives, etc. This was quite a long way from our house, but I don't believe there was ever any possibility of danger from the marvellous hill people, whatever anti-British feeling there may have been at times in other parts of India. (Even there I doubt if British *children* were often in real danger.) In the other direction we used to roam all over the hillsides up to Jalapahar, mostly along the pipeline, where we used to make dens for ourselves in bracken, or clamber across the bridge supports where the pipe had to cross a gully. I certainly don't remember being frightened, except perhaps by a Tibetan monastery along the Calcutta Road. This seemed a rather forbidding place, especially after we found a skull in a cave in the hill above the monastery. Otherwise, it was a very free and happy existence. We sometimes visited other children, and once went to a birthday party in Government House (the summer residence of the Governor of Bengal, a magnificent white building with a blue dome). I remember a large ballroom with a gallery above, from which had been built, for the party, a wide canvas chute for children to slide down. Great fun, except that the canvas generated great heat and pain if the slide was not judged just right.

ANN BURKINSHAW

I must have been one of the earliest of the evacuees to arrive in Calcutta; there were very few other children of my own age around when I arrived just before Christmas 1939, and a big search had to be made before one or two companions were found for me. I was an early arrival because my mother happened to be in England when war broke out, and my father decided to get us both out as soon as possible. I was not quite 11 years old.

The voyage out on the SS *Strathnaver*, a P&O ship – from Southampton, I think – was uneventful in that there were no appearances of U-boats or hostile aircraft. The captain of the ship was apparently beside himself with worry at having so many children on board (no doubt his first experience of this), and did not take his clothes off until we reached Gibraltar. For us children, of course, the voyage was excitement from start to finish; a wonderful holiday with daily entertainment, swimming, film shows (I took myself to see Alice Faye in *Alexander's Ragtime Band* and was enthralled!), a fancy dress party and excursions ashore at Gibraltar, Port Said and Aden. The *Strathnaver* was a splendid 1930s ship – wide staircase, enormous state rooms and even a lift, all decorated like the cinemas of our youth. There was always a thrill at seeing the first sighting of land when approaching ports, and the slow progress through the Suez Canal, where there was greenery and activity on the western bank and arridness on the eastern, was a wonderful distraction, but the emerging coastline of India in the early morning sunshine – low blue hills rising from a shimmering sea against a pale-blue sky – was magic! Finally, the view of the Gateway of India and behind it the Taj Mahal Hotel, the port with all the ships in the dock, the noise and bustle of the docks, the coolies, the luggage and the greeters and meeters were the ingredients of an *Arabian Nights* fairy-story to a 10-year-old!

My mother and I were met by a business friend of my father's who took us to his flat on Malabar Hill – a road of large white houses with verandahs and gardens full of cannas – where we spent the day. In the evening he took us to Victoria Station – a magnificent Victorian edifice – to catch the train to Calcutta. There is nothing to match the atmosphere of an Indian railway station anywhere: the mêlée of people, the coolies carrying huge suitcases on their heads, the food sellers shouting 'Pan, biri, cha', the sleepers amongst whom one had to pick one's way, the railway staff shouting orders, the cacophony of sound, the smells, the noise of the steam engines whistling and belching and the sudden gusts of smoke which the engines emitted. Then there is the excitement of finding one's carriage, or watching the bearer bring in the bedrolls and make up the bunks, of getting in the ice boxes, of seeing the ferment of humanity on the platform from the safety of one's carriage and then warding off intruders. Waking up in the morning on the train was also enthralling – seeing the interminable plains and vegetation and mud huts and colourful people passing by and having breakfast in the restaurant car. It was such fun to have to get out at a station in the middle of nowhere and walk along to the restaurant car and then have a delicious meal of bacon and eggs and the most succulent of all bananas, those small fat ones! The primitive air-conditioning was intriguing – the ice box at the open door and its replenishment along the route. And finally, after two nights and a day, arrival at Howrah Station, with Father and the bearer waiting on the platform amid the mêlée of people and sounds. The last stage of the journey was by car – a Morris 10 horsepower – to 7/2 Burdwan Road, Alipore, bottom flat. There were the servants all lined up to greet us – even my old *ayah* whom mother had *not* asked to come back because she thought she would spoil me. Needless to say, she stayed! I remember my delight at seeing the *khitmagar*, the *bochi*, the *mali* and the sweeper. I was home.

Then it was Christmas, and we were off to Puri, for me the first of almost annual visits. This was a very heaven for an 11-year-old – swimming, surfing, elephant rides, visits to the town to see the Jagannath Temple and the Monkey Temple, watching the fishermen in their pointed hats bring in the catches, the BNR Hotel and my first experience of a fruit machine! Christmas dinner was just like Christmas dinner in England – turkey and Christmas pudding, crackers and paper hats, Christmas trees and tinsel. The memory of arriving at Puri at 6 o'clock in the morning is still vivid – everywhere tinted with a peachy hue from the rising sun, the cool, soft air, the walk to the hotel along a sandy road, the coolies following with the luggage on the heads. But early morning in India was always magical.

Christmas over, the problem of education raised its head. A local school was not considered – 'You will get a "chi-chi" accent' – so my father took advice from the Education Secretary, whom he met in Delhi. Poole School in Simla was 1000 miles away – two nights and a day in a train, followed by a three-hour car journey from the foothills – but all European children went there! Poole School was housed on Jacko Hill and surrounded by monkeys – despite the netting around the verandahs. I have been terrified of monkeys ever since. Miss Poole, a tall, somewhat horsey-looking lady of uncertain age, ran her school with the assistance of three or four ladies. There were probably about 30 girls, mostly boarders, but some day-girls whose fathers were on the Viceroy's staff and in Simla during the hot weather. Simla, of course, was lovely, much like Darjeeling, and my companions were very pleasant – out-of-school activities like riding picnics out in the hills were fun, but the teaching was abysmal. Things got worse as the months of 1940 wore on, because Miss Poole's entire thoughts were focussed on her Austrian gentleman friend, who was interned in the local gaol. We only saw her when she came and asked us to contribute to the purchase of eau-de-cologne and ink for the poor chap; the eau-de-cologne was to compensate for the lack of washing facilities in the gaol. As I was not learning anything, I asked my mother to remove me. My mother was dispatched to check my complaints, agreed they were justified, and took me back to Calcutta! And back to square one. There was a rumour that a school was to be set up in Calcutta, so as a temporary measure I went to a small day-school in Calcutta run by the wife of one of my father's office colleagues.

YOMA CROSFIELD

When we arrived in Bombay at the end of 1939, we took the train to Calcutta. But, once there, we found the Company's plans had changed. We were to go instead to Burma. As we sailed away down the Hooghly River from Calcutta to Rangoon, we passed the ship carrying all our belongings from England going in the opposite direction. Months passed before we saw them again.

When we arrived in Rangoon, bereft of all our luggage, Harold Roper, the Burmah Oil Company's General Manager in the East, met us at the dock. He had not only made temporary arrangements so that we could move straight into our company house, but had brought with him Christmas presents for all of us, not forgetting Nanny.

My new home was near the university district of the city in an enclave of BOC houses known as Greenbank. It had a wide view over the Inya Lake, which had a wooded, indented shoreline. My father must have liked the house, because just before we left for India in 1941 he took a whole series of photos of it. Like the house in Chittagong, it was large, but whereas the house in Chittagong

Yoma in front of the Crosfield's BOC house in Greenbank, Rangoon, Burma, 1940.

had been built of brick, with a touch of half-timbering, this one gleamed with white stucco. It was squared off with a flat roof and wide, horizontal eaves that stuck out just below the roof balustrade and again over the ground-floor windows. The windows were tall and narrow, with a semicircle at the top. The stairwell had its own tower, which was attached to the side of the house and projected above the roofline. The main part of the house was on two floors, but a single-storey wing with garages and servants' quarters extended from the back. A large verandah overlooked the lake on the ground floor. Steps below it lead down a steep grassy bank to a tennis court, after which the ground sloped down to the lake. At the shore, there was a small jetty with a punt moored to it.

My earliest memory of Rangoon concerns the punt. I loved to sit on the damp, cool bottom of the boat and look over the edge at the little waves on the lake, or perch on the steps at the water's edge, watching the punt yaw at its mooring and hoping to get sprayed by an unusually big wave.

I loved to swim, because the water was cool. Rangoon was a humid 80–85 degrees Fahrenheit that could rise to 100 degrees Fahrenheit and rarely fell lower. During the day I always wore a cotton handkerchief tied around my neck to catch the sweat off my face and neck. Nanny would wring it out from time to time. It had a welcome clamminess when she tied it back on.

My clothes were changed three times every day, because they became limp with sweat almost as soon as I put them on. My mother brought a good many of them with her from England, so to begin with I had beautifully smocked dresses. As the War cut off supplies, my clothes became much simpler. My everyday dresses and sunsuits were made of cotton, stiff with starch, which made them stand pleasantly away from my hot skin. For the late afternoons, when I might be shown briefly to the grown-ups at tennis or drinks parties, I had dresses made of Liberty silk, pronounced as one word. I did not know for decades about the shop in London after which the silk was named. These dresses were not as cool to wear, but I consciously enjoyed their luxurious softness against my skin. I loathed my very best dresses, one in particular. It was made of stiff white organdy, with flounces around the skirt. When the dress was starched, the waist seam dug into me miserably. The only redeeming feature of that dress was a bunch of crimson wooden cherries at the waist. I wore it for a carefully posed professional photo portrait in which I appear to be standing on thin air, like an unusually robust young saint.

For the birthday tea, a tablecloth is spread on the ground with plates of food scattered on it, surely including Marmite sandwiches, then the staple food of the British child. Around it, rugs are spread out. The lake shimmers in the background. Nine small visitors, most of whom will later be at school with me in India, eye the feast. Five Burmese nannies in traditional dress attend them. I am the only one with an English nanny. She sits on the rug, visibly uncomfortable, her considerable bulk constrained in her tight European dress. The Burmese women, in their comfortably relaxed blouses and sarongs, sit with practised ease and elegance, the European children clustered around their knees.

A children's tea party at Greenbank, Rangoon, Burma, in early 1940. Yoma Crosfield's nanny, Dorothy Manooch, is at far left with Yoma to her right. All the other nannies are Burmese, and are wearing their national dress.

STAR STAUNTON

I returned home to a different world. Britain was at war. My father had rejoined his regiment. My step-mother came back in nurses' uniform, working full time in the Indian Military Hospital.

At 17, I was a year too young to join up, but now a job was available, one which, while it would earn me no pay, would give me a lot of interest and enable me to feel I was helping the war effort. A family friend, Colonel McKelroy, was a recruiting officer with the task of raising native forces to replace white soldiers needed in Egypt or Europe, and to assist in the many extra duties which the Army would now have to undertake in time of war. He kindly invited me to join his office and to accompany him, along with his wife, on the recruiting tours he would be making in the Punjab, Kulu, Kangra, Afghanistan and Tibet. Of course, I jumped at the chance.

Mrs McKelroy was a gentle, motherly, Irish woman who had left her heart in Dublin, where her two boys were in a boarding school. She was self-contained, and took little interest in the places or the people we met, whereas for me this year of my life is packed full of treasured memories, both of places and of people. We toured by car where cars would go, or, where they would not go, on horseback, with Mrs McKelroy riding in a *dandi*, a kind of sedan chair carried by coolies. I had not seen the dawn over Everest from Tiger Hill when I was an infant, but now as a girl of 17 there I was, going about from place to place in awe-inspiring country, high-up among what I have heard called 'the petticoats of God'. I believe I have been a deeper and more reverent woman all my life for that experience of being able, day after day, to 'lift up mine eyes unto the hills'.

Moreover, I had a job to do. The colonel made full use of me by sending me in among the women, where he himself could not go, to explain to them the benefits their sons and husbands would enjoy if they enrolled in the British Army. He knew very well that the womenfolk would influence the men one way or the other, so it was important to get them on his side. I could speak Urdu fluently, which many of them could understand.

The women enjoyed looking at the regimental pictures I passed around showing soldiers on parade, and soldiers at training camp learning to use guns, drive lorries, Jeeps, tanks, or even (laughter here) to ride on horseback. We always spent a minimum of two nights in each village, more if the head man was away, since the Colonel always wanted a word with him. In the evening of the first night we would show films to mixed audiences with men at the front and women at the back – our recruiting film, a Donald Duck cartoon, which was a great favourite, and an Army fighting film. Films were a novelty, and these simple people could never have enough of them.

The following night we would be entertained, often by the village storyteller. Wonderful sagas would be related out of the local folklore: tales of gods or devils or heroes, love stories, tales of family feuds, water nymphs, peris, fairies in all shapes and sizes, and ghosts. Animal stories, heroic tales, tragic sagas – all were told with a wealth of detail and a love for the music of language. For drama, you cannot beat the professional storyteller.

On tour, we spent the nights in *dak* bungalows, post-houses used by touring Government officials – whites-only before the War, but war altered many such examples of discrimination. These were well-staffed and well-stocked, so that within the borders of India one could always rely on a good hot meal at the end of the day and a comfortable bed to sleep in.

So my seventeenth year was a happy one, a kind of postscript to my childhood, an interlude before adult life began. Towards the end of it, however, occurred a little *contretemps* which in its way was ominous, and reminds me, as I now recall it, that I was already out of Eden with at least one foot in the real world. It concerned my old friend and benefactor Professor Roerich. We were in Nagur, Kulu, where he and Mrs Roerich had taken up residence, and I thought it would be pleasant to call on him, though I had had no contact with the family since I set out to school in England. My Colonel thought it a splendid idea, and said he would come with me, for the natives evidently thought a lot about the old boy and it would do us no harm to be civil to him. Would I write and tell him to expect us? I did write, saying I was the little girl, Star, to whom Professor and Mrs Roerich had kindly sent beautiful toys for so many Christmases, and the colonel enclosed his official card.

The home turned out to be a fortress palace with a uniformed guard at the entrance, armed with the short, curved sword of the hill men. We were shown into a guard room and kept waiting there quite on our own for an hour. At length, an answer came. The Professor was not at home. My Colonel was furious at the slight to HM Government, which he felt he represented, and none too pleased with me for my part in putting him in the way of such a snub. I, too, was saddened and humiliated as my fairy gold turned to moss in my hands. Of course, it may well have been the truth that the Professor was really away from home. But it never felt like that at the time.

It was with regret that as my eighteenth birthday approached I had to surrender this delightful form of war work and – as my father's daughter could scarcely imagine not doing – enlist. I presented myself at the proper quarters and joined the Women's Auxiliary Corps (India). The volunteer recruiter took the king's shilling, so to speak, and herself became a recruit.

2

1940

9 April	Germany invades Denmark and Norway
10 May	Germany invades Holland, Belgium and Luxembourg; Italy declares war on Britain and France; Churchill becomes Prime Minister
30 May–3 June	The British withdraw from Dunkirk
22 June	Northern France and its Atlantic Coast occupied by Germany
8 August–31 October	The Battle of Britain fought in the air over Southern England
6 September–31 October	The Blitzkrieg, the indiscriminate bombing of London

JOHN BLANDY

By the spring of 1940 it was time to make more permanent arrangements for my schooling, and after a good deal of thought my father took me up to Victoria School, Kurseong, where he had arranged for me to board with one of the masters, Mr Nugent. There were several very fine schoolmasters at this school. Mr Nugent taught physics, and I found his practical lessons on the Principle of Archimedes so fascinating that there and then (at the age of 12) I decided to become a doctor, since this was the kind of things doctors obviously did (e.g. weighing things in air and water). Mr Vernon Prinz taught English and history, and, what was far more important, ran the Boy Scouts. I needed no encouragement to join, and this proved to be great fun: I loved the knots and the tracking and the camp fires. Tracking was very special, because in the forest all round the school there really were bears (though I never saw one), and very occasionally the rumour of a tiger. We kept on hoping we would see one or the other or both. We learned to cook *bhuttas* over a log fire and we ran up and down these tremendous hills like rabbits, swam in the tanks of tea gardens, and went on a three-day camp over the Puja Holidays.

Of course, it rained during the monsoon. But somehow we were young and waterproof. The rain made the hockey faster. We would return from a walk in the jungle with half a dozen bloated leeches on each leg. But then a hot bath – the water heated in a 'salamander' on a wood fire – and poured into a tin tub (having first checked to make sure there were no snakes). Lighting was by petromax lights – which gave an excellent light, thanks to a gas mantle.

The gap in the curriculum at Victoria School was French, so special arrangements were made for a Father from the Belgian School at Mount Hermon to come up the hill once a week to attempt to teach me. He was a Jesuit of unusual charm, whose hobby was Indian music. The following year Mlle Bossenec tried to teach French to my sister Helen and me – she was distressed at our very Belgian accents (Helen having been sent to school near Brussels).

Came the *pujas*, and my parents and Helen came up to Darjeeling to stay in the Planters' Club for a week's holiday. I was sadly mocked for my 'chi-chi' accent – which was a little unfair after five months in a Eurasian milieu. My sister had started a secretarial course, and been given a typewriter to encourage her. I was exceedingly jealous of this.

Returning to Victoria School, I made friends with the *babus* in the school office, who most kindly allowed me to use their typewriter, left out lots of waste paper and lent me the Pitman 'teach-yourself-to-type' book. At the end of six weeks I could touch-type – a skill I have never lost. At the end of the nine-month-long term at Victoria all the boys collaborated to make a huge decoration for the school train: it was applied to the front of the hill railway engine, and transferred to the grown-up engine at Siliguri. There was a prize-giving. I had won several books as prizes, which were given away by my father – which was a little embarrassing for both of us, but he did not seem to mind.

IAN MICHAEL O'LEARY

On 10 February 1940 our ship docked at Calcutta. We had come out in a large convoy escorted by two naval destroyers, and we even had a small naval gun mounted on the stern of our ship. On 11 February we reached Dacca (Bengal) by boat and car. My father was commandant of a Gurkha Military Police battalion here, the Eastern Frontier Rifles. Our two-storey red-brick house, with wide verandahs, lay back behind extensive lawns, with wide flower-beds with brilliant red cannas blooming in them. There was a huge banyan tree at one side, and leechi trees at the back, partly concealing the vegetable garden, servants' quarters and stables.

The servants were out on the front drive in full force to greet us, the bearer and *khitmagar* in immaculate white uniforms with wide, green cummerbunds, matching the green band across their white *puggris*, with Father's silver regimental badge pinned in front. There was much salaaming, and I foresaw many happy days ahead with such obviously friendly people. The *ayah* ran up, clutching her sari, not wishing to miss the greetings. I explored the garden and tasted the delicious leechis. To my delight, Father had purchased a sleek, black mare for me, and a pony for my sister, Merula.

At this time my father was not keen for me to go to school in India, a view that I heartily endorsed, and for the next two years I revelled in the freedom it gave me to explore this exotic land – the land of my childhood. I learned Hindustani fluently, and drilled with the children of Father's Gurkha soldiers, who were most curious as to why I always had to wear a *topee* out of doors. Father was keen that I became a good shot, and I was presented with a .410 shotgun and a .22 rifle. Dun Bahadur Rai was my gun bearer when we went hunting, a young man I will never forget – I can still see his happy Mongolian features when I close my eyes at night – when I think back to those carefree days when we ran wild through the countryside, practised hockey together, climbed trees, brought home parrots, sheep, calves and on one occasion dogs. Father didn't want dogs in the house because of rabies.

I and my sister were in a Military Tattoo the boys of the battalion put on for a big *tamasha*. There were two opposing armies, the redcoats and the bluecoats – I commanded the redcoats. Permission had been granted by the Muslim *mullah* to turn an old mosque into a temporary fort, with authentic ramparts and an old cannon. Whenever the cannon was fired, droves of little boys fell to the ground as though killed – they lay motionless until the end of the battle. At the end, we all formed up in neat ranks and marched past the reviewing stand, smartly saluting with commands of 'eyes right' ringing out.

In 1941, my sister Hazel was born – she received the major share of brains and beauty in our family. At about this time, Father got the strange idea of crossing India by car, with the servants and luggage in a huge bus behind. We children were thrilled, but the servants were less than pleased – they preferred to travel by train in comfortable servants' compartments attached to the first-class carriages. On long rail journeys they made sure that no intruders from the second class, inter class or third class slipped in with them.

Back to our exciting journey across India from Bengal to Baluchistan. Father drove with quiet determination, nothing perturbed him – at one desolate area a tyre blew out (we had no second spare), so Father had the servants cut coarse roadside grass and stuff

The bus, loaded with possessions and servants, that crossed India behind Ian O'Leary's family car. His father is at far right of photo.

the deflated tyre. The bus was sent on ahead to try and locate a new tyre, while we limped along at a very reduced pace. Eventually, we arrived hot and dusty in Loralai, Baluchistan. I thought that my mare had been disposed of, but Father had kindly sent it on with a *syce*. The climate here was so dry that we had to put oil in our bath tubs each night to prevent our skin cracking and bleeding.

HAZEL INNES

When war started we were taken out to India again and put in boarding schools in Darjeeling, my twin up on a Darjeeling hilltop at St Paul's School for Boys, and I to Mount Hermon, an American co-educational boarding school down in the valley, where we spent four years, returning to England in 1944 to finish our education at 'home'.

Going to boarding school proved a traumatic experience for the first few weeks, and I would stand at the entrance gates peering through the railings for my mother, weeping and biting my handkerchief to shreds. Eventually she felt able to return to my father down on the plains, and it took me some time to adjust to the horrible realisation that I was destined to stay at boarding school for nine months every year, with only a three-month holiday down on the plains with my parents. I probably wept every day for about three months, but eventually came to terms with incarceration and learned to put up with it. My brother was up on the hilltop at St Paul's and was allowed a pass to come to our valley once a month, on 'sister Sunday', as it was quaintly called.

ROBERT MATTHEWS

Early in 1939, Father, Arnold Monteath Matthews, a professor of English at the Forman Christian College in Lahore, was sentenced to nine months in jail for sedition, under the Defence of India Act, 1916, but although my mother visited him in Lahore Gaol whenever possible, he never allowed any of his children to see him there.

Then, just before I was sent away to boarding school for the first time, he asked my mother to bring me with her. Up in the hills, my incarceration was to be nine months away from home: ironically, the same length of time as my father's sentence. Assuming that he would

Geoffrey Innes (right) and a friend 'doing *puja*' in the latter's garden. Dum Dum, near Calcutta, 1940.

be released before I returned home later in the year, he wanted to say goodbye and wish me well. It was a final goodbye, for I never saw him again. Four months later, my father died of typhoid, a victim of adulterated milk.

My father was already waiting when we were shown into an ante-room adjacent to the Prison Governor's office. A prison guard was present, but he left when we entered and stationed himself outside the door. As I recall, the room was small, hot and dusty. There was a rough wooden bench the length of one wall, a single table and two chairs. Other than that the room was bare.

I burst out crying when I saw my father who, though smartly turned out as ever, looked even thinner than I remembered. He appeared close to tears as he picked me up in his arms and hugged me close. 'Be brave. Men don't cry, son,' he said gruffly, clearing his throat. Releasing me, he said, 'Now look what I've got for you'. He fished inside his shirt pocket and withdrew a single sheet of paper. 'I've written a poem for you, Bobby. It's called "The Boy with the Green Bike". Would you like me to read it to you? It's very short, but here goes.'

'The Boy with the Green Bike, by Professor Arnold Monteath Matthews, MA (Oxon)'. My father looked up from the lined paper scribbled in pencil and smiled.

> Little Bobby Matthews was given a bike.
> A real two-wheeler, and not a trike.
> It was new and shiny and a very bright green.
> He'd soon learn to ride it and keep it clean,
> His Daddy said. And when at school, away from home,
> He'd work very hard and play hard, too.
> A champion student and very well liked,
> That little Bobby, 'baba', and his shiny green bike.

My father finished reading. He looked very sad as he handed the poem to me. Managing a grin, he said, 'Son, Daddy would like to say, "bye" now.'

He hugged me again. Almost as if it were yesterday, I can still feel the tremble in his body against my small frame. My mother gently pulled me away. My father called out to the guard, and casting a last, sorrowful look at me, he vanished through the door and out of my life.

There were other things said between us, of course. Such as: chin up, stiff upper lip, never sit on the fence, that sort of thing, but the most poignant meeting, what I've written about, means most to me.

ROBERT BAKER

I reported to the Officer Training School in Belgaum in May 1940. Belgaum is situated some hundred miles inland from the port of Goa, which at that time was a colony of neutral Portugal. There were German merchant ships caught by the War, at anchor in Goa, and their crews came ashore to frequent the Goanese cafés. I never visited Goa from Belgaum, but many cadets did, and exchanged pleasantries with the enemy in circumstances which were very extraordinary indeed.

The OTS in Belgaum processed every single prospective British-Indian Army officer in the Madras Presidency, of which there were fewer than eighteen hundred all told, between the ages of 18 and 42. While I was there, the first draft of Officer Cadets destined for the Indian Army arrived straight from Britain. Some of these young men hired a taxi, and then one of them persuaded the taxi driver to allow him to do the driving. Probably he did not know how to drive, certainly not in India, for what I heard was that an accident was caused by a bullock bandy not pulling over to the left. At all events, he was involved in a serious accident, and I was horrified to hear screams from the sick bay, which I was informed came from the accident victim.

Another British cadet went out with a rifle and, seeing a buffalo, shot and killed it, thinking it was the wild version. It transpired, however, that it was a tame water-buffalo belonging to a villager.

I never learned how much was paid in compensation, but no doubt it would have been generous.

Our course in Belgaum was only of one month's duration. At the end of that month we were sent to Murree, a hill station halfway up the *ghat* between Rawalpindi and Srinagar. Murree had a Club, but was also a military station. The Royal Indian Army Service Corps course that I attended there was of three months' duration, one month on animal transport, one month on mechanical transport and one month on supplies. How much we learned of military matters I am largely doubtful. Our instructors knew only peacetime soldiering.

After my course at Murree I was granted ten days' leave and, with two chums, went to Lahore, where we booked into Nedou's Hotel. The more modern, and perhaps the better hotel was Faletti's. To my amazement, we found there a night spot very like any European counterpart. There was a cabaret consisting of a man, his wife and two young daughters, who were Hawaiian and played that type of music. One tune I remembered their playing was 'When you're smiling, the whole world smiles with you'.

Besides the Hawaiian group, there were two White Russian dancers, Luba and Larissa. They performed a dance separately – not, I think, of great quality, but that didn't really matter – they were white, and they came and sat with us after their turn and talked. There was also a white girl-vocalist. She was a domiciled European, and Windle (I think he was called), who claimed to play the drums, used to talk to this girl on the subject of dance music. Luba and Larissa came from the wave of White Russian refugees who had escaped into China in 1917 and who had made their homes in Shanghai and on the China Coast.

After my leave in Lahore I was posted to Razmak. One day there was a begging letter in the post from Luba, and a proposal of marriage. She explained that it was imperative she have a British passport, that she would disappear from my life as soon as the ceremony was over and in the meantime would I send her some money. I replied by saying that I was not prepared to marry her, but enclosed a cheque for 100 rupees, a lot of money in those days, but I was young enough to be foolish. Not, however, so foolish as Windle, for he entered into correspondence with the night-spot singer, and eventually married her.

Razmak was a North West Frontier fort 80 miles into tribal territory from Bannu. Tribal territory was not administered, which meant that there were no courts, no schools, no post offices, no hospitals: in short, no administration. However, the road from Bannu to Razmak was of a very high standard. Tarmac all the way. I was very surprised on this trip to see, coming the other way, an open staff-car with a British officer, a passenger in it, wearing a *puggaree*, that is to say a turban, khaki in this case, with a tail to it some two feet long.

I should explain here that we Europeans of the Raj were hugely concerned to adopt nothing that was Indian, or should I say native. We ate curry on Sundays, but that was just about the only concession we made to Indian culture. Never did we wear Indian clothes – our shirts were always tucked *inside* our trousers – *pukka* Europeans never knew any Indian language, and we never mixed socially with Indians. I was a very strict adherent to all these taboos: hence my astonishment at seeing a British officer in an Indian headdress. The explanation, when it came, was obvious. By wearing the same dress as his men the British officer was less conspicuous, and thus less likely to be picked out by a tribal sniper.

BARBARA ANN JARDINE

The Second World War began, and we read in the newspaper that the India Office would help us to return to India and our father, and we joined a convoy going round by South Africa in August. Our ship's engines (the *Orion*) broke down, but we eventually caught up with the convoy at Cape Town. We were allowed ashore to visit the city and Table Mountain, the only time I have ever set foot in Africa!

We arrived in Bombay in October, where our father met us and travelled with us on the railway ('Frontier Mail') all the way up to

Peshawar. I remember the big event on the journey was stopping at Lahore Station and having a really good meal – otherwise our bearer would bring us things to eat at different station stops. India seemed very natural to me as I remembered the atmosphere and bustle!

As several families had arrived in Peshawar about the same time, the Almonds and Squires among them, the doctor's wife organised some schooling for us in her house. We acted Shakespeare's *Midsummer Night's Dream*. But a wider education was required, so my sister and I and a girl cousin travelled to Simla to Sherfield School. We were there for nine months of term and then a three-month holiday. Journeys took so long in those days. As well as studying for our School Certificate we played tennis, skated in winter and learned first aid and Russian. Confirmation was in Simla Cathedral. At the time we got our results for School Certificate, which had to go all the way to England to be marked. We were all so excited I thought we should creep out of school and see the film *Rebecca*. On our arrival back at school there was our headmistress, waiting for us and furious. I was expelled, but luckily I was leaving for home the next day anyway!

At this time our father took us trekking up the Khagan Valley to the borders of Tibet. I shall never forget the marvellous scenery, valleys, rivers, waterfalls, mountains, forest and flowers and bears. We also went hunting every Sunday with the Peshawar Vale Hunt with all the other British, and went to church in the cantonment.

DOROTHY MARGARET BAKER

When war was declared in 1939, my mother, sister and myself were in London in a flat we had regularly rented on our trips to Britain. My father was due for home leave, but that was cancelled because of the War, and my mother took us to Wales. In mid-1940, my father got us passages on one of the last unescorted ships to travel to India. Relations dubbed us 'rats jumping the sinking ship'. We were bombed in Southampton, and we saw (without understanding its meaning) some of the boats returning from Dunkirk. We were chased by German U-boats in the Bay of Biscay, and by Italian gun-boats off the African coast. We travelled in complete darkness until we reached Cape Town a month or so after leaving England, and travelled far from land once we had left the Canary Islands. I recall fear, boredom and the unbearable heat in our blacked-out cabin – we mainly slept on deck. The lights of Cape Town were like fairyland, and the beginning of a new life dawned.

By September 1940 we were living in a house in Bangalore with my mother, attending Bishop Cotton Girls' High School as day scholars. Bangalore was chosen by my parents as cooler than Madras and easier to reach (from Madras) than the Nilgiri Hills. One of my mother's sisters was a matron at the Lawrence School Hospital in Lovedale, and we used to visit her, reinforcing my concept of this area as 'home'. A year or so later, all houses in Bangalore, if an alternative existed, were requisitioned by the Army for the expanding OTC. My sister and I became boarders, with my mother joining my father in Madras.

The only brush with the law that we had was in Bangalore, when a friend and I cycled to games at school through a park, one riding pillion. Both acts were unlawful. We were stopped, names and addresses were taken, and we expected to hear no more. But a month later, the summons arrived, we confessed, and our mothers went to court to represent us. Apparently the Indian judge had great difficulty deciding which of the two over-14-stone ladies had been on the back! The court found it hilarious, but we (or rather our mothers) were still fined.

Due to the War, the school provided a social melting-pot with children of various races, colours and creeds, all living and learning together. It set the seal on any lingering notions of racial or social superiority that I retained, and I count myself fortunate to have had friends from such varied backgrounds. The school had a high-Anglican religious inclination, but I cannot recall what happened over attendance at religious services for the Muslims, Sikhs, Hindus and Roman Catholics among us.

JOAN BRAGG

I have no memories of the earliest times, as we left for England on leave while I was a baby. Two brothers were born in the early 1930s, and in 1933 they were taken back to Jhelum, while I stayed with relatives at home. The family were reunited in 1937, when the Coronation brought the Jat Regiment contingent to take part in the procession. Our dad was at home on leave in 1939 when he was recalled on the outbreak of war, and he returned to India. When Dunkirk fell, believing the danger of invasion was very real, he telegraphed for us to book a passage, and in ten days our mother had to pack up and store the household goods and get four of us to Liverpool to sail on the *City of Venice* via the Cape, a journey of six weeks.

The first memory of India was looking down on the quay at Bombay and seeing our dad standing, and being the first of us to race down the gangway and into his arms. Snapshot memories after that: crowded streets, hubbub, arriving at the railway station hotel, where a room had been booked for the night, and at last falling asleep with the precious newly bought *topee* on the head of the bed, while outside the traffic roared round the concourse, hooting endlessly.

Next day, the first of a number of Indian railway journeys – a train to Ahmedabad. Those railway memories can almost be felt and smelt. Intense heat, with a big block of ice, renewed at every station, on the floor in a tin container under the ceiling fan, and around the sizeable compartment we perched on our bunks (much competition for the top bunks) reading, playing games, squabbling and peering out through the shutters at the wide landscape, the flame of the forest trees in scarlet blossom, trudging buffalo carts, ramshackle villages, and at the stations the milling crowds and sellers of different items – the call of 'Hindu *pani*, Mussulman *pani*' seemed almost insistent. We piled out to eat meals ordered ahead at the station restaurants, a delightful and welcome change of scene. The reek of *bidi* cigarettes was everywhere, and was just one of the thrilling odours that everywhere tickled our noses: some richly fragrant, but most far from delightful. Yet, to a child, exotic and exciting beyond any previous experience.

The big bungalow in the cantonment at Ahmedabad was our home for the following few months. Grey Langur monkeys leapt around the roof and the garden. Crisply turned-out Bearer and Khitmagar saw to the more visible household needs – and, delightfully, played with us in free moments, teaching us novel and enjoyable card games. There was an *ayah* – our little sister was two. We slept under mosquito nets: oh, joy. We had to tip our shoes over in case of scorpions before putting them on, and once or twice there were shouts and men running around with sticks when a snake (maybe a *krait*) was spotted and dealt with. At dusk the cicadas set up their clockwork din. New marvellous birds flew about – hoopoes with their crests and flamboyant black and yellow, blue jays, bulbuls. One bird was heard but not seen; later in life, hearing the call described, I recognised that it must have been the brainfever bird.

Soon after our arrival, the monsoon broke. In wild excitement we leapt off the verandah into the sheeting downpour, and rejoiced as we were instantly transformed into drowned rats and the quite indescribably wonderful gusts of wet-dust smells and intensified flower fragrances assaulted us. Soon we were not so enamoured of the rain: shoes went mouldy overnight, and having previously simply felt hot, one now felt tricklingly hot, and usually experienced the torment of prickly heat blisters between the fingers.

There were lessons of a sort, with an unimpressive Army schoolmaster, struggling to manage a group of youngsters impossibly mixed in age and attainment. It was clear that education had to be a priority, and it was decided that our mother should take us up to Kashmir, where there was schooling available and a good climate. The morning we woke on the train nearing 'Pindi and actually had to put on a sweater because – miracle – one felt cool, has always stayed with me. The two-day car trip up the winding road, with my little sister being horribly sick at intervals, was broken by an overnight stay in Murree. There we experienced the forgotten bliss of snuggling under blankets against the crisp mountain air. Next day, swinging round endless bends and climbing, climbing, we emerged on to that paradisically beautiful plain and drove between the double file of Baramulla poplars, to arrive finally at Mrs Amesbury's guest house on Gupkar Road, Srinagar.

I went first to my brother's school, Sheikh Bagh, and was deeply and silently unhappy; as one pubescent girl in a class of outspoken boys I was the butt of much teasing, and it was fortunate that I only had to survive one term there, returning to the plains at Christmas when the regiment returned to Attock on the frontier near Peshawar. It was after our return to Kashmir the following year that I entered into one of the happiest times of my life. We moved into Mrs Kidd's boarding house behind the Presentation Convent, and I went into Standard Six, presided over by Sister Immaculata. One of my fellow pupils was Karan Singh, son of the ruling Maharajah, a cheeky, handsome lad who for obvious reasons did more or less as he liked. We were a predominantly European bunch; however, I have always been grateful that among our number were Indian girls, whose families valued the education offered by the nuns, and after the time of quite unconscious 'sahib-log' conditioning it was quietly effective in releasing me from any such nonsense: we were conscious of no barriers at all in dormitory or classroom. The well-structured curriculum brought me almost at once to the realisation, after years of haphazard, interrupted schooling, that I had a very respectable brain, and much enjoyed using it. There was a choir which provided music for Mass and Benediction in the white-painted chapel, and I encountered plainsong. I was very good at art, and that brought me much kudos. The music mistress discovered I had a good voice and gave me lessons, and this brought me into contact with classical music for the first time. The mysterious magic of the Latin Mass and the attraction of the life of the nuns, who made riveting role-models, began to cast a strong spell.

Home for weekends, we went on picnics over the Dal Lake to Shalimar or Nishat. I can still recapture the bliss of lying prone on the prow of the *shikara*, which was urged through the water by the boatmen with heart-shaped paddles (it would have a name plate with something like 'Here I am, where are you?'), and full spring seats. The weed-smelling water surged under my view, tangled weed visible below, and the lotus blossoms starred the lake.

This security was shattered in 1942. Our father had gone with the Jats to fight in the Western Desert, and there came a telegram telling of his death at El Adem. The world rocked. Our mother, always-imperturbable ruler of our world, cried. Fear moved into me. Her grief was novel and unbearable. Emotion had always been taboo and, totally unable to express or acknowledge my own grief, life became a grim, determined struggle to avoid a repetition of her distress. I know how selfish I was, but I had no means of knowing it then. The convent became my rock and refuge. I adored the teacher who had been in charge of me since my entering the school, and when after Christmas 1944 we left to return on a wartime convoy to England, I felt my life had ended. Had I been free to choose, I would have stayed on with the nuns and become one of them. I was 15, and those most vivid and impressionable years of my life have left a lifetime mark.

ROBERT MATTHEWS

In March 1940, at the age of nine, I was packed off to the senior boys' school of the Lawrence College, Ghora Gali, in the Murree Hills. My sister Pamela, aged seven, and brother Richard, aged five, were sent to St Denys School in Murree at the same time as myself. It remains a mystery to this day why my elder brother Geoffrey, aged ten, and baby brother, David, were both left behind in Lahore to be brought up by my grandmother, a Grey Lady Presbyterian missionary from Scotland.

I dare say this had something to do with straitened financial circumstances, and what with my father being in gaol, my mother was forced to seek help elsewhere. As an ex-ballet dancer with the

Ballet Rambert, and still only 33 years of age, she was ill-equipped to support her large brood. However, my father happened to be the Grand Master of the Freemasons 'Lodge of Light', a Scottish Lodge, and so, to Mother's relief, the Masons offered to pay for the children's education. Meanwhile, Mother buckled down and took a course in stenography, which stood her in good stead later on.

My first two years at school in Ghora Gali were a positive nightmare and, because most of the boys knew that my father was in prison, I was subjected to unremitting, unmerciful bullying. Not a day passed when I was not either caned by prefects on the slightest pretext, or beaten up by others, to the accompaniment of vicious taunts. The damage to my spirit was long-lasting. Nonetheless, I endured the bullying, sometimes giving as good as I got, and made friends along the way. In time, I learned how to box pretty well, which meant I was finally left alone.

Although the Lawrence College is set in the most beautiful surroundings of the Himalayan foothills, I found it to be a brutal place. Founded by Sir Henry Lawrence in 1860, as an asylum for the orphans and the destitute of common soldiery, away from the heat of the plains, the Senior Boys' school was run on quasi-military lines. The regime was strict, hard for all the boys between the ages of nine and seventeen, with a good deal of marching about in hand-me-down uniforms supplied by the school. The very young children

Lawrence College, Ghora Gali, Murree, the main building. (Robert Matthews)

in the Junior School, and also the girls in their separate Girls' School, set on a hill, a safe distance away from the Senior Boys' school, were rightly treated much more benignly.

One of the least-cherished recollections of my school days is of classmates receiving six annas a week pocket money, dished out to them by a master every Saturday. Because my mother infrequently remembered to send me any pocket money, I hardly ever lined up for a hand out. Thus, instead of running off to stuff myself with cakes and sweatmeats bought from a *cakewallah* with a tin box, full of goodies, I spent my free Saturday afternoons wandering about the *khud*, dreaming. Either that or confined in the dusty library devouring Henty novels and ancient, yellowing copies of *Punch*, the only available reading matter.

On a happier note, I was good at boxing, athletics and most other games. After about six years at my school I was made up to prefect, in 1946. By then, caning by prefects had been banished. Nevertheless, masters still turned a blind eye to bullying.

ROBIN MALLINSON

I was eight when I left my father and two sisters in India in 1937 to travel by sea to England to go to prep school. Holidays were spent partly with relations, partly with schoolfriends, whose mothers had no doubt been tactfully asked by the school if they could help out, and once or twice at places which cared for children whose parents were abroad – these places were not particularly enjoyable.

So when, in 1940, I was told that I was going back to India, I was very pleased – not because of the War, which was getting 'interesting', with the odd air-raid, but because I was going to see my family again. I think I had become resigned to not seeing them for some time, so the news was an unexpected and welcome surprise.

In June I was on the *Narkunda* in Southampton, with scores of other children bound for India. Before we left there was an air-raid in the harbour, which increased the feeling of leaving a beleaguered island. There were rumours that we had missed the convoy, as our propellers got fouled, and we had to return to port for two or three days. Perhaps this was fortunate, as by ourselves we were faster than the convoy, so had a better chance against the U-boats.

All I remember about the *Narkunda* is that it was crowded, not just with children, and that it seemed old and dirty, which may explain the outbreak of chickenpox, to which I succumbed. I think the ship had a very quick turn-round in Southampton after its previous voyage, and being crammed with passengers made it difficult to keep it spick and span. Our cabin had six bunks, and I think there were two matrons nominally in charge of us but, although there was little discipline, we behaved fairly well.

In Bombay someone, presumably one of the matrons, bought me a ticket and put me on the Frontier Mail bound for Rawalpindi. I was in an air-conditioned compartment with three Army officers, one of whom knew my father and said he would take me from Rawalpindi to Srinagar, as he was going fishing in Kashmir. I still remember his name, Colonel Skrine, as well as his kindness, and then hearing later that he was killed in the Western Desert.

The road from 'Pindi to Srinagar climbs to Murree and then descends to the valley of the Jhelum River and follows the river into the Vale of Kashmir. We stopped at one of the *dak* bungalows along the route, where you could stop for a night without advance notice. They were normally close to the river and the roar of the torrent was a familiar sound as one tried to go to sleep on a flea-ridden bed. Dinner was always chicken, which was chased, caught and despatched with much hullabaloo on one's arrival.

In Srinagar I was put on a bus to Tangmarg, where my mother, who must have been told of my arrival, met me. I think the whole journey took about seven weeks and, looking back on it, it was amazing that, apart from the chickenpox, nothing went wrong and a small boy travelled safely from wartime England to peaceful Kashmir.

In Gulmarg in the summer, six or seven of us were taught by a retired policeman, Fred Bartley (who taught us very well), and spent our spare time playing golf and riding. At that time there were four golf courses in Gulmarg, which included one for children. The winter was spent either in cold Srinagar or at Jullundur Cantonment, which had fine crisp weather at that time of year. Life there for a child was full of games and picnics, but our friends were inevitably from other British families in the cantonment. One year I reared a young kite which had fallen out of its nest, and trained it to fly from my wrist.

I can remember 'Quit India' slogans, but we were isolated from large towns and areas of unrest. The Indians we came in contact with were invariably friendly. One little memory: trying to explain in Hindustani, to a Kashmiri woodcutter who had never seen an aeroplane, an air-raid made by hundreds of bombers flying from England to Germany.

HEDI BRAUN

When Holland was overrun by the Nazis, my father, who was working for a Dutch firm, lost his job. In addition, my grandfather was arrested as an 'enemy alien'. There was great confusion among the British Police. They didn't seem to know what to do about Austrian refugees. My poor grandfather was very upset at being grouped with the Nazis, whom he had fled. He fell ill but, after a few days in the hospital, he was released. My father was arrested as well, but released when he promised not to leave the house, except between two and four in the afternoon. These restrictions were later abolished, but we were never able to travel more than five miles without the permission of a Police Commissioner. In Darjeeling we had a very kind and understanding Commissioner, who allowed my mother to go regularly to Calcutta once a month, to make her broadcast and spend the weekend with my father and her parents.

My father had by now found an engineering position in a factory in Agarpara, near Calcutta, owned by the Elias and Jacob families, members of a Jewish community whose ancestors had come to India from Baghdad at the beginning of the nineteenth century. My father air-conditioned their factory and my grandfather supervised the lumber mill.

Later, my father took a position with a British firm in Kamarhati, also on the outskirts of Calcutta. My mother and I spent the school holidays with him there, in a spacious flat on the factory's luxurious compound. Each flat had its own large garden, and there was also a swimming pool, bowling green and tennis court – quite a contrast with the crowded Indian living quarters outside the compound walls. While my father worked on his inventions (he successfully converted ceiling fans into powerful air-conditioners) and my mother practised the piano, my grandmother ran the household according to strict European standards. She taught our Muslim cook (the *bovachy*) to prepare complicated Viennese recipes. I remember the ceremony involved in making *apfelstrudel*: the dough had to be placed on a white, linen tablecloth, stretched until it was paper-thin and then rolled up with the cooked apples and raisins inside, as the *bovachy* and my grandmother raised one end of the tablecloth up from the large dining table. (My task was to keep our ginger tomcat, who followed my grandmother everywhere, from leaping on to the table.) There was an American Army base nearby, and my grandmother often invited one or two homesick young soldiers to spend Sunday with us, for a swim in the pool and a long Viennese lunch.

(After The New School closed, at the end of 1944, I briefly attended the Altamont School in Darjeeling, and later a succession of small schools in Calcutta. My mother was by now Director of Western Music at All India Radio, but she began to feel that our time in India had come to an end. Her father had died, her mother couldn't stand the climate, and my parents didn't feel it was good for me to grow up in a country where one had to harden one's heart against poverty. My father had been to the US once before and longed to settle in New York. So we set off there, travelling on a freighter from Calcutta to Boston, a journey which took six weeks. We arrived in July 1947, and took the train to New York.)

SHIRLEY POCOCK

After Dunkirk it was thought that Britain would be invaded. Father had been recalled to the Army in Cawnpore, and as Mother wouldn't leave him it was suggested we should join them. It was a big decision. My sister had won a place at Oxford, and I was at Cheltenham Ladies' College, thanks to her coaching me through a scholarship exam. We decided to go, and in the summer of 1940 sailed from Southampton in the last passenger ship to leave unconvoyed. We were bombed in the Channel, and had to take refuge from an Italian submarine in the Cape Verde Islands before zig-zagging our way round the Cape to Colombo rather than through the Canal to Bombay. We were not supposed to be carrying military personnel, but there were naval officers on board disguised as civilians, and my sister got 'engaged' three times on our six-week voyage!

Father met us in Colombo, where we stayed at the Galle Face Hotel. This was very grand. Women were still in long evening-dresses, and men in dinner jackets. My sister, aged 19, looked lovely in peacock-blue silk and I, aged 15, ghastly in pink-spotted net. This was my first-ever evening dress, and I had longed for black tulle. So when we took off on our journey to Cawnpore the contrast was enormous. We had a large zinc tub in the compartment which was filled whenever possible with large blocks of ice. We bought lychees from the vendors at the stations, and after a while in the ice tub they were gorgeously cold to eat. It was a long journey through southern India to Cawnpore, but it was all colour, noise, sight and smells. My father spoke both Hindi and Urdu fluently, so we had a very jolly and interesting time.

But at the end of it, to be all together in our own home was unbelievable. So was breakfast on the verandah, with cereal served in a silver dish by our *khitmagar*! We had a lovely spaniel, a pony and trap to beat the petrol rationing, and Father bought me an ex-polo pony. There were dances and parties, but it took us a little while to fit easily into this new life.

SHEILA FERGUSON

By 1940, war was raging in Europe, and my school at Battle, in Sussex, was in the path of aerial battles etc. The Army commandeered our school building, and so we were evacuated to Devon. During the move we were given a month's holiday, which I spent in Scotland, and it was during this time my father sent for me to return to India. I was 14 years old by then.

For the journey I was put in the care of a doctor who was returning to his job on the tea gardens. Our ship was the *Strathnaver*, and we sailed from Southampton toward the end of July – a shipload of children, the crew of an aircraft carrier, who were joining their ship in the Far East, and fiancées of men working in India. The carrier was later sunk by the Japanese. We set off in the company of a troopship and two destroyers, and in the Bay of Biscay we were attacked by German dive-bombers – they mistook us for the troopship and we took the brunt of the attack, but came through unscathed. For 'safety' the passengers were herded into the tourists' dining saloon, which was on the waterline! The three ships left us off Gibraltar, and we continued on round the Cape of Good Hope. We ran out of water on two occasions – it was always rationed at the best of times – and put into the Cape Verde Islands and Freetown to fill up the tanks. After about a month we disembarked at Colombo. I felt I was home again – it was marvellous to be back in the East.

We had to go by train from Colombo to Calcutta – crossing to the mainland by ferry and then changing trains in Madras. The journey took about a week.

In Calcutta I was met by friends of the family, and my dear old bearer from the tea garden – who proceeded to look after me until I arrived on the tea garden (another train journey, of course), where I was introduced to my new baby half-brother, who in due course was also made to speak one of the Indian languages (Hindi mostly). I was sent up to Darjeeling to a small school run by the minister of the Scottish church. During breaks and lunchtimes we played in the woods down the *khud* (hill) and we were always covered in leeches (bloodsuckers) on our return – difficult things to get off, usually done by something hot against the tail, so they would pull out their own heads. Horrible! Later The New School was opened in Calcutta for children in India for the War, which later transferred to Darjeeling.

India in wartime was not much different – there were shortages, of course, and one of the main roads in the heart of Calcutta (the Red Road) was used for planes to take off and land. On the tea gardens, most of the young men were in the services, and as the War with Japan progressed the other assistants were sent to help build the Manipur Road into Burma. The tea garden was then mostly run by the manager. There were more wives and children around, as the ridiculous rule about marrying had been eased – and now covered only the first agreement with the company.

Social life was lively – wartime people I suppose played hard, and lots of servicemen were sent on leave to tea-garden families or to hill stations, and in Calcutta special dances were held to entertain the troops. After leaving school in 1942 I spent about nine months of the following year with a well-known family in Kalimpong working at the Arts and Crafts Centre. One night there was a fire in the Kalimpong Bazaar, and we all went down (servicemen on leave too) to try and help put it out, passing buckets of water in a primitive manner. When it was all over we found that the local shopkeepers had been hoarding large quantities of rice (which was in short supply) under their mattresses in their strange, boxed beds – used to sit cross-legged on during the day and sleep on at night. They were not happy to be found out.

On another occasion, the daughter of the house and I had been to Calcutta for a break. We caught the train to Siliguri and then the little train *en route* to Kalimpong. Not far along this track a tree had blown down, and we could go no further. We decided to walk, leaving our luggage on the train – and wearing open-toed sandals. We had quite a difficult time, clambering over fallen trees etc., but we eventually made the 26 miles to Gielle Khola, blistered, tired and thirsty – but at least there was a phone, and we could call the family, who came and fetched us.

SALLY TOFT

I was taken to India when I was one. I can remember flying back to India in a seaplane when I was five. We had to come down every night: first stop was Alexandria, then Marseilles, and finally Poole Harbour, where my two sisters, Joan and Patricia, who had been left behind, met us.

My father followed, and must have been on leave, but when it was time to return in 1940 we all went back to India on the *Orion* in convoy, and went round via the Cape. We had the son of a friend of the family, and he was going as far as Cape Town. It was a very comfortable voyage, and as far as I was concerned we were all together, and were going 'home' to India. The only home of which I have any recollections was 9 Mayfair, Ballygunge. It was an idyllic home with plenty of animals – at one point we had 16 dogs, our own four, one of which had ten puppies, and two dogs we were looking

'This is the verandah at the back of our house at 9 Mayfair, Ballygunge, Calcutta. Photo probably taken by my father, in 1945. You can just see my mother and elder sister, Joan, sitting at the table on the verandah. The creeper was a beautiful bougainvillea. Pots of flowers were on the steps leading up to the verandah – different flowers at different times of the year.' (Patricia Toft)

after. We had two ducks, guinea pigs at various times and two mongooses. I remember it being a very open home, and my parents entertained soldiers – Bombay Grenadiers – every week. They came to play tennis, and then had baths, and stayed for tea and supper. My mother helped the WVS, and went to the racecourse, where troops went for R&R. I suppose it was during the holiday that I went with her and played cards etc. with the troops who came to the canteen.

The Saturday Club was a special place, where I learned to swim and enjoyed the annual fancy-dress party. The excitement when the fathers came back from work and pulled us round the polished ballroom floor on sacks – three or four of us on a sack. Another interesting point at the end of parties was when the large paper fish or balloon that was suspended from the ceiling was punched, and lots of 'puffed rice' and little presents fell out – what a scramble. There were duck parties, and I can recall taking my duck in the car to the party. There would be races, and you held out the wings and made the duck run – oh dear. I wonder now what we did with the ducks for the rest of the party.

One year, we spent Christmas at the seaside at Gopalpur. The waves were enormous, and we each had an Indian lifeguard, I suppose he would be called. We had to wear these pointed hats, which helped you dive through the waves headfirst! Most Christmases were spent at home. We would go to the cathedral on Christmas morning and then friends would come to lunch with us and we would go to them for dinner.

ELSPET GREY

By the time Dunkirk fell it was decided that we would be better in India, and in August 1940 we boarded the *Strathnaver* in Southampton and with a sister ship and a naval escort we set off on what was to be quite an adventurous voyage. We were machine-gunned in the channel. As we children came on deck from our early lunch-sitting, there was this extraordinary rat-tat-tatting along the deck, alarm bells ringing, and we were hustled below decks for what seemed like an eternity. We were told that we were also pursued by a submarine, but eventually said farewell to our escort at the Cape Verde Islands and, after making a stop at Freetown, continued on our journey round the Cape. We must have stopped again in Cape Town, for I remember Table Mountain in the background but after three more weeks, we finished our sea journey at Colombo, in Ceylon. Because my father was now stationed in the Punjab, in Rawalpindi, he had sent his bearer, a lovely, patient man, to meet us as well as our *ayah* and I think my mother was immediately relieved to see them both. It was early September, very hot, and of course, no air-conditioning. In the middle of the railway carriages – with long seats facing each other – there was a large metal bath filled with an enormous block of ice, replaced whenever necessary at one of the stations, with a *punkah* blowing on to it from the ceiling.

The train stopped at many stations *en route*, and this was a source of amazement and fear, as the beggars and vendors jostled and shoved to climb on to the running boards while the train was still moving. The sheer number of people was overwhelming and, of course, the deformities of the beggars. The explanation that this mutilation was inflicted on them as babies so that begging could be a source of income for the family was only accepted with incredulity and incomprehension. Our lives were, of course, completely different. Everything was made easy for the *missy-sahibs*. Paths were cleared, people were shooed away, none too kindly, just so we could get out of the train and walk along the platform. I like to think that, even then, there was a sense of unease at the inequality and unfairness of life.

The scenery must have been spectacular, but I don't recall it – only the baboons which played on the embankments of the railway line. My sister Rhoda and I played Monopoly – solidly for four days – which is how we spent the journey!

Arriving at the Bank Bungalow, which was beautiful with lovely gardens – the *mali* grew prize chrysanthemums with heads the size of dinner plates, which were his pride and joy – the staff all lined up to meet us. Our bearer we already knew, Rhustum Khan, the driver, had met us at the station, but the number of other servants was bewildering. They all lived in the compound at the back of the bungalow, and it took some time to appreciate the hierarchy that existed between the servants, with the bearer firmly at the top of the list, but I decided that there were enough people around, so I would just clap my hands for anything I wanted. My mother soon put me right: 'Get up off your lazy little bottom and get a glass of water for yourself.' A good lesson.

Our beds were covered with mosquito nets, and *ayah* always slept outside our door. Talk about another world! The insects were not a favourite – large and alien. We were given strict instructions, 'Never put your shoes on without upending them, and always shake hats or jackets in case of scorpions.' The horror of pinning down an enormous centipede with my ruler while screaming for help, I can remember to this very day – we were not very brave.

The Bank and the Bungalow were only separated by a few hundred yards, and my father would walk to work in the morning, return for lunch and his before-lunch gin, and then have an obligatory twenty-minute nap on one of the long cane chairs on the verandah. Between the two buildings was a large tree, so old that the branches had rooted themselves so many times that it made a glorious treehouse for us to play in. From this tree a screeching flock of green parakeets would leave every morning, to return, with just as much noise, in the evenings. If one continued on the path behind the Bank, it led to the bazaar, which was allowed with Ayah in attendance. My impressions were of noise, colour, lovely smells – not all bad! – but primarily I remember the kindness and friendliness from the Indians we encountered.

The Rawalpindi Club featured greatly in our lives. Apart from the social aspect of my parents' lives, for us there was the swimming pool, tennis courts and eventually the Christmas show, at which I recited Kipling's 'If' and got my first taste of applause! I remember the first drinks-party my parents gave in the bungalow to celebrate our arrival – 'nimbu pani', lime juice and sugar and water for us; allowed to hand round the drinks, I was instructed, 'Never say, "Would you like another drink?" – simply, "Would you like a drink?".' Shortly after we arrived, we were invited to a Sikh wedding, which went on for three days. Eating on the floor was very strange, and the beauty of the bride's and the groom's costume were very different from the austerity of wartime England.

In the summer – the hot weather – we went to the hills, to Murree, while my father remained working in 'Pindi. Murree was beautiful, pine forests and monkeys and pine martens. We stayed in a chalet which was part of Nedou's Hotel. The first night, we were bitten alive, and the bed bugs were clearly visible in the canvas frames of the *charpoys* when we turned them over in the morning. Large, hairy spiders would wait until we were in our bath tub and then emerge from the drain hole and send us shrieking into the living room. For a short time, we also went to school in Murree – to Mrs Ancrum's – but I can't remember dates for this period.

GILLIAN OWERS

My father went to India in 1918, having been wounded and invalided out of the Army. He worked for Sinclair Murray in Calcutta, a jute-exporting business, and eventually owned it in partnership with another Englishman. Our family had no roots in India. My father wrote an interesting history of Sinclair Murray after retirement – a vivid picture of commercial life from the 1880s.

I loved India; I still do. And I loved my *ayah*, who was, to all intents and purposes, my mother. With her I was absolutely secure. With her I worshipped the 'moon mama', went to temples, listened to storytellers, ate forbidden bazaar food, attended funerals, played in the park. She was the omnipresent figure, and the star on my horizon. My parents were vague, unimportant, rarely seen and vaguely threatening figures who could not speak my language – for I remember consciously translating into English when I was with them. It was Ayah who sang me to sleep with lullabies, Ayah who cared for me, dressed me, fed me, Ayah who came when I cried in the night. In hospital, in quarantine, with diphtheria, it was Ayah I called for and who finally spent all day squatting where I could not see her from the window, because I was not expected to live. If I were to return to India I would never find her; but she has never left me.

It could not last, of course. I remember getting into trouble in Selfridge's, on a very early visit, bargaining when buying a toy, and also feeling that everyone in England was ill – they were so pale. I loathed both of my British boarding schools (the food! The cold! The loneliness!). I was dumped in school at the age of six. I can still feel myself, standing on the steps with my hand in someone's, absolutely incredulous that my mother was walking away down the driveway, abandoning me. Fortunately, I was able to live with my maternal grandmother during the holidays, a great woman and lifelong influence. Without that safe haven…

I was rescued from school and shipped back to India in 1940. My mother had been in England when war broke out but – unbelievably again – she returned to India, leaving me behind. This trauma was so acute that, after only a year and at the age of 12, I had completely forgotten her, what she looked like, who she was, what she was like. When she met me at the end of the voyage in Colombo, if she had not known me, I would not have recognised her. In retrospect, I consider this breach never to have healed between us. The voyage had been long; I kept a diary, so I know quite a lot about that journey. I remember periods of real fear, but mostly it was a time of freedom, and the joyous knowledge that I was going back to India overcame all other emotions. I also remember trying to buy two lion cubs in Sierra Leone from a basket and a ship's officer making me give them back. Though we spent a few days in a hill town in Ceylon, it was the train journey back to Calcutta that became the overwhelming return experience. The remembered – recalled at some subliminal level, and surfacing with joy – voices, the country itself, the smells, the sounds the train made and the shouts of the platform vendors – these were not only as familiar as my hand, as welcoming as home, they have continued to haunt my dreams throughout my life. In times of stress and of trouble, I have been able to fall asleep by recreating the sounds of an Indian railway journey. The utter sense of security, and yet adventure, as my bedding roll, with its dusty odour, surrounded me on the hard, slippery bunk, of waking in the night to peer out at strange stations, the shouts of the vendors selling tea and peanuts, waking at dawn to watch the countryside come alive in that magic, pearly hour before the sun stole all colour.

TONY ORCHARD

At the age of 10 in 1936, when my parents came on leave, my father decided that it was time that I lost my regional Cheshire accent, and I was shifted to prep school at Bickley, Kent, where I remained for four years until June 1940 when, fortuitously, my fourteenth birthday coincided with Dunkirk. During that period I spent school holidays with a cousin of my father, married to a Church of England vicar in the West Riding of Yorkshire, who gave me a wonderful home. Only once in those ten years from 4–14 did I ever experience anything resembling Kipling's 'Baa Baa Black Sheep', and that was not repeated, during Easter holidays at a so-called 'holiday home' at Bexhill-on-Sea.

After Dunkirk, my parents in India decided they could, after all, cope with their offspring, and in early August my brother and I were taken up to London by a master and put on the Liverpool train to join the *Strathmore*, one of the prides of the P&O fleet. For what turned out to be six weeks' unconvoyed voyage round the Cape, we were given £5 pocket money between us, and two pairs of blue gym-shorts and two aertex shirts each. But no matter, it was escape to a great adventure, to a completely unknown land that I imagined to be one of Maharajahs and permanent sun.

In no way did our voyage disappoint. Shell was an extremely generous employer. All their families travelled first class as a matter of course. So my brother and I were allocated a first-class cabin each, with access to unlimited food of stupendous quality in the dining saloon. After 10 years of boarding school, free of supervision, surrounded by similar children that included exposure to friendly, jolly girls for virtually the first time, and with unlimited grub, this was nirvana of the highest order.

If the captain of a P&O liner was God, then the head steward of the first class was St Peter, resplendent in his short jacket with gold buttons and blue epaulettes. My brother and I shared a table with the two Johnstone brothers, whose father was with Burmah Shell in Madras. After a few days of testing the menu we asked the head steward how much we could eat. 'Just as much you can tuck away,' he replied encouragingly. So we decided to take him at his word and 'eat the menu' – soup, then fish, followed by a roast, a full plate of curry and rice with all the trimmings, some trifle, rounded off with cheese and biscuits. Bliss! After two or three days of this the head steward approached our table to ask if we were enjoying the voyage and if everything was all right, which we assured him was so. Then casually he enquired, 'Are you boys getting enough to eat?'

'Oh yes thank you, the grub's wonderful.' With that assurance he began to leave our table, but then had second thoughts and returned to ask, 'By the way, I suppose you know the arrangements for paying for your voyage?' When we shook our heads he explained, 'Well, you see, the actual passage has been paid for by your parents or their company, but as for the food you consume, we keep a record of what you eat and send the bill to your parents at the end of the voyage,' and strolled off. Consternation! Could it be true? Do we know any grown-ups that we can ask and trust to give us an honest answer?

Being the elder brother, just fourteen, with the younger brother nearing eight, I did what any other older brother would have done, and out of the £5 pocket money allocated myself half a crown a week and my brother 1/3d. On arrival at Cape Town in about three weeks the Purser's notice board announced coach tours of the drive past the Twelve Apostles, the Lion's Head, Cape Point, Groote Schuur and so on, at a cost of 10/- per head. Clearly this was too good to miss, but with the inevitable miscellaneous expenses the weekly allocation had been breached irretrievably. So I asked the purser if he could find any passenger on the list associated with Burmah Shell, and he came up with a Mr Donaldson. It is hard to believe these days that despite the War, on a completely blacked-out and closed-up ship that accentuated the stifling heat below decks, dressing for dinner was still *de rigeur*. At around seven o'clock that evening I knocked on his cabin door, which sure enough was opened by a man adjusting his bow tie on his dickie shirt. In answer to my enquiry, he confirmed that he was indeed Mr Donaldson of Burmah Shell, to which I delivered my rehearsed spiel: 'Well, I'm Tony Orchard, my father works for the company in Calcutta, my brother and I want to go on the coach tour tomorrow but we cannot afford it, so could you lend me a fiver please, and I'll give you an IOU?' Without further ado, he turned round and produced one of those crisp, white, crackly £5 notes, the first I had ever seen, and told us to go and enjoy ourselves. Colonial life developed initiative at an early age.

It is a truism that nothing prepares one for one's first arrival in India. The sheer press of people, the noise, the bustle, variety and colour, the heat and dirt, the contrasts between rich and poor, all combine to overwhelm the senses. As we docked in Bombay, this is what we looked down on from the boat deck, hundreds of children lining the rails to try and identify whichever parent, usually a mother, had come to meet us. We soon found ours, and were swept away to the Victoria Rail Terminus, that indescribable memorial to Indo-Victorian Gothic from where the Blue Train departed for the three days' and nights' journey to Calcutta. The meals were ordered at one station from a menu to be eaten in the restaurant of the next station during a halt; British Colonial food, lentil or mulligatawny soup, chicken curry or mutton, steamed sponge pudding or plum duff. And the scenes out of the windows: mile after mile of red laterite earth broken by paddy fields, peasant farmers ploughing with water buffaloes, simple villages of mud huts, sheltered by groves of palm trees, and crowds of youngsters lining the track and waving as we passed. Our mother was somewhat dismissive of the quality of the compartments provided, being spoiled by years of Shell standards, but to me it will always be remembered as a ride on a Persian carpet across the plains of India, a Kashan rug with 1000 knots to the inch.

SHEILA WRIGHT-NEVILLE

Much against the advice of my headmistress, my parents booked a passage for me to sail to India in August 1940. They paid an extra half-fare for a woman from Thomas Cook to chaperone me during the voyage: I was now 12. The woman met me on the dock in Liverpool and ticked my name off a list as I boarded, but I never saw her again. The liner was the *Stratheden*, and it was to travel in convoy round the Cape of Good Hope to Bombay and then on to Australia. As well as troops bound for the Far Eastern front, and some civilians, there were four hundred unaccompanied children on board. We spent the first three days and nights moored in Liverpool docks, with continual air-raids. The Battle of Britain was being waged. We lived in our lifejackets, and there were several lifeboat drills before we ever left port. In my ignorance, I wasn't at all frightened, and my only regret was having to leave my new bike behind at school.

Five of us children shared a cabin, with a kindly stewardess in the next cabin keeping an eye on us. I had a bout of tonsillitis during the voyage, and she wrapped hot antiphlogistine poultices round my neck to draw out the poison. Once at sea, we made a wide sweep out into the Atlantic, before turning south. All the passenger vessels were accompanied and protected by a large convoy of naval ships. Target practice from the deck was often part of the day's excitement, and we were continually warned never to take off our lifejackets. German U-boats were patrolling the Atlantic, and I only realised later just how dangerous this part of the voyage was.

We arrived in Cape Town without incident and stayed there a week for ship repairs. A brigadier's wife, *en route* to India to join her husband, with whom I had become friendly, took me and a friend ashore and toured us round Cape Town and up Table Mountain. I was finally able to send a cable to my parents to say I was on my way. It was the first news they had that I had actually sailed, as any such notification from England would have been censored ('Loose Lips Sink Ships'). We left Cape Town without a convoy, and finally arrived in Bombay after more than six weeks at sea.

In Bombay, I was met by my family friends and put on a train for the three-day journey across India to Calcutta. The railway authorities assumed that all train passengers named Wright-Neville belonged to the same family, and should therefore ride in the same carriage, which is how I came to meet some cousins I never knew I had. My father had a half-brother from his father's second marriage, of whom he strongly disapproved. No communication between the two families had occurred for many years, but I soon learned that my two cousins, Peter and Patsy, had, like me, been at school in England. Their father, a senior officer in the Madras Police, had travelled to Bombay to meet them, and we shared a carriage across the continent. Both families met on Calcutta's Howrah Station, where my uncle and cousins changed trains for Madras. The other Wright-Neville family were very nice to me on that train trip, and I regret I never saw or heard of them ever again.

MARION ALEXANDER

My return to India, unaccompanied when aged about 10, proved on the whole uneventful. The *Stratheden* left Liverpool in August 1940, joined a convoy, and arrived in Bombay after calls at Freetown and Cape Town. It took about six weeks, and I for one thankfully left behind the cumbersome lifebelt which had to be carried around all the time. I arrived with no luggage, as it had been mislaid from the beginning of the voyage (clothing had been lent on board).

My mother met me, no doubt bringing necessary garments, and we boarded the train for Calcutta. I think the journey took about two

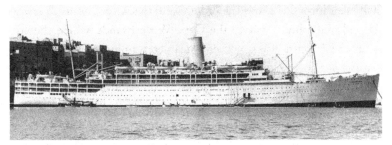

The *Stratheden*, pictured at Malta on her maiden voyage in 1937. In 1940 she transported a large number of unaccompanied children – variously estimated between two hundred and four hundred – from Liverpool to Bombay round the Cape of Good Hope. (Courtesy of P&O)

to three days, during which time I developed spots, and subsequently spent the next week or so in a Calcutta hotel with measles, and dying of heat! I remember nothing about the final stage from Calcutta to the bungalow, but I clearly remember being reunited with my case several months later – not bad for wartime.

LAURENCE FLEMING

We sailed from Liverpool on the 3rd or 4th of August. Our ship was the *Mulbera*, a one-class vessel belonging to the British India Steam Navigation Company Limited. I remember the masts of a sunken ship as we sailed down the Mersey in the afternoon. Our companion on this memorable voyage was to be Ruth Dear, originally our Norland nurse, but who had never been anything other than a great friend, and we were delighted to be travelling with her. My sister Jane was five and a half; I was to have my eleventh birthday on the voyage.

We were in convoy three days later, on the outside. It was gloriously rough, and we had 'wooden walls' put round our places at meals to prevent food, cutlery and crockery cascading into our laps. The food, I thought, was delicious and, very early on, I hoped this voyage would last forever. Then the convoy disappeared. Years later I was to learn that a ship right on the other side of the convoy had been torpedoed, and the orders were to scatter at once. We zig-zagged our solitary way to the Cape Verde Islands, where the coal – for the *Mulbera* was a genuine steamer, running on boiling water – came out on a tender, brought aboard by men with baskets on their heads. This took three days. There was blackwater fever at Freetown, so we continued our erratic course to Cape Town.

Somewhere, Jane had picked up impetigo. The ship's doctor, delightfully drunk most of the time, prescribed a castor-oil oint-ment which made it worse. So the object of our afternoon ashore in Cape Town was to find a skin specialist or similar. But it was a Saturday, and everything in Cape Town was firmly closed. We wandered drearily round the silent city, eventually finding a cinema, where we had waffles. It was the 7th of September, the day the *blitzkrieg* really began on London.

Durban was quite different. The first chemist we went into had a skin specialist upstairs. The ointment he prescribed disposed of the impetigo in three days, and I no longer had to put Dettol into my bath. I really loved those baths. They were enormous. Full of hot sea-water, I could just perform two breast strokes end to end. Then, after a glorious wallow, the bath steward, who was Indian like most of the crew, would bring in a tin tub of hot fresh water, and it was into that that I put my Dettol.

After Durban, *Mulbera* came into her own. The blackout was relaxed, and canvas swimming-pools on wooden frames appeared on the well-deck below the bows. We bought our *topees* in Colombo, but it was when we went ashore in Madras, and I felt the heat seeping up through the soles of my sandals, that I knew I was coming home. We arrived in Calcutta on the 3rd of October, and here our mother met us.

After a few days' shopping – for to the best of my recollection we had only one small suitcase each, and hardly any thin clothes – we embarked on the Assam Mail, which left Sealdah Station at 2.00, or perhaps 2.30, in the afternoon. A very broad-gauge train took us to Parbatipur, where we changed into a narrow-gauge train. Bedding rolls were unrolled; we actually slept in sheets, and the train ambled through the night on wheels traditionally thought to be square, depositing us on the north bank of the Brahmaputra in the very early morning. Here we were met by our father, who had been rowed across the river in a country boat, 'so that we could have breakfast together on the flat'.

Of all my memories of India those 'breakfasts on the flat' remain some of the pleasantest. The 'flat' was an unpowered ferry with two decks, rounded at both ends. On the lower deck was the luggage, all kinds of merchandise, goats, chickens, the occasional cow, possibly even a motor car and all the third-class passengers. But upstairs, courtesy of Messrs Framjee, were long tables covered with white cloths, on which they served papaya or an orange, cornflakes, fried fish, bacon and eggs, toast and marmalade, tea or coffee. It was always very early in the morning, so it was cool, and the crossing at this time of year took about an hour, hauled by a little chugging tug.

On future occasions we travelled on by train, arriving about mid-night, but this time we went by car. We went first to Gauhati, where we were welcomed with flowers by the Chunilals, Jain merchants selling all the products of the Assam Oil Company. 'Not wreaths, darling,' said my mother. 'Garlands.' Then we set off up the Assam Valley, rice fields and tea gardens, forests and high hills in the distance, though we never again saw that wide, calm river.

The Great Trunk Road of Assam consisted, at that time, of two tarmac strips with mud, or dust, depending on the season, between them. This was a good arrangement so long as there was only one vehicle on the road, which was the case most of the time. But when one had to get off the tarmac strips, to meet, or overtake, the dust was indescribable. We all gradually turned a pale coffee colour. Past the Lake Temples of Sibsagar, past the railhead of Tinsukia, other end of the Assam Bengal Railway, past the tea garden of Chabua where Jane was born, past the *burra bhil*, a snipe-filled marsh, and then, at last, The Ridge, with its oil derricks, the Refinery and then the Railway Station. We were there.

top The Fleming family and Miss Ruth Dear, on right, garlanded by Messrs Chunilal, Jain Merchants of Gauhati, Assam, on the children's arrival in October 1940. The Swastika, four-square, feet on the ground, is a symbol of good fortune to both the Buddhists and the Hindus. The Nazis foolishly painted it black, an insult in itself, then up-ended it, obliging it to stand on tiptoe, so that all the good fortune ran out.

middle A view of the Refinery at Digboi. (Ann Prowse)

bottom The Railway Station at Digboi, 1940. Platforms were a rarity. This is where 'Barbara' and 'Lilian' spent the night shunting. Viewed from the garden of No 1, Digboi. (Lavender Todd)

The *burra bungalow*, one of the oldest in Digboi, and certainly the largest, stood on a small hill above the railway station – not the Assam-Bengal Railway, but an even older one, the Dibru-Sadiya, completed in the 1880s – and was reached only by a long flight of steps. As I began to climb them, the last five years rolled away. The green gate at the top, the beds of cannas each side of the path, the ground orchid, the strange tree whose name nobody knew, but which was always covered with ants, all were remembered and all were still there. My sandpit had gone, but my swing was still there, painted black and white. And on the verandah, in navy blue surtout and splendid white turban, stood a well-remembered figure, after whose health I had frequently enquired in my weekly letters.

'I remember Rahman,' I said.

We shook hands. He called me 'Baba-sahib'. The last five years vanished completely. I was being welcomed, back into paradise; and I hoped my stay there would be a long one.

AURIOL GURNER

When war broke out, my parents were on home leave. My father had to go back to India immediately, my mother stayed in England. After Dunkirk my mother, who had refused my father's request that she should come back to India without us, made arrangements to take us out to India. I could not believe my good fortune – I could not believe it was actually happening when, taken away from school before the end of the summer term, Lynette and I joined my sister and mother, who took us to buy *topees* (what a thrill) and clothes for India. My eldest sister got two beautiful ball-gowns, one white, one pink, for the Governor's and the Viceroy's balls.

We sailed in August for Bombay on the *Orion* as part of a large convoy. The *Orion* developed engine trouble, and we had to return to Greenock for repairs. The ship was carrying many families rejoining parents in India, and a battalion (I think) of the Argyll and Sutherland Highlanders. The days spent slowly steaming back to Greenock and rejoining the convoy were a period of anxiety for the adults – I was just in a seventh heaven of delight. I was with my mother and sisters going to India and the conditions on board were luxurious (we were travelling first class in virtually peacetime conditions). Approaching my thirteenth birthday, due in October, I knew I was the luckiest child alive.

Initially, peacetime conditions prevailed in Calcutta. My eldest sister entered into the social life, while my sister and I went swimming at the Saturday Club, shopping with mother in Calcutta's big stores and – much more exciting – in the New Market, and walked the dogs on the Maidan after tea when it was cooler. I was, I felt, transported to another world. Where at boarding school in England I would be running 'twice round the rose garden before breakfast', always hurrying, life ruled by bells and constantly trying to do the right thing, here I was another person. There was a servant for every purpose. Mother had taken on an *ayah*, who laid out our clean clothes each morning. While one was still asleep she ran the bath (each room had adjoining bathroom), with a rag wound round the taps so that the sound of running water would not wake one. She squeezed toothpaste on to the brush in readiness, and then brought fresh orange juice to one's bedside. After breakfast, my mother sent for the cook, went through his book listing his purchases the previous day, chose today's menu and gave him 5 or 10 rupees for today's shopping. At dinner parties he sometimes produced his speciality, exquisitely woven toffee baskets with brittle-toffee handles filled with fruit. A great treat was breakfast on Sunday mornings at Tollygunge Club on the outskirts of Calcutta. There we would enjoy an enormous breakfast and afterwards sit out under two huge trees on the lawn and read the papers brought out from England, sometimes finishing with a swim before going home when the sun rose too high for comfort. In the cold weather there were races there. Periods of boredom sometimes occurred in the afternoons when my mother was out or resting and my sister and I would lie on our beds under the fan, quarrelling scrappily. My one abiding dislike was tennis parties.

PATRICIA TOFT

My parents came back to England in 1940, as my father was due for leave. The two 'aunties' from April Farm, our holiday home, were planning to take any children whose parents wanted them to to Canada for the rest of the War, and it was touch and go whether my parents would choose for us to return with them to India or go with the 'aunties' to Canada. I held my breath, and thank goodness they chose India.

We were terribly excited to be returning to India. It was a six-week voyage round the Cape, and in convoy. For the first part of the voyage we had to wear our lifejackets all the time. On arrival in Bombay I had an attack of tonsillitis, and was deemed too ill to travel on to Calcutta, so my father went on with my two sisters and my mother and I stayed in Bombay until I was better. One night apparently I was very ill, and my mother sent for a doctor, who was called from a dinner party and arrived in full evening-dress. He terrified my mother by telling her that I had diphtheria. Fortunately, he was wrong. One of the things I found utterly fascinating while staying in Bombay was watching people sleeping on doorsteps. I would get out of bed very early in the morning and sit in the window and watch until the sleeping person woke, sat up and put on his shoes, got up and went on his way. This really fascinated me.

I don't remember the rest of the journey over to Calcutta but on arrival was sent to Dr Norre, the ear, nose and throat specialist, who said my tonsils were in too bad a condition to be taken out yet, so I had a course of infra-red lamp treatment for a few weeks and had to suck vast quantities of rather horrible sweets before he could do the operation, which was done in Miss Reardon's Nursing Home in Calcutta. We were now living at 9 Mayfair, Ballygunge.

We used to ride early in the morning on the Ballygunge Maidan, where the Calcutta Light Horse, who stabled their horses on the other part of the Maidan, were also exercising. The Maidan would sometimes be shrouded in a thick blanket of mist which, as the big, red ball of the sun slowly rose in the sky, would rise gradually, and we could first see the hooves of the other horses and then their legs, then their bellies and, as the mist rose higher, we would eventually be able to see all of the horses and their riders. It was strange to be able to see part of the horses, while the rest was completely invisible, enveloped in the thick mist. There was an avenue of trees on the way to the Light Horse stables which were crammed full of monkeys, who would peer down at us as we rode under them. I was always afraid they would spring down on to my horse's back and terrify both him and me. Fortunately it never happened, but it was quite scary – there were so many of them, and rumour had it that they had killed a little boy.

At one end of the Maidan there was a huge trunk, in which lived a Holy Man. When the cover over the opening was not there I would peep in. It was always spotlessly clean and tidy, with bright, shining, brass pots, and his sleeping mat rolled up. I always thought it was a wonderful way to live, and I envied him.

On Sunday mornings we would go to the paperchase. This was a horse race over a course marked out by a trail of paper. We would watch the start and the finish, and then we were allowed to ride over the course. It was quite difficult, with jumps and ditches to

Jeremy Lemmon: 'Watching a snake charmer in the garden of our Ballygunge house. About 1940. The standing gentleman is my uncle, Harry Lemmon, a distinguished soldier. Sitting half-hidden in front of him is his wife, my aunt Bella, and sitting on the *mora* in front of her is their son, my cousin Kenneth. I am sitting next to him, and next to me is my younger sister, Jane. My brother John is on the extreme right. Behind Jane is Lizzie, our *ayah*. I think she was from Madras.'

manoeuvre. After this we would go to the Jodhpur Club, have a bath and change, and then have breakfast, which was served out of doors on the lawns. I remember small *chokras* in uniform walking around the tables holding flags on extremely long poles. This was to scare away the kites, who would otherwise dive down and snatch the cakes and sandwiches at tea time.

During the week in the holidays I would often put my little dog in my bicycle basket and ride over to the Jodhpur Club to walk with her on the golf course. There was a level-crossing on the way there, and it was always very exciting to watch the trains go through. Those walks were exciting too, with the ever-magical atmosphere of India and the wonderful sounds of the Indian birds. Later on it became a bit unsafe to cycle alone, as I can recall on at least one occasion meeting a large group of demonstrators marching along on the other side on the road, chanting things like 'Jai Hind' etc., and there had been rumours of girls being attacked by groups such as this one.

I left India before Independence and travelled back to England with my elder sister. Arriving at Tilbury everything seemed grey and damp – it was late August. One of the first things I noticed in England, and which bothered me, was that there was nobody on the streets – having been used to the teeming throngs of Calcutta I found it strange and lonely to walk along a road and see no one. Where was everybody? We must have had so much freedom in India, because in England everything seemed to be 'not allowed', or 'forbidden'. Notices everywhere saying 'no' this, or '...forbidden'. I felt very restricted, and it took many years to get used to having left India.

JOHN LANGLEY

On arriving aboard the *Stratheden*, Grandfather Clark had dutifully handed me over to a Mrs X, who was supposed to be taking care of me during the voyage, and who would be turning me over to my parents on arrival in Bombay. I have not the slightest recollection of her name, because after the first introduction I don't remember ever seeing her again. Apparently she was the matron in charge of about three hundred children who, like me, were being evacuated to India.

We suffered an air-raid as we waited to cast off in Liverpool. Fortunately, we suffered no damage, and were finally cleared for departure in the early hours of the morning. We sailed north, around the top of Ireland, and then south through the Bay of Biscay. There were about thirty ships in our convoy, and on the second day one of them, the *Orion*, developed engine trouble, and had to return to England.

Boat drill was one of the fun events on board. I am sure that the adults must have groaned and complained. Finding the correct lifeboat was a disaster. Confusion always seemed to exist, no matter how many drills took place. Adults rushing in all directions, brushing aside small, unaccompanied young boys, the klaxon horn blaring away, adding to the urgency of the exercise, and often the drills were held just after dinner, with darkness adding to the problems. I think I managed to find a different lifeboat each time. I do remember watching with great interest the destroyer escort running around like sheepdogs and looking very sleek and beautiful, with the large bow waves they created when moving at speed. They made us feel as though we were standing still, which was almost true, as we were reduced to steaming at 12 knots, the top speed of the slowest ship in the convoy.

Our first port of call was Freetown in Sierra Leone. I have no idea why we called there, although it may have been that part of the convoy broke up at this point. Part of the escort left us, and I suppose it was considered we were out of the range of the majority of the U-boat wolf packs. Whatever the reason, it gave us an opportunity to see the coast of Africa, and left me with one or two impressions.

The first was the smell. It seems to me that it was the smell of rotting vegetation, or maybe it was a pulp and paper mill, but whatever it was, the smell extended miles out to sea. The other impression was of a very hot blue sky, deep-green vegetation, yellow-white sands and very white buildings. The water was remarkably clear and, as we were not allowed to go ashore, we were visited by the local population in all kinds of boats.

Not long after we left Freetown we were treated to one of the rare sights of the sea, a clipper under full sail. It was one of the few that still remained in active service, and was bound for Southampton. We were advised of its approach over the loudspeaker, and the ship took quite a tilt as everyone rushed to the side to see the clipper go by. There was much cheering and waving from both sides. It was a marvellous sight, and we hoped it would have a safe voyage back to England. Needless to say, it was not in a convoy.

We arrived at Cape Town one glorious morning. At first we did not know whether we would be allowed to go ashore at all. However, it was later announced that we would be staying in Cape Town until the *Orion* rejoined us, and that would probably not be for three or four days. Permission to land was obtained from the local authorities after a health inspection had been carried out, and this took some time. I think it was at least two days after we arrived before the first groups went ashore.

I managed to join one of the shore parties by telling my guardian steward I had been invited to accompany my friends but, instead, tagged along with a completely strange family. They were also interested in Table Mountain, and planned to take the ride to the top. There was a type of cable car that took groups up and, by staying close to my currently adopted family, I was admitted into the car. I wonder who, if anyone, paid for me? There were spectacular views in all directions, but the one that impressed me was looking out to sea and hearing someone say there was nothing between us and South America. I overheard another group saying they were going to walk down and take the bus back to Cape Town. I decided I would once again tag along.

It was a very long way down. The trail wound down between the Two Apostles, as the hills adjacent to Table Mountain are called, and finally over the pipeline to the road. I got very tired, and gradually fell further and further behind the group. By the time I got to the road the day was rapidly drawing to a close, and I was tired, and hungry, and a little frightened at being completely on my own. However, a bus came along and I got on, and then realised that I had another problem: I didn't have any money, I didn't know where I was going, and I was getting panicky. When the conductor came to collect my fare I found out I was going in the wrong direction: apparently I was on my way to Simonstown. He suggested that I get off at the next stop and catch the bus going the other way. Fortunately, this conversation was overheard by a man and wife who were sitting behind me, and were also planning to get off at the next stop. When they discovered that I was from one of the ships, and that I was on my own, and had managed to get lost, they suggested I go with them to their house and they would arrange for me to get back to the ship. Needless to say, I gratefully accepted their offer, and I was very fortunate that they were indeed a kindly couple. They gave me an excellent dinner, and then arranged to have me driven back to the ship.

The remainder of the trip to Bombay was uneventful. We arrived there one very hot day, and suddenly there seemed to be masses of queues everywhere on the ship. It appeared to have been boarded by millions and millions of grown-ups, all dashing about looking for their children or relatives, and causing even more confusion.

By some miracle, Mother had wangled a boarding pass and had found me amongst all those hundreds of people. It was just as well that it was Mother, as I was not at all sure I would have recognised my father (or he me!). After thanking the steward for looking after me so well, my mother and I left the ship. To the best of my knowledge we never did meet Mrs X.

I was very shy of meeting Father after all my years in England. Four years is a very long time at that age, and I'm still not sure that I would have recognised him if Mother had not been there.

That evening we had dinner in a very elegant and huge dining room at the Taj Mahal Hotel. It had large, sparkling chandeliers and snowy-white table-cloths, and there were waiters everywhere in sparkling red-and-white uniforms. A four-piece orchestra with a lady singer performed quietly throughout the evening.

The following morning we went for a walk in the Botanical Gardens, which were set out in terraces on Malabar Hill. It was immaculately maintained, and was one of the tourist attractions in the city. We also visited the small church, All Saints', where Mother and Father were married, located at the top of Malabar Hill. It had a lovely setting amongst luxurious, green foliage, and exotic flowers. The church was built in warm red-brick and white, painted, woodwork trim, and seemed very English, in spite of the tropical setting. It was beautifully cool inside after the long, hot climb up from the Botanical Gardens.

We returned to the hotel for lunch, and in the afternoon boarded the train for our two-day journey across India to Calcutta, where we changed trains. Kanchrapara, where Father was currently stationed, was 25 miles north of Calcutta. It was a railway town, with various locomotive and carriage shops, as well as the design offices for this portion of the Bengal-Assam Railway. The end of the journey was anticlimactic, as almost immediately I was confined to my bed with an attack of measles, which I must have caught on board the *Stratheden*.

LYNETTE GURNER

My father was in the Indian Civil Service, joining in 1910 and retiring in 1947, on Partition. For at least the last ten years of his career he lived in Calcutta. My mother, sisters and I joined him in September 1940 after six weeks at sea, and the long train journey over from Bombay. We, the daughters, had spent the previous 10 years, 1930–40, at boarding school and a holiday home in England. We saw my father every four years for the school summer holidays. My mother managed to get over every two years, usually for Easter holidays, as well as for the summer. When with them, we always lived in hotels. Basically we were, of necessity, institutionalised, but in comfortable circumstances and with parents to write to each week and to relate to. I missed my mother, particularly, very much indeed. Leaving India at four years of age I do not remember early years there. To live as a family from 1940 was to us the most wonderful thing – so unexpected. The decision was made suddenly, well into 1940. To live in such comfort was incredible.

In 1940 Calcutta was almost Victorian in some of its social ways. Some days after our arrival Mother set out, accompanied by her two younger daughters – as always astonished – armed with my father's and her calling cards. We drove to various homes. Our driver stopped, was handed two of my father's calling cards and one of my mother's, and dropped them in the special box everyone had at their gates. One card only for my mother, as ladies did not call on men – I think that was the explanation. People responded with their cards – invitations either way then followed. Our box was once stolen from our wall – crisis! A friend spotted it in the market, solid oak with 'Gurner' in large letters on it. It was recovered.

My father belonged to the Bengal Club and the United Services Club. Both were for men only, and both were residential. But he also belonged to the Saturday Club (dinner and dancing most evenings, afternoon teas, library, swimming and tennis). Most of all I enjoyed the evenings dancing. And he also belonged to the Tollygunge Club (Sunday breakfasts, golf, small racecourse, swimming, walking and sitting under trees sometimes in the evenings, until the fireflies came out). Sunday breakfast was a big social surprise for us. Our first Sunday in Calcutta our parents said, 'Off to Tollygunge for breakfast.' We were amazed – never heard of such a thing – but so it was every Sunday. A very large cooked breakfast, all the usual breakfast foods plus fresh fish (no smoked fish). With this went the most delicious bread-rolls, coffee etc. It was a social occasion, friends greeting each other – definitely not a heads-down, read-the-papers breakfast. Then reading magazines under the trees, a swim, then home to lunch, which would be ready and waiting for us – of course!

What did Calcutta look like? There was the Maidan, a vast, green, open space. Standing on this, large, white and very splendid, was the Victoria Memorial, which housed an Art Gallery. A seriously used racecourse ran round the Maidan area, and all forms of impromptu recreation took place on it. The Tollygunge racecourse was much more light-hearted than this one. There were Australian jockeys on the Calcutta Race Course, for instance. We often went to Tolly, but only once that I remember to the Calcutta course. We walked our dogs on the Maidan Racehorses were exercised there. Much informal cricket and football took place there, and also other special events. On New Year's Day 1941 my mother took us to a military display, an official, social occasion. It included very skilled and impressive displays on horseback given by turbaned soldiers, who were dressed in very colourful, extremely smart uniforms. Chowringhee, the main thoroughfare, ran down the side of the Maidan that was furthest from the river. It was a very wide main road. Trams, two single-deckers linked together, ran regularly alongside the Maidan, between it and Chowringhee. Other public transport were rickshaws, pulled by one unfortunate man, horse-drawn gharries, taxis and buses. The 'busty' area, the most fearful slums, were away from the main built-up area.

There was also a zoo, on the way to Alipore, a botanic garden across the river and some way down it, and, at the Government House end of the Maidan, the Eden Gardens, which were ornamental, but where cricket and tennis were also played. There were man-made lakes just outside Calcutta. Its river, the Hooghly, was vast, and the reason for Calcutta's original existence. The Lall Rasta, the Red Road, ran alongside it more or less on the far side of the Maidan, and monkeys played around in the trees there. Calcutta was originally the Viceregal base. Because of this, many fine buildings were built. They were white, impressive and surrounded by much open space, though this space had, of course, been swallowed up by 1940. These buildings included Government House, the Secretariat and St John's Church, which was the cathedral in Warren Hastings's day. A much bigger cathedral was subsequently built near the Maidan. Chowringhee had two department stores, a cinema, one or two hotels and a restaurant or two. Wide roads lead off from it, in particular Park Street. This had offices in it, rather than the Chowringhee assortment.

Outside the main part of Calcutta were Alipore and Ballygunge. There were some lovely houses there. I would say many belonged to the wealthier European firms, who provided them for their most senior staff. And I would also say that most Europeans lived in flats.

Heavy wooden shutters were fitted inside all the windows to provide shade when needed. Floors were tiled, no carpets, odd mats about. We had a reasonably large garden and a longish drive with a garage in the vicinity of the kitchen (and the servants' quarters). Those buildings were specifically designed for Europeans, for the very hot climate, for households with servants and for the rigorous caste and class system that existed. As a point of interest, for our flat, with five in total in our family, we had 10 servants, and this I would say was a modest home. Each servant only did one job. Life was very comfortable indeed – luxurious after boarding school. I would like to give one illustration of the sudden, extraordinary contrast in our lives that occurred with our arrival in Calcutta. We had an *ayah* employed as the equivalent of bearer to us three daughters. A dear old lady, who worked out for herself how to make life easy for us. Every morning she came in first thing with freshly squeezed orange juice, which she put by my bed. I slept on. She went into

Chowringhee and Tram Terminus, Calcutta. (John Langley)

the bathroom, fixed strips of sheeting to both taps to silently run my bath. When this was ready she woke me with her gentle voice, 'Your bath is ready, Miss-sahib,' in Hindustani. I was a 14-year-old schoolgirl. That same 14-year-old schoolgirl the previous two terms of 1940 had undergone vigorous Swedish drill, out-of-doors winter and summer, followed by a brisk run round large, ornamental gardens, and this was every day before breakfast.

LAVENDER TODD

In September 1939 our parents arrived home on leave on the day that war was declared. As our father was recovering from an illness, their return to the east was delayed until September 1940, and they decided to take us two girls with them to India. We travelled in the *City of Simla* but we didn't get far in her, as she was torpedoed the second night out from Glasgow during a very bad spell of sinkings, which it was thought at the time was the work of submarines harbouring somewhere off the northern coast of Ireland. The attack took place in the middle of the night, just after a muster station warning. There was a tremendous explosion, and the ship lurched to one side with alarm bells ringing the order for all to get on deck. The lascars had lowered all the lifeboats, so we had to climb down ladders and jump into the small boats when the sea swell raised them to the end of the ladder. There were many children aboard travelling out to join their parents at this stage in the War. I had a small boy on my back, half asleep, and he lost his grip around my neck halfway down the ladder, with the result that we both fell into the water. Someone with an oar kept us from being squashed between the boat and the ship, and we were yanked into the lifeboat. An empty cargo boat *en route* for the US was ordered to pick us up, so we were not in the boat for more than four hours. Mercifully there were not many casualties, and the ship did not go down immediately, unlike the *City of Benares* the night before in the same place, with many travelling to the US, which sank in five minutes with great loss of life.

Back in Britain, having lost all our possessions other than the clothes on our backs, we waited for another passage, and two months later we boarded the troopship *City of Exeter*. This convoy was again attacked, and two bombs were dropped on the convoy in daylight as we watched, but this time we got away with it. By this time, of course, the Mediterranean was out of the question, and we eventually made land at Cape Town, thence to Durban and eventually to Bombay, without any further incident. Our father did his best to teach us some Hindi, but achieved little success – four women in a troopship for six weeks was too much fun for us girls, though it raised no little concern for our parents!

Quetta was our father's next posting, as assistant to the Governor General in Baluchistan. There was an earthquake when we were there, but nothing like the 1935 disaster, and anyway, the buildings had been constructed on the Californian anti-earthquake model, so houses, trees, and gardens rose and fell as if on waves. I was sent to a small, private school in Delhi to complete my School Certificate, and during the hot weather we moved to Simla, a wonderful town clinging to the hillside, with memories of monkeys, rickshaws drawn by two men as no cars were allowed, fires at night and much kindness shown to me by my parents' friends, the Glancys – he was the Governor of the Punjab, and he and his secretariat staff went to Simla during the hot weather. He lived in what seemed to me to be a palace!

I was lucky to pass my School Certificate. All our answer papers had to be written in triplicate for marking to go back to Britain in different ships in case of loss, and for the English essay I had placed the carbon paper upside-down. However, I was given an extra 20 minutes to re-write my offering, and I can only suppose that our torpedoing was a novel subject!

Our next posting was to Udaipur in Rajastan – a dream of fairyland, especially during the Diwali Festival of Light, when barges on the Pichola Lake were decorated and lit up, and parties and curry feasts seemed to go on for days. It was very hot indeed here, but the Residency was kept cool by *khas khas tatties* – screens draped over the open, exterior doors with a continuous flow of water running through the mesh of the sandalwood brush, allowing the hot desert winds to blow through the water, thus cooling the house. At night we slept on the roof of the house until the rising sun awoke us.

It was a wonderful life, with camps for duck and *teeta* (partridge) shoots and trips to see marvellous Rajastan tombs and palaces and Hindu religious festivals, with all the pomp and glamorous ceremony that the Princely States were so well known for. Sadly the Maharana, the most senior princely rank, suffered from paralysis, resulting from the treatment by imposition of a dung poultice on a boil, which had then turned septic. Tennis parties at the Residency were organised by our mother with equal ceremony: the players arriving and indeed playing, in their exotic and colourful Rajastani clothes and *pugris* – swords were worn during play! Indian sweetmeats, curry puffs and savoury dishes were served for tea at half time.

With my father and sister I rode for two or three hours every morning, getting up at 6.00 a.m. before the heat of the day caught us. I can smell the early-morning fires, fuelled by cow dung, and I can hear the village dogs barking as clearly today as 54 years ago!

ANN BURKINSHAW

The opening of The New School at the end of 1940 must have come as a great relief to many parents, and I look back upon it as a marvellous stroke of good fortune. A lot of people, and particularly many self-opinionated people in the press, radio and television, like to say that no one in their right minds can truthfully say they enjoyed their school days: they didn't have the luck to attend The New School – and I consider I am still in my right mind! I look back on the years of 1940–44 with the greatest of pleasure and gratitude.

It was an amazing feat of organisation on the part of Mr Loukes and his staff to sort out 250 boys and girls covering the gamut of school age into their relevant forms with form teachers at the ready with exercise books, textbooks, pencils and desks. I remember that first day walking up the drive from the gate on Alipore Road (does anyone remember that Rumer Godden lived next door, in the lower flat?) with, presumably, the other 249 children of all ages and sizes, to the enormous porch and into the marble assembly hall. I do not recollect any confusion, but found myself in a classroom on the ground floor on the left of the hall and near to Mr Loukes's office. Outside his office was that splendid statue of a nude nymph emerging from the water in a fountain (except that there was no water). Initially, she was shrouded in a white sheet! The school building, which belonged to Mr Gubbay (he who distilled illicit whisky and found himself incarcerated for his efforts), was really rather splendid, with large areas of marble floors and innumerable marble columns, both upstairs and downstairs. I do not think there were a great many rooms – classrooms had to be formed out of the spaces. There was quite a large area of grass at the back where I seem to remember we played netball and spent our breaks.

No 12 Alipore Road, Calcutta, first home of The New School in 1940. It had previously been the house of a Mr Gubbay, whose distillation of an illicit whisky called 'House of Lords' had landed him in jail. (Barbara Dixon)

It was decided to evacuate the whole school up to Darjeeling permanently from 1942 onwards. It was obviously less divisive, and a great deal cheaper, to have the whole school in one place for the whole year from March to December. I think those of us who remained in Calcutta during that first hot weather felt a little bit out on a limb from the mainstream in Darjeeling.

In Darjeeling we followed the term timing of the local schools and worked through from March to December. Cambridge School and Higher School Certificates were sat at the end of the year. We used to have some days off – I remember the *pujas* in October. The journey from Calcutta to Darjeeling has no doubt been described many times over: the mainline train from Sealdah to Siliguri at the foothills of the Himalayas – at most stations throughout the night one or other of us at the ready with a hockey stick to bang the fingers of would-be passengers trying to board the train through the window – and then the famous little train from Siliguri to Darjeeling with a stopover at Kurseong for breakfast (bacon, eggs and toast!).

Senior and Middle boys at The New School in Darjeeling doing physical training on the 'plateau' above Eden Falls, the school house. Kanchenjunga above, Birch Hill, Darjeeling, middle distance. (Brian Hocking)

The boredom of the journey was relieved by the many opportunities of jumping off and on the train when it looped the loop. The station at Darjeeling was a long way down the hillside, and the coolies carrying our trunks on their backs had a very long trudge up to the school and the boarding houses. In March Darjeeling was still fairly cold, but the air was crisp and clear, as it was again from October to December. Kanchenjunga and the snows were at their best during these periods, but even during the rainy season Kanchenjunga nearly always revealed herself at least once during each day.

Perhaps the most indelible memory I have of those years in Darjeeling is of the annual walk up to Tiger Hill to see the sun rise on Everest. This took place in October, when the rains were over and the days were clear and the air crisp. We set off between 2.00 a.m. and 3.00 a.m. walking up to Jalapahar – which was, I think, a British military cantonment and probably where British soldiers spent their leaves during the War – through the military cemetery, which was quite eerie, and then along the road along the north-west side of Darjeeling to Ghoom. The view of the snows from along this road was out of this world: the moon lit up the mountains on our left-hand side and the moonlight filtered through the trees on the Khudside on our right-hand side on to the road.

At Ghoom we turned left up the hill. I seem to remember starting up a rocky path, then coming across one or two large fields and after them up more rocky paths. Then we walked over the Senchal Golf Course, highest in the world, and would reach Tiger Hill just before dawn, to be given a hot drink and the most delicious, moist fruit cake which the Austrian matron of the girls' boarding house always made for us. Then, as the sun began to rise, the silvery, snowy mountain range – the 'roof of the world' I think it was called – slowly turned to peach, and the sky became the palest of blue. There was always controversy about which of the three peaks in the far distance was actually Everest, but if you looked at all three you must have seen it! The walk back always seemed an anti-climax.

STAR STAUNTON

In November 1940 I packed away my finery, my flower collection, my paint brushes, my girlish interests, donned the drab Women's Army Corps (India) uniform, and became, *ipso facto*, an adult. Eighteen weeks of intensive but unmemorable training and I was commissioned as Second Lieutenant.

They could have posted me anywhere, and to any kind of job, but by fortune or favour or because of my previous experience I was in fact attached to the Allied Liaison Office in New Delhi, the most interesting opportunity, I suppose, that could have been offered me. There was gathered there an international multitude that included representatives of all the forces that were contributing to the allied war effort, or that might be persuaded to do so – French, Dutch, Norwegians, Americans, Australians, New Zealanders, Canadians. We lived in the sprawling camps that ringed New Delhi, each cantonment flying its own national flag. Lord Louis Mountbatten, the future Viceroy, was our overlord.

I was responsible to two bosses, Colonel Lionel Wilson and the French Colonel François Gibbon Guilem. France had fallen. Pétain was keeping in with the Germans as much as his conscience would allow him. We were dealing now with General de Gaulle's Free French, who were of course very much at odds with Pétain. Whether they followed Pétain or de Gaulle, all Frenchmen were 'Frogs' to Colonel Wilson, who in this respect, I believe, was typical of the British in India, who perhaps had atavistic attitudes inherited from the days when French and English fought for control of the sub-continent and the English won. As their go-between I was much more aware of the warfare between my two colonels than of the larger struggle in which they were supposed to be co-operating. Guilem suffered from the humiliation of his country's defeat by Hitler and was very touchy about French *honneur*; on the other hand, he enjoyed the personal friendship of Lord Mountbatten. Colonel Wilson could stick out his chest at the memory of the

Battle of Britain. Ours was a liaison office indeed, but most of the liaison was done by us girls, as we played peace-maker between these two belligerents. At least we did not lack material for satirical gossip.

It was hard to take our main work seriously in that atmosphere, the more so because before the Japanese brought immediate menace by their invasion of Burma, the chief activity of the various groups that made up the Allied Liaison Office seemed to be the throwing of parties. Life in the evenings was one rather hectic round of social festivity, which, though we could superficially justify it because it furthered mutual understanding and friendship, nevertheless, I am sure, drew some of its energy from the psychological disturbance caused by the fact of war. The fall of France, the German threat to our own country, the see-saw fortunes of the War in North Africa whither so many forces from India had been directed, the horrible and unbelievable successes of the sinister Japanese and the political situation in India itself, created a sense of impending events of most serious consequence, and made our chitter-chatter of 'liaison' seem petty and irrelevant. So, 'Let's throw another party' became the order of the day in all our various cantonments. At least a party would give us something to do, and for me especially, parties provided relief from the antagonism of my superiors.

One event seems worth mentioning from the few years of my life that I spent in the liaison office. I was sent to a conference of Allied Liaison Officers at Calcutta, where I had to walk over the dead and dying lying on the pavement, and not ever stop to give help or comfort even when a hand was lifted in supplication or my glance caught the expression in a dark eye looking up at me from the ground. 'Too many. Too many. I must not falter. I must go on my way. I have a job to do.' Absurd in the mathematical sense. A problem, but no conceivable solution.

The misery of this bewilderment was enhanced rather than lessened by the jolly boat-trip up the Ganges that was laid on for the members of the conference. It was indeed a delightful journey. We were in one of the old paddle-boats that were still around, provided with every comfort – clean, padded, cane furniture, well-appointed cabins with good fly-proofing at all apertures, excellent food. The social programme kept the party fully engaged as we churned up-stream – eating, dancing, making merry in a variety of ways. How could one imagine young people spending a couple of days in a more carefree manner? But to maintain the jolly mood one had again to avert the eye. Every so often a dead body sped by us, borne by the current – a dog, a buffalo, a man or a woman. Life was cheap in India, and in this part of it you needed a strong stomach.

On my return to New Delhi the frivolous memories soon faded, leaving a deep sense of wretchedness for those passing dead and for their living brothers and sisters for whom so very little could be done. Uncared for in life or in death, the dead and the dying set up a perturbation in my spirits that remains there still, muted but recognisable, a sad counterpoint to, for instance, the exhilaration of the virgin mountains.

MOLLY MILNE

Three days after war was declared on 3 September 1939, I had my twelfth birthday. At that time my brother Robin (who was four-and-a-half years younger than me) and I were at a boarding school in Sussex, whilst our parents were in Rangoon, where my father worked for Burma Railways.

The first year of the War was uneventful for us, but in the summer of 1940, following the Dunkirk evacuation, the Battle of Britain started, and the invasion of England seemed very probable. At the end of the summer term we were told that our school was to be evacuated to Cornwall. Later I learned that instead of evacuation into the countryside our mother was flying home from Rangoon to take us back with her to Burma so that the family could be united and where, ironically, it was thought we would be safer! We were, of course, very excited to see her, and to learn that we were booked to fly out the following week when our passports and visas had been organised. This involved a visit to London which I shall never forget; barrage balloons heavy in the sky, windows sand-bagged and criss-crossed with brown strips. Sadly all this activity was fruitless, as at that point Italy declared war, and inevitably our flight was cancelled.

For the next six weeks, whilst my mother organised sea passages for us, we were lucky enough to find a double bed in a farmhouse in Crowborough. The air-raids started in earnest, and most nights we were in the air-raid shelter, which was more comfy than three in a bed! Some date in September we left for Liverpool to board the large P&O liner *Stratheden*. My brother and I tossed up for the top bunk and I lost. That night as I lay I saw that the springs above me were covered in chewing gum! I gather that Americans had been in the trip before us! Our convoy assembled outside Liverpool the following morning at dawn, and we could hardly believe our eyes. The sea was alive with ships – cruisers, liners, destroyers and armed merchant-cruisers. We set sail in formation, zig-zag fashion, the *Stratheden* right in the middle as flagship.

One liner had engine trouble and stayed at Freetown. We waited for her at Cape Town, where we had five wonderful days. It was marvellous to feel safe, for a start, but our days in the city were incredible. My mother took under her wing about ten children who were unaccompanied by parents, and the shopkeepers welcomed us with open arms. We were given souvenirs from every shop we went into, and my recollection of the town was a bower of flowers. The pavements were lined with enormous baskets, full of flowers of every colour. It took a long time to get used to life in a big ship: every day there was a lifeboat practice, and of course we were never parted from our lifebelts. 'Elevenses', I remember, was always Bovril, until we reached the equator, and after that ice cream.

The children had different meal times to the grown-ups, and every night when my mother went to dinner she was away longer than she said, and always found me in floods of tears on her return!

I was absolutely scared stiff that we might be torpedoed, as we were very near water level, and would have no hope of survival. As my brother slept I am afraid my imagination ran wild. In fact we were lucky to have an uneventful journey, although we had many scares, with depth charges being dropped.

Eventually we arrived in India, and were briefly installed in our cousins' house in Bombay. We then spent two nights and a day travelling by rail to Calcutta, followed by a few hours aboard a flying boat to Rangoon and the long-awaited reunion with my father.

In Rangoon it was a good life – security, happiness, fun. All of us together, school, holidays in the hills shooting with my father, monsoons, hot weather, Burmese festivals, pagodas and bazaars. Our original Karen nanny, who had looked after us at birth, was with us again. She used to lie for hours with me, under the mosquito net, tickling my back in return for information about the outside world, and what was happening in the War.

BETSY VICKERS

Mid-1940 brought the joyous news that we were to return to India to rejoin my father. Whilst waiting for a ship we stayed with an aunt in Croydon, not an ideal location in the middle of the Battle of Britain. We saw plenty of action and London burning in the distance. We sailed from Liverpool after two air-raids whilst we were on board – that made 58 in all – and set off in convoy. Suddenly there was a huge explosion. Our accompanying destroyer had dropped a depth charge, hoping to get the U-boat which had sunk the *City of Benares* with all those children on board. We saw a burning ship as we rounded Northern Ireland and then the convoy steamed on leaving our 6000 ton SS *Casstalia* alone. It took us three months to reach India, calling at the Cape Verde Islands and Cape Town *en route*.

How good it was to be back home! We now lived in Medak, mission headquarters, in the bungalow in which my parents had their wedding reception, next to the little church in they were married. When the new church was built, the little church became a weaving shed but still had memories for them. We now had electricity, for the compound had its own generator and many more fellow missionaries. Water still came from the well and instead of the twice daily visit from the sweeper we had septic tanks. We were 60 miles from Secunderabad and had a railway station 14 miles away. Telegrams were sent to the station and then came to Medak on the bus. Medak has a picturesque old fort. Sometimes on bright moonlight walks we would walk through Medak town and up to the fort trying not to get in to conflict with the resident langur monkeys. All around the landscape was flat, good rice-growing country. In fact it is said that the town got its name from a grain of rice.

Back to Hebron which was almost bursting at its seams with about 120 pupils divided between the kindergarten and standard 8. Educationally it was an excellent school. Boys were tolerated until the age of 10 when they went on to Breeks School in Ooty. I took my Junior and Senior Cambridge school exams whilst there, but as only a handful of us from various schools were sitting these exams, all the pupils in Coonoor had to foregather at the convent. When we were first entered for these exams we had our thumbprints taken just to make sure that no teacher would be sitting the exams for us! The exams were written with carbon paper just in case the original papers were sunk on the way back to England to be marked.

The highlight of the year was Hebron Day when we all dressed in fancy dress and paraded on the almost sacred drive, followed by a delicious meal in the dining room, where the Indian domestic staff had decorated each of the long tables with intricate patterns in various coloured grains of rice.

I was fortunate in that my mother spent six months of the year living on the hills for the sake of her health, and for those months I was a weekly boarder. She would rent a cottage, bringing a cook/ butler with her from the plains and then hire someone local to do the rough work. She favoured Kotagiri, some miles from Coonoor. I would sneak out of school during singing lessons on Fridays, as it was the last lesson of the week, and walk down to the *shandy* or bazaar, which was strictly out of bounds to catch a toast-rack bus, one with no sides, just seats the width of the bus with canvas to roll down when it rained.

Kotagiri was a quiet hill station, not posh like Ooty, situated at a height of about 6500 feet. There was a golf course on the Coonoor Road, a bazaar in the lower part of the town, the Blue Mountain Hotel, a *maidan* across which raucous music blasted, a cluster of shops, and a post office displaying a poster entreating one to 'Visit the Khyber Pass'. The picture showed heavily armed tribesmen hiding behind boulders waiting to shoot. The Danish Mission and some of the Methodist districts, i.e. Hyderabad, Madras and Mysore, had holiday cottages. The homes were well scattered along several roads radiating from the post office. Some others were modelled on English bungalows and bore such names as Windyridge, Shamrock and others that reminded people of home.

Frances Windram
(right) and two friends,
Quilon, 1940.

Tea estates surrounded much of Kotagiri, but were not as all-pervading as around Coonoor, and eucalyptus trees rustled in the breeze. Then there was the *shola*, a tranquil wood where we would go for picnics, sometimes with Australian friends, when a billy can would be used. Small monkeys peered from the canopy and ever-present picnic ants would arrive.

3

1941

22 June	Germany invades Russia
7 December	Japanese aircraft bomb Pearl Harbour, Hawaii; Japan declares war on Britain, the US and the Allied Nations
11 December	Germany and Italy declare war on the US
25 December	The Japanese occupy Hong Kong and bomb Rangoon
30 December	The Japanese occupy Victoria Point, Tennaserim, the southernmost point in Burma

PETER BROADBENT

In late 1939 my father, who was then Second-in-Command of the 4th Battalion Rajputana Rifles, was sent with his battalion to fight in North Africa. It was not long before my mother decided to pack and follow. On arrival in Cairo, however, she was told that she would not be allowed to stay unless she was prepared to work in support of the Army. As she could type and write shorthand, she took a job in General Wavell's headquarters, and I was sent to the Gezira Preparatory School. We spent two years in Cairo, and it was a good life. I remember the Gezira Club, with its polo ground and three wonderful swimming pools: I had my seventh birthday party at the middle of the three pyramids at Gizeh and for us – but certainly not for my father, who was at the battle of Sidi Barrani – and others, the War seemed rather a long way away. We did, however, have one air-raid in which the local anti-aircraft batteries shot down one of our own planes and none of the enemy's!

In January 1941 my father was sent back to a new posting in India, and we went too. We sailed from Port Said in a Free French ship called the *President Doumier*, built for 800 passengers. On this occasion, however, the ship held about 3500 Italian prisoners and an escort drawn from the Royal West Kent Regiment (the Buffs). My father was OC troops. Conditions on board were not at all pleasant. There was no air-conditioning, and with overcrowding everywhere nobody enjoyed the passage through the Red Sea. The British troops kept singing 'Suzannah's a Comical Man' in order to keep their spirits up, and the Italian prisoners, who thought the accompanying noises were directed at them, kept falling in to complain to my father. Otherwise, we got on very well with the Italians, who seemed only too pleased to be out of the War.

Peter Broadbent, aged five, looking through a porthole on board the SS *City of Canterbury* during the passage from England to Bombay in November 1938.

We had four of their officers in the cabin next door to ours, and I remember one of them drawing a portrait of my elder sister from a photograph and others sharing with me their rations of oranges. I also made friends with one of the French crew members, who made me at least two model boats from cork taken from the lifebelts! What would have happened if we had been torpedoed I am not at all sure – presumably some of the survivors would have floated rather lower in the water...

We arrived safely back in India. The Italian prisoners went off somewhere to be interned for the rest of the War, but I do not know where. We went up to Peshawar on the North West Frontier.

My father had been appointed in command of the 8th Battalion, 6th Rajputana Rifles in May 1941. It was a new battalion, raised initially in Delhi and then sent to Peshawar to train in the North West Frontier area. We arrived there in October 1941 to live in an extremely spacious bungalow at 1 Campbell Road. It was a wonderful place to live, and we all enjoyed our time there.

One day I was in the dining room having breakfast. Suddenly, the overhead *punkah* started swaying wildly. The pictures on the walls also seemed to be swinging like pendulums, and the doors and windows were rattling loudly. I had no idea what was happening, but vividly remember being hustled out into the garden by the bearer, who appeared from nowhere. It was my first and, I hope, last earthquake.

For my eleventh birthday I had the inevitable party, attended by my schoolfriends of both sexes. My parents arranged a snake charmer who arrived with two or three covered baskets dangling from a pole carried on his shoulder. He settled down on the drive to prepare for his show while the children gathered round in a semicircle. First, a rather large and sleepy cobra was produced from one of the baskets and made to sit up and open out his bespectacled hood. After a few minutes of swaying around in time with the snake charmer's reed pipe and puffed cheeks, it was returned to its basket and we all clapped, suitably impressed.

The snake charmer then produced a small yellow snake from another basket. This one was, I think, a yellow asp, and highly poisonous. It was about a foot long, very fast moving and not at all sleepy. What is more, it had clearly had enough of being cooped up in a hot basket, and made a determined bid for freedom directly towards all of us. The snake charmer lost his audience in a flash and we made an extremely disorderly retreat to a safe distance, from which I have this wonderful memory of the snake charmer desperately following the asp on all fours, grabbing at its tail every few feet – and missing! Luckily, the chase was eventually successful, and the afternoon was voted a distinct success.

I remember little of my father's regimental life. The battalion was away quite a lot, training near to the frontier and in places such as Abbottabad. Occasionally, my mother and I would be taken on sightseeing trips to places like Kohat, down to the south west, or up towards the frontier. One of my main memories of these trips is overtaking ramshackle buses, full to the brim with people and then festooned with others wherever there was a handhold. There were

left upper 'Our Bungalow at No 1 Nicholson Road, Delhi Cantonment, after returning from Egypt. The family lived here in 1941 when my father was serving at the Rajputana Rifles Regimental Centre after the battalion returned from fighting in North Africa.' (Peter Broadbent)

left lower Peter Broadbent with his mother, Mutroo, the family's bearer for many years, and his uncle, Captain Desmond Hall. 1 Campbell Road, Peshawar, January 1942.

a few cultivated fields, but as soon as one moved up closer to the frontier the hillsides seemed to be just rocky sandstone outcrops, often with a fort placed on a suitable vantage point.

ANONYMOUS

When I arrived in Madras in September 1940, my father's office was near the harbour (some miles from his home), but after the entry of Japan into the War in December 1941, he was asked to move it (since his company was much involved with contracts for the Army) away from the harbour area, as there was a perceived risk of the harbour being bombarded from the sea. He then moved it to a modern house about a mile from home. While he still worked near the harbour, I would get a lift from him as he went to work and he would drop me at the Gymkhana Club, which was on his way: I would then spend the morning in the Club swimming pool with all my friends – and be waiting at the Club gates to be picked up as my father went home for lunch. He would then have a siesta on the sitting-room sofa (the only time the room was used in the normal course of events) and then go back to work at about 3.00 p.m. My mother and I saw him again at about 7.00 p.m.

About 4.30 p.m., the men who looked after the coconut-palm plantation behind the house would start to climb the trees to tap the leaf stalks. The trees were not grown for their coconuts (though they were undoubtedly harvested), but for tapping, to make toddy and arrack – two native alcoholic drinks. The base of the leaf stalks at the top of the trees would be cut, and little pots tied on, to catch the sap that dripped out. The sap would then ferment naturally and produce the drink. The whole process was very time-dependent, and the product had to be got to the shops where it was sold in a very limited time from the initial tapping. The plantation was artificially irrigated from a deep well, and I would often watch the water being drawn up by a traditional balanced-beam and buffalo-skin bucket arrangement.

So I was sent to a Catholic convent run by Irish nuns, the Presentation Convent in Kodaikanal, another south-Indian hill station. The convent was basically a girls' school, taking girls up to 16 or 18 and younger boys. They had presumably been persuaded to take boys of 12 because of the War, but I think the nuns found the influx of 12-year-old boys too much of a handful, because at the end of the year all the parents of those boys were told to remove them.

I had chicken-pox at the convent and was banished with two or three other, younger children who had it, with a nurse, to a little isolation hospital about a mile out of the town. I think that going there – not feeling at all well – was the only time I ever travelled in a *tikki-gharry*.

The isolation hospital – no bigger than an ordinary house – was on a ridge, and about half a mile further along the ridge was a Hindu Temple. Morning and evening we would hear the temple bells, but we never saw anyone going there – perhaps there was another road that went there from the town. I remember the evenings, with an enormous hissing Tilley lamp on a table in the middle of the room and our nurse reading to the younger children. Kodaikanal is a much smaller place than Ootacamund. It is on the shores of a large, artificial lake, surrounded by low hills. It is a very pretty spot, but for some reason I never liked the place as much as Ooty.

YOMA CROSFIELD

In early 1941, my father was transferred by the Burmah Oil Company to the oilfield at Digboi, in Upper Assam, India, and so I sailed away from Burma, never to return. The country's real legacy to me is the magic of its names. The Shwe Dagon Pagoda, sheathed in gleaming gold. Pagan, home of the myriad temples to which I never went. Mandalay, with its bewitching name. And my own Burmese name – lasting witness of my father's connection with a country he loved.

We arrived in India early in 1941. Our new home, Digboi, was an oilfield town in Upper Assam, headquarters of the Assam Oil

Company, which the BOC had acquired in 1921. The field itself was a huge area, with unsightly derricks scattered through small, once-wooded hills and valleys. We were lucky to live outside the town, and well separated from The Field by a thick tract of jungle. Our house was Bungalow 73, the last on the paved road and built only in the late 1930s. With three other bungalows, in one of which lived our friends from Rangoon, the MacInnes family, number 73 made up an enclave known as 'Jungle Corner'.

The name was apt. The genuine jungle started just beyond the servants' quarters at the back of the house. It was close enough for me to see black monkeys swinging through the trees, their white faces glimmering. They were called 'hoolock' monkeys, although they were really gibbons, because of their peculiar call. One of them would start with a long, low 'hoooooo' and go up the scale to a shriek of 'lock' at the end. Then they would all howl together, shaking the jungle with their racket and swinging from tree to tree by their long, thin arms. Whenever I heard the beginning of that howl, I would run to the back garden, hoping to be in time to see the monkeys, but they moved so fast that I often missed them.

I found the gardens enormous. At the edges stood extremely tall trees, saved when the jungle was cleared. A wide lawn stretched away

A picnic in the jungle near Digboi, Upper Assam. Mrs Crosfield second left, Yoma and Nanny Manooch bottom right.

from the front of the house, looking out to the golf course, then the railway line between Dibrugarh and Sadiya and, in the distance, the Patkai Hills on the border with Burma.

My memories of my father in Digboi are golden. One of the most dramatic incidents of my childhood, and one in which he played a heroic role, was the shooting of the king cobra.

On this morning, a very excited bearer brought Nanny her early morning tea and poured out a story in rapid Hindi. Nanny hadn't been in India long and her Hindi was almost non-existent, but she thought he told her there was a barking deer in the garden. This kind of deer was a pretty and rare animal, so we got up and went downstairs to the front verandah, hoping to see it. We quickly found out that there was no barking deer. A *mali* had disturbed a huge cobra when he opened the garage door that morning. He had run for help, and my father was about to go to the garage with his gun. The household was gathered on the verandah to watch.

In his dark-blue silk dressing gown and leather slippers, my father walked down the steps from the verandah to the drive. His Indian bearer followed him, carrying his loaded gun. Without turning his head or saying a word, my father held his right hand out behind him. The bearer put the gun into it. My father walked across the drive, already glaring in the early sun, to the garage and disappeared into the dark interior. Everyone on the verandah held their breath. At last we heard a single shot. My father reappeared, beckoning. My mother and the servants poured off the verandah and across the drive. I hung back, but everyone else pushed and shoved to stare into the garage, where a ten-foot cobra lay curled around the washing machine. My father had shot it through the head, and the bullet had gone on through the body.

When the snake's skin came back from being cured, my father persuaded me to touch it. I was surprised to find it very soft and beautifully marked.

JOHN LANGLEY

Kanchrapara, a small town 28 miles north of Calcutta, was probably fairly typical of a railway community of the late 1930s and early 1940s. It was on the mainline from Calcutta to Darjeeling, but did not warrant a stop for the majestic express trains such as the Darjeeling Mail, which would thunder through the station to the delight of the small children, the indifference of the adults and the terror of the older Indians and various livestock. It was a very structured community, built in conjunction with the Eastern Bengal Railway's locomotive, carriage and wagon workshops.

The workshops were in the south-west quadrant, and were reached by crossing the main railway line about half a mile south of the station, which was more or less the hub of the community. The main road ran parallel to the railway on the east side, and almost opposite the workshops was the railway subordinates' colony, which was occupied by the various overseers and foremen and their families. Their houses were generally of masonry construction, and had small compounds.

The Institute, or sports and social centre, was located in this quarter, and we used to be expected to attend certain of the functions held there. One of these was the annual sports day, at which all kinds of races were run, from serious track events to three-legged competitions.

The Executive Engineer's Bungalow at Kanchrapara, 1941, for several years home to John Langley.

Other social activities took place at the Institute such as dances, mah jong, bridge and billiards, and I suspect many other events. Father and Mother were only expected to attend some of the larger gatherings, such as at Christmas, as we had our own Club, which provided all the facilities that we needed. It was a very caste-oriented town, as I imagine all the railway towns were, and it was expected that senior railway officials 'put in an appearance' at these social occasions.

Following the road to the north from the station, one passed Father's offices on the east side of the road before it curved, crossed the railway and the asphalt ended as one approached the Indian village. I found this a fascinating quarter. Most of the houses were built with bamboo and adobe walls, decorated with round pats of cow dung, dried on to form patterns. The roofing was generally a lattice of bamboo and banana leaf. It was a colourful, ever-changing scene, a seemingly limitless variety of saris and plenty of unusual smells, some unpleasant, some not, but always present, and a steady beehive-like background noise. Mother always found the smells offensive, and I don't think she ever became reconciled to this part of the Indian scene. I can still picture her, journeying through the bazaars with a handkerchief soaked in Chanel No. 5 or similar exotic perfume, determined to keep the smells out, both of the bazaar and the villagers, but equally determined to bargain for any of the merchandise that she fancied, no matter how long it took.

There were two ways of approaching our quarter: by the paved road at right-angles to the station, and by rail, along a spur line that allowed trolleys access to some of the homes, ours being one of them. The latter had a footpath alongside it, but where it crossed the river it was necessary to walk from sleeper to sleeper. Both the road and the railway crossed the river, called the Bundar Khal, which provided a definite boundary to the rest of the community. It was a small river, hardly more than a stream for most of the year. In the height of the dry weather it would become little better than an open and malodorous sewer, but in the monsoons it became a respectable river. Fortunately, the prevailing wind was such that the odour seldom came our way, but if it did, Mother's handkerchief was welcomed by all!

ROBERT BAKER

On or about 1 March 1941, I received orders to report to Bombay, preparatory to embarkation for the Middle East. I cannot now remember how long it took me to get to Bombay from Razmak, but it would have been three or four days. In Bombay I was billeted at the Taj Mahal Hotel.

Just before embarkation, I bumped into van Ollenbach, whom I had known in Razmak. He was also in the RIASC and claimed to have been a tea planter from Dehra Dun, but in retrospect I now realise, without doubt, that he was a domiciled European, and had almost certainly never been a planter. In any event, I don't believe Dehra Dun was a tea-planting area. Ollenbach – the 'van' part was a prefix he attached to his name on being commissioned, so I learned later – was anxious to prove his *bona fides* as a European and a gentleman, and one evening in the Mess claimed he had had an uncle who had fought in the Zulu wars. Still another officer from Madras, and not a regular, asked, 'Oh really – on which side?' Ollenbach did not think it funny, asked for an apology, and got it. He was very, very insulted. Perhaps had he been a *pukka-sahib*, he might have been less put out. Now, however, he was bound for Britain, an officer in one of four companies of animal transport, fully equipped men and mules, and was in his seventh heaven. I simply could not believe my eyes. The ship on which all this vast number of men and mules were embarked was *The Empress of Scotland*. She had been *The Empress of Japan*, but it was thought an inappropriate name when we were, if not at war with Japan (which came with Pearl Harbour only in December 1941), at least on something less than amicable terms.

In due course I embarked aboard the *Islami*, a 7000-ton vessel which in peacetime was employed in ferrying Mecca pilgrims from

Bombay to Jeddah. It was a very heavily laden troopship, but I was very comfortable with a small but very adequate cabin to myself. On opening an envelope addressed to me which I found in my cabin, I discovered I was to be sports officer for the duration of the trip. The sports equipment took the form of board games, dice and packs of cards. I issued these at the beginning of the day and collected them each night, and so far as I remember I did little else. For this extra responsibility I was paid an additional amount over and above my normal salary.

A cruiser, HMS *Belfast*, escorted the *Islami* all the way across the Indian Ocean as far as Aden, a most lavish escort for so small a ship.

ISABEL DAVIDSON

Our bungalow in Digboi was in Muliabari. The day began at six o'clock in the cool of the morning – I do not really remember the heat in India. I expect we children were just used to it. I was left to the tender mercies of Ayah and paraded with the other children for walks near the golf course and swimming pool. Ayah was kind and loving to me, but the person I remember best of all is the bearer, Amir Ali – I adored him. He was always around, in charge of the house. Looking after the *sahib* and *memsahib* and looking out for the *baba*. On occasions, his little daughter Lotte used to come and play with me in the compound. I was taken once to the bearer's house behind the bungalow and it seemed very dark compared to ours. His wife was extremely pretty, but when she went out in the evening for a walk with us she was all covered up. No one could see her, and I thought this was a great pity, as she was so pretty and had such lovely saris.

Tiffin was served at 11 o'clock in the cool dining room downstairs. The ground-floor areas of the bungalows had terrazzo flooring, and there were wonderful – and to me, very large – verandahs, both downstairs and upstairs, where the sitting room and the bedrooms were situated. Like all the bungalows, each bedroom had its own bathroom, which could be reached from the outside by stairways, as well as inside. One of the rituals of the day for the bearer was the drawing of the *sahib*'s bath when he finished work, which in our home would be at different times, as my father, John Davidson – known to everyone in Digboi as Davie – was a drilling engineer, and therefore on shift work.

One great excitement in Digboi during the War was a fire at one of its wells. Someone had lit a cigarette – strictly forbidden – and this had been the cause of it. I remembered seeing this horrendous fire when it was under control. How the fire was extinguished, I do not remember. What I do remember is being told that a message had come over the radio from the Japanese Army, to say that they had seen it, and knew it to be a decoy. They were therefore not going to bomb Digboi, they were going to capture it! It must have been around this time that an asbestos suit took up residence in our 'dooley'. It stood like a suit of armour in the corner beside the water-filter and was named 'Joe' by Father and the bearer.

JONQUIL MALLINSON

The Frontier Mail train came through Jullundur (in the Punjab) at midnight. Our boxes and bedding rolls were piled into the compartment, two top berths and a lower were made up and my mother, my sister and I slept till morning. At Rawalpindi we hired a lorry with a Sikh driver, and set off for Kashmir. We spent the night in the *dak* bungalow at Kohala, from where we could hear the roar of the river Jhelum. In the morning, we crossed the bridge over the gorge – when the snow melts in the mountains, the river rises 60 feet. Next day we arrived at Tangmarg, in Kashmir, the end of the motor road. 'But Memsahib, you cannot go. The snow is very deep in Gulmarg and no water or electric light.' 'There is plenty of wood for fires,' said my mother, 'and we have hurricane lamps.' (Water and electric light were turned on on 15 May and off again on 15 October, when everything in Gulmarg closed down for the winter. It was now late

April.) Riding ponies were chosen, and the coolies lined up for their loads. There was a steep winding track of about three miles up to Gulmarg – 9000 feet up in the Himalayas. No wheeled traffic there – only ponies in the summer.

Our hut or chalet was built, like all the others, of pinewood, with pine shingles on the roof. It soon warmed up as the tin pot-bellied stoves were stoked, and fires lit. The pinewood was full of resin, which collected in the chimneys and could catch fire. Once, we saw flames coming from the top of our chimney. An old rug, kept for the purpose, was stuffed up the fireplace, and a few buckets of water poured on the roof, and the panic was over. The snow that had slid or been pushed off the roof was high around the hut, so that we could hardly see out. Next day, we cleared a space and sat in the warm sun. All the huts were empty except ours. The air was thin and clean and smelt of pine trees. The toboggans were brought out, Ahmed (our *syce* when the ponies came up from the valley in May) pulled them up the hills for us, and we all took turns going down the steep slopes. After a few days, another family came to stay, in response to a message from my mother.

The servants were in their winter uniforms – long kaftan-type coats made from brown homespun Kashmiri wool – a change from the plains, where they wore white cotton long-sleeved jackets. Later in the summer Khan, our water-carrier, died of typhus. He used to go down the hill to the tap and carry the water back in a goatskin. This was very serious from a health point of view for the whole household, and for his family, who now had no wage earner. Fortunately, nobody else was taken ill, and soon his 16-year-old son Madh took his place.

Every day Gania, our cook, went to the bazaar to buy meat, vegetables and fruit, and then he would present his account to my mother. Rupees and annas were written down in the account book – but nearly always a few extra annas for salt.

'But we had salt yesterday and the day before,' said my mother. 'No more salt this week.'

'Very well, Memsahib.'

The kitchen was small, but separate from the house, with a mud range built against the wall, fed with pinewood. Cakes and scones were put into a big round tin with a lid, hot embers were piled on top, and it was put on the fire to bake. Outside there was a grease-trap: pine-needles were laid in the drain from the kitchen, and when they were burnt, a new lot was put down. We had wonderful food – saddle of mutton, chicken pilau, curry and rice, dhal, apricots, cherries, strawberries and raspberries. Walnuts were brought to the door and sold by the hundred in handfuls of five. No beer was taken, as Kashmir had a Hindu Maharajah, and no pork either, because the servants were Muslims. Imported tinned food was expensive and difficult to get – my brother was delighted to win a tin of sardines at a children's party. Once, my mother brought a basket of pears, too many for us to eat, so the cook stewed them before they were put into tins made and soldered up by the bazaar tinsmith.

Mohamed Butt was our devoted bearer – he had been with my grandmother. Some servants were very conscious of their position. My sister and I took a note one day to Lady M's hut. We asked the bearer at the door, 'Is the Memsahib in?' He replied gravely, 'The Lady-sahib is in.'

My brother Robin went off on his pony every morning to his tutor. My father was in the Indian Army, stationed in the hot plains, or in the Middle East or in Burma – we children never quite knew where he was. He would appear for a few weeks' leave in the cool mountain air and then disappear again.

When my mother decided we needed another bedroom, Kashmiri stonemasons and carpenters arrived. Stone foundations were laid and pine posts and planks were sawn and nailed, and pine shingles cut for the roof. Soon it was finished. Then the other end of the house was extended, and we had a new bedroom, bathroom and verandah. Our hut was on the outer, circular road and looked across the Vale of Kashmir – 90 miles as the crow flies – to the high snow-covered Himalayas. The icy peak of Nanga Parbat rose to 26,000 feet.

We slept on beds with wooden frames and webbing. The mattresses were kapok, and once a year a man came with a large wooden bow with a string across. The kapok was beaten up by twanging the string until a huge pile of soft white cotton was ready to be stuffed back in to the mattresses. What a blissful sleep we had that night!

LAURENCE FLEMING

My first term at The New School in Calcutta ended at Easter. As a boarder, I slept upstairs in the magnificent house in Alipore that the school had taken over. We had individual mosquito nets, tucked in under the mattress, and somewhere nearby there must have been some barracks, as we sometimes heard 'lights out' blown on a bugle. The two combined gave me a feeling of security that I don't think I have ever felt since.

I think it was in this Easter holiday that I began to see Digboi as the remarkable place that it was. It still did not figure on maps of India, although the Assam Oil Company was registered some time in the 1880s. Most of the old houses were built on the Assam tea-garden model, on stilts with a store room at ground level, and a wide verandah above with rooms opening off it. They were often half-timbered, as were the indigenous Assamese houses, and on the tea-gardens they were thatched; but in Digboi the roofs were of corrugated iron, painted either red or green, and the noise of the rain in the monsoon was tremendous.

The older houses were all built on the tops of small hills, the tops cut off for the bungalow to sit on; but the *burra* bungalow, where we lived, was quite unlike this. It dated from 1913 and was huge, on one storey only, opening backwards, as one might say, from an enormous verandah.

The cookhouse, the *bovachy-khana*, was separated from the main house by a covered way, but the *bottle-khana*, the pantry where all the food was received before serving, was part of the main house. It was huge, cool and tiled, like the rest of the house, in highly polished red tiles. It contained a very noisy refrigerator in which filtered water could always be found, now in old Gordon's Gin bottles.

A large flat lawn spread in front of the house, with the swing at the end of it, under the Indian Laburnum. At the bottom of the steps on the right lay the railway station and, when one woke in the middle of the night, one could always hear the shunting engines working away. They were called Barbara and Lillian, after the daughters of a previous General Manager. But the left-hand slope down to the kitchen garden was covered in pineapples, and any disturbance in the night could always be dismissed as 'only a jackal among the pineapples'. The kitchen garden grew what one might call English vegetables in the cold weather, and okra in the monsoon. There was a patch of ground in which nothing would grow; a group of papaya trees, a grove of guavas and a lychee tree beyond the pineapples; and there was a mulberry tree beside the stream that separated the garden from the Club tennis courts.

There were four Clubs in Digboi. The Indian Club catered for the Indian employees of the company – because Digboi was exclusively a company town – who spoke little English. We were once invited

An afternoon wedding reception in the garden of No 1 Bungalow, Digboi, November 1940. Jane Fleming is talking to the bride, Laurence Fleming, head in air, is just above her. The Scots Minister, Padre Maclean, who had conducted the service, faces the camera bottom left.

to a wonderful play there, centring around the adventures of a girl called Sreemati and which, sadly enough for us, was scheduled to go on all night. We were removed at midnight, leaving Sreemati in the most terrible trouble. The Sports Club was mixed, Indian and European, but of course one had to be interested in sports. These were badminton, golf and tennis. The Jubilee Sports Ground (1935) was a football field as well as a sports ground, with particularly spectacular athletics competitions in the cold weather.

The Assam Valley Light Horse Club (AVLH) was more or less the preserve of the Anglo-Indian employees, of whom there were several: telephonists, office staff and, possibly, policemen. The AVLH, of which I can discover nothing, was probably embodied very early, perhaps even in 1823, when the first tea garden in Assam, Chabua, where my sister was born, was planted. The Makum Fort, which we used to see derelict in the jungle, a miniature Tower of London, certainly dated from 1825, built by the British to keep the Burmese out of Assam – a project which, astonishingly, succeeded.

The Digboi Club, which we could see from our verandah, was open only to Europeans, company employees and tea planters from the surrounding countryside. There were grass tennis courts between us and the swimming pools, a squash court beyond them and then the Club itself. The Royal Bioscope Company showed a film on Friday nights. The Churches of England and Scotland held services there at rare, but regular, intervals. There was also a grand piano and a stage, on which, in this Easter Holiday of 1941, the Digboi Children, superbly produced against all the odds by Ruth Dear, gave a remarkable performance of *Through the Looking Glass*, which astonished everyone who saw it.

But my father's greatest triumph in the first five years of his tenure of office must have been to persuade the London office to build a proper hospital. Completed just before the War began, it had an up-to-date theatre and an X-ray machine, and was in every way a very pleasant building, not only for the benefit of company employees. For lesser ailments we went to the Refinery Dispensary, to be painted with gentian violet when we got foot rot, and I seem to remember being vaccinated there.

The great treat was always the picnic on the Dehing, or Dihing, a tributary of the Brahmaputra. It came down from the Patkoi Hills, a raging torrent in the monsoon but, in the cold weather, a lazy, limpid stream, ambling between huge sandbanks, with jungle-trees high on both sides. We would go to the bridge at Margherita and take dugouts, being poled either up or downstream. There was nothing very much upstream, beyond the magnificent forest itself. We would camp on a sandbank, under the shade of two enormous red and yellow umbrellas. We would spend the day running, or splashing about in that smiling, welcoming river, which, at that time of year, we could walk across, or swim with one foot on the bottom.

But if we went downstream, and we were lucky, we would see the elephants at the rest camp, lying about in the river, a perfect picture of contentment. Mr Belcher, whose elephants, in a sense, they were, was the local representative of the Assam Railways and Trading Company, a remarkable organisation founded in 1850. It was they who built the Dibru-Sadiya Railway to take the timber, tea and coal from Ledo down to the river at Dibrugarh, to continue their journey by river. Later there were oil products from Digboi as

A group of Mr Belcher's elephants leaving the jungle on their way to the rest camp. (Ann Prowse)

well. Mr Belcher lived in a very handsome thatched bungalow just by Margherita Bridge, but his great attraction, so far as we were concerned, was that he ran a logging camp, using these elephants. It was reached by a 'trolley', a man-propelled railway wagon with seats for four people, which took one, on a gloriously uneven line, far into the jungle, where one could see these elephants rolling gigantic logs – usually of sal, but sometimes of teak – and loading them very neatly on to the railway wagons.

The New School moved up to Darjeeling in May, and I travelled there from Digboi with the two sons of the Police superintendent at Sadiya and their mother, picking up the son of a tea-garden owner a little way down the line. I always looked forward to those long train journeys. On this one we had a wonderful dinner in the compartment – baked beans, Walls' tinned sausages, sardines, superb sandwiches, curry puffs and a great deal of assorted fruit. After which we made up our beds from bedding rolls and went to sleep.

Very early the next morning we crossed the Brahmaputra on the ferry, having a delicious breakfast on the way. Then we took another train to Parbatipur, where there was a connection to Siliguri. If we had missed this, of course, we would have had to wait for 18 hours until the next Darjeeling Mail came through, but I only remember this happening once.

The great disadvantage of our journey was that the 'little train', which connected with the train from Calcutta, had always gone by the time we arrived. So we went up in a car, or a bus: on this first occasion, it was a car. It dropped us just below the Planters' Club, and then we had to walk.

The junior boys' house that term was called Terpsithia – I think the summer residence of a Maharajah or so, and with one of the best views in Darjeeling, overlooking the whole town. It must have been a climb of some four hundred feet from the Planters' Club but, when we got there, the whole panorama of the Kanchenjunga Range was displayed before us. I shall remember forever that first view, as the sun set over it, pink, pink and pink, then orange and back to pink again – after which it disappeared completely. I remember wondering, rather optimistically as it turned out, if we were to be treated to this magnificent display every day.

Kanchenjunga is sacred to the Sikkimese, the abode of their God of War, a fearsome deity scourging the land with blizzards and wild winds. But we never saw him in this mood. We only ever saw him when the skies were clear, when he was not wreathed in cloud, when he was not raging. I came to look upon him as a strong, benevolent father-figure, obliging everyone in Darjeeling to be pleasant and prosperous as long as he was watching over and protecting them, and while we were there, he was certainly doing both.

MARK TULLY

Slow train to innocence

The servants lined the drive of 7, Regent's Park, Calcutta, waving goodbye. Nanny, from England, whose job it was to stop us children getting too close to the servants, stood on the steps. My father sat beside Willy, the driver of our Sunbeam Talbot. My mother sat on the back seat, one arm around me, the other around my elder sister, Prue. We turned right into the tree-lined avenue, which was then Regent's Park, left at the stables, right at Tolly tram station, and then we followed the tramlines into Calcutta. Tolly in those days wasn't really considered Calcutta, it was out in the country.

My eyes were filled with tears, but I tried to restrain my sobbing. My father had already told me 'to be a man', a little hard at the age of five, but when he was born Victoria still ruled, and her stern values with her. Prue, then seven, and the oldest of the family, sat silent, staring ahead. There were eventually four more Tully children, and we always regarded Prue as very 'grown-up'. It was getting dark, and there wasn't the traffic of modern Calcutta, so it took all too little time to reach our destination – Sealdah station. There we were to catch the Darjeeling Mail for our first term as boarders at The New School.

The New School had started in Calcutta as a day school for all those children of Calcutta–European *sahibs* who couldn't go back to Britain to be educated because the War had disrupted passenger shipping. Admission was limited to children of Calcutta *burra-sahibs* and those on their way to that exalted status. In those days, Europeans thought Calcutta's humid climate was a health hazard for young children, and hence the move to Darjeeling.

As we got out of the car, Prue hissed at me to 'stop blubbing, you don't want to make fools of us', and I did. In 13 long years of boarding school, I was never able to hold back my tears as I left home, but in some miraculous way my eyes always dried before I joined the school train. Later, an equally miraculous reverse process used to occur when I got home from my public school in England. Our language at Marlborough would have done a British sergeant major proud, but never once did a four-letter word pass my lips during the holidays.

On the platform I found Keith Younie, Donald McLeod, Jane Grice – The New School was co-ed – and others who had been in my class in Calcutta standing silently beside their parents outside the compartments reserved for us. There were the awe-inspiring seniors too – The New School provided for all ages. The acrid smell of steam and smoke, which was so exciting when we caught the train at Howrah for family holidays in Puri, was now dank and depressing. 'Don't kiss us,' Prue said to my mother as we were told to board the train. I shook hands with my father, clutched my mother, and clambered aboard. The member of staff escorting us shut the windows to keep the smoke out, so we couldn't wave goodbye. This was probably a good thing, because it might have brought on a shaming bout of weeping. Shrill whistles blew, and the train steamed laboriously out of Sealdah. As we got up speed, the rocking and the 'da da da dum, da da da dee' rhythm of the wheels soon sent me to sleep.

We woke up the next morning at Siliguri to find a special train of the two-feet gauge Darjeeling Himalayan Railway (DHR) waiting for us. Many years later, an Old Boy collected reminiscences from those who had been at The New School and wrote a book he called

Harrow on the Hooghly. In it, I read that some parents arranged for their children to go up the hill by car. The DHR was run by Gillanders Arbuthnot, the oldest of the major Calcutta managing agencies, and my father was one of the Gillanders *burra-sahibs.* So there would never have been any question of us going by road, not that I regretted that.

The train to Darjeeling has changed very little since 1941. The gallant engines, with their tall funnels belching out black smoke, are still operational. The carriages, according to *Harrow on the Hooghly,* were grimy, and the windows small – not much change there – and the maximum speed up the hill was 12 mph, as it still is I suspect. Ticketless travellers were as much of a problem to Gillanders as they are to the nationalised Indian railways. At one stage the DHR apparently took the steps outside the carriages away to prevent free-loaders jumping on board whilst the train was moving, but then a first-class passenger, a lady of some importance, put her foot where she thought there would be a step, and fell getting out of the train. The step was restored, but freeloaders, if my memory serves me right, were put off by the strange sight of a train full of chattering white children.

The DHR on its way down from Ghoom to Darjeeling. (Nicole Walby)

When I got a little older, I would join my seniors jumping off the train at the zig-zags, where the gradient was too steep for a straight assault and the train shunted backwards and then drove forward again. I remember we stopped at Kurseong for lunch, but I don't remember the chemist there who, according to *Harrow on the Hooghly*, kept a two-headed lamb preserved in a bottle of formaldehyde.

Eventually, the train reached the highest station on the line, Ghoom, 7407 feet high. I can't remember how long it had taken to travel the 47 miles from Siliguri, but it must have been the best part of a day. I do remember that it was a fine day, because we looked out on Kanchenjunga as the exhausted engine free-wheeled down to Darjeeling.

The New School consisted of separate houses, all but one of which had been private residences, on the road up to St Paul's. By the time I had climbed from the station to The Dingle, the junior house, the homesickness had entirely disappeared and I was enjoying the camaraderie I suspect only boarding-school children know. My father, a most efficient man, had given me a stamped postcard to report my arrival. I wrote 'I have arrived safely and was not sick,' which my father forever after quoted as an example of brevity and clarity. I am sure that if not homesick, I would certainly have been car sick if I had not travelled by train.

Ever since that first journey to Darjeeling I have resented the description of the DHR as a 'toy train'. It was a train which took me and many others on a deadly serious journey. It is sad that it has now been reduced to a tourist attraction and a vehicle for those who don't want to pay a bus fare, but I suppose that's progress. As for The New School, for all its oddities, its short life too – it closed as soon as passenger ships again became available to take its pupils back to more orthodox schools in Britain – it can't have been all that bad. When I got back to my prep school near Winchester, I was ahead of the boys of my age academically. Unfortunately, that happy position didn't last long.

JOHN LANGLEY

We had two housemasters during our one year stay at Terpsithia. The first was a very old man called Mr Woods, who had come to India as a tutor to the son of a Maharajah in something like 1894 and had been there ever since. He turned out to have a passion for little boys and, as he finally gave in to this passion, had to leave. Tony Lamarro was almost as unsuitable as Mr Woods, although for entirely different reasons, and he left at the end of that year to open a chocolate shop in Chowringhee (Calcutta) called Tony's and probably made a fortune.

During the holidays Father would sometimes be gone for a few days at a time 'up line', which meant that he was on a railway-line inspection trip, inspecting his work gangs and the progress they were making on new lines, or on maintenance of the existing ones. When he went on this kind of trip he would take his special carriage, called a saloon, that was like a home away from home. It would be hitched to the end of a train and dropped off at a siding close to the section that he was going to inspect. The trolley always went along with him, and was used for the day-to-day inspections. The railway was the lifeline of the country, and continuous track maintenance was essential to cope with the increasing rail traffic and the effects that the monsoons could have on railway beds, bridges and culverts.

Travelling by trolley was an exhilarating experience, depending on the type of trolley being used. They varied from the hand-pushed type that was used for short trips (and before the motorised types became the standard), to fully motorised ones. The hand-pushed trolleys required two *trolleywallahs*, one on each side, pushing against fixed handles while they ran along the rails. The trolley itself consisted of a wooden platform with a bench seat for the *sahib* and his assistant(s), and was equipped with awnings, which increased the sensation of speed with their flapping. An alternate design, used mainly by work parties, had a pump-handle device in the middle of the trolley which was pushed up and down by the two *trolleywallahs*, and by a series of cogs and wheels, the trolley moved forward. With the advent of motorised machines, the work of the *trolleywallah* was reduced. They were only required to push the trolley to get up enough speed so that Father could let in the clutch, and the motor would burst into life. The *trolleywallahs* would then scramble aboard and squat on the back of the machine, grinning like mad and enjoying the speed (and lack of exertion) of the trolley. I don't know how fast the trolley actually went, but it seemed quite fast when seated out in the open on the bench and apparently so close to the rails. One had to hang on to the seat edge when going round corners or over temporary tracks – but it was a marvellous way to travel.

SUSAN BURDER

In 1940, it was decided that I should be packed off back to my family in the comparative peace of Calcutta. The *SS City of London* transported us, a strange assortment of children, amongst VIPs, soldiers and merchants, around the Cape to India with a convoy of vessels to accompany us on a journey which took about six weeks.

Returning to Calcutta was, in today's terms, quite a culture shock: the flattening heat, the smells, so many bustling bare feet, bullock carts and rickshaws and people spitting, with remarkable aim, long red squirts of beetle-nut into the open drains ... but I was back home again among the familiar haunts of Ballygunge, Ayah and *burra bearer*, my guinea-pig and ducks, and the mosquito-netted bedroom, with the *punkah* slowly turning as I lay and listened to the cawing crows, and sometimes to the lilting song of the Brain Fever Bird heralding the rains.

At the end of the cold weather, the annual migration from Calcutta to the hills took place, and Kalimpong was always our favourite choice: a village 4500 feet up in the foothills of the Himalayas across the Teesta River from Darjeeling. To reach it involved an exciting overnight journey in the sleeper from Calcutta, dogs, ducks and guinea-pigs sharing our carriage, of course, followed by a four-hour haul in a little mountain train to Gielle Khola and then a really sick-making taxi-ride up the winding mountain road, frequently held up by land-slides, to our destination.

Kalimpong is widely known for Dr Graham's Homes, founded in 1900 for deprived Anglo-Indian children by the far-sighted Scottish missionary Dr Graham, and the homes still thrive today. Here our parents decided to build a house designed by Norman Odling, a family friend and architect son-in-law of Dr Graham. The Odlings kept open house in Kalimpong – they started the Arts and Crafts Centre in the bazaar, inspiring and employing dozens of local talents, and their generosity and hospitality were legendary for anyone trekking to Tibet, Sikkim or Nepal, or indeed itinerant visitors from all over India.

Tashiding, our small Cotswold-style house, was built on a hilly site chosen for a beautiful bohinea tree and the most stunning view imaginable of Mount Kanchenjunga. The hillside below us fell away in a series of maize and paddy fields, interspersed with native *busties*, each with its maize stack cleverly arranged on top of a tall pole, and sometimes a Singer sewing machine in the doorway. Papaya grew round about, arum lilies thrived in the ditches and the hedge-rows were festooned with morning-glory, vying with the pungent Lantana for the attentions of dazzling butterflies and swallow-tail worms. The fireflies danced, at night jackals howled, and everyone's chickens woke us up at dawn. We ambled to lessons on our ponies (no self-respecting hill pony would trot), our rucksacks of homework and sandwiches on our backs and the *syce* running behind. The delights of the bazaar sometimes made us late for lessons, and was a further temptation on our way to French and Latin classes at the convent. Parental control was sketchy – our mother trying to juggle her life between a husband in Calcutta and two daughters in the Himalayas meant an extraordinary freedom and lack of discipline for us. With friends we camped, and damned streams, and flew our kites in the windy season of September, and joined in curry picnics on the native festival days in a happy informal mingling of Tibetans and Nepalese families gathered round huge bubbling saucepans of curry and rice.

Archery was one of the great sports, especially for the Bhutanese, and a jolly party would come down to the Mela Ground from Bhutan House, home of Tobjay Dorji, hereditary Prime Minister of Bhutan, and Rani Chuni, his wife, sister of the Maharajah of Sikkim. They were the parents of the present Queen Mother Kesang of that secret mountain kingdom. Jigmi Dorji, eldest son of the house, was married in a magnificent ceremony to Tashi, a Tibetan princess, the occasion lasting about a week, with much feasting and gaiety. The surrounding houses filled up with relatives and friends who had trekked over the mountains from Bhutan. Tragically, Jigmi, a courageous and most charming diplomat, was assassinated a few years after at a race meeting in Calcutta.

The Mela Ground also boasted a cinema – actually a tin-roofed hut – and we sat enthralled on wooden benches as *Hellzapoppin!* flickered across the screen, but the rain poured down, and the tin roof added another dimension to the acoustics. The bazaar, too, had many other attractions, including Gompu's Tea Rooms, in the upstairs part of a dangerously rickety wooden building, and two fat rascals called Banshi Lal and Kashi Ram, who ran the Everything store and reclined on a huge white mattress, smoking their hubble-bubbles. We imitated them shamelessly, and they were the central figures in all our games of charades.

Kalimpong was the trading outpost and gateway to India from Tibet; mule trains of cheerful Tibetans would arrive from Lhasa into the bazaar, and sometimes a colourful band of them would wind up the hill and into our garden and perform their ancient plays and whirling dances, accompanied by flutes and strings and such banging of drums. A great bargaining session would then ensue as they tempted us with prayer wheels, conch horns and jewellery.

The Dalai Lama was a small boy of nine when I left Kalimpong in 1945 for school in England. It was decided that my precious set of Hornby trains should be presented to His Holiness by our High

Commissioner in Lhasa, George Sherriff (the botanist). I like to think that the little novice lamas had fun with them in the Potala, a harmless distraction from their spiritual training.

Our return to Calcutta for the cold weather was anticipated with great excitement. Our parents now lived in the *burra-sahib*'s house in Alipore with a lovely garden and grass tennis court. Part of the house had been turned into a rest centre for soldiers who had escaped from Burma, and many of them would come up to stay in Kalimpong on leave.

After the War, Tashiding was bought by George and Betty Sherriff. Prince Peter of Yugoslavia then acquired it, and finally it became the summer house of Rani Chuni Dorji from Bhutan.

ANNE PROWSE

My mother, Joan Willoughby Grant, was born in 1914 to Dr Willoughby Grant and Clarice (née Woosnam). He (my grandfather) was the medical officer to the Assam Railway and Trading Company Ltd in Margherita, Upper Assam. In 1920 they came to England on leave, where they left Joan with her aunts for schooling, first in a convent in Bexhill and later at a Parents' National Education Union school in Haslemere, and finally to St Swithin's School in Winchester. Then to Paris for six months, before returning to India in 1931. Here, Joan met Arthur Skardon Prowse (Keith), who had been in India since 1925. He was Bristol-born and trained, and went to India as the Medical Officer to the Assam and Burmah Oil Companies in Digboi, Upper Assam.

In 1934, Dr Willoughby Grant, my grandfather, resigned over the treatment of a fellow employee, and went on leave to England with his family. They returned to India via Ceylon with their daughter (my mother), and Keith (my father) came down from Digboi to Colombo to get married. They spent their honeymoon in Ceylon and returned to Digboi by boat from Colombo to Calcutta, and then by train. My grandparents went up to Ootacamund after the wedding, where they purchased Kempstowe Nursing Home, where they then worked and lived. In 1935 Rosemary Anne (me) was born at my grandfather's home in Ootacamund, Nilgiri Hills, South India, and in 1936 I was left with my grandparents while my parents undertook a world trip, after which I returned to Digboi with them. We lived in Bungalow No 36 in Digboi until father was posted to Chauk in Burma. We then moved to Yenangyaung and finally to Syriam near Rangoon, where there was an excellent zoo, and where my *topee* blew off into the otter pool and was destroyed by the otters!

In 1939, my parents went on leave from Burma, and took me to my grandparents in Ootacamund, where I went to the Convent. As I was very unhappy there, they kept me at their home. Back in Burma, my earliest memories were of the wonderfully shaped and coloured pagodas, and seeing the huge orange moon rising on the horizon. I remember with affection my *ayah*, Priscilla (from Shillong), and having sand thrown in my eyes by a young friend in the sand pit. I remember how painful it was. At this time I also became aware of snakes being around the compound. I recall also that my parents brought with them from Assam to Burma my *ayah*, the cook, the house boy and their bearer, who subsequently returned with us to Assam in 1941. Here, we lived in Bungalow No 71, Digboi, Upper Assam. My first memories with my sister at home were of sitting in the bamboo-lined open-topped air-raid shelter in the garden with some of the servants while the Japs flew sorties overhead. They never

Bungalow No 71
in Digboi, built
about 1938.
(Ann Prowse)

actually bombed the Digboi oil-fields. My six-year-old worries were whether it was going to rain, and I used to watch most carefully for the stars to 'go out', and when my mother went into the bungalow to warm up milk for my sister, I remember the 'pokes' that used to crawl out from between the bamboo canes.

The bungalow had a tennis court and a large garden with poinsettia hedges and flowering hibiscus bushes. Also in the garden were chicken runs. The jungle came up to the boundary fence, and I remember the pineapples growing just beyond the fence. There were three large Flame of the Forest trees down one side and the garden sloped downhill from the verandah to a hedge at the bottom with a gap in the middle to yet more garden. Here the passion fruits grew. Beyond this the jungle lay between us and the golf course and the railway line to Margherita.

There was a staff of four gardeners, as well as a night watchman, who would return me from the garden when I walked in my sleep and when my *ayah* did not wake up. With Dunerahm the bearer and his boy, and the cook and his boy, and the *ayahs*, there was a total of 11 staff. Their quarters were in a compound across the road in the jungle, forbidden territory for me, although I remember going daringly over the road once. When they had time off they used to walk for miles to their family homes. One of the sounds of the jungle

Father Christmas arriving at the Club, Digboi, Upper Assam, 1941. The house on top of the hill was No 1, Digboi, with the Railway Station beyond it. The area between was occupied by the Club's grass tennis courts. The schoolboy about to cross the road behind the elephant is Laurence Fleming. (Yoma Crosfield)

I will always remember were the whoops of the 'hoolock' gibbons, rising to a shrieking crescendo. When part of the boundary hedge started to die off, the gardeners dug down and found a large iguana's nest with a great number of big eggs. There were also wild boar, which we saw on the roads, but they could not get into the gardens because of the boundary fences. The males were very fierce, and not to be tackled without a gun. There was a constant battle against the cockroaches in the house.

JENNIFER BETTEN

Before Malcolm, my father, built the ropeway at Tukvar, the tea chests were carried by ponies up the steep 2000 feet to Darjeeling. In the cold weather the road was full of the porters from Sikkim carrying enormous baskets of small, sweet and delicious oranges to the rail head. They were not unlike the tangerines one could once buy.

And the fireflies. That night at Nagri when the air was full of them. How can one describe what that life was like? Silence, space, magic. I love the sound of the rain on the roof at night, conveniently forgetting the leaking drips plopping. The smell of kerosene (paraffin) reminds me of the old 'butties', and the days with no electricity. By the 1940s, when most tea factories had their own generators, we discovered that the iron or the battery charger for the wireless could only be used if all the lights were off. I remember the bathwater being heated in smoke-blackened kerosene cans, and the 'Rikki Tikki Tavi' hole for its dispersal through the wall.

With my sisters 'at home' (in England), mine might have been a lonely childhood but for the pets and my pony. I rode before I walked, as it was the best way of getting about. Donkeys and small ponies went the rounds of the families. It was discovered that Saucy Sue was not a pregnant donkey but a lazy one, and the delightful Whitelegs, a piebald pony who shied and threw me, once carried Rumer Godden's children.

Malcolm acquired an Austin 7. It chugged up the 4000 feet from Singla to Darjeeling, overheating at every *gumpti* (corner), and the plugs always had to be changed. Driving in the monsoon down the notorious Tukvar road was best avoided. Brakes stopped the wheels, but not the vehicle, and the onward slide towards the edge of the shelf-like road was determined by fate alone. A blade of grass, a tree or a stone could stand between passenger and the torrent in the ravine below. The journey down to Tukvar was always an ordeal for guests. Their choice was terror or pain from knees and blistered feet as the steep and rough gradient took its toll on the human frame.

We may have teased guests about leopards and snakes, but our respect for the wildlife, the weather and the terrain was genuine.

War broke through our isolation to reach all corners of our tea-gardens. Assistants were called up, bungalows left empty, hospitality was given to Burmese refugees, my sisters and hundreds of other children came out from England, and in Darjeeling, two schools were opened, while others were extended. My mother, with other graduates, went back to teaching. Malcolm and fellow managers went, in turn, with their labour to build the roads back into Burma. On holiday we shared our home with two French girls – whose parents were in the French Resistance – and a girl from Burma. Later, there was always a soldier or two staying, or a dozen visiting for 'tea'.

Picking tea in a garden below Darjeeling. The leaves were thrown over the pickers' shoulders into the baskets. (Nicole Walby)

Food was rationed simply: one loaf of bread per household per day. Our *rotiwallah* (bread man) could only walk the 18 miles to Darjeeling twice a week, so we had two loaves a week and lived off pumpkin jam, pumpkin marmalade and *atta* (almost like bran) scones. A primitive kind of molasses replaced sugar. It made good toffee. I only ever saw one aeroplane, and that was when a pilot flew over our school and a teacher ran out with her umbrella to wave to him!

TONY ORCHARD

The New School was at first disorganised, but free and easy, and devoid of 'bull'. The markets and bazaars of Calcutta and Darjeeling were open to be explored, a source of never-ending variety, particularly the cheerful hill folk. And we were free to roam up and down the *khuds*, learning to ride the hill ponies around the Old Calcutta Road, and visit the Gymkhana Club with its skating rink.

Another boy, Martin Pinnell, and I wanted to continue studying Ancient Greek for the School Certificate. A request was circulated to parents for anyone with such a background, and turned up Mr Cyril Gurner, who was the head of what amounted to the Public Works Department, and a graduate in Greats from Oxford. Twice a week, Martin and I went to his house for two hours' coaching, and we both passed. In 1990, when I attended the fiftieth reunion of *Harrow on the Hooghly*, I expressed surprise to Mr Gurner's daughter that her father, who then must have been in his late forties, could simply pick up Xenophon's *Anabasis* and Homer's *Odyssey* and teach us with ease. 'Oh, that was nothing,' she replied, 'the other five nights a week my father was translating Ancient Greek into Sanskrit!'

My time at The New School, in fact, only lasted 16 months until Japan entered the War in December 1941, so my experience was essentially of a peacetime British community with a war going on 6000 miles away in Europe and the Middle East. Within a couple of weeks of arrival, my father broke the news that I would attend a temporary school that was being started, which at £105 per term would be more expensive than Eton, without the quality or cachet – therefore as soon as I had sat the School Certificate in December 1941, he would be sending me on to Geelong Grammar School near Melbourne, Australia. By present-day standards, where any child that trips over a paving stone is offered counselling, that must seem somewhat callous; but, in the event, I never went to Geelong. The sinking of the *Prince of Wales* and the *Repulse* put paid to that, so my father cabled three public schools in South Africa, asking them if they would accept a 15-and-a-half-year-old boy, whose headmaster said he would get such-and-such grades. Thus, on 19 December, I found myself sailing down the Hooghly, another family separation, but a new adventure to be made the most of. I spent two and a half memorable years at a school set in an unrivalled location above Maritzburg, Natal, high up on the edge of the wide Umgeni valley. That's where I learned the real meaning of open-hearted hospitality.

MARTIN PINNELL

In May 1940 my parents decided to haul me out to India to be with them, rather than staying, in effect, as an orphan in England. The *City of London* called at Freetown, Durban and Colombo before arriving at Calcutta on 31 August 1940. During the stop in Colombo, I bought five black wooden elephants as presents for my family, but the shopkeeper carefully broke off and stole the ivory tusks as he was wrapping them for me.

On my arrival at Calcutta, my father had taken leave so that the whole family – Father, Mother, my brother and I – could go together on holiday. We stayed in a bungalow on an apple farm near Manali in the Kulu Valley, in the central Himalayas. There was trout fishing in the Kulu river, and I remember that while the equipment provided to me was strictly a fly rod, the *shikari* assigned to look after me insisted on putting a 'titla' (grasshopper) on the hook in addition to the man-made fly – it certainly helped me to catch trout.

We paid an early visit to Darjeeling, where I had a lesson in the meaning of integrity. I went one afternoon to the one and only cinema in Darjeeling, and was agreeably surprised when the manager intercepted me at the box office, refused to let me pay for a ticket, and showed me to one of the best seats in the cinema: it was quite exciting to me, as a 12-year-old, to be treated in this way. When I got home and told my mother, she was horrified, and made me go back at once to the cinema and pay the full price for the seat which I had used. It was explained to me that as my father had, some seven years before, been Deputy Commissioner in Darjeeling, he was well known there: somehow the cinema must have heard that Mr Pinnell's younger son had recently arrived from England, and he was trying to curry favour by offering a free seat. Now, the Indian Civil Service had strict rules against accepting any kind of favour: in a country where bribery was (and still is) endemic, the ICS had, over the years, earned the nickname of 'the incorruptibles', and it was almost a religion to ICS officers that they would never accept a favour. Anyhow, I hurried back and paid for the seat, so honour was saved – just.

Calcutta had had an influx of perhaps two hundred British children who had been evacuated from Britain, and the parents, with help from the authorities, had decided to start a special school for them. It was called The New School, probably because its chosen headmaster, Mr Harold Loukes, was a Quaker, and a brilliant educationalist with a great interest in new theories of education.

Years later, I came to realise that the setting up of The New School had caused great ill-feeling among the several existing schools which were run on the lines of the English public school, and which were open to any children whose parents could pay the fees: Indian, European and Anglo-Indian – in those circles, The New School was often called the 'snob school'. Entry to The New School was limited to children evacuated from Britain, or to children who would have been sent 'home' to school but for the War, and I do not know to this day whether the reason for setting it up was snobbery or just practicality.

By the middle of 1942, the Japanese Army had occupied Burma, and there was a real threat that Assam and Bengal would be invaded next. Bengal was full of refugees from Burma, both military and civilian, Indian and British. I remember that with some of the older boys at The New School, we discussed the possibility that if the railway line to Calcutta was cut, we would walk west through the Himalayan foothills to Nepal and beyond. We could all make ourselves understood in Hindi, and the hill tribes around Darjeeling and in Nepal were pretty friendly, so if it had come to the point, I think we might well have made the long trek out through the hills.

LYNETTE GURNER

One Christmas, I believe in 1941, a friend of my parents arranged a holiday for a group of friends in the North Bengal jungle area where he was based. He was ICS, and would have been responsible for a considerable area around his base position. It was a 'ghooming' – riding through the jungle on elephants, to observe the wildlife but not to shoot it. He gathered together quite a number of elephants loaned by various people in the Indian Forestry Service. Over the holiday period they would not have been needed for their usual work, I would suppose. There were eight of us in the party: our host, a married couple and their teenaged daughter, who were also our friends, and my mother with her three teenaged daughters. My father declined the invitation, and went swimming at Puri.

During the day we roamed the jungle on elephants. These had very large mattress-like pads on their backs, strung with ropes. We sat flat-legged on these and held on to the ropes. Our particular aim was to view rhino, even then very scarce in the area. As we went through the jungle, of course, we saw other birds and smaller animals. The vegetation was not always dense, and we covered a wide area each day.

Rhino were tracked by their spoors and suddenly, after a considerable hunt, we were successful – a female and a young rhino not previously known of. They were in fairly open ground, and were seen clearly. The female was very wary because of the young one; the elephants seemed nervous. Everyone gazed at everyone else, then eventually the rhino turned and went off with her young one. It was a very exciting encounter.

On another occasion, one elephant got stuck in the mud, which was alarming. It was obviously an enormous struggle for the beast as it moved constantly to and fro in the confines of the thick mud, struggling for freedom, verbally encouraged by the *mahouts*. My

left Auriol (left) and Lynette Gurner on their way to school in Darjeeling, 1941, photographed by their father. The building in the left background is the small school where missionaries taught the Hill children.

below The Mission House, Darjeeling, taken from the front, where Auriol and Lynette Gurner lived. It was below the main street with a long drive leading down to it. This placed it conveniently for the Hill children and other Hill folk to come to and fro to the mission, coming in a side entrance.

younger sister was on this elephant. My mother had heard that, in such situations, a desperate elephant will take off what is on its back to place on the ground and give some foothold. How true this is I do not know, and she kept quiet at the time, but obviously she was more worried that most of us. After what seemed like a long struggle, the beast got one foot out, and after a further struggle was completely free. It had been a tense time for everyone. These were all no-nonsense working elephants. The interaction between them and their *mahouts* was remarkable.

Being a private party, which was there for ten days or so, the elephants seemed in a way to be our elephants. It was most unusual for so many to be gathered together. They were a lovely sight, and in the evenings we would often go to the clearing where they were kept to see them. Of particular interest to us was a nine-month-old baby. It was unusual for an elephant to be born in captivity. One night, we all heard tremendous noise and unrest among the elephants. We learned in the morning that a snake had gone for the baby elephant, and it had died shortly afterwards. This was a major loss in every respect.

JOHN BLANDY

One of our perks at this time was a free pass to the two cinemas in Darjeeling that were owned by an old friend of my father's, a Parsee gentleman called Mr Dinshaw E. Avari, who had known me since I was a baby. Thanks to his generosity I must have seen almost every film that came out to India in 1941 and 1942.

As 1941 slipped by, we all returned to Calcutta for the cold weather. My mother was busy organising a fund-raising *mela* at the Dakhuria Lakes for Lady Mary Herbert's war effort. There was a great treat when my sister and I were allowed seats very near the throne of the Viceroy at Durbar. As Chief Secretary it was my father's job to read the citation for the notables who were being rewarded with various honours. I was inordinately proud, and the colours of the uniforms of the Viceroy's guard, and the pageantry of the Indian noblemen made a spectacle that I shall never forget, nor the glimpse of the bulge in my father's uniform pocket where he kept his pipe and tobacco.

I once visited my father in his office in the Writers' Buildings. He had a pipe-rack on his desk, with room for six pipes: one was always in use, another cooling off, another being scraped out and the remaining two being filled and tamped down by his *chaprassi* so that there need be no interruption to the smoke that was so necessary for concentration. He always came home in the middle of the day, had a light lunch, and slept for an hour in the afternoon, returning for another four hours' work in the late afternoon. Often, in the evenings, there would be guests to dinner, for which I was seldom allowed to stay up. Once, the guests included some visiting Greek Naval Officers with whom my father tried to converse, without success, the language of Homer being no longer current: however, they got along fine when they wrote things down.

On special occasions there would be children's parties in Belvedere if the Linlithgows were in Calcutta: I can remember the great excitement of my fancy dress as home-made Roman soldier.

But, gradually, a shadow fell over our happy family. For a long time it was kept from me. My father was an inveterate smoker, as were so many of his generation. In the cold weather of 1941–42 he was appointed Governor of Assam. It was the pinnacle of his career as an ICS officer, but there was one snag: he had to undergo a medical examination. The sore throat that had bothered him from time to time turned out to be cancer. He underwent the usual treatment of the day, radiotherapy, but it was probably too advanced to expect a cure. To get over this, he had a week's leave in the Planters' Club, Darjeeling, and I stayed with him. It was a wonderful chance for me to talk to my father, whom I hardly knew. He tried to teach me to play 'slosh', and included me in the conversation with his old friends in the Club, and with servicemen on leave, and some who had walked across the mountains out of Burma. He gradually explained what was going on, and that he had not many months to live.

During those months – during which he retired as Chief Secretary, was knighted, given a sinecure as the Member of the Board of Revenue and assigned a house in the grounds of Government House – he spent his time reading the Bible and Gibbon all through, and compiling for me a collection of useful sayings, which I still cherish, find useful and have added to. He also gave me some special coaching in Latin, for which I had no talent. I could find no real interest in Virgil, and took no interest in Patroclus or why Achilles should have been so concerned at his death. In fact, he always thought Latin a rather boring language except as an introduction to Greek, which would have opened the door to Sanskrit.

My father died on 8 September 1942: he was buried with all the tear-jerking ceremony of a public man. It was a typical grey September Darjeeling day. It was dry but overcast. There was a large crowd – I suppose most of the European community would have turned out. A platoon of Gurkhas (perhaps Police) paraded, blew the 'Last Post' and fired a salute. After the Padre had done his stuff, about six of my father's brethren in the Lodge, dressed in aprons etc., said a few words, and I was astonished to see among them not only the Honorable Secretary of the Planters' Club, but also my

Government House, Darjeeling, built after the Great Bihar Earthquake of 1934, which destroyed its predecessor, and home to Robin Herbert until 1941.

old schoolmaster, 'Verni' Prinz, from Victoria School, Kurseong. I cannot remember very much more about the ceremony, except that I was rather ashamed to have cried. Later on in the year we visited his rather bleak grave, where he was buried beside his first wife, my mother's elder sister.

JOHN JUDGE

I travelled out in the *Orion* with my step-sister, who was several years older, and had been working in London as a physiotherapist. We joined the ship in Liverpool, and shortly after sailing the ship broke down with engine trouble and had to put into Greenock at the entrance to the Clyde for engine repairs. We then set sail in company with the *Stratheden*, with an armed merchant cruiser as escort. We arrived in Bombay on about 15 September, to be greeted by my parents. The month-long voyage was most enjoyable, as the ship was full of children, and I was spoilt because I had a first-class cabin to myself. The length of the voyage and possible dangers did not have any adverse effect on an 11-year-old schoolboy.

Upon arrival, there were scenes of great jubilation: having survived the voyage and the U-boats, seeing my parents again after a long gap, the train trip to Delhi and staying at the Imperial Hotel, where I was presented with a new bicycle for my twelfth birthday. We then took a long car journey up to Srinagar (Kashmir) via the Banihal Pass, with my mother and the driver. My father remained behind to go to work in Delhi and Ramput. Time was short for me before the start of the first term at this new school in Srinagar, called Sheikh Bagh.

There was a church mission school in Srinagar, which Canon Tyndale-Biscoe joined in 1890, later becoming headmaster and establishing a high reputation for the school in India. There were about five hundred Kashmiri boys in this school. In 1940, his son Eric and his wife decided to start a prep school for all those boys who were unable to go to schools in England because of the War.

They opened the school in October 1940 with 39 boys and 6 girls, and named it Sheikh Bagh. I was one of the senior boys, at the age of 12. The numbers gradually built up over the next four years in association with a girl's school called the Garden School, also in Srinagar. My two sisters and my future wife went to it.

I left after two years to move on to my next school, Aitchison College in Lahore. Aitchison College, also known as 'chief's college', was a large Indian school (approximately five hundred boys) for the upper-class Indians in the Punjab – mainly Sikh – run by a mixture of Indian and European teachers. The headmaster was English.

This superior Indian school, with a good reputation in the country, decided to open a section for schoolboys who had been evacuated from England and Europe because of the War. This section was opened in 1940. It was the equivalent of and similar to an English public school, with a mixture of British and Indian boys. They were more integrated in lessons and sport for the Autumn and Easter terms. The summer term was an exception, because of the heat in Lahore without air-conditioning. The English boys were sent

The Tiger Patrol, Sheikh Bagh. Bob Bragg, third from left – 'knock-kneed, squashed topee'.

to Simla (Wildflower Hall – nowadays a smart hotel) via a narrow-gauge mountain railway, where the pupils were boarders and taught normal subjects.

In Lahore the Indian and English boys were mostly day-boys. I stayed with the Pakenham-Walsh family, and bicycled to the school each day. The education at the school was satisfactory, but lacked French and Latin: however, the subject of horseriding was taught, alongside our Indian colleagues. The Sikhs and the Princes were expected to be accomplished horsemen, and the English found it to be fun, if a little boring.

MICHAEL MULLER

Early in the War my father was posted to Chaklala as chief at the RIASC school there. It must have been a busy time for him – certainly, I saw little of him. I rode a lot, but only with a *syce* as company. I remember riding as far as the tomb of Bucephalus, Alexander the Great's war-horse, and we went one weekend to Taxila to see the Buddhist temples. I started going to Mrs Watkins's school in Rawalpindi: when summer came it moved to Murree and we went to Khuldana, from where I could ride to school every morning. I went back to Chaklala in the autumn, and then in the new year came a fundamental change for me.

Sheikh Bagh Preparatory School had been started in October 1940 to provide schooling for boys who either had not been sent home to England, or who had been brought out from England as the War started. There was a shortage of such schools, and a number of other 'war schools' started up. The school was based on the Church Missionary Society (CMS) schools, famously founded and run by Canon C.H. Tyndale-Biscoe in Srinagar. His son Eric had come to Kashmir in the thirties on his way to settling in New Zealand, and was persuaded to stop off and help to teach in the CMS schools. He saw the need for an English school and started Sheikh Bagh. The first term there were some forty boys who, from the point of view of the founder, were very difficult. He had to find teachers from nowhere, and start a school from scratch, with a lot of missing boys who had enjoyed a long break from the formal education and discipline of their schools in England. He called it the 'bear garden'! However, word got round, and when the school opened for its second term the numbers had almost doubled. T.B., as he was known, had also worked very hard, finding new teachers and generally bringing his ideas and organising ability into play, so that the school I went to at the beginning of 1941 was a great deal more controlled and civilised. It had not, however, lost its spirit.

Sheikh Bagh was very special. We played football, hockey and cricket and so on – but we also went mountain-climbing, sometimes on expeditions lasting several days, and we sailed and played in boats on the Dahl Lake, and there were other Kashmiri specialities. In the first summer, a mile swim was organised in the Dahl Lake. A surprisingly large number of us succeeded in this, so a year later a three-mile swim was added, and a year later a few were swimming back again – six miles!

Sheikh Bagh. Easter holidays on the Wular Lake. An outing or picnic by boat. (Michael Muller)

Holidays, for whatever reason, were celebrated with major outings. Usually we started by paddling across the Dahl Lake, and then spending the day at Moghul gardens, such as Shalimar, Nishat Bagh and Cheshmachai. Picnic lunches would be taken, and we would explore and play games. One of these was 'Kabaddi' – a sort of Indian 'Tom Tiddler's Ground', in which one could only go into the other side's ground for the length of one breath, demonstrated by muttering 'Kabaddi, kabaddi, kabaddi...'

Because of the distances many of us had to travel, the school ran two terms per year; January–June (with a short canoeing and boating break on the Wular Lake at Easter) and September– December. While I was at my first term at Sheikh Bagh, the RIASC school – with my family – moved from Chaklala to Kakul near Abbottabad. I never saw this home, because by the time term ended my father had gone to the Middle East to the War, and I found my mother and sisters living at Thandiani, 14,000 feet high, with the same Forestry Service friends that we had lived with in Kulu many years before. The Forestry Officer was then recalled to the Army, and we appeared to be homeless – but not for long. Shah Zaman, our bearer and guardian angel, found a home in Abbottabad, where my mother and sisters lived for the next two years and from which I went to school in Kashmir.

Many of my journeys to and from school in Kashmir took two or three days. Sheikh Bagh ran a convoy of buses from Rawalpindi to Srinagar and in the opposite direction at the end of term. These convoys in themselves took two days, with a night in the *dak* bungalow, usually at Kohala. To get from Jutogh to Rawalpindi took two days and two nights, and involved changing trains at Kalka, Ambala and sometimes before. Generally, Shah Zaman came with me for at least part of the journey, but latterly I was on my own, joining up with school fellows as we approached Rawalpindi. This, in retrospect, gives a huge compliment to the railway staff in northern India, who looked after me like a registered parcel and saw that I changed trains and so on. I never felt anything but safe in all

One of a dozen or so buses forming the Sheikh Bagh Rawalpindi–Srinagar convoy, at Kohala. (Michael Muller)

my life of comings and goings in India, and I believe that I had a much easier and safer life than is possible now for my grandchildren in England.

JOHN PAKENHAM-WALSH

My family's connections with India go back to the nineteenth century. My grandfather helped to build the railway system. His brother, an Anglican priest, spent the whole of his working life and beyond there – in his early days as principal of Bishop Cotton School, Bangalore (one of the houses is still named after him), and then as Bishop of Assam. On his retirement, he founded a Christian *ashram* at Tadagam near Coimbatore, to which he devoted the rest of his life. It became a centre of healing, attracting the sick from miles around, and from there developed a small hospital nearby, which still bears his name. Yet another brother ended his career in the ICS as a High Court Judge in Madras. Not to be outdone, his sister devoted the whole of her life to good works there, and was much involved with the Guides movement; I believe she was awarded their top honour, the Silver Fish!

Down a generation, my father joined the ICS in the early 1920s, initially in Burma and then in India. After the Second World War he returned to Burma as a High Court Judge in Rangoon. His brother worked in the Burmah Oil Co. in Burma and India. His sister was the wife of the head of that company in Burma, and was later shot during the agitation for Burmese Independence.

At the start of the War I was transported to Ireland – to avoid the bombs, I suppose – and then in the summer of 1940 to India to join my father, who was then the Sessions Judge in Dera Ghazi Khan (DGK), a small township in the Sindh desert. The trip to India was trans-Atlantic by ship (pretty scary with U-boats around), trans-Canada by train (great), and trans-Pacific by ship to Sydney. The ship on which our passages had originally been booked was sunk by U-boat action, reputedly with much bullion on board, resulting in some weeks' unexpected stay in Vancouver awaiting the next available ship. Finally, Sydney to Calcutta by Empire flying-boat, stopping overnight at Townsville, Sourabaya, Singapore and Bangkok, then trans-India by train to Multan.

Arrival at Multan station in the middle of an August day was my first experience of really hot weather. At well over 120 degrees Fahrenheit, the heat was barely credible to a small 12-year-old, but it was tempered by the excitement of seeing my father again after some years, and the adventure of driving westwards to DGK, crossing the Indus (about 10 miles wide at that point) by primitive car-ferry.

The Sessions Judge's house was a typical colonial bungalow – spacious and elegant in a slightly tatty way, with mosquito netting on the windows, a large compound and loads of servants. It lay in the centre of a small crescent outside the town, in company with a few other similar residences – the Police Superintendent's house, the District Commissioner's house and the doctor's house. No baths or flush toilets, just tin tubs and commodes duly emptied on command by the sweeper. For recreation, and to get a little cooler, a couple of hours' drive reached the local hill station, Fort Munro, on the road to Quetta.

Back in DGK there was a small airfield, though I cannot recall seeing any aeroplanes. Its main use seemed to be a golf course. Being surrounded by desert, there were no greens – only browns, and it was really just one large bunker with a few cactus-like plants to lose your ball in.

In 1941 my father was transferred to Lahore, and DGK became a thing of the past. For me, the next three years were spent in Srinagar, apart from Christmas holidays in Lahore and summer holidays in Gulmarg. In the first year at Sheikh Bagh school (no bullying and cold baths there!) we were taught by a tough retired Calcutta policeman called Fred, who did his best – quite successfully – with a big stick to educate a few of us teenagers in basic subjects, without any teaching experience or qualifications. 'One page ahead' was his motto, coupled with insistence on learning innumerable extracts from Ovid and Shakespeare parrot-wise. I could recite 'To be or not to be' in 30 seconds flat. The School Certificate exam was taken at the convent in Srinagar. Fred's efforts succeeded to the extent of five School Certificate subjects, which were enough in those days to secure acceptance to a university.

Early in 1944 I was carted back to England by ship to be schooled in the normal way, and the Indian adventure came to an end.

The War was not good for the education of us Indian refugees. Compared to most others it was, of course, spent in relative comfort and splendid surroundings, but it resulted in a fragmented education. On the plus side, I was left with a lasting affection and regard for India and Pakistan. But that was probably in the genes anyway.

ROBIN HERBERT

I had the unforgettable experience of being brought up between the ages of five and nine in Government House at Calcutta and Darjeeling.

Government House, Calcutta was modelled on Kedleston, albeit substantially larger, and it sat in the middle of the city in spacious grounds, where the principal flowers were cannas. I have never subsequently lived in such sumptuous surroundings, complete with all the trappings of the Raj, from Rolls Royces – which had to be high enough to accommodate my six-feet-six father in a top hat – to uniformed *khitmagar*. To visit my parents after breakfast every morning, my normal method of transport was to bicycle from one wing to another through the massive ballroom, complete with throne. I recall Christmas parties at which Santa Claus arrived on an elephant and conjurors swallowed goldfish and then regurgitated them, to the horror and dismay of my very British nanny.

Many distinguished visitors came through Calcutta, including Archie Wavell, then GOC India. His after-tea entertainment for me was to slide his glass eye in and out! I also recall my mother complaining that Chiang Kai-Shek's generals were a nightmare with whom to play poker, because their staff sat behind her and told their bosses in Chinese what cards she held. The most frightening experience was being bombed by the Japanese, when one had to go and spend the night on the ground floor.

Darjeeling was another story, where on clear days one had one of the world's most spectacular views of Kanchenjunga and Kalimpong. Methods of transport ranged from rickshaws, to riding to Singamari school daily on a pony. I suborned the *syce* to let

Government House, Calcutta, where Robin Herbert's mother played poker with General Chiang Kai-Shek. (John Langley)

Robin Herbert, a future President of the Royal Horticultural Society, sitting in the circular, tiered Flower Garden at the Viceroy's House in New Delhi, a guest of Lord Linlithgow, January 1942, and by the empty pool. 'Much too cold to swim outside in Delhi in January.'

me play hookey and we used to go for long rides until the school telephoned my mother to find out why I was not at school. There was then a ghastly row.

SHEILA WRIGHT-NEVILLE

When The New School moved to Darjeeling, at the beginning of term in March, the staff and students travelled to Darjeeling on the school train from Calcutta. One needed three weeks to become acclimatised to the altitude, so no games or exercises were scheduled at the beginning of term. In time, however, climbing the steep roads and paths became almost routine. There was a small racecourse at Lebong, near Darjeeling, where we could go with visiting parents during the term breaks. The racehorses were the same small hill ponies, usually ridden by their owners. There were often dense fogs on the racecourse, and ponies and riders would disappear from sight in the middle of a race, to surface in a suspiciously different order.

Beyond a stopping point in the lower part of the town, no cars were allowed in Darjeeling (except the Governor's car) so everybody walked. Older people availed themselves of rickshaws pulled by the strong, sturdy hill people. These people also carried all our luggage from the train station to our boarding houses; even large trunks would be slung from a headband over the shoulder and back of the porter. These porters were often women and, though tiny, they were incredibly strong.

Darjeeling was always a popular vacation spot for allied troops on leave.

Our flat in Calcutta had several large rooms, a balcony, running water, fans and flush toilets – for the first time in a home in India. Our *ayah* at that time, Kanchi, was a sweet woman from the Darjeeling area, now living in Calcutta. Kanchi often told us how she

The end of the motor road to Darjeeling. Above this, one had to walk. The road on the left, Laden La Road, went down the bazaar. The white building above it was Keventer's, which sold delicious milk shakes. The modernist building, top right, was part of the Planters' Club. The road between them was Commercial Row, leading to the Chowrasta. (Nicole Walby)

missed her family in the hills. We also employed a cook and a bearer but, unlike our previous homes, the kitchen quarters were an integral part of the flat.

We often slept on the balcony, and one of the pests we had to deal with were night-flying cockroaches, although we were on the fourth floor. The method was simple and efficient: a smack with a rubber-soled slipper when they landed, leaving the resulting mess to be completely removed by ants during the night. Mosquito nets over beds were an absolute necessity. I never suffered from malaria, although my parents did, but once had a bad bout of dengue fever which delayed my return to school. The name, loosely translated, means 'break-bone fever' which aptly describes this unpleasant and enervating 'flu-like illness.

Occasionally, there were tea dances at the Saturday Club to which youngsters went. On one of my father's last leaves in Calcutta, I remember attending one such event with my parents and dancing with my father. He liked to dance, but on this occasion he had to stop often and take one of his 'gunpowder' pills for his heart condition.

One holiday, we spent a fortnight at Puri, on the coast of the Indian Ocean, where the beaches were endless, the people few and the sea itself always a long way out. However, the hotel had a swimming pool where all the children gathered, and the weather was perfect. I met a young American nurse on leave at the hotel who surprised me by wishing to attend an Indian festival at a nearby village: it was my first intimation that some visitors might be interested in such things.

PATRICIA BANHAM

The following year, 1941, I failed my Senior Cambridge School Certificate exam. I decided to go back to school and do the exam again. This time I was able to attend St Mary's Diocesan School for Girls, in Poona. Here we had Anglican nuns and other teachers. We were right next to St Mary's Anglican church, and I went to services every Sunday. I liked being with the nuns. Everything was so peaceful. That year I concentrated on my studies with a whole new syllabus. When we wrote our exams at the end of the year we wrote in pencil with carbon copies so that there were duplicate copies, probably due to the severe bombing over England during 1941 and the sinking of shipping. At the start of 1942, not knowing what my exam results would be, I could not return to St Mary's Teachers' Training College and was trying to decide what I should do. My stepmother, from a psychological point of view, said very cleverly, 'Your mother always wanted you to be a nurse.' My immediate response was, 'Well, if my mother wanted me to be a nurse, I will be a nurse'.

There was a young Scottish lady we were friendly with who was recruiting young women to join the St John's Nursing Service. I became a St John's nurse or VAD, as we were called. All women were being recruited – elderly women, widows, single women, trained sisters and nurses. We were sent to hospitals all over India for quick training in all aspects of nursing, and then on to Military Hospitals preparing for the Burmese frontier, on hospital ships and in the Middle East. Without having a chance to say goodbye to any of my family, I was sent from a hospital in Baroda to Quetta, and after a few months sent on a troopship to the Persian Gulf. The ship used to be a missionary steamer, sailing up and down the east coast of India, before it was used for transporting troops. I was sent up to a British and military hospital. At the beginning of 1944 I went to Egypt and nursed at a hospital on the Suez Canal for a short while. Then it was six months in an Indian hospital just outside Tel Aviv in Palestine.

Unfortunately, I never returned to India, because I had now married and my husband had planned to go out to South Africa. Perhaps it was just as well because, even before my husband and I left Palestine for South Africa, all the rest of the family had settled in England. It was not until 1967, when I had the opportunity to visit England, that I saw any of them again!

FAY FOUCAR

In April 1940, my mother flew home for the Easter holidays to put Tony, my brother, in his public school and to take me back with her to Burma. The news got progressively worse, with the Germans overrunning the Low Countries, Denmark and France. There was talk of invasion, so we all three returned to Burma. We sailed from Liverpool at the end of July, having just a couple of days from the end of term to pack. As soon as we got on board, the smell of the ship was so evocative, and the smiling faces of the Indian stewards were somehow so familiar, that Tony and I grinned at each other. We knew that we were going home.

On the fiftieth day we sailed up the Rangoon River to be met by my father and Ba In, our driver.

My father had moved to a *pukka* stone-built house up a leafy, winding road in a countrified part of Rangoon. As well as a tennis court in front and the usual servants' quarters at the rear, this time we had real plumbing and running water. An extra servant had been engaged to assist the butler, and we had been promoted to 'Miss-sahib' and 'Chota-sahib'.

Then began a very happy time for us all. We were a united family in the relaxed life of pre-war Burma. As we drove about in Rangoon, we recognised the places we had known all those years ago, but they all appeared to have shrunk.

On the garden gate of most houses there was a box in which new arrivals to Burma dropped their visiting cards. On return from leave it was the custom to drop cards to notify such return. The first call was on the Governor, and then to all those senior to oneself. This time, my name was included on my parents' card, and I was invited to dine at Government House. I feared it would be an ordeal, but it turned out to be fun, as several young new arrivals had also been asked. It is possibly of some interest to record that my mother stipulated that I should not be allowed to go out with any young man who had not dropped a card – and a copperplate card at that!

We now lived in the shadow of the 'reclining Buddha', who was floodlit at night. The first time my future husband drove me home from a late party we nearly came to grief. Rounding a corner on our winding road, there was the great Buddha smiling down on us. He had never been on this road, and I had forgotten to warn him of our august neighbour. Fortunately, his nerves were of sufficient strength to keep the car on the road, but it was a near thing.

Although we were enjoying a near-normal life, we had certainly not forgotten the rest of the family at home. The news was bad, and we worried about them. Very soon our own peaceful life was to come to an end. In December 1941, Rangoon was bombed by the Japanese, and it was their turn to worry about us. When Rangoon fell, my parents lost everything they possessed. All four of us ultimately arrived in India by various routes and spent the rest of the War there.

NANCY LLOYD

My second sister was married in Rangoon in April 1937, and so my parents and I returned to England without her. I spent two years in London studying the violin at the Royal College of Music and then in 1940, just at the end of the 'phoney war', I flew out to Rangoon to marry my husband. I flew on one of the old flying-boats. They were comfortable and spacious, with reclining chairs and room to walk about, very unlike the cramped and crowded modern planes. The journey took six days, and each night we came down and were accommodated in an elegant hotel.

We were married in Rangoon. My husband had completed an Officers' Training Course just before I arrived. He was immediately called up to join the Burma Frontier Force, and we were sent to Bhamo, a small station far in the north of Burma. It was a charming and very beautiful riverine town on the banks of the Irrawaddy. There were very few Europeans stationed there and my husband, as a 2nd Lieutenant, was one of only four officers in the Frontier Force.

He found that the two elderly senior officers seemed to be blissfully oblivious of the progress of the War in the West and the fact that the Japanese were making pretty warlike noises in the East. Apart from his soldiering, our life was again one of sport and fun; we played a lot of golf on a funny little course where all the greens were made of hard, tamped-down earth. My husband coached the troops – Sikhs, Punjabi Mussulmen, Gurkhas and Kachins – in football and hockey. Our little wooden house was right beside the military lines, and commanded the most exquisite view of the broad Irrawaddy and the blue mountains. I remember glorious picnics some way out of Bhamo where a splashing mountain torrent widened out and formed a delightful bathing pool.

We also went twice up into the Kachin Hills, east of Bhamo, by pony, for my husband to inspect outlying frontier posts, which was a wonderful experience, far from civilisation. There was also a bunch of Americans who were running an aircraft factory for the Chinese in a place called Loiwing, which was just over the border in China. They were a very lively lot, and we once or twice went up there by the hazardous mountain road for a couple of nights, and the Americans often came down to Bhamo. At one stage we had a visit from a delegation of Chinese officers. These were from the Nationalist Army, which had been at war with Japan since 1937. (The Chinese Communists did not take over until 1948.) My husband was detailed to accompany them north to Myitkyina, and I was allowed to go too. Myitkyina is about two hundred miles north of Bhamo, upriver, and was the most northerly station of the Frontier Force. We went by motor-car up the very rough road running on the left bank of the Irrawaddy. We stayed a night *en route* in a Government resthouse. These were splendid, if primitive, hut-like houses built of teak or other hardwood for the benefit of those on tour. They were manned by a servant who produced an evening meal of the inevitable scraggy chicken, and there were beds and mosquito nets provided. After a few days in Myitkyina we left the Chinese there and went back to Bhamo in a small launch, by river.

This entailed going through the upper defile, where the jungle-clad hills come right down to the river, which narrows and is very deep and swift, and quite difficult to negotiate. Again, we stayed the night in a small village, this time on the right bank. It so happened that there was a *pwe* on that night, and so I had my first experience of a Burmese *pwe*. These are colourful entertainments with dancing, singing and endless comedy turns, which were full of bawdy jokes. (My Burmese was not up to understanding them!) The whole thing is very jolly and informal, lasting many hours, the audience wandering about at will and enjoying their evening meal. Burmese dancing is beautiful, very stylised, and the costumes are replicas of the old court dress. The long, narrow *longgyis* (skirts) which are the national dress for both men and women, were, for the women, even longer and narrower, ending in a sort of short train, and the girl dancers were skilful at manoeuvring these. Their hair, jet-black and gleaming with coconut oil, is dressed high in a cylindrical shape. Their hands, long-fingered and narrow and extremely supple, are moved with great elegance and significance.

I studied Urdu with a Sikh teacher, and my husband, whose Urdu was pretty good, learned Kachin, as one of the companies was composed of Kachins, who are one of the hill-tribes of northern Burma.

Then in December 1941 came Pearl Harbour and the invasion of Burma by the Japanese.

PATRICIA RAYNES

In December 1941, the Japanese invaded Burma, and the battle of Rangoon commenced. The city was poorly defended, with only a few old planes and pilots to attack the fighters and bombers coming in waves – one young pilot chased a plane up the Irrawaddy and was shot down, unhurt, near Mandalay where we lived, and was brought to stay with us until he could catch the next train down to Rangoon – he was so exhausted, he slept solidly for about 24 hours.

Early in January bombing started in Mandalay, and my father decided that my mother, sister and I, together with our neighbour and her children, whose husband had been summoned back to his regiment, must leave Burma. The planes to India left from Lashio, up in the Shan States, and it was a long drive up there, through some very beautiful country, but the road was full of Army vehicles – many of them broken down or down the hillside in pieces.

We stayed in Lashio in the house of the young policeman in charge of the area – a small wooden bungalow with a field at the bottom of the garden, slightly away from the small township. We were there about a week – a couple of times we were summoned to the airport, but there was no room on the plane. Finally, our friends were able to leave, and after a day or so we had a phone call at 2.00 a.m. to leave straight away – once again a false alarm. The next afternoon, my mother decided we would go and have a picnic tea in the field, but as we were leaving the red alarm balloon went up – there was nothing so sophisticated as an air-raid siren – so we stayed in the garden. Suddenly, a small Japanese plane appeared, flying so low you could see the pilot in his cockpit. Fortunately, it was a reconnaissance aircraft, as otherwise I might not be here to tell the tale!

Again that night at 2.00 a.m., the phone went – come to the airport at once – and this time there was room for us. It was a very small plane, with one seat on each side of the passageway, and the pilot in a seat in the front – no separate cabin for him. We seemed to fly low – you could see the shadow of the plane on the fields and jungle beneath. We finally arrived at Dum Dum Airport, Calcutta, at about 10.00 a.m. It was very hot, crowded and noisy, and by that time I was feeling very ill, and was running a temperature. We had to go through a medical examination, and my mother was terrified they might put us in quarantine, and goodness knows what we could have picked up there, but luckily the doctor was so busy talking to someone he took no notice when he felt my pulse! We got a taxi into Calcutta, in the hope of getting a hotel room, though we knew everywhere was

Darjeeling, 1941. 'A family picnic in the Botanical Gardens with my sister Christine, Father and Mother.' (Sheila Wright-Neville)

crowded. We had just been refused a room at one hotel when we met a friend, who persuaded the manager to let us have a small room in the attics, and I retired to bed for the remainder of our short stay there! All I remember of Calcutta was the crowded streets, with cows in the middle of the road when we went to the station on our way up to friends in Cawnpore – not a very favourable start to a three-year stay in India.

Lashio fell to the Japanese three days after we left, and sadly our young policeman host was killed in the fighting.

4

1942

17 January	The Japanese invade Burma
15 February	15,000 British, 13,000 Australian and 32,000 Indian troops surrender to the Japanese at Singapore
7 March	Rangoon evacuated
5–9 April	Japanese planes attack Colombo and Trincomalee in Ceylon, Vizagapatam and Cocanada in India
31 May	Japanese occupation of Burma complete
August–November	The Battle of Stalingrad finally prevents further German advance into Russia
4 November	Allied victory over Germany and Italy at El Alamein in Libya

MOLLY MILNE

On 23 December 1941, my parents were both at work (my mother had soon obtained a job at GHQ), and my brother Robin and I were with friends, he near the aerodrome Mingaladon, and me in the city with Helen McLaren.

I had had lunch, and was helping Mrs McLaren sort the laundry to send to the *dhobi*, when there was suddenly a terrible noise of machine-gun fire and explosions. We rushed on to the verandah, and right across the sky a plane was falling, smoke streaming behind. As we watched, two figures jumped from the plane, but their parachutes did not open and they plummeted to the ground.

Suddenly the sky was alive with action, and we were ordered to the newly dug trenches. Unfortunately the gaggle of geese owned by the McLarens interrupted us, and made our objective very difficult! We hardly knew whether to laugh or cry: the natives were screaming and wailing, and we were all very frightened. We got to the trench and then stayed quietly, praying that the bombing would stop. It was good, to say the least, that at the end of the day each one of our family was alive and under the same roof.

We were very shaken, and Rangoon was in ruins. The next day, and for some weeks after this Prome Road, where we lived, saw a steady stream of natives leaving Rangoon, their bullock carts, rickshaws and bicycles loaded with belongings, children, babies and animals. It was a pathetic sight, and very undermining to us children. Reports from all directions were pretty bad, but our parents tried to assure us that everything would be all right.

Christmas Day 1941 – great excitement. I was given my first gramophone, and Robin an electric train. We had hardly got over the shock of being so spoilt when we heard the noise of planes – lots of them, a dull, sickening drone. As we ran into the garden, we saw the most perfect formation of silver planes in the bright, clear-blue sky. We've never moved so fast in our lives towards the trenches, where we spent the rest of Christmas Day! I was so frightened that I got blisters on my hands from holding my mother's hand too hard. Massive bombing took place that day, all round us – an arms depot across the road was hit, so the explosions continued into the night. All electricity was cut off by the bombing, so Robin never had his train! We discovered the next morning an unexploded bomb in the garden, 50 yards from the house.

My father took me into the city in one of our cars which had not been machine-gunned; the devastation was dreadful, smoke and dust and rubble and smouldering buildings. That day I saw my first dead body.

Everyone was told to evacuate Rangoon, and the Government set up a 'walk' out of Burma, up-country to India. Most people were still certain that the Japanese would not occupy Burma for long, so went up-country for the time being. Because of his duties with Burma Railways, my father was allocated his own personal railway carriage, to enable him to travel freely and extensively throughout the railway system.

Some time in January my mother, brother and I, plus a handful of our servants, boarded this beautiful white railway carriage, which consisted of two bedrooms, sitting room, dining room, kitchen and bathroom hitched on to a train, and were taken to a hill station called Maymo. We simply walked out of our house, leaving my two Siamese cats, my aviary of budgerigars, two aquaria, all our belongings and the house intact. It must have been heart-breaking for my parents.

I cannot remember the dates very accurately, but long after we had settled our carriage on a siding in Maymo, the air-raids started again. They were always terrifying, particularly because we had no warning. The bombs seemed to fall out of the sky, and everything went berserk. In one of the many raids I first experienced what blast felt like. We were knocked flat as we ran to the slit trench, a most peculiar feeling.

The next thing I knew was that a message had been received from my father, still in Rangoon, simply saying, 'Get across the Ava Bridge as quickly as possible.' We were particularly lucky, as all we had to do was hitch our carriage on to the next train, and we packed it with as many people as possible.

This was all done at night and we crossed the Ava Bridge and parked the carriage in a siding in the village of Sagaing. If the Ava Bridge was blown up, now we could get to India. There was no further word from my father, and we lived on, in oppressively hot weather, in our carriage. Our faithful Burmese servants were still with us, but our beloved Karen nanny returned to her home town, Toungoo.

The dreaded bombing started again, but this time we had a warning device. As soon as planes were heard, a little man would rush out and bang a bit of old railway line! Hotfoot, once again, we had to run across a large *maidan* (field) into the trenches. But no bombs fell while we were there.

Eventually my father arrived, the last contingent out of Rangoon, having organised the transport for evacuation. As a treat, to keep our peckers up – and I know I still remained very frightened inside – my father took us into a nearby golf club and gave us potato chips and lemonade – the height of luxury!

Obviously, Burma was falling to the Japanese, not so slowly, but very surely, and my parents decided we must evacuate to India. One day (perhaps the next?) my mother, Robin and I went by train to the nearest river village, Shwebo, where the three of us boarded a paddle steamer packed with evacuees of every sort. The plan was to go to the Irrawaddy River to a set point where we were to be dropped, and then start the long walk to India. I believe this route became very congested later on. However, after a terrible night, everyone lying where they could find space on the deck and only one lavatory between hundreds, the boat got stuck on a sandbank. The rivers were pretty dry because we were in the middle of the hot weather. Everything possible was tried to refloat, and the last resort was to unload the boat and make it lighter. Everyone over 12 was told to trek across about half a mile of loose, deep, very hot sand to a village on the hill about a mile or so away. The plan then was that hopefully the boat would be able to get off the sandbank and round the next bend in the river where it would hoot, and we would all trudge back and continue our journey upriver.

The walk was incredibly difficult and many people passed out, and when we got to this minute village in the shade of palm trees, it was marvellous to find that the natives were friendly. They shinned up the palm trees and got us coconuts so that we could drink the milk. The best drink I've ever had! My brother, aged nine or ten, was the lucky one, as he was too young to come with us.

Some hours later, before sunset, we heard the hooting, went to the brow of the hill, and could see from our vantage point that the boat had not shifted. Disappointed, we walked back and boarded, to be told that we would have to return to Shwebo. We had also completely run out of drinking water. My parents' wonderful man-servant since 1925, Ba Thwin, was with us still, and when we got back to Shwebo sent a message down the line to my father telling him what had happened. Meanwhile we went for the night to friends of ours, stored up drinking water in every possible container, ready to travel up the river the next morning at first light, presumably with fewer people on board. However, my father had obviously not been very impressed about the whole situation and sent a message saying 'Get off and come back' – which is what we did. That meant staying in our carriage for another week to ten days in extreme heat.

By then the Government were evacuating people by air in Dakotas from a small field quite a distance from Sagaing. We turned up one day with all the other hundreds trying to get out, and eventually were put on a short flight to cross the border into India. The seats had all been stripped out, and we were packed on to aluminium benches where, while waiting to take off, we were so hot that we were absolutely soaking wet – hair dripping – and as soon as we took off, practically iced to our seats! I remember one or two people being air sick into their *topees*! Of course we carried nothing, and arrived in India real refugees. Thereupon we had a very long journey by rail and boat which took about three days from Chittagong to Calcutta. Here again my mother contacted friends and we stayed with them for a week or so while they helped us to get clean and buy a few clothes, before going to Bombay to stay with cousins.

In Bombay my brother and I were found schools and we waited for news of my father; he had to be one of the last out, as he was in charge of transport for evacuees. His escape is another story, which I have sent to the Imperial War Museum, but my poor mother must have gone through hell not knowing where he was or what was happening.

There always seemed to be contradictory news; first my father had been seen, then he hadn't been seen. My mother met many trains in the hope that he would be on one, but it wasn't until four months later that he turned up one day. His story is an incredible one of hazard and death, starvation, leeches and disease, rivers swollen by the monsoon rains and impassable. He was very lucky, as many had died on the journey, but he was ill and very, very thin.

When my father had recuperated we all went up to Simla, where the Burmese Railways had established their headquarters. My father returned to work with them and my mother joined the WAC(I).

HELEN MCLAREN

At the outbreak of the Second World War, my parents decided I would be safer with them in Burma, so arranged for me to sail out to Rangoon on the *Salween*. For some reason that was changed, and I found that I was going on the *Stratheden*. My guardian and I took a train to Liverpool, where we arrived in the middle of an air-raid, so we had to spend the night in a shelter under the station. When it was light enough, we made our way to the Adelphi Hotel, only to discover that the bag my guardian had, with all my papers, money and passport in, had been stolen. Miss Clark took to her bed with a migraine, and I took myself off to the nearest Police station. After answering a lot of questions and being taken from one office to another, I finally got a new passport. I must say, everyone was most helpful, and Miss Clark (she had managed to pull herself together) was able to get me down to the docks and see me aboard the *Stratheden*. To this day, I have never discovered why I was switched to this ship and had a first class cabin all to myself! There were several hundred children on board, and I think we were in one of the largest convoys to have left Britain.

The journey out to Bombay was thankfully uneventful, but enjoyable. I was very lucky to meet up with Mrs Milne and her daughter Molly and son Robin, who were also going to Rangoon, and knew my parents well. She contacted my parents to let them know she had met me, and that I would be travelling with them to Rangoon. I was very relieved about that, as I was not at all sure what I would do when I reached Bombay. At Cape Town, the *Salween* happened to be in port at the same time, and looked awfully small compared to the *Stratheden*.

On arriving at Bombay, Mrs Milne, Molly, Robin and myself took a train to Calcutta. That was a very hot and dusty two-day journey. On arriving in Calcutta we stayed with friends of the Milnes while arrangements were made to take the KLM flying boat to Rangoon. That, for me, was quite an experience. We landed first of all at Akyab and then went on to Rangoon. It was wonderful to see my mother and father again, and also to be back in Rangoon and see all the familiar places. A school was started by parents at Rangoon University for all the British children. It was very well run and gave us a chance to meet and make new friends.

In May 1941 my father was due to take his six months' leave, and had been thinking about going to New Zealand. He didn't like what was going on in the Far East, so we went to Gulmarg, Kashmir instead. I really enjoyed our stay there, and there were quite a few teenagers who had come out from Britain to join their parents. We all had ponies, and after morning school (most of the girls attended a school run by a Mrs Ancrum, and a few of the boys had a tutor) we would get together either to ride up one of the valleys for a picnic or else play golf or tennis. Once a week there was a tea dance at Nedou's Café. Nedou's Hotel was the main hotel in Gulmarg, and all the big dances were held there. They also had an excellent Police band, which was led by a Mr Chapman, who my father met in the final of the Northern Indian Golf Championship. I'm happy to say that my father won. A very nice ending to our holiday.

On our return to Rangoon, everything was fairly peaceful, and then at the beginning of December the Japanese started bombing us. It was almost a daily occurrence, and usually at lunchtime. I re-member going Christmas shopping with my mother and my friend

Molly, and while in Rowe & Co., the only large department store in Rangoon, the air-raid siren started. We grabbed all our parcels and headed for the main door, where our wonderful driver Po Soo had stuck his foot in the door, and would not let them close it until he had got us out and into the car. I think that was one of the fastest journeys I have had from the town to our home in Churchill Avenue. We could hear the bombing going on in the town, but when we saw a Jap plane coming down in flames near our house we felt it was time to get into our trench. We were worried about my father, and very relieved when he was able to phone us to say that he was fine and the office had escaped damage. Our school was closed, and eventually, in the New Year, my father and mother decided that they would like me to leave Rangoon. I went up to Maymyo with Mrs Milne, Molly and Robin. Mr Milne was with Burma Railways, and had the use of a very nice guesthouse. Life was fairly peaceful there, but it was not long before my father brought Mother up to Maymyo. Father had a cousin, Touser McLaren, who owned the Mandalay Brewery and was taking his wife up to Lashio, to get a flight out to Calcutta. My father asked him if he could possibly get two seats for Mother

Mrs Ancrum's School for Young Ladies, Gulmarg, 1941. Mrs Ancrum third left, middle row. Helen McLaren on right of middle row, Joan Bragg standing behind her.

and me sometime soon. He had received a telegram from Mr and Mrs Chisholm in Calcutta. We had met them in Kashmir, and their daughter Daphne and I had been at Mrs Ancrum's together. The telegram said 'Send Helen to us in Calcutta,' and Father replied, saying 'Sending Helen and Cathie'. We stayed with Touser in his lovely home in Maymyo for a week, and then it was time for us to leave. Daddy (sorry I have to change, Father and Mother are a bit too formal) saw us off at the station in Maymyo and the journey was peaceful, though Mummy was worried about crossing the Goktek Viaduct in case the Japs would bomb it before we got there.

We were lucky, and arrived in Lashio in the afternoon. We went straight to the airport, but when the plane came in the pilot said they would not be leaving before the next day, as they had come through some very rough weather. These were the American Volunteer Group (AVG), who were coming over from China and flying people to safety in DC3s. We were bombed that night in Lashio, and the journey to the airport the next morning in a bus was over a very potholed road. Mum and I had to support a very pregnant lady between us to prevent her from being bumped around. At the airport, the plane was ready to go. Everyone started boarding, and when they came to Mum and me they said they could not take any more because of the weight. The other passengers said they would not go without us, so the pilot said, 'Everyone must leave a suitcase behind'. All the passengers agreed, which was marvellous.

Mum and I were very pleased and relieved to hear later that all the luggage left behind, including our own, came on the next day. The Chisholms were so kind to us, and I was pleased to see Daphne again. Mr Chisholm was the head of the Imperial Bank of India, and after a few weeks in Calcutta was transferred to Head Office in Bombay, so of course we had to go with them.

After Daddy had seen us off at the station at Maymyo, he heard that the evacuation sign had gone up in Rangoon, so he was unable to return there. He tried to phone the servants to tell them to get in the car and head north, but it was just impossible to get through.

Daddy then went down to Mandalay and managed to get a seat on the last plane out of there. However, before it could take off, a military official came on board and asked if there were any civilians, and Daddy said that he was one so was told that he would have to give up his seat, as a Colonel had to get back to India. Daddy then joined up with some friends, one being Jock Morton, who I think was with BOC – but I am not sure. Anyway, they walked along the Manipur Trail to Calcutta, which took them over a month. Daddy carried his golf umbrella and a pink mosquito net, which he put up every night under a tree.

By this time, Mummy and I were very worried, because we had no idea where Daddy was. Fortunately, I met up with friends from Rangoon, a Mrs Hislop and her daughter Joan. Mrs Hislop said that she was expecting a phone call from her husband who had just arrived in Calcutta, so I asked if she could spare a few seconds to ask him if he had seen Daddy, which she said she would be only too pleased to do. Mrs Hislop called that evening and said that her husband had seen Daddy: he was fine, and should be in Calcutta soon. As you can imagine, we were so relieved and happy.

In May the Chisholms went to Gulmarg, where the Bank had a very nice house. We, of course, went with them. It was not long before we had a phone call from Daddy, and in June he joined us in Gulmarg. He was looking a bit thinner, but otherwise quite fit. It was the most incredible experience, and one that I will never forget. We may have lost everything, but at least we were together again. Daddy joined Ferguson & Co. in Lahore. Mummy was very involved with the Women's Voluntary Service (WVS), for which she received the Kaisar-i-Hind Medal for her work in India, and also the MBE. I finished my schooling, ran a small kindergarten, and was involved with the WVS and the St John's Ambulance Service. I thought about joining the Women's Auxiliary Service, Burma (WASB) and going back to Burma, but Daddy said no very emphatically. Burma was such a beautiful country, and the Burmese such lovely people. It is so sad to see the situation there now.

PATRICIA RAYNES

We arrived in India in January 1942 as refugees from the Japanese invasion of Burma, where I was born, and my father was District Superintendent of Police, Mandalay. We went to stay in Naini Tal, in the foothills of the Himalayas – a lovely spot, with a deep (some said bottomless) lake surrounded by the mountains, and at the far end of the lake were the flats, where part of the mountainside had fallen into the lake and filled it in, within living memory. You drove up from the railway station by the foothills – two hours by coach – and when you got to the beginning of the valley, you could go no further by car – you either walked, went on one of the small hill ponies, or *tats*, or were carried in a *dhooli* (a type of sedan chair). The hill men could carry immense loads – I can remember one with a piano on his back – but they died young. The first year while my mother was staying there I went to a local school, but the next two years, when my parents were living in Indore (Holkar State, Central India), I boarded at the Hallett War School, which had been opened for the duration for children who could not return, as they had done pre-war, to school in Britain. It took me two days and two nights to get to school, and we stayed there for nine months at a time, having two breaks for a fortnight each in between. As my mother did not come up to the hills, I, with others in the same position, stayed at school during those two weeks, but we had a marvellous time, with special cinema visits, picnics etc., arranged for us by the 'chief' – our headmaster, Bob Llewellyn. We thought him very old, but in fact he was only in his thirties, and he was one of the best teachers I have known – we all liked him, but we also had a deep respect for him.

One of our treats was when the 'chief' read to each class in turn, one evening a week, up in his study. If you had misbehaved you couldn't go, and that was a terrible punishment. I still have fond memories of *King Solomon's Mines* – I was most disappointed when I saw the film!

I enjoyed most lessons, but I hated art – we had a White Russian art master, whose idea of teaching was to make you draw a still life of some cones and triangles and shade them to his satisfaction – as I never satisfied him I spent two years doing that, and hated art ever after.

When December came we all went home for three months – I went with the contingent heading for Bombay. We got the bus down the station, where we caught the little train that went overnight to Muttra Junction, which was a big railway junction and Army cantonment – there was a small cemetery just beside the station, and the fact that so many small children of Army families had been buried there over the previous hundred years or so made a deep impression on me. We waited until about midday in Muttra, when we caught the Frontier Mail. On one occasion we all bought ourselves catapults from a local trader and armed ourselves with a pile of stones, which we duly took on the Frontier Mail. As the carriages were not connected, and there was no teacher in our compartment, we amused ourselves by aiming at hapless passing Indians – luckily, I don't think our aim was good! For lunch we had to disembark at one station, get into the dining carriage and have our meal, and then wait until the next stop to return to our own carriages. At about 9.00 p.m. we arrived at Rutlam, where my father met me – we spent the night in a carriage on the local train, and it was another four-hour trip in the morning to reach Indore and home.

MAEVE KELLY

There were eight of us: my mother, Betty Kelly, Peter Courtenay – a British officer evacuated from Lower Burma away from the fighting on account of his malaria – my seven-year-old brother Desmond, four native servants, three ponies, a string of mules and myself, aged nine. The date was 6 May 1942.

We were leaving Tiddim, where our family had lived for the past three years. My father, Norman Kelly, was Resident, and administrator of a large area of the Chin Hills along the Burma/Assam border with India. Word had come through the previous night that the Japanese forces were 50 miles away, and with the exception of Father, we were all commanded to evacuate. There was no railway for hundreds of miles, no airstrip, no metalled road; we were expected to get out as best we could. The village of Tiddim, HQ of the area, boasted a Baptist mission school, a hospital and a Club, but besides ourselves, the only Westerners were an American missionary couple who had been evacuated months earlier.

Now orders had come for us to move at once, so move we did. Father had already rallied the local tribes to fight a guerrilla war along-side the scattered remnants of the British forces. Armed initially with knives and ancient flintlock rifles, these Chin tribespeople, led by Father, helped to hold the hills against the enemy until Allied forces returned. They were later to be known as the Chin Levies and, as such, in the words of Brigadier Sir Bernard Fergusson, 'built up a formidable achievement and tradition of their own and became a legend in their short lifetime'. The Chin Hills was the only district of Burma that remained unoccupied by the Japanese in 1942.

The village of Tiddim found itself on world maps, as head-quarters for the famous 17th Indian Division in 1942–43, then for the Japanese. It was eventually bombed to the ground, before it was recaptured in 1944. But that May dawn, the monsoon was breaking. As we trudged down the narrow slippery track which was to lead us westward across the frontier, the rain, which had been no more than a haze on distant smoke-blue mountains, became a dense mist. My last memory of Tiddim is of shuddering vapour and stark black pines, dripping. At Tuibel we crossed the mighty fast-flowing Manipur River by a 300-feet rope suspension-bridge.

The day's programme was always the same: up at six o'clock with a breakfast usually of burnt scrambled egg and tea made with condensed milk, drunk from chipped enamel mugs. Then the day's march would begin. The baggage, which only included – besides food for the animals and ourselves – two small suitcases and two rolls of bedding carried by the mules, went ahead with the servants, and we followed. We usually averaged 15–20 miles a day, walking and riding. Clothing was simple: khaki shorts and shirts, socks and sandals. We each carried a rucksack; among other things mine held a tin of bullseye sweets into which rain invariably leaked. They tasted strongly of the tin.

Peter (related to aristocracy) carried a quantity of treasury notes, and slept with them under his pillow with a revolver. His Army stories were fascinating, and so was his language: he would entertain Des and me with both as we skidded down steep, glass-hard muddy roads, while black, gleaming leeches crawled unnoticed up our legs. They dropped off unfelt from trees and sucked blood until, too satiated to withdraw, they had to be burnt off with salt and tobacco juice. In spite of the leeches, our travelling through the steaming green jungles, crags and ravines which loomed in the mist, and the incessant whisper of raindrops on sodden leaves, were forgotten. Des and I adored Peter. Soon after we left Tiddim, however, he had another attack of malaria, so severe that he had to be carried on a litter, delirious. Mother, nearly frantic with worry, now kept the revolver herself. To make matters worse, the bamboo huts in which we camped were not ideal for a malarial patient: rain seeped in at every crack, spiders, snakes and squirrels infested them, and the weather was depressing.

The day came when we eventually waded across the Tyao River between Burma and India, into Assam. I remember the clear water of it, glinting with the colour of wild honey under the tropic sun. I also remember sleek black water snakes sliding amongst stones on the river bed. Des remembers looking back for the last time at Burma, and thinking, 'This is where I was born; one day I will come back'. (He did, in 1986.)

Then one day we reached an oasis in the wilderness of jungle. Aijal was one of the main towns of Assam, and there we stayed a day or two with the British Resident and his wife. (Major A.G. McCall was Superintendent of Lushai Hills, and Aijal was the District HQ.

He was the author of *The Total Defence Scheme of the Lushai Hills*.) What luxury that was – to sleep on a bed and not the floor, to bathe in a tub and not in a river, to eat fresh food and to see a well-cared-for garden. With the McCalls we left some of our glass and plate, family wedding mementoes, hoping to retrieve them when the War was over. We never did.

Leaving Aijal, the last and worst part of our journey followed. For three days and nights we travelled northwards downstream by native boat on the Dhaleswari and Katakhal Rivers. And those boats were terrible. Shaped like long canoes, shelter was provided by a piece of bamboo matting bent over the craft like a tunnel. Inside, these were so dark, one had to grope one's way around, but so cramped there was no space in which to grope, and so stuffy that the only hope of survival was in crawling out and sitting on boards by the stern or bows, where the native boatmen who punted ran up and down. Their bare brown feet provided most of the view as one sat in the tunnel, so it was worth the risk of being trodden on to dangle one's hands in the river and watch the jungle slip past on banks of rubbery grey mud, and to stare at the stork-like birds wading in the shallows on their red sticks of legs.

That river was full of rapids. The agony of sitting in the tunnel of matting, seeing bright sheets of water rising over the sides of the boat, towering up before us and dropping away with a sickening thud, of feeling stones grating along the bottom and seeing the sweat of concentration on the men's brows, was unbearable. But shooting rapids during the day was as bad as sleeping at night. Then the boatmen ate garlic and smoked rank tobacco – opium too – and the fumes drifting into the blackness of the tunnel, mingling with the sweet smell of fresh bamboo, was suffocating. It was far more restful to stumble out into the clean night air away from them, and listen to the waters running past us and the ceaseless hum of cicadas in the jungle.

Then one daybreak, as light was just beginning to steal along the river, we looked out to see a dim line of grey humps above the high bank. Elephants, I thought. But I was wrong. After 19 days' travel through tropical forests we had found the first tentacle of civilisation: the railhead at Lalaghat and the Bengal and Assam Railway. We left for Calcutta on 24 May. Odd that I didn't consider it important at the time, which may indicate how much more intense were those other memories, but my legs were covered with boils and infected insect bites, for which there was absolutely no treatment except applying salt or neat peroxide.

Empathising with my mother's intense anxiety 61 years on, I feel nothing but admiration for her. Here she was, fleeing with strangers to an unknown future with two young and vulnerable children, possibly never to see her man again. Later on, she was to make an unauthorised and equally dangerous trip back to visit him – behind the Japanese lines. She had much courage. Of course, to Desmond and me, it was all a great adventure; pretty good training for life, too.

And so we arrived in Calcutta. What happened to Peter I'll never know – but he shines like a beacon in my childhood. Memories now of a grand hotel, with lifts, and ice-cream! Of hosts of people, bazaars, and a train journey across the continent to the foothills of the Himalayas; lumps of ice packed in straw were loaded on at railway stations to keep the carriages cool. Mother, a teacher, had been offered a job at an American school in Mussoorie, where we stayed a year. It was named Woodstock and, of it, I mostly remember endless rains and school misery: being totally unused to being with other children, discipline of classrooms and general teasing. Mother had taught me to read and write – Des (now an eminent psychiatrist) was dyslexic and mastered neither till the age of ten. But we also learned to roller skate – on one foot, as skates had to be shared – along endless concrete verandahs which snaked among school buildings.

I enjoyed small moments of glory in winning races in school sports, being well used to living in high altitudes – the Chin Hills stood at 8000 feet or more. And I high jumped well too. But other horrors were of unsuccessfully trying to eat a bun on a string in a relay race, and of having one's hair pulled by bullying boys and having it savagely washed in carbolic soap by a long scratchy-nailed *ayah*.

Then came the Hallett War School, in Naini Tal, opened for British children and run on more academic lines than Woodstock. Mother was offered a job, and we moved to a picturesque hill station, with a beautiful lake (Tal). The school was a range of buildings along a high ridge, backing the snows of the Himalayas with Nanda Devi on one side, the other rimming the dark, silent, volcanic, cratered lake of Naini. Brother Des boarded with the boys, I with the girls; our shared childhood began to split, and for years we became virtual strangers to one another. More than once I tried to run away – I can't imagine where to, but authority must have created misery.

Headmistress Mrs Mary Austin – pale-skinned, flaming-haired, thin-lipped – slippered us for misdeeds with a flippy gym shoe on bare bottoms after a hot bath. Mother, I saw briefly at weekends; her room with a kettle and toaster a small haven of comfort and familiarity in an alien world. Headmaster Reverend Bob Llewellyn, whom we called 'chief', was a tall, kindly man in a sweeping black habit (he has since become an authority on Julian of Norwich). He held confessions; what moved me, aged 11, to kneel at his feet confessing to my greatest sin of impatience, with a truly contrite heart? That sin is with me still, though life and events have helped me to control it.

Father was a distant memory. The enemy had a price on his head of 1000 rupees, and many of his men died speechless at their hands rather than betray his whereabouts to the Japanese. For over a year Mother had no word of him: he was with his tribes in guerrilla warfare harassing the Japanese. Swoops down to the plains, raids, fading back silently into the jungled hills again. In May 1942, Father was made a Lt Col. in the famous 17th Indian Division, which won more Victoria Crosses (seven) than any other division in the British Army. From the seat of his Jeep he killed with his revolver the Japanese commander in Kalemyo. His conscience racked him even on his deathbed. This time I was privileged to care for his last few months of life thirty years later – it was I who took the confession and absolved him.

NANCY LLOYD

Late January 1942
I left Bhamo on a cold and misty morning, catching the 'ferry' – really quite a large river steamer, which plied between Bhamo and Katha. I said goodbye to Chris my husband, wondering if we would ever meet again. The river journey was about 12 hours and then one caught the train south to Mandalay. That took about 24 hours. At Mandalay I met my sister, Molly Drake, whose husband Rodney was a member of the Bombay Burmah Trading Corporation, which was organising this whole evacuation trip. I am allowed to join in because I am her sister; and my husband thought it would be the best way for me to travel to India.

From Mandalay we, and several other Bombay Burmah wives, travelled to Monywa, and after a day or two there, joined by quite a lot more wives and children, we set off upstream on the River Chindwin to go to Mawlaik.

If only Molly and I were alone on this very nice boat with Rodney and Chris, how perfect it would be. I expect everyone is thinking that!

3 February
Reached Mawlaik about 5.30 in the afternoon. Geoff Bostock and Jonah Jones met us there and there were also various other women. Found a letter from Chris, and two wires so felt most cheered. Poor Molly had nothing – I can't think why as Rodney is a most energetic writer usually. Walked to the Bombay Burmah houses which are some way from the river, and set in what looks like parkland with gravel roads and rows of small trees. Most delightful. We were staying with Muir and Lois Wright.

We stayed in Mawlaik for about a fortnight, awaiting orders from Rangoon to set off over the hills.

25 February
Up with the lark, i.e. about 6.15 a.m., and of course a mad rush to get everything into our *pas* (Burmese basket containers) and bed rolls – all we are allowed for luggage. Went up to the Chummery after breakfast and got off incredibly quickly compared with the first party who left two days ago. (The first party was led by Jimmy Williams – 'Elephant Bill' – with his wife Susan in the party, and their young son Treve.) The walk was easy going and very short; when we were just thinking a halfway halt wouldn't come amiss we were in camp! It was very hot as the camp was pitched on paddy fields and in the sun. Also they had made a mistake and given us a tiny little tent and as we are four grown-ups it was a ghastly squash. We were all in good form, except for Fiona, Lois Wright's four-month-old daughter, who missed her nanny very much and consequently howled all day. To bed without much difficulty as we were given a pressure lamp for compensation for the small tent.

26 February
Up at 6.45 a.m. – quite a nice time, as it got light just in time to do one's face! Breakfast by a roaring fire just as the sun got up. A very short march again, got into camp about 11.00 a.m. and found we were in Room One of a very smart wooden forest bungalow which was most luxurious. Next was Peggy James and children whose nanny is a real terror – English and foul-tempered to the unfortunate children. Food was under the bungalow which was thick with flies. That is the worst of being the second party as all the first party's rubbish brings so many flies.

27 February
Everything slightly quicker this morning and we were off at 9.00 a.m. A lovely shady path most of the way which crossed and

re-crossed a rocky little river which was not running fast, but had lots of deep, green pools. In places the path was right above the stream and one looked down on to the rocks.

The camp for the first time was in a cleared space of the jungle and so was lovely and shady, and with Jonah's tent in place of the little one we were very happy and in complete clover. I wonder if I will get a letter by the runner who will catch us up today. I doubt it, and if I do it will be the last one for a long time from Chris as he is now on active service somewhere down near Rangoon. The Japs are perilously close to there and it is a constant worry in my mind, and so makes this trip quite the worst thing I have ever done in my life – every step takes me further from him, but on the other hand I couldn't see him if I stayed in Burma and I know he will like to think of me in Delhi – if we ever get there! Calcutta is already evacuating and if Rangoon falls they will be bombing Calcutta by the time we arrive! Who would ever have thought of me being a refugee?

In the afternoon Molly and I went for a swim. It was very hot and extremely difficult to reach a suitable pool as we had to clamber over slippery rocks and we were only clad in dressing gowns. The pool was nice but the bathe not particularly successful beyond cooling one off, as it was very shallow and one barked one's knees with every stroke.

The best part of the day is when you have had your bath and are in slacks sitting round your table outside the tent with a whisky and water under the stars. This is the only alcohol we allow ourselves as we have such a limited supply.

3 March
An early rise – 5.30a.m. and off before the elephants at 7.30a.m. A much nicer way of doing it as you walk while its cold instead of freezing waiting for them to load. They passed us after about half an hour. An eight-mile walk today – the longest yet but all on the flat through patches of lovely green kine-grass with blue hills in the

background, and then through scrub jungle and lastly across some very dusty hot paddy fields, and so into camp about 11.30 a.m. A foul, dirty camp round an old bungalow, and right on the top of the village, very hot and fly-y.

We are now nearly halfway to Imphal, having come 34 miles from Mawlaik. I can't believe though that we will ever get there. Dinner under the bungalow watching a large, orange moon oozing over the hill.

4 March

Up again at 5.30 a.m., and the moon was still brilliant until after breakfast. Off again before the elephants through jungle most of the way, some quite impenetrable jungle. Crossed the Yu river in a *lundwin* (small country boat), and then found ourselves in the camp. Tiny and jungly and leafy. Very lovely.

7 March

Up early but only a short march, along that dusty road, but it wasn't so bad as it was settled under a heavy dew. By and by we passed through Tamu, which was at last stationary (we decided it must be on rollers, as its distance from us has always been changing – and always increasing!). No shops, no cinema and no hotel! On another mile or so across the river which looks lovely here, and so eventually into camp. Here we are staying two nights, in tents for the last time, as they and a lot of our kit will go back into Burma with the elephants. With any luck the mat shelters for the Government evacuating scheme will be built and we can use them.

Molly and I brought the precious remains of our whisky along to the table after dinner and gave Jonah one in return for last night, and then Jim Davies, who is here (with various other Bombay Burmah people), joined us and we had quite a party, with our bottle dying a glorious death about midnight.

8 March

A day of rest. But not very restful. We had to re-pack everything, reducing our luggage to under 60lbs for the coolies to carry. Our old cook turned up – also on the way to India. We chatted for a little. He said that Chris had been sent to Syriam.

9 March

And so starts the real horror! It was terribly cold at 5.30a.m. and I was not feeling at all well with tummy trouble. Also a bit of a cold. Off at 8.15 a.m. – a foul march, although it was very pretty and we climbed up about 1000 feet and got a lovely hazy view of the valley. Crossed into India quite early on. I wonder if I'll ever be in Burma again during my life. I sort of feel I won't. We reach camp about 11.15 a.m. We are to sleep in the rush sheds built for the Government evacuees. It was right down in a little ravine by the stream, a tiny site. Felt terribly depressed when we saw it – such a come-down from our tents. However, it wasn't too bad when we were settled in as Molly and I had a 'cabin' to ourselves. Very small, but four bunks (made only of slats of bamboo) so we were able to spread. It was much cooler than the tents during the afternoon. Couldn't have a bath, but had a most uncomfortable wash. Dinner without a table and very dark. Rather depressing, and the news very bad as the Japanese claim to have taken Rangoon was denied. That means we shall hear tomorrow that it has gone. They have cut the road and railway at Pegu. Could it be worse? And where is Chris?

10 March

A much nicer camp than the last, lighter and a roomier site. The bunks seemed comfier too; lovely tinned salmon for lunch. Heard on the news that Rangoon had fallen. We are carrying on the fight in central Burma but I'm sure it won't be for long.

11 March

Up at 5.15 a.m. and a rush to be in time for porridge, which was lucky as there were no eggs. Off at 7.00 a.m. Up the most staggeringly steep hill, the one we saw yesterday. When we eventually reached the top the air was superb and the scenery vast and magnificent. From then on we kept on going down and up until we got into camp. It was an unfinished camp on top of a hill and we had no bunks or partitions; the worst so far, though it was cool and airy. We had our blankets put up for privacy and our bed rolls on the straw on the ground. I'm not all that good at sleeping on the floor, in fact I don't think I've ever done it before.

12 March

Getting up was the worst yet – a ghastly mess and rush and breakfast a total brawl. Today was reputed to be the worst march and there certainly was a lot of uphill, which was made difficult for me by my cold, which is now in my chest and my voice half-gone. It was very windy and fresh. But the camp was down in a combe so that you couldn't see the vast, rugged, mountain-like hills at all. There were two planters at this place. There is no water here, except for a small stagnant slime-covered pool, so washing is a bit scanty. We have certainly gone down the hill in civilisation. Jonah drank with the planters which had us all envious, but he told us afterwards that the planters were awful!

13 March

This was certainly the worst day yet. We got up at 4.30 a.m. and wore coats for the beginning of the march, which was in darkness. Soon the sun got up though and lit up that wonderful, huge range of gaunt, rather terrifying mountains with a very red light. After a good long time we reached the top of a rise and there before us stretched what looked like the promised land; far, far below a flat valley into which ran spurs of hills (the plain of Imphal.) We wound gradually down to the valley during the next five miles. On the hillsides there were beautiful white bauhinia tress which gleamed like wild cherries in a wood at home. At last we reached the level and found no lorries as we had expected. We sat for half an hour and then trudged on along a stony road to Palel.

At Palel, which was nothing in the midst of a barren plain, we found a Government rest house made of rushes, with two men there who were coping with evacuees and who were very nice and hospitable. They had tea ready for us – it was 11.30a.m. and we had walked 10 miles so we were glad of it. Soon after we had lunch – our own, which was excellent. Had to wait for about an hour for the buses. Eventually they arrived and we all piled in – there were four altogether. The buses in fact had obviously never heard of the word 'spring' and we were quite convinced that the tyres were solid. I suppose the road wasn't really too terrible, but you felt every little bump. Also the dust was a close imitation of a sandstorm in Libya and when we eventually arrived at Imphal, more dead than alive, our faces were coated with grime. I have never felt so filthy or so tired, depressed and uncomfortable.

To make matters worse the camp at Imphal was absolutely foul. Huge sheds with large double-beds of bamboo and no partitions. Also filthy, stinking lavatories which made you quite sick, a huge communal dining room and a thoroughly depressing atmosphere. We didn't think much of Imphal, I must say. The dinner was quite foul and resulted in four people being sick in the night, one of whom was poor Molly.

14 March

We are staying here one day and going on to Dimapur tomorrow. A long conversation with Maung Pu (our servant, who has been looking after me all the way), who was practically in tears, and I was feeling very miserable at leaving him too. He says if only I had let him know earlier he would have come with me to India, but now he has no arrangements made for his family. Rather a shame but, although it would be grand to have him for the rest of the journey

I don't think he would be very happy in India, in view of the way Burmans have treated Indians in Burma.

15 March

We had lunch at a very smart, stone-built PWD bungalow and there discovered how dirty we were. Our faces were, once more, literally black. After lunch, the road became more jolty and more dusty and we began to feel very sorry for ourselves. We passed through Kohima – the only town of any size on the way; it was rather a sweet place clinging to the side of a hill.

At long last, after dark, we reached Dimapur. There was an evacuation camp where a good lady called Mrs Turnbull had a marvellous tea and Dettol for us to wash our hands. Felt much better, especially after whiskies and sodas. After dinner all the mothers and children were put into the train. The special coach we had been promised was nowhere to be found, but the mothers had a coupe per family. We couldn't find our train at all for some time and walked up and down for what seemed like ages until it eventually shunted back into the station. We found we were in an 'intermediate' carriage which was filthy dirty with only wooden ledges to lie on and nowhere to wash and no lights. Didn't attempt to undress, but lay on the hard ledge in my clothes and beautiful white camel-hair coat, which by this time was not white, with one tiny cushion. Was so tired that I did sleep for a few hours and at 4.00 a.m. we started moving, and it was so cold that we had to open our bed rolls and get out a blanket each.

16 March

Managed to get some tea at about 7.00 a.m. and then we just sat till we reached Gauhati, where the other three got off, as they were going to Shillong. Molly and I felt rather light-hearted when they left! And even more so when a little man came up and handed us letters that had been sent through the Chief Commissioner at Shillong. They told us to get in touch with some people called Townend in Calcutta who would put us up. Molly got out to send the Townends a wire and all but missed the train. The next station was where we got off to cross the Brahmaputra river and we found ourselves on the most lovely steamer where we had a cracking good lunch and spent the rest of the day till 8.00 p.m. when our train left. Things were looking up! Dozed in the afternoon, and then after tea we all had cold baths and got off one layer of the quite astonishing dirt that was on us. Felt wonderfully refreshed.

Had a first-class compartment on the train – what luxury! Slept like a log.

17 March

Arrived at Parbatipur at about 7.30 a.m. Negotiated our change quite neatly. We were in a non-sleeper which was rather a pleasant change and we went along to a very nice restaurant for the most enormous breakfast. Read a bit after lunch and then went to wash and change for the arrival in Calcutta.

I was just putting on my lipstick – as the train was in a station – when a shadow came across the window and a voice said, 'Can I come in?' I looked up and for a full second didn't recognise who was standing at the window. When I did I understood the meaning of the saying, 'You could knock me down with a feather' – it was Chris! Things *were* looking up! Chris and his column had been cut off near Syriam, outside Rangoon, and had been evacuated by sea to Calcutta.

DENNIS POWELL

We were back in Burma rather sooner than any of us expected. Hitler saw to that. In 1940, the British Government appealed to all parents overseas with children in Britain, to take them out of the country. The upshot was that the three of us – Nancie, Daphne and Dennis – were aboard the *Stratheden*, part of the largest convoy to leave this country at the time. We were amongst three hundred unaccompanied children aboard; in addition there were a hundred accompanied children and a Naval draft of three thousand men. We finally disembarked at Bombay. My elder sister was only 16 at the time, but she had coped with shepherding us so far, and now she had to see us across India to Calcutta. Two days and a night on the train, a night in a hotel in Calcutta, till about 4.00 a.m., when we breakfasted and then boarded a boat to take us out to the C-class Empire flying boat on a mooring in the Hooghly River in the pearlescent dawn.

Taking off at dawn on the Hooghly and breaking our journey at Akyab in the Arakan, it must have been evening when we landed on the Rangoon River. My second sister, Daphne, had had measles on the voyage, and now it was obvious that I had got it. This put my parents in a quandary, as Father, Mother and I were to have stayed overnight with the Moodys; however, John Moody, who was about my age, was a diabetic, which made staying with them unthinkable. The following day, Father travelled north to MyitNge with Nancie and Daphne, while Mother and I stayed with 'Tiny' Carrier, the railway doctor, until I was able to travel. As the reader may guess, 'Tiny' Carrier was at least six feet four in height – I think he was actually six feet seven!

Life at MyitNge was very sweet. My mother tried to educate Daphne and me with the aid of courses from the PNEU (Parents' National Education Union), but without knowledge of what level we had each reached, and without some experience of teaching, she had a very difficult task. This was made no easier by the fact that there was a swimming pool nearby, built largely through the efforts of my father and by subscription from the various railway officers in the Mandalay district. They were all entitled to use the pool, being shareholders, but the pool was no more than a hundred yards from my father's railway bungalow, so that it was virtually our private pool. These halcyon days were rudely shattered by the outbreak of the Pacific War and Japan's attack on Pearl Harbour. Actual daily life altered little at first. For some time past, the railway had been running many heavy freight trains north to Lashio for transhipment to the Burma Road into China. Soon they were balanced by troop trains carrying Chinese troops southward to bolster the few ill-trained and ill-led British troops facing the Japanese invaders. I remember the first Japanese air-raid on Mandalay. There were five twin-engined bombers, which flew close enough to us sheltering in our slit trench in MyitNge for us to see and count them. I heard, too, five bangs and 20 thuds, which later we imagined to be duds, but which may well have been incendiary bombs. Certainly, the raid caused fires and panic in Mandalay.

About the only air cover available at this time came from flyers of General Clair Lee Chenault's Flying Tigers, a flight of which touched down at a rough airstrip which had been made at MyitNge – 'Say, is this Mandalay Field?' Needless to say, I was on the spot almost as soon as they touched down. I was fascinated by the young men with their trousers slung on their hips and 0.45 automatic pistols in their belts. Not long afterwards, we were told that we were to be evacuated from an airstrip at ShweBo, a town in the Mu Valley roughly north west of Mandalay. All we were allowed to take was 36 pounds of luggage: indeed, for me as a child of ten, I think the baggage allowance was only 24 pounds.

My father was to stay behind for later evacuation, if possible, so he drove us to Mandalay, where we were to catch the train to ShweBo. I think it was the only time I can remember, with one or both of us travelling by train, that my father and I did not go and inspect the engine. We found seats in a 'native' third-class carriage – wooden slatted seats, and not much comfort. When we reached ShweBo, ramshackle Burmese buses took us to the former Police barracks.

If official prior organisation turned out to be absent, incompetent or both, ShweBo showed that one thing we were good at was *ad hoc* organisation. If the Government of Burma had given little or no thought to civilian evacuation, the people running the camp and airstrip at ShweBo made up for the deficiency as they went along. Most refugees flew out on Dakotas to the airstrips in Assam, but our family group made just the plane-load for an Airspeed 'envoy', which was flying communications between Chittagong and ShweBo. Actually, we were one person too many, but I sat on the main wing spar, where it passed through the passenger cabin; I dare say we were over the weight limit too, but the aircrew might have stretched a point in wartime. Flying over the Arakan Yomas was dangerous, exciting and boring!

Landing at Chittagong, another admirable *ad hoc* organisation took over. Compared with the evacuation of the majority over the 'hump', there were few arriving in Chittagong, but we were looked after royally all the same, until our departure by train from Chittagong. This was to Chandpur, where we caught a river-steamer for the 70-mile journey to Faridpur (or was it Goalundo?), across and along one of the arms of the Ganges-Brahmaputra delta, where we transhipped to a broad-gauge train to take us to Calcutta. To anyone used to the metre-gauge railways, a broad-gauge train was enormous; of course it was accentuated by the fact that we were boarding not from a raised platform, but from the trackside ground level, something like five feet six below the carriage floor level!

The next morning my mother was seen by the Evacuation Committee, or some members of it – did she know anyone in Calcutta? – and mother mentioned Ted Blanchard, formerly of the Burma Railways, now working in the Government Supply Department, and her sister-in-law, Dulcie Kendall, who had arrived from Burma a day or so before. When asked whether she would prefer to stay in a hotel or with a family, Mother opted for the latter. My two sisters, Nancie and Daphne, stayed with a couple named McLaren in Alipore, while Mother and I stayed with a Mr Brodie, whose family was in Darjeeling. From this point on we were no longer being shepherded by Evacuation Committees, but were once more the masters of our fate.

PATRICK GIBSON

I was born on 25 October 1928, in England. Aged one month, I was taken to Burma by my parents. At the age of three, I returned to Britain with parents for a few months, and then, still aged three, my parents were posted to Siam (now Thailand). After three years in Siam, I returned to England and was placed in boarding school for the next three years. In October 1938 I was put on board the *Canton* by my grandparents. It was the maiden voyage of the *Canton*, and I was to join my parents in Bangkok. The ship suffered various problems, but I disembarked at Penang on 3 November and made my way to the Eastern and Oriental Hotel which I had been booked into by my parents.

The following morning I went to the airport and caught the KNILM – the predecessor of KLM – flight to Bangkok. The aircraft made an emergency landing not far from Ban Don near the Malay/Siam border, with black smoke pouring from the starboard engine. The passengers eventually arrived at Bangkok the following day, having caught the train that goes from Singapore to Bangkok, where I was met by my parents.

In January 1939 I was sent to board at Highlands School, Kabandjahe, Sumatra. This was founded and run by Mr W. Stanley Cookson, BA, JP, and his wife. It was a truly cosmopolitan school, with pupils from Britain, the US, Holland, Switzerland, Czechoslovakia and no doubt others that I cannot remember, whose parents were employed in the Far East. The teaching was in English.

Because of the distance, most pupils had to fly to reach the school, and the terms were approximately four to five months long, with two holidays a year. I attended Highlands School for three years, by which time the War in the Far East had started and, unbeknown to me at the time, my parents and younger brother had been caught in Bangkok and interned. Most of the pupils returned to their homes, and when I eventually left only the headmaster, his wife and I remained.

Early on the morning of 9 February 1942, I was woken by Mr Cookson, rushed to a waiting lorry full of red chillies, and taken to Medan airport. A KNILM aeroplane was being stripped of all its front seats, which were replaced with fuel tanks. I could hear the Japanese artillery bombarding the outskirts of Medan and became very nervous. After about two hours the few passengers for Rangoon boarded the plane, and we took off. Fortunately, a Japanese fighter plane which came after us decided to give up the chase, for unknown reasons. Ten hours later we landed at Calcutta's Dum Dum airport, having been diverted from Rangoon because of the advance of the Japanese Army.

When I arrived in Calcutta, I was met by a Director of my father's company and promptly told that my parents were dead and I was now an orphan. I had been brought up not to show my feelings. Somehow I forced back my tears until nightfall, and in bed I wept my eyes out.

I soon made friends with eleven Quakers who were staying in the same house, and were there to drive ambulances on the Burma Road. After two weeks I was sent by train from Calcutta to Bombay, and after a short stay with the Managing Director of my father's firm in the Far East I was sent by train to Naini Tal and The Hallett War School. Once more, due again to the distance and no doubt the War also, there was only one term a year of roughly nine months, with a two-week break in mid-June and mid-September.

Having no home to go to, I remained in Naini Tal during the winter months. I was very fortunate, however, in that the mother of one of the pupils remained in Naini with her son and young daughter, and she regarded me as though I were her own son.

In the winter of 1942 I received a letter from Lourenço Marques, Portuguese East Africa, from my mother, saying that she and my brother were being exchanged for Japanese women and children. The letter had been forwarded from the Bombay office of my father's firm, as my mother had no idea if I had got away from Sumatra. I was not an orphan after all. However delighted I was, I have never really got over the feeling of being alone, and more than ever tend not to show emotion, but bottle up my feelings.

In March 1944 I returned to Bombay, and in April set sail in convoy back to Britain on the *Otranto*. We docked outside Liverpool on 31 May but did not disembark until 1 or 2 June. On the boat was Group Captain Fuller-Good, my uncle. We met by chance, as he had a list of the passengers. Also on board was Ralph Reader's Gang Show and a large contingent from La Scala, Milan, together with instruments, but no piano.

My father was a chartered accountant, and worked for the Bombay Burmah Trading Corporation. He died in 1944 by lethal injection given by a Japanese orderly. My mother just received a death certificate from the Siamese Government.

PAMELA ALBERT

One very sad happening occurred in June 1942: my mother died of typhoid fever, and was buried in Calcutta, near Tollygunge, I believe. Sadly, I was not told this news until much later. I was sitting for mid-term examinations, and the news of the tragedy was withheld from me, as it was felt that it would upset my concentration at this important time in my life, almost as if the death of my mother was *not* an important event in my life. It was supposedly decided to do this for my own good.

It had been arranged that I was to leave school for the weekend with one of my mother's friends to comfort me in my grief, but to return Sunday evening ready for school on the Monday morning. I was devastated, but somehow calmly packed for the weekend at the Metropole Hotel. A stiff upper-lip was expected at all times from the children of the Raj, and one had to be that solid little brick even at fourteen years of age.

My father was in Burma with his regiment, and as my grand-parents had retired to Ceylon, I spent the Christmas holidays of 1942–43 with friends. I returned to school in March 1943, and did not see my father until May 1943 when he returned from Burma, his 7th Raj Regiment wiped out in the War. He had walked out with his batman and, after a hospital stay in Calcutta, he came up to Naini to claim his teenaged daughter. I was so pleased to see him. We needed time to get to know one another again after our long separation, and adjusting to life without my mother was the hardest thing to do.

DAVID MICHAEL THOM

Father was employed by the North Western Railway, having worked his way up from being an apprentice engineer to his final position of Divisional Mechanical Engineer 1 – Karachi Division.

Father was seconded to the Army during part of the War – transport in Iraq – but when home he always tuned in to the BBC for the world news. Looking back, it was a quiet childhood – no family around except one of Father's brothers, who was also working in the railway based in Lahore. There were occasional trips down to see three cousins – Mark, Ivor and Greta Thom. I loved travelling around by train – always looking out not wanting to miss anything – tunnels, bridges, catch sidings in the Bolan Pass in case of brake failure. Father had his own carriage (inspection car) complete with kitchen, bathroom, lounge and a verandah at the back.

As a family, we did accompany Father on one of his tours of inspection to Zahidan in Iran. This lonely, single-track extension leaves the Sibi–Quetta line at Spezand, and runs westwards towards the border for about 450-odd miles. We were coming back on this occasion – it was dark, and we were in bed – when the train stopped up a slight incline. Great discussions must have taken place outside, with Father coming back and saying that we had to leave the carriage and squeeze into a much-reduced length of train. The reason became apparent when we got outside to step into a swarm of millions of locusts, who had pitched everywhere, including the tracks. Apart from the night everything was black! Because of the terrain, both the locomotives had to carry extra water in three water-tank wagons behind their own tenders, apart from the bogies.

There were trips to Simla to see my brothers, Peter and Barry. It seemed to take days. We took the narrow-gauge from Kalka – the train we used to catch left early in the morning. I remember counting the tunnels – was it 108? We stopped for breakfast about half way – was it Barog? It was exciting – fried or poached eggs and beautifully laundered table cloths and napkins. Off to Simla, we stayed in the Railway Rest House, with wonderful views of pine-clad hills. Monkeys everywhere – nothing was safe from their grabbing paws.

LAVENDER TODD

In 1942 our parents were posted to Kerala, another exotic part of the continent, this time in the South. My father was Resident to the Cochin and Travancore States. This required him to live half the time in each State. In Cochin the Residence was the erstwhile Dutch Governor's house built in 1776 on the island of Bolgotty, in the Cochin Harbour. The other was a lovely old colonial house at Trivandrum.

Both had beautiful gardens, and indeed Bolgotty Island sported a nine-hole golf course. Cochin is a very old township where many invaders first stepped ashore in India – Dutch and Portuguese – and Vasco da Gama's grave lies in the old churchyard, although his coffin was subsequently moved to Portugal. There is a very old beautiful Jewish Synagogue lined with blue tiles which belongs to an old sect of White Jews who landed there in the eighteenth century; but my saddest recollection of Cochin was the prevalence of philaria – a mosquito-borne disease which enlarges and swells human limbs.

In 1943 I sought some way to make myself useful, and for a short period I acted as my father's secretary, but it was evident very quickly that this was not going to work. My sister and I, and another European lady, packed our bags and went North to Assam to join the 14th Army in a unit called the Women's Auxiliary Service, Burma – the 'Wasbies' for short. This was a unit of several mobile canteens travelling with divisions, and indeed on occasion with the brigades of the 14th Army back into Burma, where the unit had its origin in 1941 under the threat of Japanese invasion.

After training in Shillong we set up store camps, and with three girls and a British Army driver to man the six-ton lorried canteen we travelled ahead, sometimes pretty close to the action, delivering cakes, soap, aspirins etc. to the various units under command of the divisions as they went forward. It goes without saying, of course, that the jungle in which the 14th Army operated had little to offer in the way of NAAFIs, which were so welcome to the troops in other theatres. We served Indian, African and British troops, but not the few Americans, as they were so well looked after by their PXs. Sometimes the temptation to see a white-faced European girl proved too strong, and they also lined up for anything that they could persuade us to sell – indeed, one enterprising GI offered to buy the whole canteen, provided we came with it!

After helping one West African to recover from home/lovesickness by prescribing aspirin and Sloan's Liniment (the only medicament in our stock) which he washed down in one gulp with no apparent ill effect, we caught up with his unit later in the campaign, and I was greeted by him with a huge grin and a newspaper parcel. His officer advised me not to open it, despite the great honour he was according me, as it contained a trophy – a Jap head. My reply was instantaneous – I thanked him gratefully, and said that he must send it home to his wife, as it was she who must receive his wonderful war trophy. Honour was satisfied all round!

Finally our 'Wasbie' canteens all landed up in Rangoon for the VJ celebrations, but not before I had met my husband, who was in the Burma Rifles and Intelligence. We were married in 1945, in Calcutta. We returned home in a troop ship in June 1946 after six to seven years away, accompanied by our four-month-old son... We were interested and somewhat dismayed to note that nobody seemed to want to know about the 'forgotten army' – VE Day had happened some time before our War had ended.

ISABEL DAVIDSON

My first real school at the age of five was Darjeeling's Ida Villa, a small school run by two English ladies, Miss Pierce and her assistant, Miss Evans. We stayed at the Mount Everest Hotel, from where I went to school on a pony called Brownie and owned by a Nepalese girl called Pama, who led us sedately along! Another time it was the Windamere Hotel, and my father seemed to be there, as we took ponies and rode round the hilly park – Birch Hill.

We took visits to the Planters' Club, with its worn-out wicker chairs – even then! And the scenery – the scenery, even as a small child, was awe-inspiring. The magnificent Kanchenjunga range. The colours of snow turning from red, pink, molten gold, deep purple – magical – unbelievably beautiful. I remember a procession of Buddhist monks in their vivid yellow-orange robes, and some had wonderful mitre-type hats. They carried drums and gongs of brass, and their long elegant musical horns that carried sound for miles around. Durley Chine was the name of a guest house we also stayed at one time owned by a very irascible Irish lady with a heart of gold called Mrs Brooks, or 'Brookie'.

On one journey to Darjeeling, my mother took cholera and was extremely ill for a long time. My father was given leave of absence to be with her for a while, and I stayed with Chris MacLeod, a friend of Mother's and a French teacher, at 'the school at Jalapahar'! I stayed with Matron and Chris in the sanatorium until the danger of infection was over. Then it was back to Miss Pierce's as a boarder at the tender age of five or six. A visit to the American dentist – only if I was allowed to ride back in the rickshaw alone! Poor Ayah and Mother walked alongside. A visit to Firpo's – or was it Pliva's? – for tea and wonderful cakes. The Chinaman who made my doll a beautiful pair of little leather shoes – I have them today.

JANE GRICE

While my brother and I were innocently chugging up to Darjeeling to go to The New School as boarders, we were totally oblivious of a near-suicidal mission being carried out by eighteen Calcutta businessmen, led by our father, who was the Commanding Officer of the Calcutta Light Horse and the Managing Director of ICI in India.

In 1942, when Allied fortunes stood at their lowest, German U-boats began to decimate shipping in the Indian Ocean, thwarting attempts by the Allies to build up supplies of war materials to counter any Japanese attack. The Japanese, having taken Hong Kong, Malaya and Burma, were now ready to swoop down on Calcutta. It became obvious that the U-boats were receiving information through coded messages relayed from somewhere along the West Coast of India.

The task of pinpointing the source of these radio signals was given to the Special Operations Executive under the command of a Colonel Pugh, and they tracked it down to somewhere in the Portuguese colony of Goa – in fact from Marmagao Harbour. When war broke out, four Axis merchant ships, three German and one Italian, had taken refuge in that harbour. The Portuguese, neutral but pro-British, insisted on dismantling the radios of all four ships, but one transmitter, aboard the *Ehrenfels*, had remained undiscovered, and it was from it that the coded messages were being sent. Portuguese neutrality was vitally important, and any military action to put the hidden transmitter out of action was ruled out as disastrous. Other methods would have to be tried.

Colonel Pugh, formerly of the Indian Police, was an honorary member of the Calcutta Light Horse. This was an honourable and voluntary organisation dating back to 1759, when it was formed by Robert Clive as the Volunteer Cavalry to repel an invasion by the Dutch. Their military activities were limited to an evening parade once a week, but on 3 September 1939, every man in the Calcutta Light Horse volunteered for active service. Naturally, only those young and fit enough were accepted, but a pool of perfectly fit men in their thirties and forties remained behind, doing their everyday jobs.

It was to them that Colonel Pugh now turned. The Calcutta Light Horse had not seen military action since the Boer War, but when my father called for volunteers to mount 'a damned delicate operation against the Germans', everybody wanted to go. They chose 18 men, from the CLH and from the Calcutta Scottish. They were warned that the mission involved severe risks. They would undertake it in their own time, at their own expense, and without official backing. If anyone was killed or injured there was no hope of a pension, and there would certainly be no medals. They would not even be able to talk to anyone about their exploits. Despite this, no one stood down. They told their firms they would be 'on a special course' for the next fortnight, and left their office desks.

Colonel Pugh acquired the only seaworthy transport available, in the form of *Phoebe*, a Hooghly River barge. She was virtually a large, floating, iron tub with an engine. Her length was only 206 feet, and her top speed under nine knots. Commander Bernard Davies, a retired naval officer, was roped in as captain. He hired a crew of twenty lascars, filled *Phoebe*'s hold with coal, and lengthened her funnel to disguise her. *Phoebe* was to sail around the coast from Calcutta to Cochin, where the 18 volunteers who had left by train from Calcutta would meet her to sail the last 400 miles north to Goa. We were later to discover that the mother of another contributor to this book, Elizabeth Leigh, was involved in the project as a Wireless Telegraphist stationed somewhere in Southern India.

It was only on this last stage of the journey that my father told his men what the operation was all about. In short, under cover of darkness, they were to board the *Ehrenfels* and destroy her transmitter. The men were divided into groups, with specific tasks to perform. One group would seize the bridge, one destroy the secret transmitter, one blow up the anchor, and one stop the German crew from interfering. Everything went perfectly. The secret radio transmitter was discovered and destroyed. The frightened crew of the *Ehrenfels* decided to scuttle the ship. They opened the valves, and seawater rushed in. Within minutes the ship began to sink. When the crews of the other three ships in the harbour saw her keeling over they assumed an attack had been made by a much larger British assault force, and their turn would be next, so they followed suit and scuttled their vessels as well. In all respects, the operation had proved a complete success. There was only one fatality – that of Captain Rofer of the *Ehrenfels*. No one was seriously injured. Without details of the position of the allied merchant ships, the U-boats were eyeless hunters seeking their prey across 28 million square-miles of ocean. Allied losses dropped dramatically, and supplies of war materials began to build up. This meant that Japanese armies had to postpone their invasion of India for another year. By then it was too late. The Rising Sun was beginning to set.

After 30 years, when the official secrets bar was lifted, this whole unlikely tale was told in the book *Boarding Party*, by James Leasor, published by Heinemann. It was also made into a film, *The Sea Wolves*. But sadly my father died in 1973, before the book or film were completed.

In the report that he wrote, on 'where he had been for the last fortnight', he said, 'It was a splendid adventure – a schoolboy's dream come true. We even blacked our faces!'

PHILIP BANHAM

With the Japs and Jifs (that is Subhas Bose's Indian battalion) advancing into North Burma and threatening Assam, and with Gandhi initiating a period of non-co-operation, the Government of India were alarmed, and decided to place Gandhi and other leaders into custody.

My father was now a Superintendent and stationed back again in Poona. He was given the job of doing the arresting. He knew that Gandhi was travelling by train that night from Bombay, and that there would be thousands of his devotees at the station to greet him. He telephoned Victoria Terminus Police station and found out his whereabouts on the train; then he took a taxi, with one policeman, to Kirkee Station, which at that time of night would be deserted. He arranged with the signalman at Kirkee to stop the Poona Express, and waited. When the train pulled up – the red stop light at Kirkee must have astonished the engine driver! – my dad was standing more-or-less right by Gandhi's compartment. Dad apologised for any inconvenience, explaining he had to do his duty and carry out orders.

'So, Sir, would you please come with me?'

With the policeman in front and Gandhi and Dad in the back, the taxi went back to Poona. The road went right past Poona Station, but the crowds on and around the station, and thronging the streets, were oblivious of the fact that in the taxi trying to get through them was Gandhi himself!

Of the date I'm not sure; detail is hard to remember. It was about half-way through the War, I know.

PADDY SMITH

Saidpur was a typical Indian railway town, which owed its existence to the Eastern Bengal Railway choosing it as the location for the large metre-gauge workshops to serve the network of the metre-gauge system in the province of Bengal.

The town followed the usual layout in railway towns, in providing distinctly segregated officers' and subordinates' colonies, each with their separate facilities, including golf courses and swimming pools. A Club was provided for officers, and the Railway Institute for subordinates. There was little difference in the quality of the accommodation and facilities provided, but as said, physical boundaries existed, and there was little social intercourse between the colonies. The conventions of the day were rigidly observed.

In part, this was because officers were recruited by the Secretary of State's Indian Office from qualified professional engineers in England, whereas the subordinate grades were recruited in India from qualified Anglo-Indians who had learned their trade in India. These men were invariably very competent, and took great pride in their work. It was accepted that the Anglo-Indian staff really ran the railway system in India. The workforce were entirely Indian, and many were very highly skilled men, accomplished in the use of sophisticated machinery in the locomotive shops, and the casting of large and complex castings in the foundry. The more traditional Indian skills were well employed in the carriage and rolling-stock workshops where the fitting-out of passenger coaches was carried out.

The outbreak of war in the Far East changed the whole situation, however. Initially it appeared to be quite distant, but very rapidly the situation became increasingly serious, and I can recall the sense of shock and disbelief when news of the abject capitulation of Singapore reached us following the appalling loss of the *Prince of Wales* and *Repulse*.

Worse was to follow with the rout of the British Army in Burma and the threat of the Japanese invasion of India. Assam and Bengal were declared a War Zone, and the whole railway system was taken over by the Army.

This entailed the immediate commissioning of officers into the Indian Army with field rank – for example, major – and the commissioning of subordinate staff in company rank, that is lieutenants and captains. A very hurried training in basic military procedures and skills was given, and many officers such as my father were thankful for the training given by the OTC at their British schools!

Perhaps the most significant aspect of being in the war zone was that the military superseded the civil administration for the duration of hostilities. Thus my father, a Works Manager, and the senior person in the community, found himself to have the additional task as the Military Commander not only of Saidpur but of a large area surrounding it. His eventual promotion to Colonel acknowledged in part at least the considerable extra workload involved, particularly as the metre gauge became the main line of communication and supply to the front line at the border with Burma. This involved a massive expansion of the workshops in Saidpur, and of course the workforce.

A particularly important neighbour was a Mr English. I remember him very well. He was in charge of the Police Department at Saidpur for some years in the 1940s, though I do not remember ever meeting his wife and daughters, who were in England. I think perhaps that they had separated before he was appointed to Saidpur. I remember him as an austere, greying old gentleman, living in a large bungalow just over the road from us. Occasionally he would send a 'chit' to me by his bearer, with a formal RSVP invitation, to take afternoon tea with him. My mother told me how to make the correct response by return, and I would hurriedly smarten myself up and then present myself at his residence.

The ice, if ice there was, quickly thawed, and I like to think we managed a genuine rapport despite the vast difference in our ages – I suppose I might have been 11. Looking back, I realise what a lonely old man he was. The separation from his wife had been acrimonious, and I am sure he must have missed his daughters dreadfully. Sadly, Mr English died at Saidpur, in his sleep, I believe. My father, as the senior officer of the area, had to attend to all the formalities and arrange the burial at the local Christian cemetery. I was at school at the time, and remember being very upset when informed of his death. I still have a vase of his at home.

Another visitor of a different kind was the Irish shoemaker, who lived in the native quarters, but who was obviously very happy with his choice of lifestyle. Be that as it may, his shoes were beautifully made and much envied by my chums at St Paul's. I have never had hand-made shoes since!

A real treat was to go 'on line', or inspection with Father. This was invariably on the metre-gauge section of the railway, and we were often away several days visiting some very remote stations in the Terai or wild country. Often at night, parked on a remote siding, we would hear the jungle sounds; an elephant trumpeting, the rasping snarl of a leopard and, once, the unmistakable roar of a tiger. And of course, the constant 'India' noise of insects, howling jackals, etc. I once woke in the night and saw an inky-black shadow glide past in the bright moonlight only feet away from the saloon, Bagheera himself, Kipling's panther – or so I convinced myself! A very wonderful moment.

A favourite time of the day during the cool weather in Saidpur was the early morning. The freshness of the air, the tang of woodsmoke from the village beyond the *maidan*, and the hundred other scents of India gave this time of the day a special magic. The quiet of the evening was also a pleasant time, and my parents would enjoy their *chota pegs* on the verandah as the sun set on the Kanchenjunga massif, an incredible 135 miles distant, but only visible in the clearer air of the cool weather.

Back at school in Darjeeling, and practically under the shadow of that most magnificent mountain, it was pleasant to think that at times it was also visible to my parents at home in Saidpur.

LYNETTE GURNER

I left The New School in Darjeeling in 1942, aged sixteen, and my father decided to send me to the Young Women's Christian Association's (YMCA) secretarial college in Park Street, Calcutta. This was a revolutionary idea, to train seriously and then get down to a job proper. The YWCA college principal, Mrs McNab, a Scotswoman, trained Eurasian girls for secretarial work. It was an excellent training, and I was receiving full benefits from it until I got typhoid in the final term.

A fearful famine hit Bengal in 1942, and particularly Calcutta, because people flocked in from the province in the hope that they would find food. Rice prices went sky-high. My father and others purchased rice for their servants, but the majority did not have this. They died on the streets on a daily basis. Many were children and babies. The despair and misery of so many was visibly enormous. Rice was their basic food – almost their only food – and crops had failed. Countless thousands who came to Calcutta hoping that there they would find rice must have died there over the worst months; but, as this was the time when I had typhoid, I no longer witnessed their extreme plight.

My father was Financial Adviser to the College on a voluntary basis, and I was joined there, to my great delight, by an ex-schoolfriend. Her step-father, Colonel Murray of the Indian Medical Service, was chief surgeon at the Presidency General Hospital in Calcutta, and she was a remarkable girl, with whom every situation proved to have a funny side, in the nicest possible way.

After convalescence, and some coaching to make up missed studies, I started my working life in the autumn of 1943 in an excellent job, making the previous year very worthwhile. It was in one of the many 'hush-hush' organisations in Calcutta. It came under the blanket term 'Foreign Office', and was staffed entirely by military or service personnel, except for the female support staff. Everyone (service staff) was a number, 007-style, and I still have a memo telling me of a pay rise and signed by number only. My immediate boss was Royal Signals, our business a communications network. All the comforts of Calcutta went with the job. We were ferried to and fro, and provided with lunch, seeing the cook each day to order the next day's meal! Our pay was excellent. During this time, my mother was in Darjeeling throughout the school year, with my younger sister.

There was one air-raid when Japan was approaching through Burma. They attacked the docks. We heard the dull crumps. All our heavy wooden shutters were rapidly closed, but there were no cellars to go to, and it was not near the residential areas. One raid only, as I remember it. When Burma was invaded, some women and children turned up in Calcutta after trekking through the Burmese jungle, evading Japanese forces. One girl I worked with survived this ordeal, the only such one I met or got to know. Troops flooded into Calcutta after Japan entered the War. My mother served in the canteen on the Maidan, as did many other wives. Our contribution, working in the day, was troop dances. These were held in the Lawn Room at the

United Services Club, the only place where women were allowed. They were organised by a friend of my parents. She would arrange for as many girls as possible to attend, was always present throughout the evening, and saw us all safely off at the close. On every occasion, the last dance tune was 'Who's taking you home tonight?', but we all swept off in the family cars sent to collect us. They were very cheerful evenings, though there was no alcohol.

I joined the Swimming Club when I started work. Here, one could spend the whole day, if one wished. Officers could become temporary members. There were always a large number of them there. There were two large pools, one open-air, one under cover, perfect swimming weather, and food and drink available at the poolside. Sunbathing was out of the question. The intense humid heat of Calcutta was always a considerable trial, and one longed for the cooler weather.

My father spent every evening deep in his books, Sanskrit works being his particular interest. He was not a practical man and, in my mother's absence, I was delegated to 'run the household'. My older sister, with us in Calcutta, was not interested in taking this on. By 1942, I was no longer so amazed by life in India, and happily deputised for my mother. I saw the cook each evening to arrange the next day's meals. I then gave him money, appropriate to the choices made. All food was bought by the cook, fresh each day. He shopped early each morning in the market. There was only one wartime food restriction: one day a week was meatless. We had vegetable curry on this day, the only time we ate curry in India. I also paid the servants each month. I happily handed all this back to my mother on her return in the cold weather. Our household ran very smoothly. My role was a minor one.

SHIRLEY POCOCK

I went to the Hallett War School in Naini Tal for six months to take Matric, and then, at 16, went to the Sophia College for Women in Bombay, a Catholic establishment affiliated to the University of

Bombay, which catered for girls from all over India. For a time I was the only European.

It was a beautiful place, all marble floors and open archways screened by pale pastel curtains which billowed in the sea breezes. Mother Superior was Swedish; another, a Doctor of Philosophy, was American, and there was a lovely Irish Sister who taught music. Those I remember best, as well as an Indian lady who taught world history in a way that was a revelation to me; I had thought the British point of view the only one! The nuns were brilliant teachers but handicapped by the English classical curriculum, which had to be taught to girls whose first language was not English, and who had no experience of England. English poetry, for example, meant little to them.

I don't know when it was established, but it is likely that the Order of the Sacred Heart had had teachers in India for some time.

The Sophia College for Women, Breach Candy, Bombay, 1941, attended by Shirley Pocock and Barbara Ann Jardine. 'It was run by a teaching order of Catholics – the Order of the Second Heart. I think the building was the palace of a Maharajah at one time. The left-hand doors in the interior picture opened on to a flat roof and let in all the sea breezes. The right-hand doors were to classrooms. The chapel is at the end.' (Shirley Pocock)

The building was opposite the open-air swimming pool at Breach Candy and was once, I believe, the palace of a 'petti-maharajah'. The swimming pool was great, with a back wall built into the sea. I think it was just for Europeans only – I certainly don't remember any Indians. Just before I left Bombay, another English girl arrived from Cawnpore, as well as a Swedish girl, whose names and circumstances I don't remember.

The girls came from all over India, each in their own style of dress. In peacetime they might have followed their brothers to universities in England. The college was not supposed to teach religion, but we had a lecture called 'moral instruction' which was pure Catholicism. This could cause dramas, particularly among the Parsee girls from the Bombay area, who were tempted to become Catholics. Their own Zoroastrian religion was very obscure, with its teachings written in Sanskrit, which they could not understand. If parents suspected their girls of defection, they were literally locked up, and not permitted to return to the College.

I faded comfortably into this life. There were social days when parents and friends were entertained, and so that I didn't feel left out I was lent a sari, and the girls included me in their parties. I was also invited to attend their religious feast celebrations, when they were allowed to bring in special food; they enjoyed my inability to eat some of it! But I was not invited to their homes, perhaps because, as a particular Muslim friend explained, they might be thought to be 'licking my boots'. I also wore a borrowed sari when I went with my friends to 'Quit India' meetings, open-air affairs which were conducted in English, the only universal language in India. I thought I might pass as a Parsee with my fair complexion and nondescript hair tied back, but Mother Superior put a stop to these outings as she thought they might be dangerous for me. A pity, as I was really interested. In class I tried to keep a low profile, but we had a popular and lively Debating Society in which the girls relied on me to stir things up!

College rules were strict, and my parents had to give Mother Superior a written list of people who might take me out and with whom I might visit. Bombay was a lot more interesting than Cawnpore; my parents' friends invited me to their homes, there was swimming, and now and then a dinner dance at the Taj Mahal Hotel with somebody's brother or friend *en route* to or from the War.

I became unwell whilst at the college, and was sent to a girls' convent in the nearby hills to escape the heat of Bombay. I shared a dormitory with the Indian children, who seemed quite used to doing everything by the bell, which often caught me unawares. I got accustomed to having holy water sprinkled on me before sleeping, but disliked being under the eye of a life-sized figure of Christ crucified, which hung on the dormitory wall. Meals were eaten in silence, and there were prayers throughout the day. The children were friendly and happy, with no more than a natural curiosity in my presence. None of this did me any good, and I had to return to Cawnpore to have my appendix out. As all able doctors had been called up, this operation was performed by an elderly medical gentleman who had been catching butterflies in the Himalayas since his retirement. He gave me a four-inch scar, and I had to stay 'doggo' in the hospital bed for ten days!

It was while recuperating in Simla that I was offered a job with Associated Advertising Agencies, and decided to take it. I had been happy at the Sophia College, but felt I wasn't really learning enough to justify spending four years to get a Bombay BA. I felt sorry for the Indian girls, some of whom really wanted to learn, while others were sent to college because it was fashionable. In any case, a BA gave an Indian girl a better chance of a 'good' arranged marriage – she was unlikely to be allowed to use her degree otherwise.

A Bombay BA took four years to achieve, and was recognised only by London University, who would take graduates as first-year students. So the offer of a job in Simla was attractive, and in October 1943, at 18, I became secretary to the manager of Associated Advertising Agencies (AAA), although I had no secretarial training. I grew up fast. I seem to remember learning shorthand, and typing out of books. AAA handled all Government advertising, civil and military, and its members had been called up from the major advertising agencies in peacetime India.

Apart from the relatively few single girls, there were many 'grass widows', whose husbands were away at the War. My sister was among them, and I shared a flat with her and her baby daughter in 1944–1945 while her husband was in Burma. A year on my own had rid me of some of my romantic notions (gleaned largely from the cinema!); I knew that grass widows were considered fair game, and was very protective of her. I didn't see much of my parents. My father was back in the Army and my mother worked herself into a state of ill-health helping to run thrift shops and canteens for the thousands of troops passing through Cawnpore.

There was much to enjoy in Simla, but underneath a lot of heartache and unhappiness. War with the Japanese was close, and news from Britain was worrying. People had different ways of coping, and the gay life was one of them. I was, perhaps, too young and idealistic. I got engaged and disengaged, fell in and out of love, and began to wish I was in England and doing something more heroic!

GRETA THOM

My grandfather was sent to India via the Great Western Railway to help on the North Western Railway. He was stationed in Quetta and Peshawar, and was in the team who were building the Khyber Pass Railway. He took his family with him, and most of them returned to England when they left school, but my father and his brother stayed, and were apprenticed on to the railway. They drove engines and worked all the way up to becoming mechanical engineers.

I was born in Rawalpindi, and my early memories are vague. I was sent to a kindergarten, and remember coming home from school to hot chappaties and golden syrup. We had a faithful servant, a *mali* – officially a gardener – and he was very good at his job; he was Brahmin, which is a high-class Hindu. Although unable to read or write, he could take our wireless to pieces and put it together again (days before radio when wirelesses had valves and we could get the BBC Overseas Service and Radio SEAC [South East Asia Command]). He could also completely service Dad's cars. I can remember the Morris Cowley. We would go out for picnics with us in the front and the *mali* and the bearer in the 'Dicky boot'. The *mali* had to turn the handle to get the car started.

As all white folk were termed Europeans, we were deemed not to be able to stay in the plains during the hot summer months. So the railway funded our parents to send us to the hills. I was six years old when I was first sent, and I can recall it to this day, clutching my teddy bear and going on the train with all these strange folk, and seeing my parents waving goodbye on Lahore platform. The education we got was second to none; our school was run by the 'grey ladies', an Anglican group of gentlefolk. By the time I was there War had started, and many children were sent to India to avoid the bombing. As a result, we had quite a mixed bag, but we were soon all brought down to size. We mixed with Maharajahs' daughters and girls whose fathers were on the Burma front.

I loved Simla, it was a most beautiful place, the hills full of rhododendron when we went up to school and, as the year progressed, wild violets, cosmos and orchids. Our servants were mostly Tibetan, and they were gentle folk. We were always hungry, and often stole down to the servants' quarters to cadge a bit of bread and onion – can you believe it! Because the War was on we had an influx of top entertainers in Simla, because it was a convalescent station for injured troops. I can remember when we were about 13 we had to have a 'birds and bees' lecture, in case any of us got involved. We were more interested in the boys from Bishop Cotton School, our brother school at the other end of the town.

I spent nine months of the year in Simla, and nearly every year went to different stations for the holidays as Dad was on the railway. Multan, Jhind, where there was no electricity and the local church was under the water tower. I can remember the Maharajah of Jhind had a most beautiful palace – they had money, and certainly knew how to spend it.

I can remember in the school holidays the Christmases, where there was a whole week of celebration between Christmas and the New Year. We all went to midnight service, then the next day it was open house and folk drifted from house to house while the servants prepared the meals. First thing in the morning the 'pooh-pooh band' would come up to the house playing things like 'Colonel Bogey', and Dad's men would bring garlands and drape them round us, and bring gifts of fruit and nuts. Some folk in India did accept bribes and expensive gifts, but fortunately my Dad and his brother were known as the Thom Brothers, who didn't.

Throughout the week there were tennis gymkhanas known as the 'Tins and Bottle' – everyone brought these, and they were the eventual prize. Talking of bottles, when the War was on we never saw English chocolate or Scotch whisky, and Dad and the other guys drank arrack, which nearly ended in Dad having a serious liver problem. By the end of his stay in India, he was virtually teetotal.

FRANCES WINDRAM

I was always surprised how many bearers moved thousands of miles to be with their officers when the regiments moved. My longest journey was when the regiment moved from Wellington to Meerut. This took five days, and meals were always ready when we stopped at the stations, and the bearers brought the food to us in 'dixies'. A vivid memory is of the vast crowds asleep on the station platforms as we passed through. Our home in Meerut was in a very different style, a large colonial white building with a vast, disused well in the garden. I often used to wonder if anyone had been thrown down it during the days of mutiny! After my father came out of Burma, we moved to Nasik, near Bombay. We had a lovely home there, painted light green, with a big garden full of orange and lime trees.

I had the usual illnesses – chicken-pox, mumps, two lots of dysentery and a major ear operation, but judging by the gravestones in many cemeteries, I was lucky not to have had anything more serious.

On our arrival in Wellington I went as a day girl to Hebron School in Coonoor, which was near, and which I enjoyed very much, making some good friends, some of whom I still see. Hebron was set amongst the tea bushes and we often went to Lamb's Rock for picnics, which we ate off banana leaves while gazing at the plains miles below. Holidays were spent with my family down on the west coast at Quilon and Cannanore, which I remember as being extremely happy times.

With our move to Meerut and the subsequent departure of my father for Burma, I did not feel I wanted to go right back down south to board at Hebron, so I went to a nearer boarding school in Naini Tal, Wellesley School. I was most unhappy there, partly because the majority of the children were Anglo-Indian, whom I had not come across before, and partly because of the worry over the Burma campaign. Also, the food was awful – an early breakfast of a few raisins on an oatcake, and then a curry brunch. To try and keep her

'The Doll's Wedding', performed at the Club, Nasik Road, at Christmas 1943. The parents of all these children were in the Army, either at Nasik itself or at Deolali, or were employed at the Mint. Mrs King, the producer, was 'one of the Mint people'. Frances Windram, seated in the chair on the right, was herself the Doll, the Bride.

mind off Burma, my mother took a job as Matron at Hallett School, Naini Tal, and I soon joined her there and ended the year on a happy note. I have memories of riding back up to school on the top of the hill, and almost being thrown off my horse. There always seemed to be crows squawking in Naini Tal, and even now, when I hear these birds I am right back in India.

For my last two years, I went back to Hebron School as a boarder, as my parents had moved further south after my father came out of Burma. I remember these as happy years with a lot of sport, and tennis coaching in the holidays, music and concerts, with of course some work for the School Certificate.

Holidays during these last years were spent either in the Nilgiris with family friends or back home at Nasik. During the long Christmas holiday at home I used to help my mother at the WVS canteen, as the Nasik area was a very large Army transit camp. How proudly some of the young soldiers showed me signed photographs of Vera Lynn.

The full realisation of the War did not really hit me until my father went to Burma in 1942. The memory of seeing him off will remain with me forever. We had gone to the station but, due to security, the point of departure had been changed at the very last minute, and my mother and I had to be rushed by lorry at full speed to see my father depart. I shall never forget the sight of the train pulling out and how we felt, and one can only hazard a guess as to how they felt, many of whom never returned. There was no news from my father for three months, and when we did eventually hear, I was in the isolation ward at Wellesley School. Naturally, we were overjoyed, especially as he was expected to come to Naini Tal on sick leave. From a position just outside the ward, I could see right down to where the buses arrived from Kathgodam, and each day I sat hoping to catch a glimpse of my father arriving. Then I had a message from my mother saying she had rushed down to Meerut to be with him, as he was dangerously ill – though thankfully he recovered – but these memories rather clouded my short stay at Wellesley school.

KRISTIN SQUIRE

I was born in Mount Abu in 1930 and grew up in various small stations in India, as my father was in the Indian Political Service. Later he was seconded to the Foreign Office and sent to Iran. My older sister Hazel was in England at school, and I remember a rather solitary life in Meshed and Zabul, as I was seven, and my younger sister Gillian only two. My parents tried to remedy this by taking me to a mission school in Teheran, staying with other boarders in a lively international school where everything seemed somehow alien to me, from the methods of teaching to the leisure-time pursuits. I was shattered when I found I was actually going to be left there, and all I remember is thankfully ending up in bed with mumps!

Mother then took us to Simla, and Gillian and I went to Auckland House School – a hard time for her, setting up home, with Dad far away in Meshed. We had a house half way up Jacko Hill, reached only on foot or on ponies (*tats*, as they were called), where the monkeys stole the bananas from the dining-room table, and to this day I love golden-hair fern, which grew in profusion on the wooded hillsides. The views were magnificent of the surrounding snow-capped mountains of the Himalayas. We ran down the hill to school, and rode back up again on the *tats*. I had my special favourite which was brought to school every day by its owner, who plodded up the hill with us.

Once, Gillian and I went to an aunt's home in Peshawar where she and a friend organised a little 'school' for a number of children to keep us occupied! Mostly music, drama and sport. I was a fairy in *A Midsummer Night's Dream* and Gillian, also a fairy, had to open the play by saying, 'Your Excellency, ladies and gentlemen.' She could never pronounce 'Excellency' right. We played netball against the local mission school, where the lively Indian girls beat us hollow. My aunt had unusual pets, a monkey who loved to travel on the back of their cocker spaniel, and a mongoose called Winnie, whom the monkey used to tease by pulling its tail.

Back in Simla, one Sunday, I was told that a message had come that my parents wanted to fetch me and were coming – I couldn't go to church with the others, and must wait for further news. I waited all day with mixed feelings of disbelief and hope, but no further message came. However, some weeks later a friend of my father's arrived with his mother to take me with them to Iran. So began, in 1942, an unusual journey that took many months from Simla to Liverpool! The Indus was in flood, and we went by train as far as the raised railway line could go, punting across the flooded fields in a flat-bottomed boat, a very dusty station wagon and a carriage attached to a goods train, where we had a large block of ice in a tin bath to keep the carriage cool. It must have taken several days. Finally, by car into Iran and to Teheran, where I was safely delivered to my parents.

They were anxious that Mother, Gillian and I should go back to England, where Hazel was a boarder. They had heard that troop ships coming out to India were going home empty, and we could easily get a passage. We set off in November 1942 in an old Hudson Bomber across the desert to Cairo, sitting knees-to-chins down each side of the plane. Gillian was sick, and paper bags were duly passed from hand to hand down the plane for disposal; it nearly set me off too. It was a very bumpy ride. Arriving in Cairo, we found that the war situation in North Africa had changed, and troops were returning on the ships, so civilians had to wait their turn on the few passages available to them. But we had a two months' wait, and spent Christmas in Cairo before we were given a passage on a boat going round the Cape. However, arriving in Durban we were told the ship went no further, and we must disembark! Three months in Durban, where kind friends had us to stay, and Mother sent us to school, new uniforms and all! Three months later, at 24 hours' notice, we were off again, first in convoy, and later alone, finally arriving in Liverpool about six months after I left Simla!

Amongst the things to keep us amused on the ship, Mother had brought a crepe-paper flower-making kit, and gradually every table in the dining room was adorned with daffodils. We also made a wreath of apple blossom for the cook, who wanted it for a wedding cake he was making. In thanks, he gave us a huge fruit cake in a tin. In Liverpool it sat on top of our trolley of luggage. In the station turmoil, we lost track of our luggage, and when we found it again, the cake was still there, much to my mother's amazement. 'But of course,' said the porter, 'this is England!'

BETTY PAKENHAM-WALSH

In 1940 we could be found in Lahore with our parents, with many other teenagers, similarly evacuated. The demand for family accommodation was acute, and Father was fortunate to be offered the Maharajah of Patiala's guest bungalow, close to Lawrence Gardens, where there were tennis courts. I joined my friends there most days, and danced in the Gymkhana Club at night.

In 1942, when I was 16, I joined the Women's Voluntary Service (WVS) and helped to run the coffee shop opened for the troops in Nedou's Hotel, and supported tea dances for them. Plenty of subalterns on sick leave from Burma! In the hot weather, 130 degrees, Mother took me up to Kashmir by road – renting a houseboat on the Dhal Lake, Srinagar. It was blissful. My brother John finished his term at Sheikh Bagh School, and the family moved up to Gulmarg, 9000 feet high, for the rest of the hot weather.

When Burma was overrun by the Japs, my parents did a lot to help their old friends, who had escaped by air or who had walked through the jungle. My uncle stayed behind to blow up the oil wells at Yenangyaung, but he got out safely in the end. A friend of mine, who joined the WASB (Women's Auxiliary Service, Burma) in 1944 was killed in a road accident in Burma and is buried in the Military Cemetery in Rangoon.

I returned to England on a troopship in 1944, and at 18, joined the Women's Royal Naval Service, the Wrens. I served at Bletchley Park, decoding German high-command traffic during the D-Day landings – but that really is another story!

EVELYN ROSE HADLEY

When war was declared, Father was in India, while Mother and her three daughters were in Scotland. Ruby, the eldest by 13 years, had just left school. Mother and Ruby travelled back to India in 1940, leaving the two younger children in the charge of their grandmother and a nanny. Months later, our parents remembered about the two children, and we were delivered to a refugee ship in Liverpool. The voyage to India took six weeks, and we sailed via South America and the Cape of Good Hope. One of my first memories was meeting this strange over-emotional lady in the Great Eastern Hotel in Calcutta... the mother I hardly knew.

The family was reunited in Digboi in No 37 Bungalow. Ruby became engaged to be married to an engineer in the Company, and the two younger children were sent to Mrs Marr's school. A few weeks before the wedding, with bridesmaids' dresses to the ready, the Japanese moved too close to Digboi for comfort, so all children were evacuated to the hills. We were sent up to Darjeeling, where we enrolled at Singamari School, and we lodged with a Mrs McAlpine at an establishment called The Hermitage. Memories of happy times in Darjeeling include riding on little hill-ponies to school and from the Chowrasta, views of the magnificent peak of Kanchenjunga and of blossom against a very clear blue sky, Firpo's ice cream, and all manner of things Tibetan. The time in Darjeeling ended when it was decided that the altitude was affecting the health of my younger sister, so once more we were uprooted and we were put into school in Ootacamund in the Nilgiri Hills of south India. Here we attended Nazareth Convent. I remember the quaint hill folk, the Todas, with their buffalo, the strange antipodean vegetation and, again, the flowers. Madras was very far from Assam (in those days it was three days in a train), so after a year we moved for school to Naini Tal, a beautiful hill station built round a magnificent lake. Here, school was the Loreto Convent, with sailing and riding for playtime activities. It has been said that we would have remained in Naini at school for the duration, but my parents were convinced the War was about to come to an end, so we were not booked in for another year. When the time came for us to return to school after the long winter holiday there was no room for the Hadley girls, so we changed hill station once again and landed up to end the War in Shillong, again at the Loreto Convent.

Most of my wartime memories are of holidays in Digboi and the friends that we had there. I particularly remember how the nannies, *ayahs* and children used to congregate every afternoon on a green on the golf course that had had to be abandoned in its construction at the beginning of the War. I can almost reel off the names of the children who used to be there, and the bungalows where they lived. I remember swimming at the Club, and panic French lessons with the Couret family, who were to return to France with three children without a word of French between them!

In 1946, my father decided to retire, and we returned to Scotland. I remember a voyage home on a troop ship with Mother, and I remember that it seemed as though all the colour vanished from my life. Scotland seemed very grey, our home (and everyone else's too) seemed so small, and we were put into boarding school in Stirlingshire. Two thin, yellow-skinned (from anti-malaria tablets) pathetic creatures who spoke to each other in bungalow Hindustani. A hateful, very unhappy period of my life.

ELSPET GRAY

In 1942 we were moved to Kashmir, to the Presentation Convent in Srinagar, where it was hoped, I imagine, that the nuns would be able to instil enough audience and discipline for us to pass our School Certificates. During the War the English examination papers were sent out to India and then returned to be marked by the English examination board, so that roughly the same level of education was achieved. The Convent was an imposing building, on the opposite side of the Jhelum river from the Bund, with its variety of shops and workplaces, and to reach it we had to be rowed across.

Our school term was long – through the cooler months from October to May/June the following year. We did not return much to 'Pindi, as I remember, as it was a very long journey. The nuns were strict and I was a rebellious girl, but I always had my sister to battle for, so no doubt my worst impulses were kept in check! We played hockey with the nuns – I was left wing – who would dribble the ball along the pitch under their skirts so that we could not get at it! There was a swimming pool inside the convent which we all used – the nuns in long white shifts. They were quite jolly! Of course, there was an enormous amount of prayers – five services on a Sunday – and my sister thought seriously of becoming a Catholic. We did a school play every year – I played Mr Sampson, because I was tall. It seemed an unlikely piece for nuns – Mr Sampson had two wives. I remember that when I told Sister Vincent that I was going to become an actress she crossed herself hurriedly and said, 'Ah – God, you'll go to hell.'

For the three summer months of the hot weather we left Srinagar and went up to Gulmarg. At 9000 feet above sea level it was high up in the mountains and cut off from motor transport of any sort. The bus took us as far as Baramulla – I remember the avenues of poplar trees as we left Srinagar – and then we hired horses for the further two-to-three-hour journey. Such were the selfish needs of some of the Gulmarg residents that I can remember a grand piano being carried up a pathway – strapped on the back of three bent-over coolies.

On one occasion, we planned an all-day expedition up to the Frozen Lakes – 12,000 feet up – about eight of us, all on horseback. By mid-afternoon, it was clear that the project was too ambitious for one day, and the adults were all for turning home. However, two young men in the party wanted to leave the horses and climb up to the lakes. I begged to be allowed to go with them, and having promised faithfully that they would look after me we set off up through the forest. Well, of course, I couldn't keep up with their pace, so it was agreed that I would wait, in one place, for them to come back. They were convinced that they were only a short distance from their objective. Aware of the promise they had made my mother, we agreed they would shout hello – and I would answer – every few minutes! I soon stopped hearing them, and by this time, extremely nervous as dusk was falling I decided to make my way down to find the horses. I was very frightened by the time I reached the bottom, and the horror on the *syces'* faces when they saw me on my own is hard to describe. 'There are bears up there,' they muttered in horror! Eventually, the two young men arrived back, even more disturbed to discover that I had gone – I can't remember if we told my parents the whole saga!

We returned finally to Rawalpindi early in 1945 – though we were very young, we had a marvellous time with parties and dances and picnics with the young paratroops and Air Force officers who were based at Chaklala. There was such a shortage of women that these – very handsome – young men seemed happy to join us and include us in the fun.

After the European War ended in May 1945 plans were made for us to return home that summer. We sailed from India in a troop ship – the *Orangii* – in July, and this time the Suez Canal had been re-opened so the journey only took ten to twelve days. England seemed very grey and drab. I think the contrast for my mother was enormous. Her life in India had been very glamorous, and now she was faced with food and clothes rationing in a small semi-detached in suburbia.

My father stayed on in India and lived and worked through Independence and Partition, and all the agony which that involved. He finally retired in 1950. In 1954, he died very suddenly while ironing his handkerchiefs. He was 57, and had never really adjusted to the reality of being 'home' for good – where he was no longer someone of importance.

BOB BRAGG

We were a typical Indian Army family of the Raj. My father graduated from the Military Academy at Woolwich, joined the Jat regiment, was awarded the MC during service in Mesopotamia, married in

1926, and served around the world, punctuated by periods of home leave every two years or so.

Our family followed the pattern dictated by the conflicting demands of Father's service postings and children's education and welfare. My older sister was born in Rawalpindi in late 1927, I followed during a home leave in May 1930, my brother in Hong Kong in January 1932, and finally my younger sister in Bedford in January 1938. In 1937 the family moved to Bedford, and my father returned to India alone after commanding an Indian Army contingent at the Coronation Parade.

I have little memory of my earlier years in India. I was in Jhelum when about five or six, and was then left behind (along with my older sister) with relatives in England when my mother returned to India after a home visit in 1936. In June 1940 my father sent for us, and at very short notice the family packed up and sailed from Liverpool for Bombay on the *City of Venice* (a small ship with one large gun, manned by an ancient Royal marine, on the rear deck). The voyage, via the Cape, took six weeks, and we landed in Bombay at the end of July. We then went by train to Ahmedabad, which is where my memories of India really begin.

I have happy memories of Ahmedabad. I had my own pony which I rode most mornings, my sister and I played tennis on the Club courts when the grown-ups were siestering, and we had riding lessons on the regimental horses which, along with the mules, were still part of the regiment's support. It ended for me when we were sent up to Sheikh Bagh School in Srinagar (Kashmir) in about September. My remaining time in India was all spent in Kashmir, except for a brief visit to Attock (near Peshawar) at Christmas 1940.

Kashmir was a wonderful place to be. Snow-capped mountains all around, lakes and Moghul gardens providing a magical background for daily life. The school was led by an original thinker and enterprising headmaster in the person of Eric Tyndale-Biscoe, whose father had founded the Church Mission Schools throughout Srinagar. Many of the pupils completed the annual one-mile swim across part of the Dal Lake; quite a few of us did the full three miles of the whole lake, and a very few intrepid souls did the return swim, making seven miles in all. Another annual event was to climb Mahadeo mountain (13,000 feet), which was done by some twenty boys each year. Sleeping under canvas at the halfway stage (the tents and cooking gear being carried up by coolies), bathing naked in the icy mountain streams, sliding down the snow fields on tin plates; memories that will never fade.

Away from school, the year was divided between Srinagar (which is 5000 feet above sea level) for most of the year, and Gulmarg (8000 feet) for the summer holidays.

Our world was shattered in June 1942, when my father was killed in action. Through the generosity of the school we were able to

left The Sheikh Bagh boys on the summit of Mahadeo, among them Bob Bragg.

below Sheikh Bagh 1st Crew on the Dal Lake, Bob Bragg third from left.

continue there until my mother was able to arrange our passage back to England. It is one of the ironies of war that when a man makes the ultimate sacrifice, his family's income is immediately drastically reduced. We sailed from Bombay in January 1944 in the P&O liner *Strathaird*, we were one of the first convoys to use the Mediterranean after Rommel's defeat in North Africa, and we docked in Glasgow in mid-March, but not without some excitement on the way. For reasons which we were never given, we were offloaded at Suez, and spent some three weeks in a transit camp. The camp was managed by a formidable lady (who informed us in a very authoritative manner that weevils in the porridge would do us no harm!), and serviced by Italian prisoners of war, who were all charming people who treated us very kindly. Throughout the period in the Mediterranean we had to be prepared for attack at any time, and slept fully clothed in case of emergency during the night.

The rail journey from Glasgow to London was long, dark, food-less and waterless; and we arrived to stay with a grandparent in Croydon in time to experience a bit of bombing and Doodlebugs before returning to Bedford to go back to school and get on with the rest of our lives. Academically, the time in India did me no favours. In 1940 I left prep school at Bedford in the top stream and returned in 1944 to the lower-middle stream. For whatever reason I seemed to lose confidence, and was not at all settled when I returned to Bedford. I really don't know what India did for me. I will always be glad I had the experience, and I retain a warm regard for the country and a keen interest in what goes on there. I would love to go back; and despite the changes would love to see Kashmir again. I grieved for my father, but realised much later in life when I had my own children, that what I really resented was never properly knowing my father. That must have been a common feeling among the children of the Raj.

Views of Kashmir taken in 1932 and 1940. (Sheila Wright-Neville)

above Village women milling flour.

below Spear fishing on the Dal Lake.

right Village girls carrying water.

below Fishermen throwing nets on the Wulla Lake.

bottom Clearing the weeds and water lilies on the Dal Lake.

JONATHAN LAWLEY

By the time I was six, in 1942, we had been living at Bannu in the North West Frontier, and in the summer, Nathia Gali, for six years. My father was the Chief Civil Engineer at the North West Frontier Province (NWFP), a time-consuming job at any time, but particularly so in the unstable conditions of the frontier during the War. A major factor was communications, including roads and bridges, to cater for potential threat from Russia: for his work on these he was awarded an OBE. Despite this, there was time for relaxation, and he played polo, golf and tennis, fished for trout up the Khargan Valley and shot *chikor*. My mother came from a long line of Indian Army officers, ICS administrators and judges. She was never the conventional *memsahib*. She loved painting, especially wild flowers, and enjoyed the company of intellectuals in the ICS and Political Service. Having been born in the Andaman Islands, she came back to India as a missionary teacher, but with a reputation for climbing the college wall to go out on dates, scarcely fitted the missionary stereotype either. She was happy with our role in India, and was very much part of the British establishment there, endorsing the snobbery *vis-à-vis* businessmen or *boxwallahs*. Yet she also accepted that the British would have to go. Neither she nor my father were among those who resented Mountbatten.

We led a very social life with other British children, especially Army children, including the children from the sergeants' quarters, mostly in the trenches prepared in case the Japanese attacked across the north of India. They taught us to smoke, told us about sex and got us into stone-throwing fights with the *chikos*, the local Indian boys, in one of which I got hit above the eye. Knowing servants' Hindustani or Urdu, we could exchange insults with the best. I think the officers and other British children joined in these sessions. The exceptions were the rather priggish children of the District Commissioner.

We, but not the sergeants' boys, had ponies. My main memory of riding is of my hanging by one stirrup hurtling across Bannu golf course, and my sister doing the same on the road at Nathia Gali, from which some Governor of the NWFP had fallen to his death. We persuaded the Gurkha guards at the Bannu Fort to let us blow their bugles. We were also fairly trigger-happy: aged seven or eight I managed to get hold of a revolver an officer had left behind in his car, and blew a hole in the tarmac.

My parents never seemed to worry that we might get lost or kidnapped. They never had any real idea of what we got up to. We could eat anything, including what we could buy or were given in the bazaar. My mother wasn't bothered about what we ate. That doesn't mean that she was unconcerned about our health. She felt we would gain immunity by getting used to local bugs. But she did worry that we weren't getting enough vegetables. Nor did she like us to wear *topees* like other Europeans. She was sure that there was no such thing as sunstroke. What was important was that we had enough salt. She did occasionally worry about the effect of those sessions with the sergeants' boys in the trenches on my younger sister.

The servants seemed genuinely to like us children, and the *chota-sahib*'s word was law. My sister remembers that I once suggested we should throw the sandwiches at the servants of a bachelor friend who had invited us to tea, if they were not our taste. I have no

Jonathan Lawley on 'Sugar' with his sister and their *syce*. Bannu, 1941.

recollection of this, but I feel that if I had, the servants would have taken it in good part.

Another reason that we were left to our own devices was the War. Bannu was full of troops – whether to deal with unrest in the bordering tribal territory, or to resist a Japanese attack over the North of India, I am not sure. This was a time of much 'playing around'. Husbands were often away, wives were on their own, and unattached soldiers and young intelligence officers, civil and military, with classical educations, had every opportunity to exercise their charm. Even as a child, one had the feeling that there were all sorts of goings-on. My sister remembers how we were bribed with chips and tomato ketchup to keep out of the way of their flirtations at the Club. Our Anglo-Indian nanny didn't miss out either. She had us looking for earrings lost during a tryst in the woods with an Army sergeant. We were too young to worry when the same soldiers went to Burma or Borneo, or to grieve for those who did not return. Nor did we suffer from wartime shortages, except for tyres for children's bicycles, for which adult tyres had to be cut up and rejoined, creating a bumpy effect every time the wheel went round.

5

1943

26 July	Mussolini arrested; Italy collapses; Germans still occupy Italy
9 September	Allies invade Italy at Salerno
20 October	Field-Marshal Viscount Wavell becomes Viceroy of India
4 December	First Japanese air-raid on Calcutta

LAURENCE FLEMING

We first went 'on trek' in Sikkim in the Puja holidays of 1941.

Our *sirdar* on that tour was Ang Tsering Pansen, a Sherpa who had accompanied Eric Shipton most of the way up Mount Everest in 1937. He was always smiling, never at a loss and, as long as he was there, one felt that nothing would ever go wrong. So when, at the end of 1942, the women and children were evacuated from Digboi – separated from the Japanese only by a range of very high hills it was, nevertheless, in the front line – we had to go elsewhere for our Christmas holidays. Gangtok, the capital of Sikkim, was chosen, and Pansen came to look after us there. He lived in the Toong Soong Busti, just below the Old Calcutta Road in Darjeeling.

There were three *dak* bungalows in Gangtok, and we lived in the middle one. In one of the others lived a Mr Baker – known by all as Bakerjee, to chime with Bannerjee and Chatterjee, Mukherjee and Bonnerjee, well-known Bengali names – who was a wireless telegraphist constantly in touch with Mr Fox in Lhasa, the capital of Tibet. We must have asked Bakerjee to tea a dozen times, but he never came; and of course, we never discovered exactly who Mr Fox was.

The British Agent in Sikkim, Bhutan and Tibet – surely the most desirable post ever invented by the British Empire – was Sir Basil Gould, a widower whose only son had been killed on active service. He was, consequently, quite pleased to find a family of two women (for Ruth Dear, now a matron at The New School, was with us) and two children – we cannot have seen our father for more than a few days in 1942 – on his doorstep. He invited us to his Residency for Christmas but, more excitingly still, he decided to give an eighth birthday party for my sister Jane on the 1st of January.

The Residency was a handsome stone building, not unlike a large rectory built in the 1890s. It stood beyond a huge, immaculate lawn, which had a very small pond in the middle. And on to this came, in brilliant sunshine, the Maharajah of Sikkim himself, in yellow brocade, his sons and daughters in dark greens and purples, and the family of his sister, Rani Chuni. She was married to a Bhutanese Raja, Raja Dorje, large, kind and genial, in every way delightful. Their son Jigme, who came with them, was to become Prime Minister of Bhutan and be assassinated; and one of their younger daughters, also there, became Queen Mother of Bhutan. But on that day there was no menace in the air. They wore their brilliant brocades, rich plum, beetroot, navy blue, acid green, very pale yellow, and they smiled. We exchanged scarves. White silk scarves were laid across the forearms of the two people to be introduced, who faced each other. The senior person then laid his scarf on the forearms of the other person who, in his turn, laid his scarf on the forearms of the first one. The hands did not touch. There was, in fact, no contact. I do not remember what we did. I am sure there was a birthday cake.

It is the memory of that assemblage of colour on that green lawn, with Kanchenjunga – in profile here – smiling at us over the hill, that remains.

Sir Basil I remember as being very tall, and almost always dressed in grey. It was he, I am sure, who gave us the passes we needed to go trekking that winter. But the other person who made our stay in Gangtok so memorable was Rai Sahib Fakirchand Jali, who must have come from Western India, as he always wore a particularly magnificent *puggaree,* or turban, one end of it making a fan at the top. It was he who introduced us to Sikkim in the first place; it was he who lent us beautiful rugs to put on the bare boards of the *dak* bungalow; and it was he who solved any problems of a day-to-day variety. He lived in the Public Works Department's bungalow, so I must suppose he was one of their senior officials.

Gangtok at that time was the end of the motor road. You could drive up to the Palace, or to the Residency, but after that you walked or rode. The Palace, and its attendant *gompa,* or monastery, was at the end of a spur. If you walked back along it, the road divided, the right fork going to Lhasa – a march, I think, of 28 days – and the left one to the Residency via the post office. The Palace Guest House, Dilkhusha, lay between them. But down on the left was the White Memorial Hall, built in memory of Sir Claude White, the first British Political Agent there.

It was of dressed stone with an arcaded verandah and was, on my not infrequent visits to the post office, invariably empty. Once, I ventured in. There were sofas all round the wall, a billiard table covered in a cloth, a snooker table, cues in a rack and a great many books – Henty, Kipling, Newbolt, Scott and Stevenson, neat and untouched on the shelves. It had the smell that all books had in India, and I had the inescapable feeling that, even on a sunlit afternoon, it was haunted – I suppose by Sir Claude himself. I never went there again.

Our first trek was up to the Natu La, 14,500 feet, the principal pass into Tibet. There were two marches to the lake of Changgu, a very surprising thing to find at that height and in those steep mountains. I suppose it was about 12,000 feet high. It was eight miles from the bungalow there to the Natu La, and my mother and I set off early with our lunch and two ponies. The last ascent I remember as being very long and very steep, and our arrival at the top as very sudden. And there was no one there. Nothing. The good road stopped, the mule track continued down the other side. I think one could have stood with one foot in Sikkim and the other in Tibet, both on a downward slope. In the distance was Chomolahri, a goddess mountain to the Tibetans; and, in front of us, the track plummeted down to the Chumbi Valley, 6000 feet below us.

Our second trek was to Kalimpong, and very different. We had tea with Raja Dorje and his family, who lived there. We visited the Kalimpong Arts and Crafts Centre and lunched with Mrs Hughes, one of Dr Graham's daughters. She had recently married, as a second husband, George, Major Sherriff, who had been stationed in Digboi for some time, and whom we had got to know very well; but I don't remember that he was there. As a botanist, it was he who, with his friend Frank Ludlow, introduced many Tibetan plants to European cultivation, many from the Chumbi Valley.

Our return journey to Gangtok began more interestingly than usual. We could drive to a place called Melli, a border town back into Sikkim, but then we had to walk. However, an Austin Seven now appeared, conjured up, I rather suspect, with the help of Mr Jali. It was the only car small enough to go over the suspension bridge at Melli, and had to do so unloaded. So we all got in at the other side and were driven up the valley of the Great Rangit River to Manjitar, where Pansen waited with the ponies. It was midday, and the entire village was asleep. I remember the dozens of Datura bushes, then in full bloom, and their sweetly narcotic effect. We were glad to leave them behind – we started climbing immediately – in case we fell under their spell too.

One of the great treats for me, in the Sikkim *dak* bungalows, were the bound volumes of *Punch*, mostly from the 1920s, which existed in each one. Our trek consisted of walking from one to the other, usually about 15 miles apart; but very often we had to go right down into a valley and then up the other side. The bungalows were always beautifully situated, for the view, and only had essential furniture – four beds, four chairs and a dining table – and occasionally some reclining chairs in the bigger bungalows. We took all our bedding and our own food, though sometimes the *chowkidar* would supply eggs.

The great social event of that winter in Gangtok was the laying of the foundation stone of a Girls' School to be named after the Maharajah's eldest son, killed on a training flight in the Indian Air Force. There were many visitors from Kalimpong, the whole Royal Family of Sikkim, and the Dorje family. The stone was blessed by Buddhist monks in gold robes and scarlet hats, accompanied by much blowing of long horns; by the Church of Scotland minister, and then by the Hindus and the Muslims, the whole ceremony lasting an entire morning.

NANETTE BOYCE

In sharp contrast to The Grim, which was the name given to the North West Frontier by generations of British soldiers, was Delhi, Old and New. On my father's return from the Middle East he was posted to Military Intelligence at General Headquarters, New Delhi. Delhi of the Moghul dynasties, Delhi of the Indian Mutiny, Lutyens's Delhi. Our first home was a series of tents, but this was certainly not camping. Furniture was uncrated, Persian carpets covered the coir matting floors, crystal and silver were back on the sideboard and dining table. Khitmagar, Ayah and Khansama were in attendance.

For the first year, I commuted to school in Darjeeling. Those wonderful Indian trains; on one occasion I remember the conductor being asked if the train was ever going to reach Calcutta. He shrugged his shoulders and replied, 'Maybe...maybe.' I can hear now the hissing of steam, the slamming of doors and the cries of the hawkers: 'Hindu pani', 'Muslim pani', 'Gurram char', as the train lurched to a halt in some wayside station. By the time my Darjeeling journeying was over we had moved to a 'Baker's oven'. (Sir Herbert Baker was famed for his design of stately residences but he had scant regard for the heat they generated.) The lounge was air-conditioned, but the only relief in the bedrooms at night was to soak a sheet in the bath and lie under it with a fan playing from the ceiling.

Lord Amherst had decided in 1827 to move the Secretariat to Simla for the hot season. The custom had remained, but now included married women and children. My mother had taken my two younger sisters to the cool of the hills. I was to be initiated into the running of the house. By this time I was familiar with so much of Delhi – seen on horseback or bicycle. The Purana Qila, Safdar Jung's tomb, the Jamma Masjid; the list of exploration was long. I had not, however, seen inside the Viceroy's House.

An invitation from Lord and Lady Wavell for dinner was to fill this gap. In retrospect, I think one of the reasons for this invitation was a shared love of poetry. I know my father and Lord Wavell had been discussing the *Rubaiyat* of Omar Khayyam. (My father had also discussed this work with Sir Winston Churchill in Teheran at 2.00 a.m., with Churchill smoking the inevitable cigar, and pacing the room with only a towel wrapped around his waist.) I was to order my first evening gown. I wish I could remember the name of the couturier. I think it might have been Mrs Phelps. With all the assurance of a 17-year-old, my choice was to be a sophisticated black. No, I was told, 'Definitely not... too plump, yes, too plump.' So red it was; her choice, certainly not mine! Maybe she had in mind the mingling with the brilliance of the scene at dinner. The splendour of the Viceroy's Bodyguard, the retinue of servers with their crimson sashes, the myriad colours of the various mess kits. Golds, blues, scarlets, greens – chests glittering with miniature medals. I don't remember a great deal about the meal, but we did have the dessert the *rom-khansama* of India so deftly and delicately wove. Baskets of spun sugar filled with fruit and cream. I believe on one occasion a guest cracked her sugar basket, but sugar it was not. She had cracked Venetian glass.

ANONYMOUS

I experienced my hottest times in India in the first part of 1943. I learned to write my essays and do my translations and calculations with my writing hand resting on blotting paper to mop up the sweat and to avoid the sweat dropping from my nose and down on to the paper. By this time I was the proud possessor of a bicycle, and I would cycle all over the town – hitching a pull from a lorry as often as I could. I would cycle down to the harbour workshops to have woodwork and metalwork lessons from the English foremen of the workshops and cycle back in the dark with a little coconut-oil lamp on the bike, stopping midway at the Madras Club to tell my parents, who were playing bridge there, that I was okay. It is perhaps a commentary on India in those days that I felt quite safe to do this.

By this time, the War was a serious business in Madras. My father was almost exclusively engaged with military projects, and my mother was working as a voluntary secretary in the local British Army headquarters. Through an officer who was posted from Madras to Calcutta, they heard of The New School, which had officially been set up for English evacuee children in Calcutta and had then moved to Darjeeling. They were sufficiently impressed with the personal recommendation and the prospectus they obtained from the school to send me there. I joined The New School after the mid-year holiday in 1943 and remained there until the school disbanded at the end of 1944.

To get to Darjeeling from Madras, I was put on the Calcutta Mail at Madras Central Station one evening, travelled in that train that night, all the next day and a second night, arriving at Howrah Station the second morning. I had strict instructions from my parents not to buy from the food vendors who walked up and down the platform when the train was stopped, and I had my breakfast, lunch and dinner at the station restaurants, where the train stopped for the purpose of the passengers getting off for their meals. I do not remember whether the Calcutta Mail (or the Madras Mail in the other direction) had a dining car – but I remember being on trains in India which had dining-cars, and using them. The standard was very high and the food good.

I remember once sharing a table with two English Army officers, a General and his ADC. They polished their cutlery on their napkins and the senior office said to the junior, 'We must remember not to do this when we get back to the Savoy!' I found that they knew my father, or knew of him, because of his work on Army contracts.

I was to be met at Howrah by an Army officer (my mother's friend or a friend of that friend), and taken to his Mess in some leafy suburb of Calcutta, and then put on the night train to Siliguri at another station. The next morning one would arrive at Siliguri and then take the mountain railway up to Darjeeling. The first time I did this the officer did not appear at Howrah Station to collect me – he had malaria and sent a deputy, who missed me. Not knowing more than a few words of Hindi, I had to persuade a rickshaw man to take me, my tin trunk and my bedding roll to the address of the Officers' Mess in a large city of which I knew nothing. Somehow or other it worked, and I made sure that the rickshaw man was well remembered. Going over the Howrah Bridge on a rickshaw with your feet on your trunk and feeling that at any moment you are going to be stopped and have your throat cut is an experience I will never forget and never regret.

As for the train journeys, they were endlessly fascinating. I did not travel first class, but second, which meant that one occupied a large compartment with, say, seven or eight other people, most of whom would be middle-class Indian people. There would be four bunks, so that more often than not I would sleep on the floor on my bedding roll. I couldn't do it now, but I did it then and thought nothing of it.

BRIAN HASKINS

My father was a chartered civil engineer who gained his degree at Trinity College, Dublin. After a couple of years on the Dublin and South Eastern Railways, he joined a privately owned railway company operating in Bihar – the Bengal and Nagpur Railway; this later became the Oudh and Tirhout Railway, after some amalgamation or other. His job was to design, plan and organise the maintenance of all the railway infrastructure, such as the embankments, cuttings, innumerable bridges (many of which were enormous structures across the Ganges and its many tributaries), river training works, culverts, station structures, signalling and much else. He would have to organise the labour to carry out these works, obviously to a budget. This could be difficult, I imagine, when one couldn't forecast the quirks of monsoon flood-damage. He was responsible at one stage of his career for constructing an entirely new railway-line into the foothills of Nepal to bring out a newly found source of much-wanted limestone, I think it was. I and my mother went with him on one or two forays into Nepal, which wasn't all that 'legal' in those days.

The majority of the construction work was done by contractors who employed 'coolie' labour. I seem to recall that the vast majority of earth-movers were female, who would carry material on their heads, in baskets; they got paid in cowrie shells for each basket delivered, checked by an overseer, which they would convert into annas (possibly rupees, but I doubt it) at the end of each day. By the time I was really taking notice of what was going on in the railway world, my father was probably well into his career, and had some of the 'trimmings' that went with that. His/our houses were certainly fairly grand by any standards, in India or Britain, but I don't recall any discrimination once somebody had 'made the grade' as it were.

Most of the senior posts were occupied by Brits, and the assistants, supervisors and foremen were mostly Anglo-Indian or Indian. Station-masters, engine drivers and guards, were largely Anglo-Indian; quite a number, however, were Indian too. Signalmen were Indian, clerical staff (*babus*) too were also Indian, with a smattering of Anglo-Indians. I think only the more senior staff were allocated company houses, but I do recall that one or two Anglo-Indian assistant engineers lived close by. What I also recall was a tendency to look down on, and not socialise with Indians and Anglo-Indians. At one location, Gonda I think, the only boy of my age nearby was Anglo-Indian. We used to play together and I got on with him very well, but I got the impression my parents would rather I didn't.

I was taken to India aged three months in November/December 1933 and have no recollection of life there prior to 1936. I am told we all survived the Dharamsala earthquake in February 1934, although many of my father's railway structures didn't, and he and others were no doubt very busy thereafter repairing them. He eventually became the chief engineer of the privately owned Oudh & Tirhout and the Bengal & Nagpur Railway Companies, which were mostly metre-gauge.

My father came from a farming background in Ireland and my mother was an Admiralty civil servant's daughter from Kent. They were married in Bombay Cathedral in October 1931. Why one or both of them decided to go to India, I have never established, nor how they met. They cannot have thought through the problems of bringing up a family in India, even though it was undoubtedly exacerbated by the War. I went to local schools in the plains in whichever town father was posted to (Mansi, Sonepur, Gonda, Gorakhpur, Benares and one or two others). Latterly, from 1940 onwards, I went to Woodstock School in Landour. Initially, I went as a day scholar with mother renting a cottage in the hills nearby, but later I was a boarder. I hated it. It was principally a school for the children of American missionaries, and they were big and brash and made life for others difficult. I was also small and shy and got bullied a lot, which I don't think my parents realised, or if they did, perhaps they thought it might be good for my character.

On the other hand, there were very many pleasant times; hikes to absolutely gorgeous locations, cubs/scouts, camping, making rhododendron jelly, sliding down hillsides on pine needles, finding and collecting rare ferns (which I still do), watching langurs leaping in the trees and on to our tin-roofed houses, flying squirrels, beautiful birds and much else.

On the plains in the winter (December–March inclusive) there was monotony at times, being an only child in out of the way places. I have very happy memories of going with my father on some of his railway inspections, often on a trolley pushed by four *trailerwallahs* who would run along the track in their bare feet. The trolley was demountable, so when a train came along the four men would haul it off the track until the train had gone by. We had some lovely trips seeing neilgai, deer, various monkeys and often crocodiles. I loved making dams in the streams which led to rivers over which my father built and repaired railway bridges.

Latterly, father had his own railway-inspection saloon with a verandah on the back, which he would take us out on occasionally. It was always tacked on to the back of a train, so we had super views of forests, animals, bridges and the like.

My parents did join in the social life, such as it was in small out-stations. To help the war effort they didn't have a car (!) but

The Haskins's Bungalow in Sonepur (early 1940s).

cycled everywhere, my mother often in long evening-dresses. They also arranged social evenings in their house for some British troops, mostly 'other ranks' who were stationed nearby on their way to or from the Burma campaign. We would play games such as cards or mah jong, but gave up 'pick-up sticks' especially for those coming out of Burma as I recall their hands trembled so.

Brian Haskins's father was Chief Engineer on the Oudh & Tirhout Railway. This was his Inspection Trolley, *above*, and this was his Inspection Saloon, *below*.

I watched a few *melahs,* especially in Sonepur, but don't think I saw 'the big one'. The elephants fascinated me. For one of the Sonepur *melahs* Father helped to design and construct a huge pontoon bridge across a very large tributary of the Ganges, which was used by tens of thousands of people, animals and bullock carts.

Two of the winter holidays were very happy occasions when we were joined by the Kellys, Patricia and Desmond and their mother Betty, while Norman was in Burma. For me it was terrific fun; they were super people, and we keep in touch. Father stayed on until after Partition and came home in 1947/1948.

ANN MARINDIN

My father joined Burmah-Shell after leaving Cambridge – the family has had a long association with India since at least 1800; my great-great-grandmother was the sister of George Eden, second Baron Auckland (1784–1849), who was a Governor-General of India. The father of my grandmother served with the Indian Civil Service, and my father's father Charles Randall Marindin was Financial Commissioner for Eastern Bengal. One of my father's brothers, Brigadier John Francis Marindin, served in the Indian Army in the 5th Royal Gurkha Rifles in the 1914–1918 War, seeing service in Afghanistan and remaining in India until after Independence in 1947. I well remember my grandmother, Edith Alice Marindin, née Atkinson, regaling her grandchildren with stories of their progress through my grandfather's district by elephant. I believe many of her family had served in India in the ICS.

We left London soon after my birth for India, where we remained, except on leave in 1937, until 1945. We had many houses, and stayed in many places – always going to the hills for the hot weather and returning to Bombay or Calcutta for the cold weather.

My father had joined his regiment at the beginning of the War; he was a territorial in the 5th Royal Gurkhas, as a Captain, later Major, and we all decamped from our home to the lines outside

Delhi in, I remember, a series of tents and marquees, all of which were fully furnished as various rooms, plus all the servants. We still have a very nice Persian rug with a hole in the middle made by a tent pole.

Our servants were of great importance in our lives. We had Ayah (Emmy) and Lattif, who had been with my father as his bearer before his marriage. Ayah came to us recommended by her previous family, with whom she had been until they sent their children off to boarding school. She had visited England twice and had seen the King, of which she was inordinately proud. She and Lattif wrote and spoke English, as well as many other Indian languages, so unlike many of my contemporaries I failed to speak Hindi fluently. Lattif came from Madras and Ayah from a matriarchal sect in South India. Both servants remained with us until my sister left for boarding school (she is ten years younger than myself), and they were pensioned off by my parents. Lattif must have been with my father for nearly thirty years and Ayah nearly twenty. Their relatives informed us of their deaths in the 1950s.

Ayah wrote regularly to me in England until she died, and I felt that she was my second mother. I still have her letters. She was a small lady who was very strict, and a stickler for protocol; we were always Missy-baba and then Miss-sahib and my brother was Chota-sahib. When my father left for the Middle East with his regiment he said 'Lattif, look after Memsahib, Babas and Ayah for me,' and this he did, smoothing the path for my mother and protecting us from the many trials flexing their muscles prior to Independence.

When my father left, we five departed to Mysore to a coffee estate owned by an uncle. It was up-country from Bangalore. My uncle soon left for duties in Burma, leaving us and the estate in the charge of an Indian manager, the 'Writer'. So my mother was effectively left on her own in the middle of the estate surrounded by coffee and jungle with a workforce of coolies, with Ayah and Lattif.

Our only form of communication was by runner, and in this way letters arrived and were sent, supplies were ordered and delivered.

If we needed to visit Bangalore, a car was ordered by the runner, and it took us there and back. I remember the jungle and coffee crowding up to the bungalow verandahs, and the spiders being huge, their webs stretching from tree to tree to catch insects and small birds. My mother walked with a stick held high in front.

Vipers and many small snakes abounded and a baby cobra was found on the verandah – where were Mum and Dad? My mother had the coffee beaten around the bungalow, but many years later they were found living behind the chicken house – or it might have been their descendants! I well remember lying in bed watching the sheets which lined the rafters of the roof forming a make-shift ceiling, and seeing the movements of the rats running squeaking away from the slithering rat-snakes, and the agonised squeak at the end of the hunt. Enough was enough. My mother gathered us up and the five of us left for the Nilgiri hills.

I think we remained at Kotagiri for three to four years. I went to a small dame school, Miss Hill's, and learned to read, and experienced the great joy that brought. I also spent a short time at St Hilda's at Ooty. We walked everywhere, no transport, and my brother and I were taken to school by Ayah and a small wiry Mongolian known as 'Kuncha the Buncha'! He was a bearer in the house rented by my mother from a Parsee family, perched on the edge of the *khud*. Kuncha the Buncha's special claim to fame was his method of dusting – which

'My brother and I in our only transport on the coffee estate belonging to our uncle, Mysore, 1940.'
(Ann Marindin)

was blowing, unfortunately rather strongly, and many ornaments ended up on the floor.

We were surrounded by eucalyptus trees – the Nilgiris were known as the Blue Hills. Our house had no running water or inside sanitation. Our water for baths always smelt of eucalyptus, and our bathrooms were shared by toads. My mother said that if the toads remained it meant that we didn't have to share the bathroom with snakes.

Lattif, who until now had been our butler – a magnificent sight, tall and immaculate in white with a huge *puggaree* with a white plume – now in Kotagiri became the general factotum. He discovered that he loved cooking, and managed to make delicious meals on an open fire with a kerosene can as an oven. I can still remember his carrots and dumpling, and his light pastries – and I have never tasted the like of his Irish stew!

Kotagiri, like many other hill stations, had a large European population consisting entirely of women and children – the refugees of the steady advance of the Japanese Army. Many had been evacuated out of Burma, Malaya and the Islands – they had no idea where or if their husbands were alive, and all were poor, the services only paying half pay, and the civilians having their bank-balances frozen, as they did not have joint accounts. The Club was the centre of their lives. I asked my mother many years later why she did not play bridge, and she replied that she had seen so many upsets and rows over the game – which was played for money which was really not affordable if the players lost, such was the importance of even small sums.

There was a rabies epidemic while we were in Kotagiri which spread to the jackals. All 'European' dogs were kept indoors, except for essential visits outside. Everyone carried large, heavy clubs for protection. I was seven or eight and I have a very clear memory of an associated incident which has left me very aggrieved to this day! My mother and I and Frederick, our dachshund, were in the village square when the cry of 'Mad dog' was taken up. My mother, with great calm, walked into the middle of the square to pick up Frederick, when suddenly the mad dog ran through the square, luckily missing my mother – though the stones thrown at the unfortunate animal did not – and into the small post office, biting seven people. What happened to them I do not know, for I had retired to the top of a pile of carpets screaming in fear, only to be chastised severely by my returning mother for 'showing fear in front of the natives'!

The dreaded injections for TAB occurred every six months, leaving us feeling ill, and a couple of young Australian dentists toured the district regularly, with their chair and pedal-powered drill tied on the top of their old car. I can still feel that drill, hear the grinding and smell that cordite-like smell of burnt tooth to this day, even if I am in the most up-to-date surgery. My father was invalided out of the Army, and spent more time at the military hospital in Poona – we visited, and went straight into a smallpox epidemic. We were all vaccinated with a vaccine that I can remember my mother saying 'came straight from the cow'. It was ground into our upper arm with a small, toothed wheel. The scar still remains, and we were all so ill from it at the time.

ANNE HENRY

I do not remember my early years in India, having been sent to Britain at the age of five or six. In 1939 my mother returned to Britain but decided to remove us all to India in 1940. We sailed in August on the SS *Orion* in convoy, but the boat developed engine trouble and, when it was fixed, we set sail for Durban on our own.

We duly arrived in Karachi. My father, at that time, was stationed in Rawalpindi, so we entrained at Karachi. Our first journey in an Indian train – the ice block on the floor with a fan, getting out at one station to walk to the dining car and having to wait until the train stopped again to get back to the carriage, the monkeys at the stations and the little green bananas. My father left as we arrived to serve a year in Chitral. We went up to Kashmir, living on a houseboat, and actually spent a winter there in a house next to the hospital – icicles 18 inches long hanging from the verandah.

I attended a convent in Srinagar, the only Briton at that time, but not the only European. My abiding memory is that of the betrothal of the Uveraj at the age of ten, when we were allowed to go to the palace to meet the Maharani, at that time still in *purdah*. The Uveraj attended the convent and when we played tennis with him we had to make sure he won. Having gained School Certificate there, I attended the Hallett War School for a year, after which I left school and joined my parents in Simla, living at Jutogh. Going to the station in a rickshaw, taking the little train to Simla, where I had a job in an office – monitoring broadcasts from Russia, I think. After that, my father went to Iraq and my mother and I went back to Rawalpindi, where I joined the WAC(I) as a Radio Mechanic, Class Two. We were given an allowance of 150 rupees to buy our uniform – any fashion that you fancied – and I don't remember ever going on parade or doing any drill. I duly spent the money on mufti clothes, and had to repay it when we returned to Britain in 1944.

I remember little things like my mother always watching the servants boil the drinking water, washing lettuce in 'pinky *pani*' – permanganate of potash – sitting outside the wood store in Kashmir checking that the delivery was correct and my father being incensed because I would not go to the dance at the Club with him – he glared at me the whole evening across the floor! He also counted all my shoes once when I was out, and I was in trouble for having so many – typical teenage reactions.

We had a horrendous journey back to Britain in 1944. The convoys ahead of us and behind us were torpedoed. At Suez, we were all taken off the ship until another convoy could be formed. My mother and I were under canvas in one camp, my three brothers lived in style in the Officers' Mess! My eldest brother was taken to the British Military Hospital there with cellulites in his neck – no penicillin at that time. He was only allowed back on board if he could walk on. This he managed, but he spent the rest of the voyage in the hospital. On arrival at Glasgow, he and my mother were taken off first and I was left with my two younger brothers, aged 15 and 16, to make our way by train with a warrant to Cornwall! No station signs, no information. We got to Plymouth about 16 hours later, at night, to find the train went no further. I found a friendly porter who pointed us in the direction of the YMCA. They took us in, but we were separated into male and female dormitories. In the middle of the night, there was a Police raid – looking for unauthorised personnel from ships or camps, but I was not questioned – I only had my passport and rail warrant. The next day, we were able to ring relations and get on a local train to our destination. What a home-coming!

JEREMY LEMMON

While my elder sister and brother were at boarding school in Darjeeling, my younger sister and I went to Hilltop, the small Kalimpong school kept by Diana Leffler, most magnificent of headmistresses. I have the impression that, though many of us were very young, Miss Diana insisted on 'real' lessons – atlases, spelling bees, the learning of tables, and David Copperfield, as well as Raggedy Ann and Raggedy Andy. It was during an arithmetic lesson out in the sunshine that my head began to ache under my *topee* and I found myself shaking strangely. I was hurried home and put to bed with a nasty attack of malaria. To this day I can taste the quinine, more terrible even than the castor oil with which we were force-fed when we had eaten too many guavas.

It seems extraordinary to me now that I lived through so profoundly disturbed a stretch of history and yet, insulated by childhood happiness, remained so little aware of what was going on. In the summer of 1939 we were holidaying with my mother in England while my father, in Calcutta and growing anxious about the imminence of war, cabled urgently that we should return. Eventually we made an uncomfortable last-minute dash across Europe, so that when war was declared we were in Venice. There we stuck for some days until we found a passage aboard the *Conte Rosso*, an Italian liner bound for Bombay. It must have been an anxious time for my parents, but for us it was a holiday, memorable because my sister and I made such a hit in the ship's ballroom with our toddler's rendering of 'Boomps-a-Daisy'. On her return journey the *Conte Rosso* was sunk. In Calcutta the War was chiefly interesting because it brought so many servicemen – British, American, Dutch – to the house, buzzing round my attractive sister, strumming the piano and handing out chewing-gum. I remember an air-raid while we were playing on the Maidan, and the unknown lady who hurried all the children into her house so that we could take shelter under her dining table. There were minor privations: to save petrol, the Buick was fitted with a gas-fired engine, which uttered disturbing bangs and made the car difficult to start; one of the drivers, getting ready to take my father to work, was knocked unconscious by the fumes. Miss Diana became fierce about making us eat everything that was put in front of us, even the dreaded *bhindis* (ladies' fingers) whose slimy innards always made me sick. Instead of cornflakes at breakfast we were reduced to a nasty semolina concoction called *suji*. But there were intimations that the War could be more serious and horrible: in Kalimpong we gave shelter for a time to a family who had made the appalling trek from Burma; the mother had not survived, and the children were skeletally thin and completely bald (because of the bamboo beetles, my mother said). During the Bengal famine of 1943 we were forbidden to leave the house, presumably in case we saw the misery of the streets. I was told that my father had set up a soup kitchen; the phrase summoned up an incongruous picture. I had heard tell of Gandhi – Lizzie, our *ayah*, said he was a nasty man who blew up trains somewhere far away. I never suspected that there might be any bitterness between the Indians and British; perhaps this was because the ambit of our family affairs made us Indian as well as European contacts. Indeed after Independence, and after my father's long illness and retirement, his company began to totter, and that anything at all was salvaged was chiefly due to Indian generosity and skill.

While my father remained in Calcutta for a time, the rest of us left India just before the end of the War. The voyage home was on the *Winchester Castle*, a troop ship that moved in slow convoy. My brother, enviably, was old enough to be billeted with the troops; I was under 12 and consigned to a cabin which would have been in peace-time a medium-sized stateroom, and which now contained 20 women and children. We were in mid-voyage when we heard Churchill's voice over the loudspeakers, announcing the unconditional surrender of Germany; at Port Said all the small boats piped and hooted to welcome in the peace.

When, several weeks later, we steamed up the Clyde, a submarine bobbing up ahead of us, the houses on the banks looked tiny and quaintly shaped, like houses in a storybook, and everything – sky, water and landscape – was dream-like in its greyness.

CLARE HAYNES

My father was in the Indian Army. He, my mother and us four daughters went out to India in 1928. Very fortunately, it was too difficult to send us all to England for our education. We were sent to school at the Jesus and Mary Convent in Murree. We took our Oxford and Cambridge exams in Lahore in November, having spent nine solid months at school. You can imagine our three months with our parents on the plains was a very happy time for us all.

In 1943 I joined the Red Cross as a VAD. A group of us were taken by boat from Calcutta to Chittagong, then down beyond Cox's

The Convent of Jesus and Mary, Murree, where Clare Haynes and Thelma Smart were at school. (Thelma Smart)

Bazaar area to a field hospital with a small airport nearby. The hospital and living quarters were composed of *basha* huts. Conditions could be very uncomfortable, especially during the monsoon. In spite of that there was a great sense of camaraderie. The troops, British, Indian and West African, were very brave and, as you can imagine, some of them were badly wounded.

We did have an enclosure for Japanese prisoners of war. Male orderlies looked after them, and they were carefully guarded. It was a very strange experience to walk through a ward of Japanese patients, being aware of their reputation. Besides the wounded arriving at the small airstrip, there were reinforcement camps in the area preparing to go up to the front. There was a General Officers' Mess where we had our meals and of course there were parties. Especially, there was cheering for the people waiting to go to the front. We had the South East Asia Command news sheet, which kept us informed, and was much appreciated. Lady Mountbatten paid us a visit.

When the War ended, we were sent to Cochin in Kerala, where we looked after mainly naval patients. When we were demobbed, I joined my parents in Naini Tal and returned to England in 1946. I was awarded the Burma Star, 1939–1945 Star and World War II Medal for my service in Burma.

PAMELA ALBERT

In August 1943, my friend Audrey Razzell and I decided that the good life was all very well, but there was a war on. We felt that we really should do something towards the war effort. We decided to join up, and agreed to join the Indian Royal Navy. Both of us signed up on the same day and, without telling our parents, we were to go into signals, and the Cipher Office in Fort William, in Calcutta. Initially we had to report to Bombay for a three-month course, and were given serial numbers: 26688 for Audrey, and 26689 for me.

On 1st September we were to report to the Commandant at the then billets at Mission Row, located behind the St Thomas Roman

Catholic Church in Calcutta. Now that the deed was done, we decided to go home and tell our respective parents. The Razzells were happy with the news from Audrey, but not so my father! He ranted and raved and threatened to stop my naval training. However, in view of the fact that Audrey was also going, he calmed down. We all celebrated at Firpo's that evening.

Another surprise was awaiting me on the following day: I met what was to be my first love at the pool at the local Swimming Club. Both Audrey and I had finished our swim and had ordered tea to be brought to us at the poolside. I looked up and saw this handsome man coming out of the men's dressing room. He had to be six feet tall, with a mass of blue-black hair and very blue eyes. He wore a burgundy-coloured bathing suit and had a towel flung over his shoulder. I just could not take my eyes off him! He walked to the far side of the pool, the deep end, then threw the towel on a chair and dived in. 'Heavens,' said Audrey, 'he's a bit of all right!' I was speechless, and just kept staring at him as he swam at least four lengths of the pool. I knew that somehow I had to meet him. Neither of us had seen him before. I got up from lying on my towel in the sun, put down my book and dived into the water, making a bee-line for him and hitting him gently on the chest under water. I then popped up in front of him and said, 'Oh, I am sorry. That's what I get for keeping my eyes closed under water.' He was a Flying Officer (Bill) from Ontario, Canada, attached to 681 Squadron RAF stationed at Dum Dum Airport. He was a newcomer, and this was his first visit to the Club.

I asked him to allow me to make amends and invited him to have tea with us, and this he very graciously accepted. This was one teatime I had hoped would never end. He explained his squadron's part in the Battle of Britain and that his 681 Spitfire Squadron had now been transferred into the Japanese theatre of war on reconnaissance missions. I just listened, and hung on to his every word! I asked him to join our party at the Club dance that evening, and he said he could not promise but would certainly try to attend.

My father had planned for a quite a large seating for his party that evening. I told him about the new young man I had met that day and said that I hope he did not mind my inviting him to the party without first informing the major-*sahib*. My father, naturally, did not mind a bit. I dressed with great care and had butterflies in my tummy all evening, so much so that all noticed it.

The evening dragged on. Bill was nowhere to be seen. I gave up on seeing him this night and picked up with my old way of having fun, dancing and flirting with all the men. Of course my father understood I was upset and disappointed, and he beckoned me to come sit close for a caring hug. I sat down, reached for his cigar and had a puff, just to be amusing and funny. After a great deal of laughter from the party I looked up, and to my horror saw Bill standing in front of us, smiling! He was dressed in his Air Force blues, the DFC and Bar adorning his uniform with the top button undone, as was the rule of RAF Spitfire fighter pilots. I must have looked a sight! Cigar in hand, mouth wide open, and sitting on my father's lap, I felt sure that whatever impression I had made on him that afternoon at the pool was slowly vanishing, but he held out his hand, smiled, and whisked me onto the dance floor. All approved of this young man from Canada!

I had only two weeks really to get to know him, as now I was in the Navy I was expected to go to Bombay on a Signal course. The very thought of having to leave him was heartbreaking, but there was a war on and I had signed up to be a part of it. It was sad.

GILLIAN OWERS

After I left The New School, which I did the day after my exam results arrived, I was then accepted at the Calcutta School of Art, I believe the only European to have attended at that time. The school was in – or perhaps attached to – a museum, which is how I received my first adult understanding of the wonder that is Indian art. Not that the curriculum reflected that noble heritage – or at least not in the early classes. The school had an overwhelming number of male students, so the few women – girls, we were – had to have special protective arrangements. We had our own rooms where we spent any time when were not actually in class. The entrance was guarded by an elderly Sikh – chosen, I imagine, because age had made him impervious to our youthful charms. Unfortunately, though he had an enormous *lathi* (stick) with which to defend us from attackers, age had also made him infirm; it was our duty to assist him to his feet when he banged the floor with the *lathi* as he was incapable of performing this feat unaided. He was a charming old gentleman with the manners of a prince, so that at the first call or bang we would all fly out like a covey of butterflies in our saris. His memory was not of the best so he called us all 'Baba' (child), and he was certainly our 'grandpapa'. But perhaps it was as well that no one actually felt like doing more than send small notes in class as attacks on our virtue.

In addition to the guard we also had a chaperone. An interesting woman, a Swiss silversmith married to an Indian doctor – I still have the bracelets and the necklace I bought from her. I wish I had been more interested then in her story, for it was certainly unusual but I was, in fact, absorbed in my classes and also in my peers, for this was the first time I had been with Indian girls of my own age. Looking back, they seemed much like any other young girls except that their lives were caged about with custom and prohibitions – but then, so was I. And a major decision had been made for all of them; they were, without exception, to marry, and to complete strangers, which they took with, as far as I could see, complete equanimity. They giggled and chatted and speculated, apparently serene in the knowledge that their future was decided.

After the day ended at the Art School, I went on to work for the Red Cross in the hospital. Here the lessons to be learned were tough. After so many years, one tends to let lie fallow all the many simple, daily chores I performed: writing letters for those who could not write; teaching leather work; finding wool for the shell-shocked Punjabi who could only knit, in brilliant colours and feverish haste, scarf after scarf, holding them between himself and the ultimate horrors; shopping and gathering salads at the American vegetable garden. Instead, I tend to remember the monkeys who loved to wrap themselves in red Army blankets and lie in warmth on the verandah beds, and the squirrel whose broken front legs were successfully splinted and healed and who, in turn, healed the desperately ill soldier who cared for him. And I remember the sorrow of the Sikh taxi driver who brought Ron, newly blinded, to our house for lunch; I had never, in all the carnage and wreckage, seen a grown man weep for another, and had hardly known that I, too, could weep – India, in spite of all, had lessons for those of us who could learn.

Living now in the US, I find that people hardly believe that all through the time when India was trying to rid itself of British rule, we had no locks on doors in my home; that the verandah opened on to the driveway and that the spare bed was always there for anyone who needed to sleep at any time of night. In that time there seemed to be no sense that we, as individuals, were responsible for the Raj personally, and might have to pay the price. Nor did I even consider that I should not take my pony out by myself to ride through villages and along paddy fields every morning, finding friends everywhere; even more strangely, neither did my parents, who otherwise kept so tight a hold on all my activities. My mother and I thought nothing at all of taking off for weeks into the Himalayas, out of all reach of phone or post or telegraph. Indeed, we were safe. Of how many places could this be said when the society was engaged in the struggle for a national identity? Or, for that matter, of most contemporary major cities?

HAZEL SQUIRE

It was not until 1943 that I saw my family again. I had remained at school in Oxford when war broke out, my mother and sisters returning to my father in India. But an extraordinary set of circumstances brought us together for a wonderful summer in that year. In 1942 my mother decided, with great courage, that she must get home to see me. She set off with my two sisters and flew in an Army transport plane to Cairo, there to try and catch a boat home via the Cape.

People she knew took pity on her, and invited her to share their tiny flat. Hotel prices were exorbitant, and money would have soon run out otherwise. After a wait of three months she finally got a boat as far as Durban. This time, not knowing how long the wait might be, she enrolled my sisters in a school. They were there for ten weeks. Finally they got a passage in a convoy, which zig-zagged its way to Liverpool, with a week outside Cape Town and a further week off the coast of West Africa. In the meantime, my father had been appointed the British Minister Plenipotentiary and Envoy Extraordinary to Afghanistan, and was flown home to 'kiss the King's hand' before taking up the post. He turned up at school during the summer term, and I was allowed ten days off to spend with him. During that time we managed to find a flat through the mother of a schoolfriend of mine – a difficult task, as Oxford was a safe area, and many people had been evacuated there. Within ten days my mother's ship had docked at Liverpool and 48 hours later she was learning how to make scrambled eggs with dried-egg powder on a gas stove, not having cooked for years.

BLAKE PINNELL

I remember little about wartime in India, other than a Japanese air-raid on Calcutta, which I believe created more noise than damage; and rifle practice, which involved the boys from The New School on the grounds of St Paul's School in Darjeeling. To the best of my recollection no shots were fired, but I remembered our teachers telling us that if necessary we would be put on a train which would take us towards the northwest of India, that is away from Bengal in case it was invaded by the Japanese. Fortunately that proved unnec-essary. In 1943, coming up to the age of 18, I was told by the Army Board in Calcutta that I would not be called up into the armed forces for physical reasons. So I left India and went to South Africa; but my time in India had taught me two things, surprising enough to mention here.

Firstly I learned something of what the Indian Civil Service was trying to do for that country. The ICS men had worked long hours and were scrupulously honest: all of them had undertaken not to accept money, valuables or other inducements from anyone they might have contact with on official business. Salaries do not appear to have been over-generous, and I would be surprised if any members of the ICS became rich as a result of their work.

Secondly, that I had grown up in an India which, at a high level, was free of racial discrimination. There were Indian cabinet ministers, Indian generals, Indian judges and Indian Police chiefs working together with their British colleagues; and many of my parents' personal friends were Indian families.

ROBIN MALLINSON

In the summer of 1943 it seemed that the tide of war had turned, and my parents rather bravely asked me if I would like to go to school in Britain sooner rather than later. I said I would, and in September, at the age of 14, I found myself on board the SS *Ormonde* in Bombay with two other boys, both older than me, who were also travelling along. There were also some families on board, and we were supposed to sail through the Mediterranean to Britain. However, at Suez the ship was requisitioned to take troops to Palestine, and we were all put in transit camps. The three of us said we were too old to go to the camp for women and children, and we were taken to the officers' camp.

There we stayed in tents for several weeks, not surprisingly forgotten by everybody except our families in India, who could not do much about us. Life in the transit camp was, of course, a new experience for us, and with everyone being friendly and helpful we found it enjoyable for the first few weeks. We were in large tents on sandy ground. Once, we were taken on a trip to Cairo, which was a long drive on a straight road through the desert. I can't remember much about Cairo except that it was very crowded and full of soldiers.

There was a cinema in the camp called Shafto's – (was it run by Sidney Shafto, and did he get an OBE for providing entertainment throughout the Middle East?) – and a different film every night was a great attraction for us. We played a bit of football and many games of Monopoly, but the only other memory I have is of the primitive loos, which were a long line of thunder-boxes placed over holes in the sand – very social!

Eventually we came to the conclusion that if we did nothing, we would stay in the camp 'for the duration', so we got on a troop train to Port Said, as we had heard that a troop ship was leaving from there. Arriving there we got into the dock area before anybody questioned us, and when they did we told them that our fathers were all on active service and we were just trying to go to school in Britain. Fortunately they allowed us on board, where we were the only civilians. It was a Dutch ship, the *Volendam*. We sailed to Taranto in the heel of Italy, where we squeezed through into a large, inner harbour. There were a number of sunken warships, some sunk two years earlier by Swordfish biplanes. Our next stop was Catania in Sicily, below Mount Etna. As on the way out to India, we were usually on our own and so going fast, but we joined a convoy in the Atlantic which brought us safely round the north of Ireland to Gourock on the Clyde. A briefing to the effect that we should not talk about the troop movements and other details of our journey, a rail warrant to my uncle's home near Winchester and an overnight train from Glasgow and the journey was over.

The Britain that I returned to was a very different place from the one I had left in 1940. Now it was very much in the grip of war. The summer of 1940 seemed to be part of another age. Now it was midwinter, everything (almost) was rationed, trains were packed, with even the corridors full of servicemen with kitbags, there were long queues and drabness prevailed – but despite everything, people were cheerful and confident of victory. Tennis courts had been turned into vegetable plots or chicken runs, but apart from the extras produced by such means the food was dull and the sweet ration was eagerly looked forward to each week.

PAMELA ALBERT

A fortnight later, Audrey and I were all packed, dressed in our Number Two uniforms and ready for travel to Bombay.

Number Ones were dress blues, Number Twos were whites and Number Threes were the working clothes. The dress blues comprised double-breasted serge jacket and skirt, long-sleeved white shirt with detached collars with studs, black ties, serge bloomers (comically referred to as 'blackouts'!) with white-cotton panty-liners, black stockings, black shoes and navy-blue rating hats. We rarely wore Number Ones, as the Indian heat kept us out of them. The Number Twos were the uniform of the day, with white short-sleeved shirts, white twill skirts and a white canvas belt, which included a change-purse built into it. White shoes and the same blue rating-hat completed this outfit. The coolest to wear were the square-necked tunics of the Number Threes. On every occasion the number only was the dress code of the day. No jewellery of any kind could be worn, other than a wedding band.

Audrey's friend Arthur had a Jeep, so he offered to pick up Bill first then drive us to Howrah Station, where we reluctantly said our goodbyes, promising to write to one another, and begging them to try to get leave to Bombay. Otherwise, we asked them to pick us up on our return. So it was that, amid floods of tears, we took off to do our bit for the war effort on the 4th of October 1943.

There were eight of us from Calcutta, and we would be joining others from different parts of India, all due to sit the course. How long a duration the classes would last, no one appeared to know. Classes were to be held at HMIS *Talwar* in Colaba, and we were to be billeted at a place called Marble Hall, in the Breach Candy area.

Word had it that the Hall (I would call it a palace) was built by a millionaire Parsee. It was entirely of marble, set up on a little hillock with a spectacular view overlooking the Indian Ocean. The hallway had the most beautiful staircase I had ever seen; it divided into two halfway up to the first landing. The stairs rose on either side to a semi-circular balcony with crystal chandeliers, large and obviously imported. There was no furniture, however. Our beds, string-tied *charpoys*, were provided in the twelve bedrooms and baths located off the balcony.

Apart from Saturdays and Sundays, each day we were awakened at 5.45 a.m. Physical training was held at six o'clock for thirty minutes. Then followed a welcome cup of tea in an old enamelled mug. We then washed and dressed in preparation for breakfast, which

Pamela Albert in the uniform of the Royal Indian Navy, Bombay, 1943.

was served at seven o'clock, and by eight o'clock we were aboard the lorries to travel to classes, and for attendance at the parade ground for nine o'clock Divisions, the Naval version of Parade in the Army. Classes followed at ten o'clock until noon when we broke for lunch provided by the school. Back to classes at one o'clock, we were given a break for tea and a biscuit at four o'clock, then we boarded the bus at five o'clock to drive back to Marble Hall.

Cyphers, I could soon see, was not to be my forte, as I was really weak at mathematics, and it required adding and subtracting to come up with the coded messages. I did much better at semaphore, morse code and telegraphy, but I was resolved that, if ever an opening in another (and different) naval expertise came up, I would apply for it. My father had forewarned me never to volunteer for anything, but I did opt to be trained as a drill instructor for our band of budding naval types.

The course ended in the January and we were sent to Poona for a large parade and recruiting drive before being sent back to our various naval posts. Everyone passed the course, and was issued with the leading-seaman insignia badge, to be worn on the left sleeve with crossed flags and A/C between them.

I was presented with my crossed flags and the famed tri-cornered hat, and was to return to Calcutta with the rank of Petty Officer. This was a great honour and I felt overwhelmed, as I had no idea this was to happen to me. It must have been my very loud voice on the parade ground.

On the way back from Bombay to Calcutta, Audrey and I wondered if Bill and Arthur would be there to greet us on arrival. I felt sure Arthur would be there but I did wonder about Bill, as we had only known one another for a mere two weeks before I left. The journey seemed endless, but at last we pulled into Howrah Station. We gazed out of the carriage windows, hoping and wondering – and there they both were, and it was such a wonderful reunion. It was so good to be back. I was, of course, teased about my new hat. The news that Bill's squadron had moved from Dum Dum to the Alipore airport was wonderful, as it was much closer to our billets. Arthur's unit also had moved to the Maidan, smack in the middle of the racecourse. Only during wartime could this have happened.

CAROLINE BURDER

The house for the head of Jardine Skinner in the 1940s was a very grand, white three-storeyed affair, with wide, balustraded verandahs and cane blinds to shade them. The drive in was through wrought-iron gates, where a *chowkidar* sat outside his lodge, leaping to his feet to open the gates and saluting as we went past. Up a short drive shaded by beautiful trees, and under a wide, pillared porch, thoughtfully built to keep the *sahib* dry during the monsoon rains. Wide, stone steps led to a marble-floored hall and an impressive curved mahogany staircase coming down from the floors above – as children we could slide all the way down the bannister rail. The main rooms – a small study, the only room with air-conditioning, a large drawing room, a dining room and a billiard room with full-size table – all opened on to a large marble-floored verandah overlooking a spacious garden. Our parents were both keen gardeners, and 9 Alipore Road must have had one of the loveliest gardens in Calcutta.

There was a fountain and pond, with ornamental ducks and a pair of flamingoes, which they brought from Ballygunge Park, their first house. The *mali* and several small boys swept the lawns early in the morning with long, bamboo canes to disperse the dew into the roots of the grass before the sun evaporated it.

Upstairs the marble-floored bedrooms again opened on to wide verandahs with cane blinds. The *gussal-khanas* (bathrooms) to each bedroom were very modern for the day; a huge copper-and-brass geyser hung on the wall, beautifully polished and rather frightening, with its little blue pilot-light always burning and a loud explosion of flames when first turned on and a distinct smell of gas, but very efficient. A proper Shanks pull-and-let-go, we had a box to stand on in our bathroom to enable us to reach the chain.

During the War, our parents had between eight and nineteen convalescent soldiers to stay, who much appreciated the home atmosphere and good cooking of the *bobajee* after the horrors of the Burma jungle, and also the billiard table. At Christmas, the senior Indian staff of Jardine Skinner would call with wonderful gifts of sweetmeats (most of which the servants ate) and always something for us; Monopoly one year, and Totopoly the next.

After my sister Susan had returned to England, I used to bicycle round the roads of Alipore quite alone, but never felt threatened by anyone except the lorry loads of GIs who appeared towards the end of the War. A visit to the zoo was a doubtful treat, but the flying foxes (or fruit bats) hanging upside-down in the trees by the entrance were a great source of interest. Pets were a great part of our daily lives, both in Calcutta and up in the hills at Kalimpong. Two white rabbits and an ever-increasing number of guinea pigs all had to be fed and cleaned out – the dogs were the sweeper's responsibility; they were 'unclean', so had to be brushed and de-flea-ed by an 'untouchable'.

Our pride and joy were two ducks – Jimmy and Simon – whom we found one morning in the kitchen, the *bobajee* having bought them in the market. They were sitting on the floor with their legs tied together, quacking confidently to each other and anyone passing, unaware that they were on the menu for dinner that evening. This was too much for us, and we got them reprieved, and they became charming and amusing companions. We gave 'duck parties', and dressed them up in gaiters and boot-ties, and other friends brought their pets to tea. They travelled backwards and forwards to and from Kalimpong to Calcutta in the bathroom of our sleeper, along with a hutch full of guinea pigs, two rabbits and the dogs. When we left for England, Betty and George Sherriff took them to Lhasa, where he was Political Agent. They travelled in their basket on the back of a mule, and rumour has it that someone laid an egg *en route*. They spent many happy years in the Sherriff garden, and even got their pictures in George's excellent film of life in Lhasa – before the Chinese invasion – seen scurrying into a flowerbed at a grand diplomatic garden party. In Kalimpong, we also had two goats who followed our ponies to school, Snowdrop and Blackout, but they were rather bolshy and altogether too difficult to take in a taxi and then the train, so they remained behind with the ponies and a rather unwilling *syce*.

JANE BIRKMYRE

My grandfather, Archibald Birkmyre, went out to India as a young man in 1894, and my father was born in Calcutta in 1898. My great-grandfather, Henry Birkmyre (1832–1900), was a director of the Gourock Ropework Company at Port Glasgow. Around 1880, he became convinced of the financial advantages of manufacturing in India rather than importing jute to his sack-making company, which was a subsidiary of the Gourock. The machinery was loaded on to a sailing ship. In 1884, he and his younger brother Adam arrived at Kishna, 12 miles up the Hooghly River from Calcutta. There they purchased a plot of around 12 *bighas* with a house once owned by Warren Hastings. The title deeds were in Persian, as Bengal had once been part of the Moghul Empire.

They and an able Scottish engineer, Jim Kinnison, set up the manufacturing of jute sacking and hessian cloth. During my father's youth, the mill at Hastings employed about a thousand, with a European staff of eight, all Scottish, and was very profitable. My grandfather was made a baronet in 1921; he died in 1935. The mill was sold in the 1930s, but my father retained part of the compound for a canvas and belting factory. With the launch of the Burma campaign, the Americans wanted an HQ for their Air Force – but this had to be supplied with 125-volt AC electric current, in which all their signals then operated. By a stroke of luck, this was the voltage of the power supply (installed 1904) at Hastings Mill. Indeed, it was the only suitable place the Americans could find in the whole of India. The mill compound became the South East Asia Air Command, and my parents were given a de-requisitioned house in the very desirable suburb of Tollygunge in Calcutta.

My father was able to retain his factory in the compound, making tarpaulin covers for trucks, waterproof capes, bedding rolls, and battle dress anklets, under contract for the War Department. The business was sold in 1946, and we all came back by troop ship to England.

NETTIE LAMONT

The Army decided that a new WAC (Women's Army Corps) India platoon should be started in Cochin, mainly doing clerical work, acting as telephonists, plotting aircraft and working in stores arranging goods in and out.

After completing Senior Cambridge Examinations at Hebron, and to fill in time, I took a shorthand and typing course, and when the Platoon Commander heard about this, she suggested that I join the WAC(I).

It was found that more officers were needed for the various platoons, and some of us were asked to fill in forms and go to interviews before being chosen for training. We were sent to Dagshai, which took a week to get to from Cochin via Madras, Bombay, Delhi and Ambala. We had a great mixture of religions; Muslims, Parsees, Hindus and Christians of various denominations, and we all got on very well together. I cannot remember much about the food, but as I also cannot remember any complaints, there must have been dishes which suited us.

We were in rooms for two, and you could have a friend share with you, but as most did not know each other we just doubled up. The Common Room was where we all met and arranged to go out together, or talked. I know there were games but I cannot remember them.

I was posted to Cochin to take over as Platoon Commander, which I found daunting to start with, but everyone was most helpful. My biggest problem was the WAC(I) hostel where the girls mostly from South India lived, and they did not like the food, which was

European – they wanted a variety of curries. I could not see why they could not have the food they liked, as long as they had a balanced diet, so we changed. I did not realise that sometimes the kitchen was inspected, as I thought I was responsible for the cleanliness and overseeing the menu. The inspectors were also not impressed with all the curries being served, and contacted our Brigadier, who called me to his office, where I explained they should eat what they liked. However, some officers from the Army Catering Department arrived and wanted the menu changed. Fortunately, our Brigadier agreed with me, provided it was a balanced diet, as the girls would be much healthier and enjoy the food.

ANN MITCHELL

There was an internment camp for 'enemy aliens' the other side of the lake in Naini Tal, and we often walked around to see the Austrian and German friends my parents had known in peacetime. Coming back along the dark hill-road at night was quite frightening. We talked and sang loudly, hoping to keep the panthers away from our dogs, which we kept on a short lead between us.

I was expecting to go to the Hallett School, but in 1941 my father was transferred to Dehra Dun, at the foot of the Himalayas, near the hill station of Mussourie. So I went to Woodstock School in Landour, not far from Mussourie. This was a school for American missionaries' children, but was now accepting others whose parents had fled from the advancing Japanese, or were from other war zones. There were many nationalities in my class, but I was the only English pupil. Two elderly English sisters taught music: they were the Misses Isles, and so inevitably were known as the 'British Isles'. One of them taught me the violin until my instrument disintegrated in the monsoon, an event for which I was deeply grateful.

The school comprised several buildings on different parts of the hills around; the main building was on the road from Landour to Tehri and housed the schoolrooms, assembly hall, gym, music

above Ann Mitchell and her parents garlanded at Christmas, 1941, at Dehra Dun, with the Sub-Inspectors and Office Staff.

below left Ann Mitchell at Lachchiwala camp.

below right Castle Hill Estate Leave Centre, Landour. (Ann Mitchell)

rooms and small children's hostel. On another spur some distance away was Ridgewood, the small boys' hostel and further away, the senior girls, and down in a dip, the senior boys' hostel. Further down the *khud* (hillside) was a large, flat area known as Midwood, where all the sporting events took place, many against the other schools in Mussourie.

It would take about 20 minutes or more to walk from the various boarding hostels to the main building, and in the rains (monsoon) we would pick up leeches, which would later be seen inching their way across the classroom floor, having fallen off, fully fed, from some unsuspecting child, who would find his leg trickling blood. In the monsoon it never stopped raining, and the trees grew enormous ferns in their branches. Nothing dried, and everything smelt of mould. The good part was collecting huge stag or 'rhino' beetles, and organising races between them. One had to be careful too, that the roads had not been washed away in the night.

In Dehra Dun, my mother was much involved in entertaining the troops, particularly those who came out from Burma, either wounded, convalescent or on leave, but also the young officers sent out from England to the Indian Military Academy in Dehra Dun. They were very glad to come to a private house and get some home cooking, as they were often very homesick. Dances were organised, and parties in the roller-skating rink in Mussourie, where we cooked what seemed like tons of bacon, eggs and sausages, and gallons of tea. At the height of the Japanese invasion of Burma my mother received a message from a friend in Maymo to say she was sending her three children and governess to us, as things were very bad. They stayed with us until their parents were able to escape from Burma.

Later, in Landour, there was a large leave-centre run by the missionary parents of a schoolfriend of mine, and we enjoyed helping equip and decorate this centre, which was comfortable and much-appreciated after the horrors of war in Burma. There was also a convalescent home called Mullingar on a spur across the valley from our house. Here we used to visit the wounded soldiers and help with occupational therapy for those who were well enough. Some made and embroidered beautiful skirts and aprons for their wives and girlfriends at home. The more active ones were allowed to come to our house to play Monopoly and mah jong, and have tea and listen to the BBC. They did not have a wireless, and as at the time we were all waiting for the Japanese surrender, we told them that as soon as we heard the news we would put up our Union Jacks, which they could see clearly from Mullingar. That was how the soldiers in Mullingar heard that the War was over.

While he was in Dehra Dun, my father continued the tours of inspection around the outlying villages, and since this took place in the cold weather, I was often on holiday and could accompany him. The best places were Lachiwala, Rikkikesh and Hurdwar, the last two being holy places on the Ganges River, with many temples and hordes of monkeys which would come into the tents or forest bungalows and steal anything.

My father had to go shooting partridge or peafowl for the pot, for we could get no fresh meat and had no fridge. One day, my father was walking along a path in the jungle with the beaters spread in a line parallel to him; I was behind him and my mother last in the line with our spaniel on a lead. My father fired a shot and immediately there was a deep 'woof woof' just to the left of us, and the monkeys started chattering and the birds screeching. My mother, who knew the jungle, said, 'That sounds like a tiger'. Later in headquarters (Dehra Dun) we recounted the episode to Jim Corbett, the famous *shikari*, who said, 'You were lucky that no other shots were fired. That was the warning of a tigress with cubs, and if there had been another shot, she would have been out on you.'

JOHN LANGLEY

1942 was the year of the famine. It did not affect the white community, as it was the rice crop that failed. I suppose it must have been a drought with the monsoons either not doing their normal great job of raining heavily during the rice-growing season, or else there were areas that did not get their accustomed rainfall. Whatever the reason, the Indians, who were dependent on rice, were starving and dying in great numbers. The tragic thing was that those that came to our compound were offered all kinds of food but we had no rice either. They would not accept any substitute, preferring to die rather than eat Western food.

Christmas 1943 turned out to be our last in Kanchrapara. There was an air-raid. I was asleep at the time that the siren went off, and it did not awaken me, as I was used to sleeping through heavy thunderstorms, and an air-raid siren couldn't compete. The raid was actually on Calcutta and very little damage was done.

I think it was this raid that saw the destruction of three of the Zeros in a rather unusual air-fight. No doubt the facts were exaggerated by the time we heard them, but apparently when the warning came that the Japanese were on their way to bomb Calcutta, the pilots of the duty squadron were at a party. Most of them had had several drinks and one lieutenant, whose name I believe was Pringle, jumped into his plane and by some stroke of luck arrived at the right altitude and location at the same time as the Japanese. Without hesitation, he attacked them and shot two down. A third one was forced to land, which it did near Kanchrapara, and seemed to be intact. Father and I were invited to go and look at it a couple of days later, and we were surprised that it did not seem to have any bullet holes or any sign of damage, and with some petrol could probably have taken off. Maybe it just ran out of fuel and had to land! I am not sure what happened to the pilot that shot the two down. I seem to remember that he was later transferred to Burma, where he in turn was shot and killed.

PAMELA ALBERT

On my seventeenth birthday, Bill invited me out to the Great Eastern Hotel for dinner, with dancing to follow at the Green Shutters, a local Club. It was the most beautiful summer night, and after dinner, we decided to walk to the dance. The moon was full, the skies full of stars and he stopped me, reached into his bush-jacket pocket and pulled out a box, telling me to close my eyes. I felt him pin something on to my dress. He kissed me and said, 'Happy Birthday!' When I looked down there was the most beautiful pair of gold Canadian Air Force wings. The Royal Crown was composed of rubies and the RCAF insignia was finished in small diamonds. I had never seen anything quite so lovely, or had anything that would come to mean so much to me. It was an unofficial engagement, and I was so happy I could do nothing but laugh and cry at the same time. He then handed me the blue velvet box in which I could keep the brooch.

My father held a party at Firpo's for us and our closest friends. There were about sixteen of us, a lively lot, and all approved of the match. My father was very fond of Bill. He had to inform us that night that he had been transferred to a post called Multan in the Sind desert, a holding and enquiry camp, sort of hush-hush, so no questions could be asked. He had been given a promotion to Colonel, which delighted us, but we were all sad that he was going so far away. At the end of his little speech, he turned to Bill and said, 'Take care of her, she is just a young girl and my only child.' I wished many times he had not said that, as it was indeed taken very seriously.

But we did settle one thing. We would not marry until after the War ended, and then would live in Edinburgh until I got my degree from the veterinary college. Bill wished to stay in the Air Force or to obtain a job as a commercial pilot. We would most likely live in England and go to Canada for holidays.

PHILIP BANHAM

At the Cathedral High School in Bombay, I passed the Senior Cambridge Exam, but was exempt from London Metric. The War broke out; I wanted to get out of schooling and into the Army.

I had been a cadet since I was 13, trained in infantry warfare. But Colonel Hammond, our real headmaster, said, 'England will need teachers after the War. I've decided to book you into Chelmsford Training College, at Ghora Gali in the north west, for two years only. Get your diploma, then join up and, after the War, go and teach in England. This War will last easily for six years, if not more.' His son, a captain, was killed in Burma.

Viscount Chelmsford was Viceroy of India from 1916 to 1921, so presumably the College was founded in his time. It took about ten students a year to do a two-year course. One was expected to specialise in two science or two arts subjects, do a basic course in English and maths, take a subject called military science, do school practice in the nearby Lawrence College, take a subject called educational psychology and teaching theory, join the Punjab Rifles and keep up military training in order to be ready to go to the aid of the military or civil power.

Ghora Gali was close to the hill station of Murree, summer headquarters of the Punjab Government. The campus had a boys' boarding school, a girls' boarding school and our teachers' training college. There were about twenty of us. It was set up in a belt of pines at 6500 feet. For me, the first experience of a temperate climate. The term began on 1 April and finished on about 20 December. No half terms! Only because, come 25 December, Christmas Day, the first snows began and just continued, day after day. Murree, 1000 feet higher up the *khud*, was soon covered in snow to the rooftops. Only servants were left there to look after property. I'd come back from the south, walk up the mountain path from college to Murree, and then walk across the town at rooftop height across the snow bridges joining one house to another! My first snow and icicles!

All the staff of the schools and the college lived on the premises through the school year. Some stayed on through the winter. Just think, living so long in an enclosed community with no contact with the outside world – through the whole year. What an achievement. Automatically, all students were enlisted into the Punjab Rifles.

We had regular parades at daybreak three mornings a week, regular shooting-range practice and regular manoeuvres in a readiness to go to war – and the War was on. All this with our teacher training. After all, we were not far from the Khyber Pass! We students were rather jealous of a Mike Harding. He had been expelled from the college because he had made a date with one of the 16-year-olds in the girls' school, and was found out. So he enlisted, and with his *élan* got himself a commission in a Punjab regiment. He came and flaunted his superiority – plenty of money – and independence; it was a matter of 'snooks to the authorities'. He waited for the girl till she left the school. They married.

I met a college master in Burma later: Mike Harding (not sure I've remembered his name right) died on active service. The master was Rogers. He became a padre in the forces. I met him one Sunday, visiting a Devon Company in the jungle: he was taking the service. Before a bamboo cross he gave me communion. I went on to examine the state of their ammunition. Next night, Japs attacked.

IAN O'LEARY

1943 was an exciting year for me in Naini Tal. I was at the Hallett War School, and my special friend Mike Bruce and I were always looking for adventures. We would spend evenings sitting outside our dormitory gazing out over range after range of the Himalayan mountains – a distant valley was of particular interest to us, as we had heard of a lonely English monk who led a solitary life in a monastery he had built far from any civilisation. The monk's name we found out was Brother Michael Warwick, and we were determined to meet him, even though it would mean a march of about 15 miles through the mountains.

To cut a long story short we set off, one weekend, with our schoolboy friend Johnny Nielson; and after a long tramp through the jungle we arrived, tired and hungry and surprised to see the beautiful St Michael's Mount monastery more imposing than we had ever expected. It was built of carved grey rock from the nearby mountains, with hand-hewn heavy beams supporting an overhanging roof.

Brother Michael's servants had had word of our approach, and alerted their master, who came out to greet us. He seemed very old, with closely cropped white hair, a long monk's robe and sandals on his feet. His face lit up with a most welcoming smile, and he led us in to the main hall.

We were soon having tea with him, served in a book-lined library, handsomely furnished with heavy dark mahogany furniture. He was curious to learn how we had heard of him, and what news had actually reached us.

After a hearty tea of toast and cake he gave us a tour of the monastery; and even as teenagers we were a little surprised to find that there were no other monks – only Brother Michael, his servants, and a native pharmacist to dispense medicine to any sick passing travellers.

Major Michael Warwick.

There were comfortable bedrooms for us to sleep in, with luxurious carpets on the floors. At meals Brother Michael kept us entertained with tales of his worldwide travels; and he explained how he had built the monastery with the winnings from the prizes he received from international crossword puzzles. Even this did not strike us as strange.

On another occasion we spent a week with him, and were sad to leave at the end of our visit. We had left it later than we should have, and as we walked through the jungle on our way back to school we heard the padding of a large animal keeping pace with us. We drew our *kukris* (Gurkha fighting knives), sang loudly and quickened our pace. There was a saying in this valley that once a year there was a strange death or ugly murder.

However, our visits continued and this friendship developed; only to be cut short when we three left India for good.

Some years later news reached us that Brother Michael had died, and been buried in his hidden valley. However, the Indian Government were concerned that his death might have been a 'strange one' so they had the grave dug up, and the body exhumed. To everyone's astonishment it was found that the corpse was female! There were even some local newspaper articles about it; but nothing more developed for many years, until my friend Mike Bruce returned to India two or three years ago as an older man, and visited the hidden valley and was shown Brother (Sister?) Warwick's grave. The gravestone just has the surname 'Warwick' and the initials of the christian names on it. During Mike's visit this last time a rich Indian approached him and explained that he had bought some of the fine monastery library books, and they were inscribed to 'Major M. Warwick'.

The other adventure of note in 1943 was a trek that eight of us teenagers took through the Himalayan mountains to the Pindari Glacier near the Tibetan border. We were away for about two weeks with no adult supervision, and we took about fifteen coolies.

We climbed higher and higher into the mountains each day, doing approximately 15 miles a day as far as I can remember. Crossed the Rapts torrent on a very long perilous leg. Swam the river at Biggeswar, trudged up from Karcote to Loharkhet; past Bageswar at one point. Went over another make-shift bridge between Khati and Phurkia. Each night we tried to reach a *dak* bungalow where we could sleep the night, and have a cooked meal.

When we finally reached the Pindari Glacier it was much colder than I expected, and we had no mountaineering clothing or equipment of any sort. (I wore my pyjamas under my day clothes, and luckily had a pair of heavily metal studded leather shoes). We all got on to the glacier and Mike, Tim and I climbed to the top (14,000 feet) and got a spectacular view of snowy mountain ranges going on and on to the end of the world!

6

1944

22 January	Allies land at Anzio in Italy
6 June	Japanese finally routed at Kohima
	The Allies land in Normandy
22 June	Imphal relieved
26 June	Mogaung, Burma, captured by the Chindits and the Chinese
3 July	British troops enter Ukhrul, last Japanese base in Manipur
8 July	The Russians enter Poland
4 August	Myitkina, Northern Burma, finally falls to Allied and Chinese troops
25 August	Paris liberated
11 September	American First Army begins invasion of Germany
6 October	The 14th Army captures 'The Chocolate Staircase', the 3000-feet-high road into Tiddim

PAMELA ALBERT

On New Year's Day, Bill told me the sad news that some of the squadron would be moving up to Imphal in Burma in February and he, unfortunately, was to be one of them.

I now had a new job and a new badge for my tricorn hat, the crossed anchor removed from my left arm and replaced by three gold buttons across the sleeves of my blue number ones, plus a crown, and I became Chief Petty Officer Pamela Albert.

February 1944 came all too soon. Bill and I said our goodbyes. My father rang in April, from Multan, to say he would be coming down to Calcutta for a fortnight's leave. Audrey's parents offered to put him up in Cossipore, some miles north of Calcutta, but he chose to stay at Fort William, where he had some business to clear up while he was down. He promised to spend the weekends with us all, at Cossipore.

One Friday, Arthur, Audrey and I decided to have dinner at Firpo's before heading to Cossipore for the weekend. It was quite late when we finished our dinner and, as we got up to leave, Brick, a fellow officer from Bill's squadron, stopped us and said to me, 'Hey, Pam, I will be flying up to Imphal in the morning to deliver some parts and the mail. How would you like to come along as ballast?' I jumped at the chance, not giving a second thought to the danger of flying over enemy territory to get there. 'I will pick you up at 3.00 a.m. as we have to be airborne by 6.00 a.m. Wear your naval uniform in case there are any questions.'

Audrey argued with me all the way to Cossipore. 'What will I tell your father? And the family?' I did not really much care at this moment, for I was going to Bill, and that was what mattered to me. Brick picked me up in the squadron Jeep at three o'clock outside the compound gate in Cossipore, making sure that nobody heard us, and drove to the airstrip.

The plane, a two-seater, was waiting for us. I was handed a leather flying-helmet, and climbed into the cockpit behind Brick. He advised me that there would be no communication between us as we flew, as we would be going over enemy territory, but we could see each other via a mirror which was mounted to the right of his cockpit. I donned the helmet, climbed in and was ready for take-off. The ground crew buckled us in and off we took into the early morning sky. It was six o'clock.

This was the very first time I had flown, and it felt wonderful. After a few banking turns, including one upside-down, we headed towards Imphal. We landed to refuel at about nine o'clock, about halfway, had a cup of coffee, then continued through enemy territory. How did I know? Brick got my attention in his mirror when he pointed downwards with his index finger and mouthed 'Japs.' I laughed and shrugged my shoulders because I was much too happy to care! We landed at the airstrip in Imphal about noon. I could see Bill and three others waving their arms about telling us where to park the aircraft. They all knew Brick was flying, but had absolutely no idea who the passenger might be. As Bill slid back the top, I took off my helmet and he was clearly taken aback. The first words out of his mouth were, 'Oh my God! It is Red. I do not believe it!' He leaned over the cockpit and gave me a long and tender kiss. He was glad to see me.

Trying to climb out of a small cockpit with a skirt on is not the easiest thing to do gracefully, but somehow I got to the ground amid hugs. Brick informed me we had until 3.00 p.m. to visit and that our take-off time would be 3.30 p.m. at the latest for our return to Calcutta. Three hours! Such a short time for such a long ride, but so much better than no time at all! We would have to cram all we could into the time available to us.

Lunch consisted of bully beef curry and rice; one did not expect much else. We caught up on all the news of all the goings-on in Calcutta, and that Audrey and Arthur had decided to get married in November. He listened with interest, and I suggested that it would be a good thing if we talked about getting married ourselves, as this long separation was really getting to me and that I missed him dreadfully. He insisted that we would not talk about it at all until the War was over and when some sense of security could be seen on the horizon. I could not get my point across, and he was adamant.

Three o'clock came all too quickly and, as I climbed into the cockpit, we kissed and said goodbye. I put on my helmet and he slid the top shut, and he blew a kiss and waved as we took off.

I cried all the way home for three reasons: I did not get my firm commitment from Bill, I had to face my father and I had the most terrible feeling that I would never see Bill again.

It was ten o'clock in the evening by the time we got back to Cossipore. We were met by a very worried and angry reception. They had been anxiously awaiting news of our arrival, and were so glad when we had come to no harm. My father hugged me closely, but we did get a telling-off, and promised never to do such a thing again.

Words cannot describe my horror when, in April 1945, Bill was shot down by enemy fire and killed. His Group Captain came to tell me.

LAURENCE FLEMING

We spent the cold weather of 1943–1944 in Digboi, as it was now defended by the numerous Bofors guns of the 66th Leeds Rifles. There was an emplacement on a hill behind our bungalow, so they could come in when off-duty and use the bathroom and bedroom at the back of the house. The bathroom still opened to the outside, although there was running hot and cold water, and a pull-plug, on the inside.

There were by now three military hospitals in Digboi, one British, one Indian and one American. There were also three canteens, which my mother, as senior WVS lady, was organising. The officers used the Club, but everyone used the swimming pool, and there were frequent dramatic presentations on the Club stage. I was not there when Noel Coward came to entertain the troops. He was suffering from dysentery at the time, and spent a week with my parents, leaving a particularly inaccurate account of his time in Digboi in his second volume of autobiography, *Future Indefinite*. The only other names that I remember were Marie Burke, mother of Patricia Burke, and Stainless Stephen – I believe the gloom that fell when it was heard that Vera Lynn was unable to get there lasted for about a week.

We went for our picnic on the Dihing. I think my father must have been only too happy to have a day off. The production of oil from the Digboi field reached its highest point ever in 1944, but it was still not exactly enough to fuel the entire Burma campaign. The only other oilfield in India was at Attock, in the Punjab, 2000 miles away. Whatever could not be produced on the spot had to be flown in, or brought up on the single-track railway.

So, outwardly, things were much the same. Our two cows, Clarabelle and Snow White, who lived in bamboo sheds on the way to the new golf course, were alive and well. The two shunting-engines, Barbara and Lillian, were busier than ever. The wife of Rahman, the butler, had had a son. The vegetable garden was even more productive than usual, and the annual flower show loomed as always.

We went, Jane and I, to tea on one of the neighbouring tea gardens. The Irvines were a childless Scottish couple, who always invited us over when we were there. Their garden was called Pengaree, and it was reached through a wild and beautiful forestry reserve, full of hoolock monkeys and chattering birds, along an informal road impassable during the monsoon. The teas were always memorable, served on the huge mosquito-proofed verandah at the front of the house. It was on stilts and it was thatched, with a splendid view over the tea. Acres and acres of identical bushes, clipped flat at waist height, and with tall,

No 1 Digboi. A later photograph taken by Lavender Todd, whose husband became General Manager there after Independence. The Fleming family had to walk up a long flight of steps.

graceful shade-trees planted at intervals, the tea gardens of Assam were a wonderful sight, and Pengaree was no exception. Afterwards, we would go round the garden, and we always came home with the car full of superb fruit and vegetables.

We had two other interesting excursions during that holiday. The first was to go to the headquarters, jointly American and Chinese, of the military forces who were building the Ledo Road, intended to go right into Chiang Kai-Shek's China, with a branch into northern Burma. It was being made at enormous speed, with bulldozers, and it was there that we first saw Jeeps. We were told that they had originally been called GPs for General Purposes, but this had soon turned into Jeep. I remember the clouds of bright red dust and how surprised everyone was to see two children there. We had a colossal lunch in a huge tent, and I also remember my father wondering, when we were safely inside our own car, whether that earth road could possibly survive the monsoon. It did, eventually reaching Burma, but I don't think it ever got to China.

Our driver on that occasion was Burmese, Maung Ohn, wearing his national costume, which was much admired by the road-builders. It was he who drove us on our other excursion, which was to Pasighat, beyond the Inner Line, absolutely the final outpost of the Empire. We were poled across a river, which I think must have been the Brahmaputra itself, on a wooden ferry with room for one car only. Then we drove for what seemed to be a very long time, mostly through natural forest.

Pasighat was situated on the west bank of a river called, at that point, the Dihang, or Siang, the Tsangpo of Tibet and the Brahmaputra of Assam. There was one handsome forestry bungalow, on the tea-garden pattern, with a circular bed of pale-pink gerbera in full flower in front of it. There were two other much smaller bungalows a bit further along and, as far as I remember, we occupied them both. They faced the river, which was bordered by a row of bauhinia trees, also in full flower, but with branches on one side of the trunk only, indicating the ferocity of the prevailing wind.

We went to the bazaar, which lay behind the bungalows, two rows of bamboo stalls selling fruit, vegetables and hand-woven objects, chiefly large, loose bags which could be slung over the shoulder, or if really heavy, could be passed across the forehead. The people were principally Abors, copper-skinned and of no particular religion, who lived by cultivating a little and spearing the river fish. The other local tribes were the Mishmis, darker-skinned, and the Daphlas, darker still. We bought several of their bags.

We went to one of the Abor villages, on the other side of a very swift stream crossed by a bamboo bridge, which swayed alarmingly, but which was perfectly safe so long as one didn't look down. We went to the house of the headman, on stilts of the huge bamboo which could be found in the forest but which also dotted the plains, looking like great clumps of green ostrich-feathers. The walls were of woven bamboo and the roof was thatched with palm fronds. My father managed to hold some conversation with the headman which, considering that, so far as I know, he spoke only Hindustani and Burmese, was clever.

We set off the next day for a picnic, up the road on the west bank of the river. Pasighat was built at almost the exact point where the river emerges from the hills and, after a few miles, we could go no further. So we left Maung Ohn and the car and walked on by ourselves, climbing at once, and in quest of a view we had been told about. But, suddenly, we found ourselves descending very sharply, the path disappearing between the rocks. There was a wonderful smell. There were white violets in full bloom on either side of the path and there, below us, a sand-locked backwater had been created by the river, which flowed beyond it at incredible speed. There was no longer any question of the view. As one, we made our way down to the beach and spent the day there. There were huge blue-and-black butterflies. The backwater was deep enough to swim in and not at all cold. Occasionally a passer-by on the path above, almost as naked as we ourselves, would wave, and we would wave back. It remains in my memory as one of the most magic days I have ever spent.

SHEILA FERGUSON

Early in 1944, my stepmother, little brother and I had to return to England – not easy to get a passage with the War still on. We were told to gather in Bombay – six liners were leaving, and we had great difficulty finding somewhere to stay. We found a room in an Indian house but had to think again when we found bed bugs crawling over my brother. Each day we had to report to the shipping office and were finally told to board. The ship was packed – two thousand Italian prisoners-of-war below-decks – and we were 12 to a cabin. The saloon bar was turned into an officers' cabin – their bunks were four deep – and troops slept on stairwells wherever they could find a place. Water, of course, was rationed to one hour in the morning and one hour in the evening, and blackout was strictly enforced. The officers did a rota system of manning the guns and helping as lookouts. All six liners left Bombay together, and at Port Said the rest of the convoy joined us, about 32 ships in all, each sporting a barrage balloon – as storms erupted in the Mediterranean they quite often burst. We were the first convoy through the Mediterranean in January 1944, and it was cold and miserable.

We docked in Liverpool on a cold, bleak early-February day, the most depressing sight I had seen for years, not helped by the fact that one of our own trunks was inadvertently dropped into the River Mersey while being unloaded – our clothes were ruined.

I joined the Wrens soon after arriving home, but I returned to India for the cold weather of 1948–1949. At that time, after Partition, things had quietened down and there seemed very little change – but until I returned I had forgotten how snobbish Calcutta could be. There was a definite 'pecking order', and it was frowned upon to overstep one's place. Some of these people looked upon themselves as the élite, and it was not until some of these people retired, and the younger ones moved up the scale, that the snobbery eased.

SHEILA WRIGHT-NEVILLE

Early in the 1944 school term when I was 16, my mother telegraphed the news that my father had died suddenly. He had been on leave in Kassauli, a small hill station in northern India, and one evening had collapsed and died without regaining consciousness. He was buried there. No transportation was available for my mother to attend his funeral, and the telegram announcing his death did not reach her until two days later. She came up to Darjeeling to be with Christine and me, and we tried to comfort each other. When he died, my father was 46 years old.

One year previously I had passed my School Certificate exams, and was presently studying for the Cambridge Higher Certificate exams to be held in December 1944. Four students were taking Highers that year. School Certificate exams were being held concurrently for the class below ours, so a dozen of us were housed together for two weeks in one of the school's boarding houses. It was bitterly cold, I remember, and as the school itself was due to close, we knew we were all about to separate. But in many ways it was still a memorable and happy time, a fitting conclusion for my four years at The New School – a time that had influenced all our lives and provided us with an excellent education and grounding for whatever lay ahead.

When I left school I was 17, and although the end of the War in Europe was in sight, the fighting still raged in the Far East. I joined the local censor station as a civilian (although in uniform), and worked there until VJ Day in August 1945. Several friends did the same thing: we all wanted to contribute to the war effort, but our youth precluded us from enlisting in the armed forces. Both the people and the station itself made the work interesting. Calcutta teemed with the armies of many countries: British, American, Australian, Poles and others, either stationed or on leave. With all the parties and social events, it was a good time to be young. I learned to drive (illegally) in an American Army Jeep signed out to a young US officer in the Intelligence Corps.

The US Army had built a superb Club for their people and their guests, where a group of us often gathered. They were very hospitable to British officers and civilians, and the entertainment they provided was exciting, with famous entertainers from the US appearing live on stage.

Signs of civil unrest were beginning to surface in Calcutta, signs which would later escalate into horrific riots and killings between the Hindu and Muslim populations. The 'Quit India' graffiti that now appeared everywhere was aimed at the British. I recall one occasion when, after a party, I was unable to get home because we suddenly found ourselves on the outskirts of a riot, with mobs of screaming, fighting people, burning trucks and throwing rocks. We hurriedly turned the car around, and I spent the night with a girlfriend who lived on the other side of town.

On another occasion, while riding my bike on Chowringhee, Calcutta's main street, I collided with another cyclist, an Indian man, and was badly cut and scraped on the arms and legs. The Indian was unhurt, but immediately began complaining loudly that I was to blame and had wrecked his bike and, as a result, owed him money. Within seconds a large crowd had gathered, but nobody helped me. They were clearly hostile to me and joined in the tumult, shouting insults. I was hurt and frightened but, with as much dignity as possible, limped across the road to a shop where I was known. There they kindly patched me up and sent me and the remains of my bike home in a taxi.

ANN BURKINSHAW

My memories of Calcutta during the three-month school holidays in the cold weather, and during my last six months there, are many and happy. I enjoyed particularly my regular early-morning tennis coaching at the South Club with S.J. Smith, one of the premier coaches in India at the time, taking the tram from Alipore into town with my mother (petrol rationing was in force) to go shopping and the courtesy of all of our fellow travellers, visits to the various cinemas (nearly every Saturday night, and often during the week in the afternoons), cycling all over the place, but particularly along the Strand where all the ships were moored, cricket matches in Eden Gardens and watching various ceremonies on the Maidan. I remember one attended by Field Marshal Wavell. Then there were the various Hindu and Mohammedan festivals, which were intriguing: Holi, where they sloshed red paint at each other, Diwali, where in Darjeeling the hills around were alight with flickering candles, Mohurram, celebrated on the Maidan, and one connected with the Goddess Kali, whose images were thrown into the Hooghly.

The only sour note in my memories is the social stratification in Calcutta. A person's educational background seemed to matter greatly to a lot of people. I cannot say that I was affected by it, but I am sure my parents felt it. The gulf between the Europeans and the Anglo-Indians was rather shameful. I was particularly aware of this, as my aunt had married an Anglo-Indian gentleman. Although he had a good position and was a major during the War, my mother and I were not allowed to acknowledge them in public in case it got back to my father's firm. My one unpleasant experience happened during my last six months, when I began being invited to dances. An officer invited me to the Saturday Club, of which we were not members. At dinner the Secretary came to the table and told me I was not to come again. At 17 this was truly humiliating! My father decided he would make amends, and applied to join for my sake. He was black-balled – by a parent from The New School! My mother was always amused by how many more people spoke to her after I had gone to Oxford!

AURIOL GURNER

Life in Calcutta began to change after the Japanese War began. No more Governor's Balls or New Year Parades, and eventually even the arrival of petrol rationing. No one could, however, call our life Spartan in any sense. When the car was no longer so readily available I cycled through Calcutta and enjoyed it. Mothers and grown-up daughters were now all doing war work, hospital visiting and troops' canteens, generally on a voluntary basis for some; others joined branches of the Services or worked in wartime offices. Having earlier taught myself to type on my father's old typewriter, I went to work in the Psychological Warfare branch of SEAC, where I earned 300 rupees a month. There I typed English translations of the leaflets to be dropped on the Japanese, and did various clerking jobs. For the first time, I mixed on terms of friendship with people other than those in the same privileged position as myself. In India from 1940 till 1946 I never had an Indian friend; here I worked with Anglo-Indians, girls of my own age (17/18), and made a friend amongst them.

Altogether I would have to say that my knowledge of Calcutta and its people was limited. We lived on the first floor of a large house in Lee Road, off South Circular Road, rented by my father from an Indian landlord. I do not remember ever travelling by bus or tram. When I became more independent, after leaving school, I cycled or occasionally, when with a friend, took a rickshaw. When still a child, the bearer took us very occasionally with him to see an Indian film, confusing but a treat. We learned enough words in Hindustani to address the servants with requests, but that was all. They were discouraged, perhaps not permitted to speak English. There was no air-conditioning, except in the cinema. Houses were built and furnished for coolness. We got ill fairly frequently. All milk and water was boiled, floors in the flat (red tiles) were washed every day with lysol in the water, and the usual rules of hygiene in India were strictly kept, but bouts of dysentery were unavoidable, and kept us thin. Bouts of dengue fever were not uncommon. The area I knew well in Calcutta comprised the main shopping street and all the streets round home. These were tree-lined. Beggars of all ages, from babies to ancients, and of every degree of deformity seemed to frequent every street in Calcutta. We were strictly forbidden to give even an anna. As I remember, one band of beggars came into Calcutta round the corner of our street and, if one was awake early enough, they could be heard chattering away as they passed on their way.

The Indian efforts for Independence reacted on our family, primarily in the extra stress and work it brought my father. When the Bengal Cabinet of Ministers was dissolved by the Governor, my father took on the job of Finance Minister in addition to his work as Chairman of the Calcutta Improvement Trust. The stress was enormous, I did not appreciate it then. In my last year in India, processions with their banners of 'Jal Hind' became frequent, and eventually we were picked up for work and brought home in motor transport with armed soldiers on each vehicle, but I left before Partition.

The voyage home in June 1946 was very different from the outward one. Now there were four of us I was travelling with my mother and two sisters in a cabin originally meant for two. No swimming pool or library or first-class comforts this time but the voyage, via the Suez Canal, lasting only three weeks instead of six.

If I had been asked what India did to me in the first year back in England (I got married in November of the year I returned), I think I would have said it made me a completely useless person. I could not cook, I had no idea how to keep a flat clean, I had no idea of budgeting, and washing up, washing clothes, making fires etc. seemed insuperable tasks, which I often gave up. Worst of all, it had made me forget what cold was, and the agony of chilblains. But like others I learned gradually the skills necessary in a servantless life. India and the life it forced on me both before and during the War, I think, gave a self-sufficiency and ability to adapt to circumstances.

NICOLE WALBY

After my Higher Exams at the end of 1943, I had a six-month wait for a ship home – my father had to return on business, and felt that my brother, then 14 years old, should go to public school, and I should come too. In the months waiting for the ship, I had a chance to travel in India. The first trip I did was with my father, who was going to

Delhi on business. He had booked an air-conditioned sleeper, a rarity, and when we boarded the train we found it was four berth, and had two other men in the compartment. Nothing could be done to change it, and I had the fascination of watching a Sikh carefully rolling his beard and moustache into a net before going to bed.

In Delhi, a girlfriend and I cycled around viewing the monuments. We toiled up all the steps of the Kutab Minar for the view from the top. As the passage was narrow there was a continuous procession of Indians up and down, and the buzz of excited talk. They took us in their stride. We stopped off in Agra on our way back to Calcutta, to see the Taj Mahal. It is all it is claimed to be – beautiful and serene. Unfortunately, the dome was covered in scaffolding – we were told that the reason for this was camouflage, as the brilliant gold could have given it away.

Later, I went on my own to Madras – no air-conditioning this time, but the usual enormous block of ice in its container in the middle of the carriage – very useful on long journeys for food to be

The Chowrasta, Darjeeling, 1943, Nicole Walby second left. Six roads led out of the Chowrasta – hence its name: Mall Roads East and West; Rangit Road, leading to Lebong and Sikkim; Old Calcutta Road; Jalapahar Road and Commercial Row.

kept on. I had three Indian ladies in my compartment – two were very shy and hardly spoke, the third was a headmistress who had done a lot of her training in the US and spoke English perfectly. She made an interesting companion and made me sample different fruits I had never seen before, some bitter, some sweet as honey. My mother used to give us a whole fruitcake and a bottle of sherry to take on these journeys, and for the rest we bought fruit and food from the vendors at the small stations.

At one point we crossed a troop train and both came to a halt. In no time at all they knew an English girl was on board our train, they could not understand that I was travelling with Indians. It was the first and last time I met discrimination and very embarrassing. I went up to Ootacamund from Madras, another hill station, but utterly different from Darjeeling – gentle, undulating hills – a very English landscape.

Towards the end of June, after D-Day, we joined our ship in Bombay – it was a captured German ship, the SS *Dusseldorf,* 5000 tons and twenty passengers – five of them captains whose ships or submarines had been sunk. We hit the monsoon in the Indian Ocean, and I didn't appear on deck for several days. When I came up for air, the ship was sliding down into troughs and then juddering up waves as high as houses and certainly taller than the ship.

We came through Suez and picked up a large convoy. We were the commodore ship, and had a disabled submarine on either side. They could no longer submerge, and needed our protection. A hawser was fired across to them regularly to send fresh bread and food. We also had a Greek ship in the convoy, which couldn't keep up and made a lot of smoke, and after several warnings had to be sent back. We watched it turn around and sail off, still belching smoke.

We had one bit of excitement. A German plane was spotted, and the possibility of it warning its submarines meant 'all stations'. At the time we were fooling around in the small swimming pool with some of the young officers, who responded to the alarm with such speed that I fell backwards on to the ammunition boxes that surrounded the pool. The passengers gathered just below deck on the stairs, but no further alarms came. We were supposed to be a very safe ship as we were carrying monkey nuts in the hold, and were told that if we were hit by a torpedo we would stay afloat!

Because of the activity in the Channel we sailed up round Scotland, leaving most of the rest of the convoy behind us. We stopped off at Loch Ewe and Scapa Flow and finally landed on Grouse Shooting Day, 12 August 1944, at the port of Methil in the Firth of Forth.

We waited all night on Waverley Station, and then caught the train for Cambridge. It was so crowded we stood in the corridor, or sat on our suitcases. My father, knowing Cambridge well, found us lodgings and gave us time to get used to wartime England – because of the War the Slade School of Art was evacuated to the Ashmolean in Oxford, and my first year was spent there. I still remember all the planes going over for the tragedy of Arnhem – little did we realise, we just cheered them on.

That Christmas 1944, we joined my father in London. It was empty. Doodlebugs came over regularly, and we got used to their growly noise. We saw New Year in with friends at a Canadian Club near Piccadilly (we had a small flat in Oxford St); afterwards about 12 of us did the Palais Glide all the way up Regent Street, with only a 'specials' to see us. We felt we owned London. My father returned to India, and for the next couple of years my brother and I organised our holidays.

What India did for me was give me a strong sense of colour – the clash of orange, red and yellow, the mix of designs, have influenced my art and my home. It has also given me a love of the Indian people; so gentle, so humorous, they are never crude or vulgar. I think it has influenced my thinking in that I accept, perhaps more easily, what fate has to chuck at me. I enjoy so much suddenly finding in Tooting a haberdashers filled brimful with goods even hanging on the ceiling, and behind the counter in her lovely sari, placidly knitting, the wife sitting whilst her husband rushes forward to help. They are delightful people.

STAR STAUNTON

New Delhi was my first and only posting in the Army. At the Riding Club, where I spent a good deal of my spare time, I met a young officer of the RASC called Don, in whose company I found myself both beloved and in love. Soon I was writing to my father to tell him about Don and say that we were intending marriage. I told him that Don lived in a North Yorkshire village with his father and grandmother, and that his father was a stockbroker. My father's reply was discouraging: 'Marrying into a bucket shop! My God!' That was my last contact with him. Shortly after, I had a letter from my stepmother telling me that he was missing, presumed dead. He had gone off in a Jeep with some of his men on a reconnaissance patrol from which no one had returned. At that time Rommel had command of Tripoli and the vast sands.

Don and I were married in 1944 in New Delhi. The church was packed with an international congregation including representatives from both sides of our inter-office divide, the English and the French. One of my colonels would have to give me away now that I was orphaned. Colonel Gibbon of the French side was a Roman Catholic, which made me shy of taking an active part in the service, though he was present, so Colonel Wilson kindly consented to be the bride's 'father'. Colonel Gibbon kept his end up however, by insisting on paying for the wedding reception, a generous action for which I was particularly grateful, having now no longer my father to supplement my pay. My standard of life for the future would be considerably more modest. Farewell, a long farewell to all my greatness! But it was a rather splendid farewell, with all those international representatives and our head boss Lord Mountbatten himself honouring us with his presence. It was quite a wedding.

Don was in the process of making a training film, with the technical assistance of a Frenchman who knew no English. It was concerned with the transportation of animals. The stars, and stars they were, were mules, horses and camels. Their handlers were all Punjabis. The work continued during our honeymoon with me doing my bit as translator in both languages, an unwelcome distraction for which I found much consolation, in that the film was shot in the beautiful Kulu and Kangra valleys, in which I had done my recruiting.

One episode provides quite a pendant in my memory to those very happy days. We were miles from nowhere when we met an acquaintance of mine, let me call her Lady Blank. She passed near enough to where we were filming for an exchange of greetings. 'Off to the hills with me cats,' she yodelled. She herself was seated in a palanquin supported by four stalwart bearers. Behind her came a similar conveyance similarly supported and carrying her *ayah* and cats, a second with her *chaprassi* and cats, a third with her *khitmagar* and cats. It was a bizarre example of that cosseted existence at the expense of Indian labour and goodwill which I myself had shared, in a past that was fast disappearing.

As though to give me another reminder of these fading glories, fate and the exigencies of a wartime railway service decided that Don and his camera crew should be accommodated on their way back to New Delhi in the Viceregal train in a carriage specially constructed with proportions to meet the requirements of Viceroy Lord Linlithgow, a man who was six foot six in his socks, with a Vicereine to match! The train was both vast and ornate, for in India the Viceroy had to live up to Indian standards of royal display. There were Persian rugs underfoot, the wall-covering was of satin, we used silver cutlery, cut glass and the finest porcelain. All this was new to the filmmakers. To me it was nostalgic.

During the first few months of our marriage my stepmother gathered together some objects and documents which had to do with Skinner's Horse, the unit of the Indian Army which my father had joined on his return to active military service at the beginning of the War. Skinner's Horse, I believe, has a place in history, and I will say no more about it than that it was raised by the original Skinner at his own expense at the time of the Indian Mutiny, he being an Englishman of sufficient wealth to do for his country that great service in her time of need. My stepmother felt that the regimental archives would be the proper resting place for the regimental mementoes my father had left behind him, so she wrote to the then head of the Skinner family offering to send them to him. Arrangements were made, and I received a charming invitation to visit the Skinners in their home, which was still the palatial establishment built by the original Skinner in the mid-nineteenth century.

It turned out that this Skinner had 'gone native', and married an Indian lady all those years ago, and his descendant was himself an Indian in all but name, with an Indian wife, and a tribe of khaki-coloured children and other relations. The family was still rich, and domestic arrangements were not dissimilar to those I had met when travelling with my father as a child among the Maharajahs. There was a butler and footmen in livery, elaborate and expensive furniture, heavy silver and spotless napery, everything you might have found in the palace of a nineteenth-century English duke if the duke had still been rich enough to afford it; but it was all Indianised, exaggerated, too much of a good thing, and except for us two the company were all of the wrong complexion.

Poor Don was most embarrassed. Indeed he was horrified, as a primitive must be who discovers that he has broken a strong taboo. His conditioning in the Army tradition had not given him the responses needed to cope with this situation, for in his milieu it was not the done thing to accept the hospitality of the natives, and he could not conceal his discomfort. Accustomed as I was to the company of an expert diplomat whose speciality was making himself at home with Indians I suffered fairly intensely both for Don, our hosts and myself. The weekend was a disaster. Years later I was solaced to hear Don regret that he had wasted the opportunity of such a contact. The Skinners, he admitted, though they had Indianised, were still Skinners, and bore a name that was justly famous. At the time I was perplexed and a little frightened. My husband's acquired reflexes were so different from my own.

One more event of a similar kind and this matter had to come to a resolution. We met a certain Major Hill, a descendant of the Hill who was responsible for introducing the Penny Post in England, the representative of another English family of note who had 'gone native'. The major was charming. He was handsome, tall and slim, and the colour of dark seasoned oak. He took us to a good restaurant in the bazaar in Bombay and gave us an excellent dinner, Indian-style, apologising that his wife could not be present because she kept *purdah*. After dinner he invited us to his home and Don accepted, though as I could see, he did so nervously and with reluctance. Another disaster. Again, there was no lack of affluence, but the major, for all his English name, was clearly an Indian by culture and in his domestic arrangements. There were a lot of children around, more surely than a single wife could have produced, and there was no doubt that they were very far from pure-bred English. I was taken into the women's quarters, where I met the women of the household and enjoyed their company, while poor Don was left in deep embarrassment engaged in man-to-man conversation with his host. He did not like the arrangement.

On our return to our flat he made it very clear that he did not think it becoming in me to hob-nob with Indians or to let it be known that I was fluent in the Indian languages. People would suspect that I was Eurasian, and that would be very bad for us in all sorts of ways. Now that I was married, I should make up my mind that I was an English woman and behave as such. Would I please give up my contacts with the natives and behave like the wife of an English Army officer?

For me that was the parting of the ways. I thought carefully about what Don had said and then agreed. I said I would do as he asked. I had married him with my eyes open. I loved him. My whole future lay with him. So I promised. I promised that I would try not to embarrass him again. I would forget India, my lovely Indian friends, my up-bringing in this alien land. I would be the kind of wife he wanted. I do not think I realised at the time how much it cost me to make the trouble-shooter's daughter give way before the Army officer's wife, but I kept my promise, in principle if not always in detail.

Soon after this my son Christopher gave notice of his intention to enter the world, and I shared the ward in Delhi with a 13-year-old white girl called Bella, who had given birth at the same time. Poor child, she needed a little company and sympathetic consolation, for her baby was the product of rape committed on her by her own father. We got on famously together, though which of us did the other the most good, I have never decided. Certainly, Bella enlarged my understanding of human nature, its potential courage and dignity. She brought home vividly to me the truth of my father's dictum that what counts in a human being is not the culture or class that bred him but his personal integrity.

Our second son, Andrew, was born exactly a year later in a military hospital in Naini Tal, a hill station north of Mussoorie, and again I enjoyed comparative luxury, though for a different reason. The hospital was fully staffed in preparation for the Burma campaign, but had not yet received any wounded. I was the first patient, which was wonderful for me and my new baby. Andrew had at his infant disposal the services of one consultant, one other doctor, eight nurses and four orderlies, among whom there were so many Andrews that his name was scarcely a matter of choice. Mr Andrews delivered him, Nurse Andrea was my personal nurse, Sister Andrews was in charge; so Andrew it had to be. I hoped Don would approve.

YOMA CROSFIELD

When my mother retired from being the Girl Guides' Commissioner for Assam, she was presented with a most beautiful Address of Farewell. It is on a single piece of thick paper, 18 by 13-and-a-half inches. The text, handwritten in black ink, is surrounded by a thick, black line. In the first three paragraphs, the lines starting, 'Oh our beloved', 'Oh devotee' and 'Oh our Sister Guide' are extended to the left, and stand out from the indented main text. In the top left-hand corner and down beside that first paragraph, the guides glued a beautifully painted cut-out representation of a sunflower with stalk and leaves, with one stem reaching up to a paper version of the Guide badge, coloured in golden yellow with black outlines and glued to the top centre over the black line.

AN ADDRESS OF FAREWELL TO MRS M.E. CROSFIELD, GIRL GUIDES COMMISSIONER, ASSAM

Oh our beloved commissioner! On the eve of your departure from Digboi, we fare you well with mixed feelings of joy and sorrow. Sorrow, because we are going to miss forever the happy and pure company of a genuine lover of the Womenhood of our land. Joy, because you will get wider and better field for your Social activities which are so dear to you and will have much more comfortable and happy days.

Oh devotee of social service! In you are always found a genuine and earnest desire to help the suffering humanity. Your very many endeavours in aid of the India Red Cross Society for the relief of the sufferings of the Indian soldiers will ever be remembered by us with gratitude. We also remember with awe and admiration your anxiety for the fighting soldiers at the different fronts and your day and night toil to send handmade garments and other necessities to them for their protection against trying Climatic conditions and diseases. Your efforts were not confined to our society only but you came down to us as an ordinary worker and infused in us the Spirit of Service for the Suffering idealists who are hankering after a lasting peace in the new great world to come.

Oh our Sister Guide! You have been the nerve centre of the Girl Guides' Associations and its activities of Digboi and you attracted us to this association as if with a magic spell and we understand the Philosophy of the movement by precepts as is usual the case, but by living examples from your life. It will remain to us a treasure to us for the years to come. We always feel how badly we fail in our duties as a Guide or Blue-bird but you never took our shortcomings. Otherwise you acted as a Guide, Philosopher and friend, and we will always remember your sisterly behaviour with the best of the Spirit they were used.

Before we part, we pray to the Almighty father for your long and peaceful family life, and wish that you will always keep our memory in the Sweet Corner of your heart.

Yours forever,

Girl Guides and Blue-birds of First Digboi Guides Company

Dated Digboi, the 15th September 1944

My mother, as Guide Commissioner, used to travel second class by train in order to save money for the Guide Movement. Few Europeans at that time would deign to be seen in anything but a first-class compartment. She used to travel long distances over India in crowded and sometimes insanitary conditions, an indomitable and rather wonderful person.

JANE GRICE

In October 1944, my parents came to Darjeeling for a fortnight's leave. My brother and I were at school there for the war years, but we had a short holiday over the *puja* festivities in October. We went on a trek to 13,000 feet to view Mount Everest. This was a wonderful experience. We had a merry band of Sherpa porters and some sure-footed ponies, and climbed up to Tonglu, Sandakphu and Phalut. We stayed in *dak* bungalows overnight. The porters always arrived before us, however much they had to carry, and always had our beds and tea ready and waiting for us. The Kanchenjunga range of mountains must be one of the most beautiful sights in the world, and is very impressive from Darjeeling, but the views on the trek were magnificent. Everest in comparison is rather disappointing; it looks a bit like a licked ice-cream cornet. The villagers all along the way would rush out on to the mountain paths to yell greetings, always smiling and giggling, the little girls attired in their bright new *puja* dresses, usually of flowered cotton.

Shortly after this holiday it was time for us to return to England. The New School was to be disbanded, as the War was drawing to a close. I was just nine years old by this time, and was dreading losing all my friends and going 'home'. The school had been like one big happy family to me, and the community club life we led in the holidays drew us together in a strong band.

When we returned to Calcutta, the flat was full of packing cases and trunks waiting to be filled. It was time to go. We travelled by train to Bombay and embarked on the SS *Ranchi*. We had my brother's thirteenth birthday, Christmas and the New Year on board ship, but in spite of these exciting interludes the trip was very uncomfortable. The ship was divided from bow to stern down the middle; the port side accommodated returning troops, the starboard side civilians. All the cabins had been converted to hold as many as possible. My mother and I were in a converted two-berth cabin, which now held eight. My brother was in what had been a four-berth and now held twelve. We travelled in convoy with several other ships, and had to carry our lifejackets with us all the time.

We arrived in Glasgow on Sunday 6 January 1945, and it was snowing. I was thrilled to see the snow on the hills as we sailed up the Clyde, but my mother was not. We had few warm clothes; I suppose we wore our school uniforms during that first winter. I remember a long wait in the Central Hotel, where everyone was very silent. I suggested a game of cards and was shushed and tutted – it was not done to play cards on the Sabbath. We had an even longer wait on Central Station, but we finally caught the overnight train to London, and I spent the night in the luggage rack.

YOMA CROSFIELD

In 1944, my parents were transferred by the BOC from Digboi to Calcutta. They and Harold and Nora Roper, their friends from Rangoon days, each had a flat in a large company house at 18 Alipore Road until Sir Harold retired in early 1945. This was the official residence of the Manager of Burmah-Shell, which marketed all the oil the BOC produced. When BOC and Assam Oil Company staff and their wives visited Calcutta, they automatically stayed there. With Nanny, I joined my parents there during the school holidays over Christmas 1944–45 and 1945–46. It was an extraordinary contrast to both Digboi and Darjeeling.

First of all there was the city itself. Crammed with people, deafening with horns and the clanging bells of trams, dusty, hot and humid. Out in the suburb of Alipore, we were fortunately protected from the worst of the crowds and noise. The other major contrast was that, compared with our life in Digboi, I hardly spent any time with my father. There was no equivalent of our walks in the jungle. Perhaps he was too busy. Nanny was my companion, as always, but my mother was with me more now, even though she was as busy as ever with the Guides.

I now learned that my mother could be utterly different from the person I remembered. One evening I was already in bed when she came into my room to say goodnight on her way out to dinner. She was wearing a long dress made of purple velvet. Pinned on her bosom was a sparkling brooch. As she leaned down to kiss me I could smell her perfume. She seemed magical, so unlike the mother I'd been used to seeing in her starched Guide uniform or her tennis whites.

Nanny and I would go into the centre of Calcutta on the tram, which ran on rails in the middle of the street. The Alipore tram was marked fore and aft by an orange and a yellow circle, which Nanny expected me to recognise from far away. The tram would come clanging along the line, a vehicle of delight. I would cling to my wooden seat as it swayed and bumped, glad of the slight breeze set up by the movement. In the busy streets I could see crowds of people on the pavements and in the roadway, rickshaws, carts drawn by bullocks and other trams, thundering by on the parallel track. We would pass the bleached expanses of the Maidan, a huge park that was one of Calcutta's only 'green lungs'. My favourite destination was Firpo's, a famous teashop that sold wonderful nutty macaroons. I still have a smart red Firpo's tin, which holds loose stamps from my early Indian collections. On its lid is a gold panel which reads, with self-conscious style, 'Firpo's the Confectioners of Calcutta'. The delicious macaroons it once held are long gone. No macaroon I have eaten since, and I have tried many in hope, has tasted as good as the originals.

right Yoma Crosfield on a hired pony in Darjeeling with a local *syce*, whose striped apron indicates that she is married. Perhaps 1942.

below The Burmah Oil Company's Calcutta House, No 18 Alipore Road, with Yoma Crosfield's mother in front. 1944.

ANN BURKINSHAW

At the end of 1944 The New School closed down. As I was halfway through my Higher School Certificate I went down to the Loreto Convent in Darjeeling to finish it off. The War was not yet over, and my father did not wish to send me back to England. This was an interesting experience, firstly because the method of teaching was so different from what I had been used to, and because for the first time I was mixing with Indian and Anglo-Indian contemporaries. And, of course, I was exposed to Roman Catholicism, which until then had been a closed book. As regards teaching methods, great influence was placed on learning by rote, and information was fed to us. If one had a good memory one could not fail to pass examinations! I used to go for walks so that I could learn various things off by heart aloud. The only people I would meet would be Buddhist priests mumbling away whilst revolving their prayer wheels! The other bonus of going to the convent was that my walk there and back took me through the bazaar, where I got to know the sellers and their wares and all the myriad little shops.

It was with sadness that I left India in June 1946 with my parents. My father was going on his first home leave for nine years.

Manor Lodge in Darjeeling. This was the senior girls' boarding house at The New School from 1941 to 1944. A typical Darjeeling road can be seen zig-zagging its way up the hill beyond it. (Sheila Wright-Neville)

I think that as a result of India gaining her independence I felt – and still feel – that I lost my 'home', and in a way my roots. Even now I do not feel that I quite belong here, despite being English and considering myself very lucky to have been born so. I still sometimes feel not quite integrated, especially when people show a certain surprise and uncertainty when I say I was born in India. Indians are invariably delighted to hear it, and never show any animosity, contrary to what many modern commentators on the British in India would like the world to think! I do not think India harmed me in any way, and I am very grateful that chance put me there.

JOHN LANGLEY

Father was transferred from Kanchrapara in the spring of 1944 to Haflong, a small town in the Naga Hills and not too far from the Burma border, as the crow flies. Father was responsible for the maintenance of the railway from Lumding in northern Assam to Kalaura, in southern Assam. The latter was a junction where the troops retreating from Burma were routed to camps in the Calcutta area. The tea planters' wives had a stall at Kalaura station, which they manned every day to help feed the troops as they arrived from Burma. However, as far as the railway was concerned, the most interesting link was the 115-mile metre-gauge section between the plains zone across the Naga/Cachar hills to the mainline in the Brahmaputra Valley.

The line, traversing as it does some of the worst jungle and mountain country in Asia, was fraught with operating difficulties, among them dangerous, spongy track in a bad state of maintenance and very subject to washouts and landslides in the monsoons, disease and fevers, which at the worst stations brought down 90 per cent of the staff, earthquakes, difficult gradients, including a gruelling 11-mile stretch of 1-in-37 and long sections which cut down the maximum capacity of the line to nine trains a day. (It was a single-line railway with double track only at stations.)

When we were in Haflong, Father inherited a unique trolley. It was a Model T Ford that had had its motor wheels replaced by railway wheels, and was the only completely enclosed trolley I ever rode in. It was terribly temperamental, and even though it had a battery starter it often refused to work, and we still often had to rely on the jump-start. I think that it also had carburettor troubles which put it out of commission for long periods while we waited for spare parts to be sent up from Calcutta. Nevertheless, we used it as often as we could in the rainy season as the rains in the Naga Hills were torrential. Six months of the year were a drought and six months would see an average of 500 inches of rain.

The Hill Section was never intended to carry heavy war-traffic, but by the exercise of patience and ingenuity the section became an essential lifeline. Some of the finest work of the campaign was done there. Accidents, some of them serious, were the inevitable result of the big push to drive the Japanese back into (and ultimately out of) Burma. Because of the demands on the line there was no time to recover wrecked rolling stock in the normal way. Vehicles were simply left where they fell, or were lifted clear of the track and deposited nearby for collection later on. By VJ Day, 14 August 1945, the Hill Section had the appearance of a battlefield! Father was kept busy with the derailments caused not only by the spongy tracks and the wrong type of locomotives, but by rogue elephants who, in the mating season, would challenge the train to a duel. While the elephant would be killed in the effort the trains also suffered, and the line would have to be cleared in a hurry for the next supply train to get through.

Father was given the rank of major in the Indian Army, and had a colonel and a battalion of soldiers under his command to assist in improvements to the track and in the operation of the system, as well as protection from potential sabotage. About the time of the battle of Kohima a contingent of Americans also arrived, complete with air-conditioning and ice-cream, to install an oil pipeline for their air-bases. Since we did not have electricity this luxury made the rest of us very jealous!

In 1915, a severe earthquake damaged the hill section so badly that it was closed for two years, and a committee was formed to determine whether it should be reopened. The astonishing thing was that it was kept open, and after 1942 became such a vital link in the campaign to protect India from invasion.

When Assam suddenly became a war zone, due to the rapid and unexpected advance of the Japanese through Burma, the normal cargoes underwent a radical change. Pineapples, jute and tea became of lesser importance to oil for the new airfields in the Brahmaputra Valley. Food of all types was required for the troop concentrations being built up all along the border. None of the lines in the Bengal Assam area were well equipped to handle the sudden heavy volume of traffic, least of all the Hill Section.

LAURENCE FLEMING

In December my father retired, after 25 years with the Burmah and Assam Oil Companies. His principal connection was with Dibgoi itself, and the two farewell addresses that he received, contained in the most beautiful silver cylinders, engraved and pierced, must have given him a great deal of pleasure.

FAREWELL ADDRESS TO W. FLEMING ESQR.

Sir,

We have assembled here tonight with mixed feelings of joy and sorrow to bid you farewell on the eve of your departure from our midst. Sorrow, because we will be missing a true friend and a trusted guide; joy, because you will be back in your Home to enjoy the much-deserved rest in retirement after long strenuous years of heavy responsibilities.

Your association with our Club is so full of memories that we can not conceive of its present status without you. You had the lofty ideal of making it a suitable common meeting ground for all the Indian Communities linked together through its various activities – social, recreative, artistic and philanthropic. The present extended building compared with its humble beginning will tell the story of your sympathy for your employees, your magnanimity and your liberal outlook concerning the gradual development of a club life for us in Dibgoi. We realise that you will have a painful feeling to leave us and the Indian Club which you have nursed up to its present stage, but at the same time you shall have a consolation when in that distant home of yours you will hear that the Club, through the collective endeavours of its members and the benevolence of the Company, has developed to cater more extensively for the needs of recreation and other amenities of the Indians in Digboi.

We know that you have always tried to make Digboi a healthy place. For the general welfare of the employees of the Company you have improved hospitals and schools and created Maternity and Child Clinics and many such institutions for which you will always be remembered with gratitude. We expect that as a result of post-war reconstruction we will be able to enjoy still greater advantages in the form of better housing, still greater opportunities for education and care of our children and other facilities, the beginning of which has already been pioneered by you.

We all remember with admiration your endeavours towards raising funds for the relief of hungry millions of Bengal during the last famine, the homeless people of the flooded district of Nowgong and the earthquake-stricken people of Behar, Quetta and Turkey. Your anxieties and consequent efforts for the aid of the Indian Red Cross and for the comforts of the fighting Indian soldiers have endeared you to us all the more. We shall also miss very much the charming personality of Mrs Fleming, who has been closely associated with you in all your benevolent activities.

We pray to God Almighty that He may bless you with many more long years to continue your good work in the world. We hope that in your home you will have a soft corner in your heart for us and remember us with kindness whenever you get a little leisure amidst your still-busy life.

With the kindest regards,

Affectionately yours

The Members of the Dibgoi Indian Club

Dated Dibgoi the 2nd December, 1944

The second, from the Members of the Digboi Sports Club, was in similar vein, and my mother, too, received a farewell address from the Guides and Blue Birds. She had already been Mentioned in a Despatch for her work with the Women's Voluntary Service in Assam. She left Digboi a little ahead of my father, in time to nurse both Jane and me through an attack of measles in the Windamere Hotel. Mrs Bearpark, the manageress at the time, fed us on rich vegetable broths, specially made I am sure, and we recovered as quickly as possible.

Mrs Bearpark was reputed to be the daughter of a sergeant in the ill-fated Garrison of Senchal. Some time in the 1860s, the legend ran, this garrison – on what is now called Tiger Hill – was left unrelieved for 20 years. Probably someone in London mislaid their file. One morning on parade, the bugler blew The Retreat, and the entire garrison committed suicide. One version is that they fell upon their swords; the other is that they roped themselves to gun-carriages and hurled themselves down the *khud*. One could still see the foundations of their cantonments on Tiger Hill and we used to go there, when the school got up early to see the sun rise over Everest, to see if we could not surprise the odd ghost or hear that final bugle call. Recovered from measles, we trekked to Gangtok, and our father was able to join us there on Christmas Eve.

MICHAEL BRUCE

My father was now a Deputy Inspector General, first in the CID and then with the Central Intelligence Office, probably because of his excellent command of Hindi, Urdu and other languages, at all levels. He was stationed at Patna, in Bihar.

In the hot summer months, we children were up at the relatively cool Himalayan Hill Station of Naini Tal (6000 feet), not far from the western border with Nepal, in the Kumaon Hills, as interns at the Hallett War School (7000 feet). Despite the ongoing World War, with the Japanese threatening to invade from Burma to the east, and most of our forces, including the Indian Army, engaged in the west, with the confidence (naiveté?) of youth I remember having little concern that our world might crumble.

Holidays (October to January) we were at Patna. Against the above background, and despite walls beginning to be inscribed with 'Quit India!', I remember cycling through the bazaars without qualms. The Hallett War School was a mixed residential boarding school, high in the Himalayan foothills, by a beautiful lake, with lovely views of the main Himalayan range (other than during the monsoon). There was a high standard of teaching. It was founded by Sir Maurice Hallett, the United Provinces Governor – incidentally, heartily detested by my Uncle Gerald, of whom more later. The Hallett closed in 1945, having achieved its object.

Four incidents stand out. Firstly I, my sister, brother and one or two schoolfriends were invited over to Government House, on the hill on the other side of the lake, to enjoy the swimming pool and have a picnic. This involved each teenager being conveyed in a chair called a *dandy* by a five-man team (four lifting, and one in reserve) down the *khud* and up the other side. This meant six children, 30 carriers, one policeman and a supervisor, the last two probably being armed, or a total of 38 persons. I remember the pool being wrapped in mist, very cold, and green with weeds.

Next, our headmaster, the Reverend Llewellyn, allowed our Scout troop to engage in an expedition, entirely on foot, from Ranikhet, the last locality with roads passable by vehicles, to the Pindari Glacier, below Nanga Parbat, one of the Himalayan peaks (over 20,000 feet). We had a small army of Kumaoni Sherpas, who carried most of the food over successive ridges (9–10,000 feet), going from one *dak* bungalow to the next, to the last one, at about 13,000 feet, at the snowline. A Hindu *sadhu*, in a saffron robe, tagged along in the early stages of the journey, on his way to his periodical fast-and-contemplation session in a cave. He must have been reinforcing himself for this ordeal, as the Sherpas could deny him nothing, so our rations soon became depleted to the point where, on the journey back and three days from Ranikhet, we remained with a very few tins of bully beef and the makings of some very small *chapattis*. It was years later (in England) before I could bear to look at a tin of bully beef.

The third incident occurred when 'Jungle' Jim Corbett, an ex-white hunter, but by then confining his shots to those with a camera, came to our school to show us very close-up movies (there were no zoom lenses then) of tigers in the Kumaon Hills Nature Reserve. This included groups of up to six grown tigers, which is rare, if not unique. Also, every night in Naini Tal, and even more so at the Scout

The Hallett War School's expedition to the Pindari Glacier (1943). *above* Michael Bruce on right of group. *below* A rest by the wayside between Bageswhar and Kapcote. *bottom* Crossing the River Pindar. (Michael Bruce)

camp at Saht Tal, we heard the authentic savage jungle sounds, with the constant chattering of monkeys crashing around the trees.

Finally, in 1943, when it was only in the cities that there was some semblance of control by the Raj, my father arranged for me to be a passenger on the weekly mail flight from Patna to Raxaul, on the plains, just inside the Nepal border. This was virtually the only means of written communication with the area at that time. Two things stand out in the memory of that flight: the whole Himalayan range in the far-distance as we approached Raxaul (so I can say that I have seen Everest from a Tiger Moth), and the very hairy, smiling *kukri*-bearing Raxaulis coming to greet us at the place the pilot had recognised as being the airfield – it was flat and had a large white cloth across it.

In January–February 1944, going ahead of my family, I returned to Britain, through the Canal this time, to complete my education in England. Some German planes remained in the south of France. I recall very clearly that at breakfast they were announcing that we were about to say goodbye to fresh eggs and fruit, when there were alarms sounded, and the ship swung round to present the smallest possible target to the torpedo that went past us, and I was horrified to see my bacon and eggs had slid to the deck. Disaster!

My uncle, Major General Gerald FitzGerald ('Ged'), CB, DSO, MC etc., was the very epitome of the Raj at Flagstaff House, Lucknow. He almost certainly had more servants under his command than the King Emperor at that time, but not many troops, since the majority had been sent to active theatres of war. However, dressed in his regimentals, six feet four tall, in a scarlet tunic with a chestful of medals and a sword, and mounted on a 16-hands horse, it was said that he was worth on his own at least one division of infantry, if not cavalry. His ADC was one Captain Booth, who must have suffered much under my uncle's aegis, but got his revenge when he ran off with my uncle's brigadier's wife to Calcutta.

When Ged retired, about 1947, the event was generally acclaimed as the 'second relief of Lucknow'.

JONATHAN LAWLEY

In 1944, aged eight, I was sent to a prep school in Srinagar in Kashmir started up for boys who would normally have been at boarding school in Britain. It was called Sheikh Bagh, and had evolved from a Church Missionary Society school established partly to introduce Kashmiris to sport, including boxing, athletics and mountain climbing, and generally to inculcate the values of muscular Christianity, influenced by the ideas of Kurt Hahn and summed up by the motto, 'In All Things Be Men'. It encompassed such things as 'owning up', telling the truth, not blubbing in front of others, avoiding 'smut' and bullying and respecting character rather than birth or colour. The head, Eric Tyndale-Biscoe ('TB'), the founder's son, very much exemplified these virtues, only once allowing himself a cigarette at the VE Day celebrations.

At Sheikh Bagh we led a very physical existence, being required to swim a mile on the Dal Lake aged eight, three miles aged ten and six miles aged twelve. We climbed the 13,000-foot mountain, Mahadeo, and having climbed the Twin Peaks came down on our bottoms through the steep gullies, full of leaf mould. There was skiing and various outward-bound type games, and continual inter-house sports, including paddling *shikaras*, hockey and boxing. It was competitive in the sense that you got a point for each sporting or athletic achievement, or completing a stage in exploring or mountaineering. At the boarding house, new boys, called 'squeakers', had to descend from the top to the ground floor via a slippery pole, rather than the stairs. There wasn't much time for reading, but there was very little beating either. The only time I remember being beaten was when I had openly and flagrantly disobeyed the head after being asked three times to desist from making a noise outside his study window.

The school's values, combined with the physical freedom we enjoyed and the setting in the most beautiful part of the world, was deeply influential on the lives of all who went there. My English prep school that I went to on our return to Britain in March 1947 I found stultifying by contrast. We wore house shoes and tiepins, were not allowed outside and went for walks in crocodiles. The result was that I was very naughty on several occasions, and was beaten regularly.

I remember almost nothing of our leave in England in 1938–39, but post-war England was very different to what I had expected. I suppose I was still the *chota-sahib*. When we were staying at an inn in the Lake District I remember ordering the landlady to 'get out' when she accused me of taking too much butter. My godmother was shocked that I had never cleaned my bath in my life.

I missed India dreadfully, especially the freedom, and I hated the way I was suddenly cut off from it. In some ways it had made me grow up so fast that I did not have a lot in common with school children in England. I felt I had insights into life which set me apart, not as a better person, but just different. I didn't like being different, I just knew I was. I think it's generally true that the British at home never understand Britons who live abroad.

In 1947 my parents moved to Southern Rhodesia. One strong reason was that they couldn't afford a good public school in Britain and from Rhodesia were able to send me and my sister to public schools in South Africa. They also endorsed Britain's imperial mission, and the idea of building a non-racial Federation of the Rhodesias and Nyasaland. My mother hated the all-pervasive racism of whites in southern Africa, and frequently defied it. My mother also hated the local accent. There was a feeling that few of the white settlers were '*pukka-sahibs*'.

For me personally, Rhodesia was easier to adapt to than England. I wanted wider horizons, more freedom, and more air to breathe, though after India I couldn't accept the generalisations white Rhodesians and South Africans made about Africans. I already knew that the world contained a multiplicity of cultures.

India made me proud to be British, and aware that history and circumstances had given us a special role in the world. The public-service ethic I acquired there, plus the family tradition of imperial service, led me naturally into the Colonial Service.

HILARY VIRGO

In 1940 my father was seconded from the Imperial Bank of India to wind up enemy firms in Calcutta. We got a lot of perks from this – bottled mineral water from Italy, scissors and cutlery items from (maybe) Siemens and various other goodies. We moved from Alipore to a flat off Park Street, top floor with a marvellous view over the rooftops, particularly good at Diwali when our verandah had little chatties of oil lit along it, and seeing the lights all over Calcutta outlining buildings.

I went to The New School, which moved permanently up to Darjeeling in 1942 and, in the year of the great famine, we all went out on the streets of Darjeeling with our collection boxes. We found that the Indians gave very generously, but also discovered that there was nothing left to buy with the money we raised.

My father had, by this time, wound up all the enemy firms in Calcutta and, because he was by then seriously ill with heart trouble, he had been retired from the Imperial Bank. He was desperately bored and irritable but was offered a post as Personnel Manager with Bata, the Czech shoe company, whom he had helped out of difficulties as 'enemies'. So we again moved, this time to the Bata shoe factory at Batanagar, some 10 miles out of Calcutta, towards Budge Budge and by the river. My mother started an allotment and grew, successfully, tomatoes among many other things. The local Indians would squat for hours on the river towpath to watch this Memsahib working on the land.

Here I was living amongst Czechs and Indians, with a few English who were married to them. The Far Eastern War was getting closer and there were some leaflet raids by the Japanese. The Americans were starting to be in evidence and would come out to Batanagar, socially.

Driving into Calcutta we had to pass an abattoir which was always closely attended by vultures and sometimes the car had to drive into them to get them to clear the road. I remember from this time too, the lepers thrusting their maimed limbs through the car windows.

In January 1944 my father died suddenly and we had to wait several months for a passage home. In the meantime the Japs were advancing and there were bombing raids. One night they dropped a bomb at Budge Budge, only a few miles from the factory. There was a terrific blaze and the planes departed, but they had only hit the grain market and not the oil pipeline to Burma which started there and was their target.

We had trouble with passports, as my mother was born in Shanghai. There was much hard work and persuasion to convince the *babus* that she was not Chinese.

It was getting hotter and hotter, but finally we were on the train – three days and nights to Bombay. We had a steel thermos which got so hot outside it couldn't be touched. In Bombay at last we staggered into the Taj Mahal Hotel longing for showers but were told to get on board immediately. So we rolled up our bedding rolls and made for the ship that was taking troops back to England.

We sailed on D-Day in convoy. The World Service was relayed regularly and to this day the tune 'Lillibulero' brings it all back to me.

One night my mother couldn't stand the cabin any more and took a pillow up to sleep on the deck. She found herself surrounded by troops. The men took it in turns to sleep on deck so what they suffered in accommodation doesn't bear thinking about.

We came back through Suez and had a smoke screen past Gibraltar, finally arriving in Liverpool. We were met by some organisation that night and were taken to a transit hotel at Hoylake, where we were given Spam for supper and thought it delicious!

I find that an Indian childhood is a bond with others who have experienced it also, whether they are passing new acquaintances or children I have played and grown up with and who have subsequently remained friends. But I realise I didn't have too much close contact with the Indians themselves. I only had one close Indian friend, the daughter of our doctor at Batanagar, and I regret it now. But at the time the opportunities didn't seem to arise.

7

1945

3 May	Rangoon recovered by the British
8 May	Germany surrenders unconditionally; the War in Europe ends; VE Day
6 August	The Allies drop an Atomic Bomb on Hiroshima
8 August	Russia declares war on Japan and invades Manchuria
9 August	The Allies drop an Atomic Bomb on Nagasaki
10 August	The Japanese surrender unconditionally; the World War ends; VJ Day
21 November	Police fire on rioters in Calcutta: two killed, 75 injured

BARBARA ANNE JARDINE

When my father was transferred to Baroda State as Resident, I started my studies in history of art at Sophia College, Bombay. I was the only white girl there, but everyone was friendly. Outside the city it was a different atmosphere as 'Quit India' was in full swing, so travelling on the bus to college and back was dangerous, and also going shopping. Another danger for a teenaged white girl was the British troops on leave in Bombay before going to the Burma front. We were lucky in India that we had no rationing and we could have our clothes made by the *dhirzi*. But before leaving London my mother bought us some clothes at Harrods I well remember.

In 1945 our mother took us three children back to England, partly as war seemed nearly over, and also our grandfather had just died. I think too our father foresaw a lot of conflict about to happen in India. He believed much could be done by building bridges between Hindus, Muslims and British and arranged to meet their leaders, even spending a whole day talking with Mahatma Gandhi, which was much appreciated by the Indians.

Our journey was on a troopship, *Straithaird*, back to England, this time through the Suez Canal. I remember getting my exercise by pushing my little brother in his pram round and round the deck. Our ship arrived in Liverpool in January 1945, and the ship nearly keeled over as everyone on board rushed to look at the shores of England! The captain had to call us back over the loudspeaker.

We travelled down to Surrey and our grandmother. Life in England was a great shock to us – the drabness and the severe rationing. All the women with their heads tied up in scarves as factory workers. The Doodlebugs, which no one knew where they would land. There was a prisoner-of-war camp for Germans near us, and if we met one in the street we were terrified. We children would be sent out to pick nettles to cook as a vegetable, and we inherited a lot of rabbits from our grandmother so we could eat them. Our father joined us in time for VE day, and he took us to celebrate outside Buckingham Palace.

LAURENCE FLEMING

We spent New Year's Day in 1945 in the *dak* bungalow at Yatung. It was a large double bungalow with a fine view of the town, which lay across the River Chumbi. Yatung was further up the river than the town of Chumbi itself, and it was in this valley that Messrs Ludlow and Sherriff discovered so many interesting new plants.

We were two marches into Tibet. The snow, in general, did not fall until the end of January, and we had hoped to complete the four marches to Phari, on the edge of the Tibetan tableland and as far as tourists were allowed to go, before that happened. But the snow was already falling at Yatung, though not very heavily.

It was Jane's birthday and Pansen, who was with us as always, made some scones in her honour. Eaten hot, they were very good; cold they turned instantly to concrete. It was here too, that we learned, from telegrams sent on from Gangtok, that our father had been made a Companion of the Order of the Indian Empire, a very high honour for a *boxwallah*. He was, of course, one of the last to be so honoured, as the Order came to an end in 1947.

The next day the snow stopped, so we set off for Gautsa, in bright sunshine, past the old Mint, on the other side of another river, and across a strange entirely flat area suspended, like some spectral football field, in those very steep mountains. I do not remember any terracing, or any sign of cultivation. There were very few trees and we passed no one. No sooner were we inside the next bungalow, however, than the snow came down in earnest.

By the time it stopped, some time in the night, the road to Phari had been blocked by an avalanche, and the road to Yatung was just blocked. We stayed a day at Gautsa while they unblocked it. But I received a political lesson there that I have never forgotten. The bound volume of *Punch* was for 1905, and one of the full-page cartoons was of the 'Plucky Little Jap' triumphing over the 'Fallen Russian Bear'. It was perhaps by Bernard Partridge, or by L. Raven Hill; but whoever the artist was, it made the strangest viewing at the beginning of 1945.

So we never got to Phari. We went back two marches, to the bungalow of Champithang, perched on the side of a hill at 13,000 feet. On the way we had been given tea by the *chowkidar* of the Kaju Monastery, who let us all warm ourselves at his brazier and showed us round his huge monastery. They were all very similar in design, two or three floors, with the sacred statues behind glass, the rooms almost bare of furniture. But this one was built round a courtyard and, in the last room, high and very narrow, there were three seated statues, their hands raised in blessing, larger than anything we had ever seen before. I remember them as two male and one female, and turquoise in colour – perhaps a trick of the light. We gave the *chowkidar* a chocolate, which he ate, silver paper and all…

We spent a week at Champithang. The snow fell relentlessly all that first night. The Natu La was closed, and so was the road to Yatung. We were in a small bungalow, three rooms round a central chimney and two bathrooms. The earth closet was at the bottom of the garden, now two feet deep in snow. The great disaster for me was that there was no bound volume of *Punch*. There were two copies of the *Strand Magazine*, or perhaps *Wide World*, for 1912, which had the first two instalments (of five) of *The Phantom of the Opera*, and it was to be years before I discovered what happened in the end. Otherwise, we played rummy, read *Pride and Prejudice* to each other and had only one meal a day.

Laurence and Jane Fleming, on either side of their mother, rest by a chorten on their way out of Tibet in January 1945. The standing figure on the right is their wonderful *sirdar*, Ang Tsering Pansen, veteran of at least one Everest Expedition.

We were rescued after six days by the Head Clerk, who came to re-open the pass. He was tall and spoke excellent English, dressed in magenta brocade, with one turquoise earring and a magnificent hat. He escorted us along the road to Natu La on the seventh day. The snow had been cut into blocks, like railway sleepers, and the steep slope up to the pass into steps. Jane was carried up by one of the porters, whose previous load, I suppose, we had eaten. I had another behind me in case I slipped, which might have involved a slide of several hundred feet, there being nothing to hang on to. However, we all got quite safely to the top and were bidden a gracious and smiling farewell by the Head Clerk. His courtesy was unfailing and, whatever he may have thought, he treated us like honoured guests.

Two days later we were back in Gangtok, invited to dine at the Palace. My mother washed her hair and I put it up into curlers for her; she produced an evening dress from somewhere – though I am sure it had not gone to Tibet with us – and my father his dinner jacket. In my best school suit, and Jane in her best dress, off we went to dinner with the Maharajah. He and his second daughter Kula were charming and smiling, as always. They only said that they were very glad to see us, and remarked that the snow had fallen very early that year.

We paid a visit to the Residency, but Sir Basil had gone and, with him, all the objects which had made that house so unique. Without them it suddenly looked dull, forlorn, even official. Only the servants in their scarlet, braided coats and straw hats with peacock feathers were the same. I think that was really where the long farewell to India started. We had already, almost inadvertently, said goodbye to Darjeeling. Now we said goodbye to Gangtok and to Sikkim, as we crossed the border at Rangpo. But the worst was yet to come. We had to say goodbye to Pansen, whom we had known for four years and who had calmly arranged all our erratic travels, including this last one, with his never-failing smile.

There was a branch of the Darjeeling Himalayan Railway to a place called Gielle Khola in the Tista Valley, on the other side of the river from the road to Kalimpong. And here our farewell took place. Pansen's English about matched our Hindustani, Jane's and mine, but the blend of smiles and tears on both sides needed no words. We got into the little train that would take us to Siliguri. He got into the bus that would take him to Darjeeling and, of course, we never saw him again.

DOROTHY MARGARET BAKER

My father died in Ootacamund in 1945, so my mother took a job in the Lovedale School Hospital with my aunt. They had both been allowed, against all odds, to take nursing training after leaving school. I left school in early 1946 and took a job for six months as a governess to two children on a tea plantation, who were spending time with their parents before being sent to boarding schools in England, and I then joined my mother in Lovedale while my sister completed her schooling and took her exams. My feeling that Lovedale was 'home' was reinforced during this period, but we all realised that in an independent India there would be no place for three nearly penniless English women, so we came back to Britain for good.

ANN MARINDIN

We returned to Bombay, where my sister was born, and to Burmah Shell, who had been so supportive during the War, making up the Army pay my father received to the same salary he had had in the company. Just before we left we had our usual hot-weather holiday in Kashmir. The Gulmarg Pony Club was run by a fierce lady called Di Beer; she was a colonel's wife. There I learned to ride. She was a marvellous teacher and her lessons stood me in good stead later when I joined a pony club in England. I still have my badge of the Gulmarg Pony Club. We children of Gulmarg were not very popular with the golfers: rather than hack around the course we used to ride slap-across the greens, and many an angry Army officer would wave his golf club at us. I remember my brother in his best party-clothes landing in a dead cow, splosh, when his pony refused to jump a ditch in the middle of the golf course.

When people ask, 'Where were you when the European War ended?', I can say in Kashmir, at Gulmarg. My mother said that 'The War in Europe is over, which is wonderful, but you must not forget that we are still at war with Japan.' This made a great impression on me.

We went back to Bombay to pack up and go home. We lived then in the married quarters of a very old, established Club called the Byculla, which had been a strict men-only Club until the middle of the War. While living there, I remember getting up early and riding before breakfast, *chota-hazri*, and rats coming up the loo-bend and being flushed away.

We packed up for England, leaving a tearful Ayah and stoic Lattif, both of whom I did not see again until I was 17. Our dog, Frederick, was shot, and I was made to leave my very large doll, Christine, behind – I now see her, or something very like her, on the *Antiques Roadshow* every Sunday.

We all – Mother, Father, myself, brother and sister – embarked, with my sister's *dhooli*, on the SS *Strathmore*, no Ayah, no Lattif, and had a small two-berth cabin and the 14th Army, the Forgotten Army. They were so many that they had to be brought up on deck in shifts for fresh air. We children were so spoilt by these men, who had not seen their own families for so long: Mars Bars, games and singsongs; and I saw *Sweet Rosie O'Grady* 14 times in the cinema – the only film on board, and it took so long for all to see it. *Topees* were thrown overboard after Suez, and then we were in Southampton and meeting our relatives. I met a new aunt on the boat train and had my first taste of milk, so creamy and delicious after the milk of India, and at last we were at Waterloo, where two ladies (still alive at 96 and 86) bounded over the luggage calling wildly to their sister, my mother, who they had not seen for seven-and-a-half years. The

London flat was cold, with no meat and the cottage in the country with oil lamps. I ask, 'Shall I make my own bed?' and my six-year-old brother stands waiting to be dressed. My mother's hands bleeding from wringing nappies. She had never cooked or done housework before. Then off for Christmas in Devon in a large house, with new cousins and uncles returning from the War to an austere post-war life, and no Ayah or Lattif. We just got on with it.

LAURENCE FLEMING

As my father had now retired he was, more or less, a displaced person. His job was being done by someone else; the house that went with the job was occupied by someone else. In previous times the polite thing was to 'get on the next boat', but this, in early 1945, was not so easy. However, arriving in Calcutta from our adventure in Tibet, we found ourselves invited to New Delhi to stay at the Viceroy's House. The Wavells had once stayed in Digboi, and Lord Wavell had been there on at least one occasion by himself.

The Viceroy's House was a large, rectangular block, three storeys high, with a circular throne-room in the middle, the whole height of the building under a dome. At each corner of the building there was a block, more or less square, separate from each other but joined to the main block. On the top floor of one of these, looking over the garden, we found ourselves. We went up in a lift, though there were also some stairs. A huge marble-floored corridor faced us. To the left, my parents each had a bedroom with a circular sitting room between them. To the right, and after a right-angled bend, Jane and I had bedrooms opposite each other. Our sitting room, where we had all our meals except when summoned to 'the presence', was next to Jane's room as one turned the corner.

They were, of course, the most luxuriously furnished bedrooms I had ever seen, though I realise now that it was really the best kind of hotel furniture of the time, such as The Dorchester or Claridge's might have had. We each had a bathroom and a separate loo, with a handle that pulled up – which did surprise me – and a crown on each sheet of lavatory paper, very fine Bronco. The soap was similarly stamped. There were bearers all over the place. Our clothes disappeared as soon as we took them off. Our shoes were cleaned; and, as we sat together at supper that first night, in the sitting room of the family of Mr and Mrs W. Fleming, we were visited by a very nice housekeeper called Mrs White, who wanted to know what our favourite foods were. As I don't think we had ever been asked this question before, I am not sure how helpful our replies were.

JANE FLEMING

While we were staying in the Viceroy's house, I wrote part of a letter every day to our dearest Ruth, Ruth Dear, who was by now back in England having accompanied four motherless children on the voyage. She kept the letter, and so here is most of it.

Dearest Ruth

I am starting this letter from the beginning of our stay here. Arriving on 28 January at nine o'clock at night. We arrived at Delhi station up to time. There was an ADC to meet us. He had one of the Viceroy's cars, so we all got in. The luggage all came behind in a lorry. When we got into the house, we were absolutely amazed the rooms that we had were all single but quite big enough for a double, or even a treble bedroom. I will try and draw a plan of my bedroom. I think the others are too difficult. They are lovely bedrooms. There is nothing in them that looks as if it was Indian except the fan, which you cannot help. Anyway we had all had supper because we had been told the train was late and was not going to arrive until ten o'clock. It was due at nine or half past but it made up. (I am sorry, I have tried to do a drawing of my room and I can't but I will ask Laurie to.) Well, we settled down for a good night's sleep and we all slept very well.

I did ask Laurence to help me, and a plan resulted on a very indifferent piece of paper, marked 'MSV 141', whatever that means. 'Sorry the paper isn't better, but it would have been a waste of the other', is my comment round the edge of the plan. The 'other' was, of course, the beautiful – I should think hand-made – writing-paper with 'The Viceroy's House, New Delhi' engraved in the top right-hand corner. The plan reveals that there were two enormous carpets, their colours not noted, and that the curtains were patterned with exotic birds not quite sitting on their nests, in blue, pink and green on a pink background. The door was in one corner, with the bed diagonally opposite it. There was a fireplace, but I don't remember a fire being lighted in it. My letter continued:

29 January. Next morning, I put on my yellow skirt, the one you gave me. We had breakfast, then Laurie and me went to look round the gardens. But we were stopped by the police, because we hadn't a pass. So we went back and got one. And at the same time were told that we were having lunch with Lord and Lady Wavell; we were thrilled. When they came along, we all shuffled into line. Lord Wavell came first. He came along the line and shook hands. The men (and boys) had to bow, and women and girls had to curtsey to both of them. Mummy and I only did a bob curtsey, which struck me as being rather odd, but suppose it's not. We started lunch and it began to rain. But we didn't go in, we finished lunch and then went in. After it stopped raining Miss Wavell took Laurie, Mummy and me shopping. I got an Arthur Ransome book called *Swallows and Amazons*. After that we came back and had tea. Daddy and Mummy went out to dinner, so Laurie and I had supper in our sitting room, as usual.

30 January. We got up and got dressed. I put on my grey skirt and coat: it is a new one, and very nice. We went to lunch with Colonel Rose, then we went to the Red Fort, it is a fairly new one. Because there was water, and underneath it were all sorts of coloured stones. And the floors and ceilings were lovely too, with their coloured stones. Then we came back and had tea, supper and then bed.

LAURENCE FLEMING

We had luncheon on the terrace on two days, and we were introduced on the first one. 'I don't think I have met your family,' said Lord Wavell to my father, and then passed on. We bowed, we curtseyed. Lady Wavell smiled, that wonderful *burra memsahib*'s smile, and said nothing. As the youngest male I was served last. Lady Wavell did not linger over her food and, as soon as she had finished, everyone else's plate was swept away. On the first occasion there was, in any case, nothing on the plate when it was offered to me; but on the second I had the good fortune to sit next to two of the ADCs, who engaged me in conversation about Darjeeling, Sikkim and Tibet. I am not sure that 15-year-old boys are very interesting, but they allowed me to feel that I was; and, when we were served, at last, they just said, 'Now just stop talking and eat.' I think we all managed to finish. It was one of them, the Earl of Euston, who showed us round the house. All the ADCs were recovering from war wounds.

The garden of the Viceroy's House was entirely artificial, squares with stone surrounds, planted that season with petunias, either purple or white. There was a large circular flower garden, arranged in tiers like the Dutch Garden at Hampton Court, and all the trees were clipped. We were allowed to roam wherever we liked, but our most satisfying activity was playing hide and seek on the roof.

JANE FLEMING

31 January: I put on my yellow skirt again, and we had breakfast. Then we went to lunch again with Mrs Peace. Were you there when they were in Digboi, with the lovely big Alsatian, Myra? Myra has died, but they have her daughter, her daughter's puppies, and they have her grandson. The daughter's name is Kate, and the grandson, Abdul. Mr Peace is in Calcutta. After we had lunch, Mr Armstrong took us to another court – it was a lovely one, all sorts of passages. Then we came back, and three American girls were coming to tea, so we had tea, Mummy took the girls round the house and garden, and Laurie and I took Daddy and Mr Armstrong to the Dome. Then supper, bed.

1 February 1945: I woke up after a fairly good night's sleep and put on my grey coat and skirt. Then Mummy, Laurie and I all went to the Purana Kila, which means 'Old Fort'. Then we came back and Daddy took photos of the garden. Now I am upstairs in my room writing to you. Tomorrow we go to Agra. I am now on the day that I am living in. We are going to have lunch with 'Their Ex's', so Mummy and I have to do a curtsey not a bob, and Laurie and Daddy have to nod. They do not bow.

I wonder who all these people were? My brother thinks the Peaces had something to do with the railways. Colonel Rose was an American, previously stationed near Digboi, and involved in the Ledo Road. He had got to know our parents very well. It was he who was to arrange our transport to Agra, most probably at the expense of the American people. The 'three American girls' were either nurses, or in the Army, and one of them, Miss Severn, escorted us to Agra. Mr Armstrong was a very old friend from the Burmah Oil Company in Calcutta.

2 February: Everything went right. The car arrived, with one of the American girls. She was coming to Agra to see the Taj Mahal, and going back the same day. Well anyway, we started off. The journey wasn't bad, not dusty. Soon we reached Agra, went straight to 'Laurie's hotel', had lunch then went to the main thing, the Taj Mahal. It was the most marvellous place. The screen round the graves of the two people used to be pure gold, with all the other stones in it. But they took it down for fear of theft. But I should think they still have it locked away somewhere. We couldn't stay long, as Miss Severn was going back the same day. We talked to the man in charge, and he said the moon would be up by twelve. So when we went back to the hotel, we saw Miss Severn off and made the arrangement for a tonga. And the night watchman was to call Daddy, and then he would call Mummy and me. (I won't try and draw the Taj, because it would be an insult.) This all went well. The tonga arrived. We all got up again (it was 11 o'clock) dressed, put on coats. And then snuggled into the tonga, Laurie and me in front and Daddy and Mummy behind. We soon got to the Taj Mahal. The moon wasn't quite up yet so we waited. After a bit we saw one of the world's most beautiful things by moonlight.

3 February: It was two when we got into bed. And we all slept soundly till quarter past nine. Mummy had breakfast in bed, so Laurie, Daddy and I all rushed into breakfast. After breakfast, Mummy and Daddy went to see a doctor about a vaccination. He said he would do it tomorrow. Then we went to lunch at the airport, with a friend of Colonel Rose's friends. American. After lunch we went round the airport, it was very interesting. We saw many planes take off and land. Then we came home, and had a sleep, and tea. There are two dogs who I constantly play with, that's all I have to do.

4 February: Today we went to Fatehpur Sikri. It is an absolutely marvellous place. There is a tomb of a saint in it. The story is that Akbar

very much wanted a son. So he went to a holy man and asked him what he should do. The holy man said to bring his wife near him. But nobody really knows the answer he really gave Akbar. Anyway soon he had a son, and in celebration he built this little city. In this place he put the tomb of this holy man. It was a very beautiful place. The actual place where he was buried was lovely, with a mother-of-pearl covering. It was beautiful. I was sight-stricken. After we had seen everything, we came back home. Rested in the garden, and had tea. And now I am writing to you. Tomorrow we are going to see the fort, and the next day we go back to Calcutta to collect our luggage and take it over to Bombay, and then go to Pachmarhi, which is the place Mummy and Daddy had their honeymoon.

5 February: We went to Akbar's Tomb this morning, and the fort. The fort was nice, but Akbar's Tomb was very boring. Akbar was the man who built Fatehpur Sikri. He built part of his tomb, and then thought it so hideous that he pulled it down. He left only the main gate and one lamp that Akbar had had made. The gate was lovely, but the main tomb was very gloomy. The fort had a lot of lovely things. We crossed a bit of a drawbridge. There is a story that one of the kings jumped on his horse from a very high wall of the fort. And his horse was half in the ditch and half on the road. He cut the middle of the horse with his very sharp knife. And now there is a statue of the head of the horse. Akbar also had a favourite horse and there is a statue of it over its grave. I have had to start more paper, as the paper I brought from V. House is finished. Tomorrow we go, and tomorrow I send this letter off to you.

LAURENCE FLEMING

We went back to Calcutta and were sent on to Bombay, told it would be at least three months before a passage could be found; and so my parents decided to spend those three months in Pachmarhi, where they had spent their honeymoon. We stayed in the same hotel, now called the Pachmarhi Hotel rather than the Hill Hotel, but I hardly suppose that anything had been altered in those 17 years.

It was a fourth kind of magic for me; not the green, smiling acres of Assam, or the sheer tree-covered mountains of Sikkim and Darjeeling, or the embroidered, jewelled buildings of Delhi and Agra. Here was a dry, undulating tableland to be bicycled over. Then one hid one's bicycle under a bush and descended, perhaps even a thousand feet, down a steep cliff face, to where, even in February and March, streams still flowed. They had been given faintly laughable names, Fairy Pool, Pansy Pool, Irene Pool, Duchess Falls, Waters Meet; but nothing could impair the charm of the places themselves, and we visited them as often as we could. At the bottom of the rift it was cool and shady, the sun falling on the water perhaps only at midday. But one had to be back up at the top before the sun set, because of the panthers.

I remember the flag at Government House flying at half-mast for Franklin D. Roosevelt. Then, all too soon, we were given a week to get to Bombay. We embarked in the morning, all my father's luggage from his 25 years coming with us. There was such a crush to get on board that we didn't manage to say goodbye to Rahman, who had been with my father for the whole of those 25 years. In some way my suitcase was taken right down to the hold, and when I retrieved it

Laurence and Jane Fleming at Fairy Pool, Pachmarhi. March 1945.

and got back up to the fresh air again, we had sailed. I rushed up on deck to say goodbye to India, to blow it a kiss if nothing else. But it had gone. I stood there, almost crying. 'I will come back,' I said; but I did not do so for 28 years.

The *Winchester Castle* was converted as a troopship. My father and I shared the tourist dining saloon with some 200 other males; my mother and sister shared one first class cabin with ten other females. We spent VE Day at Port Said, but were not allowed to go ashore. I remember being surprised at how drunk people could get on one pint of beer, which was the ration. In the Mediterranean something went wrong with the engine and we limped into Gibraltar, where it was put right. We left Gibraltar in a magnificent convoy, perhaps the last ever to leave there, of first-class passenger liners. I remember the *Caernarvon Castle* and the *Samaria* as our neighbours. We sailed to the Clyde, spending three days anchored off Gourock. Then we sailed up to King George's Dock, with those amazing green fields apparently six inches away – not at all like the Suez Canal – and disembarked in a gentle drizzle.

As we left the ship, we were given a white paper bag with picnic food in it. Food rationing was strictly in force at the time. About two hours later, seated on top of our mountain of luggage at Glasgow Central Station, we decided to open those bags. After a very short while, I heard Jane saying to me, rather indignantly, 'I thought you said that people in Britain didn't stare as they do in Tibet.' I looked up. We were sharing an orange and were the centre of attention. It was probably four years since anyone at Glasgow Central Station had seen an orange.

JOHN LETHBRIDGE

Those of us boys who were evacuated to India from England in 1940 and were still in India on their eighteenth birthday normally had to enlist in the armed forces. This could be a very stressful change, from an easy, pampered lifestyle, to the rigours of an Army barrack-room, perhaps not as hard as it would have been in England, because even privates in a British regiment in India would share a bearer between three or four of themselves. This servant would do many of their chores, such as polishing their brass and keeping their equipment clean. However, I was one of a number of English boys who had a rather more gradual and perhaps easier introduction to military life.

At the age of 16, after passing my School Certificate at The New School in Darjeeling, I was sent to the Prince of Wales Royal Indian Military College (RIMC) at Dehra Dun. This was a school started by the British to inculcate military virtues in Indian boys from the age of about 12 so that they would become good officer material by the age of 18. The boys wore Army uniform and had to salute the masters, who were almost all Oxford or Cambridge graduates, and often Blues as well. In 1941 it had been decided at GHQ in Delhi that 30 English boys could be admitted, and so a 'Wavell section' had been formed.

The teaching and facilities were of a very high standard, so it would have been possible for me to have taken my Higher School Certificate there, but being fascinated by the Army – probably unwisely after one term in the HSC form – I elected to join the Army class. The only academic subjects we studied there were English language and Urdu. The rest of the time we spent on weapon training, fieldcraft, infantry tactics, map reading, arms drill and learning how to instruct in these subjects. Like the rest of the college, we had a tremendous amount of exercise: physical training every morning except Sundays, and PT or games every afternoon, including Sundays. After two years I was certainly physically fit, and almost up to the standard of Sergeant Instructor in military training.

Near our eighteenth birthdays, the military authorities allowed us cadets to attend a War Office selection board for selection, if we were suitable, for training as officers without having first served in the ranks, which was the normal rule. I was fortunate in passing and being selected to be trained for a commission in the royal engineers. I then went home on holiday to Calcutta to spend Christmas with my parents. Early in 1945, I was instructed to report to Fort William to formally enlist in the Army. After doing this I was told to go back home and wait until my course was due to start. This was preliminary infantry training at the Indian Military Academy (IMA) in Dehra Dun. It was not very different from the RIMC, except that we were paid and that many of the other gentleman cadets were a good deal older, having already served for some time in the Army. Very little of the instruction was new to me and we had servants to look after our kit, so the life was relatively easy, except that the Coldstream Guards Regimental Sergeant Major required a rather higher standard of drill than any of us had been accustomed to before. VE Day occurred before the course was finished, and our company, having the highest standard of drill, was initially selected to carry the flags of the United Nations 20 miles through Delhi on the Victory Parade. Fortunately the iron law of seniority prevailed, and the most senior company had the honour. Shortly afterwards those of us who were going into the Engineers were told that we would miss the last few weeks of the course so that we could join a new course at the Engineer Officers Training School (EOTS) at Kirkee near Poona.

The EOTS was attached to the Bombay Sappers and Miners, who provided the instructors. Life, although strenuous at times, was much more easygoing with less formality than that at the IMA, which was modelled on Sandhurst. Our course was the last one at the school, and we numbered about thirty officer cadets. In eight months we skimmed over most of the activities of military engineers. We also endured a course of so-called 'battle inoculation', in which live rounds were fired near us as we charged up hills and through barbed wire at supposed enemy positions. The climax of the course was a period of jungle training to prepare us for Burma; this was held further south near the border with Goa. The camp was on a beautiful river in which the water was so pure it did not require treatment before being fit for drinking. It was most enjoyable, especially as the snakes and wild animals seemed more afraid of us that we were of them. Before the course was finished the Japanese surrendered, so we knew we would not have to fight in Burma. In January 1946 we were commissioned as officers, and I heard that I was to be attached to the King George the Fifth's Own Bengal Sappers and Miners at Roorkee, about 100 miles from Delhi.

PATRICIA RAYNES

The Hallett War School had closed in December 1944, and my father had joined the Army General Staff in Calcutta prior to returning to Burma. My mother, younger sister Jill and I were waiting to get a passage home to England – it took months, and we sat and waited in Indore. Finally, the letter came in June 1945 – we were to go down immediately to Bombay to catch the ship. We were told we had to get permits to take several items we owned out with us, such as a Kashmiri table lamp – why, I still don't know! I have vivid memories of waiting hours in various offices and being sent on to yet another one, walking through crowded, dirty streets filled with beggars, but we finally triumphed. After five days we were told to go to the docks to board the *Johann van Oldenbarnevelt*. She had been the crack liner of the Dutch Navy before the War, but had not had a thing done to her in five years, including her engines being overhauled, and we kept breaking down in mid-ocean. As the Japanese War was still on, we were sitting ducks for any lurking submarine. We were on board early, which was just as well, as we discovered each cabin contained twenty women and children, in rows of bunks – with half the underneath of the lower bunk for one case, plus a six-inch shelf over the bunk. We managed to get spaces by the portholes, which was a boon on hot tropical nights. There were about six hundred women and children on board, and the rest of the ship was packed with troops. There were two baths for every two hundred people, and a large washroom with drainage holes in the floor – every evening the first contingent using it was the children – all filthy from the very dirty ship and heat, and then mothers followed suit later – you poured water over yourself as a makeshift shower.

When we got to Port Sudan, the engines ceased yet again, and we sat there for about four days – gazing at the shore, for we were not allowed to disembark, and it was terribly hot, without the benefit of any sea breeze. However, they obviously did a more reliable job on the engines there, as once in the Mediterranean, we did not break down again.

We finally reached Southampton on a dark and rainy day, to be met by my uncle and taken to stay with him and my aunt. We had to queue once again for food and clothing coupons, and then try and find some warm clothes for winter. We were going to boarding school in September. As far as I can recollect it was warm and sunny that summer, and we spent a lot of time in the garden – without having to wear a *topee*! Winter was a different matter though, and I spent my days coughing and spluttering, with chilblains on my fingers and toes. It was a far cry from the heat of the plains of India.

SHIRLEY POCOCK

In the early summer of 1945 the European War was over, but the War with Japan dragged on. As a priority was required to get a passage home, and I didn't qualify, I advertised and got a job as a nanny to an RAF family with a two-and-a-half-month-old boy. His mother had been ill, hence their permission to take me. There was only one other family on board, with two small boys and a nanny like myself. The fathers had berths a long way from us, and we four women and three children were given a converted passageway as a cabin – dreadfully hot and uncomfortable. My job was particularly difficult, as the mother of the baby was mentally unstable and the father couldn't help except on deck.

The ship had been tied up in the dock for ten days, and when we got on board it was red-hot. There was nothing to sit on on deck except our life-jackets, which we had to keep with us at all times for fear of drifting mines. This was an RAF troopship and very overcrowded. The men had a hard time amusing themselves during the three-week voyage, and I remember them daring each other to climb in and out of portholes! We docked at Greenock and I somehow made my way to London, where my erstwhile holiday-home friends had a new home. I had not been able to tell them the date of arrival but they greeted me, after five years, as though I had never been away.

I decided to go to Pitman's Secretarial College in Southampton Row to learn shorthand and typing properly. Most of the other students were young wives who were going to have to support their demobbed husbands while they went back to university, or young widows who needed to find work. We used to queue at a British Restaurant for a three-course lunch costing a shilling and sixpence, one-and-six. Sometimes the smell of the monotonous food was too much and we blew the whole one-and-six on a slice of lemon meringue pie at Fuller's across the way.

In the following years I had several secretarial jobs, in the City, in commerce and in the film industry. After Independence in 1947 my parents, with my sister and her family, left India for England. My ex-fiance, who had been in the Gurkhas, came home; we got engaged again and should have been married that year. Everything seemed fine until ten days before the wedding, when my mother worried that I looked so unhappy. When I asked her what I could do at such a late hour she replied, 'What late hour? You can get right up to the altar and still say "No!"' The wedding was called off.

PAMELA ALBERT

On 15 August, the War was over – it was VJ Day, but four months too late for me. The US had dropped the atomic bombs on Hiroshima and Nagasaki. A Victory Parade was held and we all marched with an unusually happy pace down Chowringhee. We were all very anxious to find out when we were to be demobbed, and began closing some of our various departments. There was no need for gunnery now, thank God.

Audrey and Arthur were married on 14 November. I was one of the bridesmaids. By 19 December, I was demobbed and on my way to Multan to be with my father to await repatriation home.

NANETTE BOYCE

We were in New Delhi when the bomb was dropped on Hiroshima.

A Victory Parade was held in New Delhi to commemorate the cease of hostilities, to honour those who had fought and survived and to remember those who had not. A seemingly endless column marched down the Vista that led to and from the Viceroy's House. Gurkhas who had won so many Victoria Crosses, Punjabis, Pathans, Mahrattas, Gujuratis, Sikhs, Punjabi Mussulmans, Bombay Sappers and Miners, Cavalry regiments now mechanised, The Mountain Artillery, possibly with a mule as a mascot.

The parade was followed by a searchlight Tattoo. An unforgettable spectacle with the great red wall of the Red Fort with its magnificent gates as the backdrop. No matter that no longer was the Palace attired in its rich silk awnings. No matter that English lawns now replaced the Moghul gardens. Flames of the fires flickered on the flashing swords of the Pathan dancers in their heavily embroidered waistcoats. In almost eerie contrast, a musical ride by the Bikaner Camel Corps. A salute from the Indian Air Force crossing the barriers of time. An offering of peace and gratitude from the length and breadth of India. Sadly, a peace that was so soon to be broken with the train riots.

ANN MITCHELL

In 1942 my father was transferred to Meerut, where the 'Quit India' campaign was in full swing. There was an armed Police sentry guarding the house at night, and when we came home after dark, it was exciting to be challenged, 'Halt! Who goes there?' and to think we might be shot or bayoneted if we did not give the correct answer, 'Friend,' to which came the reassuring reply, 'Pass, friend: all is well.'

My father had his office in a part of the house with a separate verandah where the *mulacartis* waited to see him. These were villagers or townsfolk with any sort of grievance. The cookhouse was a separate building ruled over by the *khansama* and aided by the *masalchi* in the preparation of vegetables and the washing up. The food when carried from the cookhouse by the *khitmagar* was sometimes stolen by kites on the way. On the dining room verandah was a big *dhooli*, or meatsafe, with its feet in saucers of water to keep the ants out.

My favourite was the *khitmagar*, who had been with my mother since before her marriage. Like all Indian servants he spoiled me, and also intrigued me because he had an extra thumb on one hand, which he said was very useful when carrying plates.

The fact that there were so many servants is always a mystery to people who have not lived in India. In fact, the number of servants depended on the rank of the *sahib*, and when he was promoted, the number of servants would naturally be increased accordingly – if not, the *sahib* would lose face. Included in the large compound were the servants' quarters, where they lived with their families, the stables and various godowns or storerooms.

There was a well at the bottom of the garden with a banked-up mud slope on one side, up which walked the patient bullocks drawing water for the garden, the house and the servants. As the War dragged on, petrol was rationed, and so my mother adopted one of the rescued pack ponies from the SPCA home which she ran, and we trained him to pull a small basket-trap for errands and short visits. Friends who lived nearby also had a small pony, and we used to have races over small mud-jumps until the ponies had enough and tipped us off.

In the Meerut District too, my father went out into the villages on tours of inspection. Independence was approaching, and the villagers were uneasy; they would implore him to stay in India and look after them. They feared they would all be massacred – the Hindu villagers by the Muslim villagers and vice versa. We hoped to the end that Partition would not happen, or at least not too quickly. Gandhi was against it, but the Government in London, as so often happened, would not listen to the men who had worked all their lives in India, knew the problems and tried to prevent the communal riots wherever they began, and to calm down the hatred stoked by the politicians. After 1947 the British officers in the Indian Police had to leave India, and the villagers' fears became a reality.

In October 1945 my mother took me back to England once again to finish school. It was difficult to get passages, and we sailed on a troopship, a Cunarder built for the Atlantic crossing, without fans, blowers or porthole scoops, and very little deck space. We had a two-berth cabin, but we were eight in it. The hundreds of troops being repatriated lived in much worse conditions. The heat was terrible. The CO who ran the ship was a tyrant, issuing orders all day on the tannoy and treating the civilians like criminals. The soldiers called it the 'Belsen ship'. But we were going 'home'.

My father remained until August 1947, and my mother went back to join him. They eventually had the sad task of overseeing the destruction of all our animals, as there was no one left to give them a good home. To our *khitmagar* and his family they gave a *tonga* and a pony, so they could escape if they had to, and also a sum of money. He and all his family survived.

ISABEL DAVIDSON

Back to Digboi from Darjeeling and by road to the main railway line past the falls of the Puggla Jhora (waterfall). Visits to Pengaree.

The Durga Puja – the festival of the Goddess Durga. The statue of the goddess after various rituals and processions finally went down to the river, and the statue was thrown into the water.

The boys of the village dived in after it to retrieve the crown, bringing good luck to the village. The Diwali Festival of Lights, all round the houses of the villagers. Tiny oil lamps or candles all round the windows, very beautiful to look at.

The journey across India for days and visits to the Grand Hotel in Calcutta and the Great Eastern, culminating finally in 1945, after a tearful farewell with my beloved bearer, who I did not realise I would never see again. We sailed from Bombay after a wonderful two-day stay in the Taj Mahal Hotel. We shared a suite of rooms with two other ladies and their children. The bathroom was huge, with an enormous black-marble bath right in the middle of it. I was very impressed.

My last thought of India was throwing my *topee* over the side of the ship – this I did not want to do, but it was the 'done thing' for people going 'home'. I, as a child, was not going home – I was home!

We sailed from Bombay on the troopship *Strathaird* in 1945. This time we went through the Suez Canal, and I remember seeing the statue of Ferdinand de Lesseps, the Frenchman who engineered the whole project. This tiny waterway and the huge liner sailing through. Once it could almost touch the banks on either side.

We sailed home in convoy. The *Strathaird* was in the middle row behind the leading ship, zig-zagging our way across the oceans to avoid torpedoes. Our arrival in Britain was quite a disappointment to me – everything seemed so grey! But it was in winter, and wartime! I did miss the colour and sun of India.

BETSY VICKERS

To arrive in the Vale of Kashmir was to be reborn. Behind lay the hot dry plains of the Deccan, where the temperature had crept up to 103 degrees in the shade, and everywhere was dry and colourless. The brainfever bird had been repeating its monotonous note, so it was time to escape to somewhere cooler. On the 2nd of April 1945, we headed for Kashmir, stopping *en route* to visit Agra, Delhi and the Golden Temple at Amritsar. A week later, after getting on and off trains and in and out of *tongas*, we arrived at Rawalpindi station, where my mother and I spent the night in the ladies first-class waiting-room sleeping on couches, whilst my Father balanced himself on a table in the men's. During the night some kind Indian lady had put her shawl over me, for it was cold in 'Pindi.

The next morning we boarded a bus for Srinagar, almost two hundred miles away. As it was not the middle of April, this trip had to take two days for the roads were tortuous and liable to landslips. We were not in the super bus, as used by most of the Europeans, but an ordinary Indian one, piled high with luggage and livestock and full of friendly inquisitive travellers, no doubt wondering what three whites were doing on their bus.

Kashmir was a native state with a Muslim population ruled by a Hindu Maharajah, so there was strict control on the import of any forms of beef, the cow being sacred. At the border between India and Kashmir there was a customs post at Domel where luggage was likely to be searched for any beef product. Marmite was permissible, being vegetable, but Oxo or Bovril were not. On one trip we discovered that we had inadvertently taken into the state a tin of K rations which contained beef, so by dead of night we slipped it furtively into the lake.

The Super Bus was always met by a seemingly riotous throng of cut-throats, who were merely touts trying to make one hire their particular houseboat, but by arrived in the Mail Bus we did not have this trouble. A British Army hospital matron, who arrived on the Super Bus was surrounded by such a crowd. She looked up to one particularly villainous face and asked, 'Are you the man from Paradise?' That was the agency through which she had booked her boat.

The next day my father and I inspected seven houseboats and decided on the *Dar es Salaam*. The houseboats were extremely comfortable, with a porch, a sitting room, dining room, several bedrooms, each with its own bathroom, and a flat roof where a canopy could be put up. All the internal doors were sliding, and the tin tubs hung on a nearby tree when not in use, so there was more room in the bathroom. The boats were beautifully carved, and smelt of new wood. An attendant cookboat was moored alongside, where meals were cooked and the staff lived. I cannot remember the cook, but the owner and manager was Dundoo, a likeable and obliging youngish man with a damaged hand. He kept a wary eye on us, shooed off the most persistent of the hawkers and gave us advice. His younger brother, Sultan, waited at table and cleaned the boat. Both were bright and cheerful, and greatly added to the pleasure of our stay. Each houseboat was snugly fitted into a *nullah*, a mooring space between two spits of land, hence the handy trees for tin tubs and cycles. We had our own taxi *shikara*, *The Prince of Wales*, which was at our beck and call for as long as we wanted. When not in use, the paddlers sat in the back patiently gossiping and smoking their *hookahs*.

The taxi *shikara* is an elegant, punt-like boat with a roof, embroidered cushions and coloured curtains, propelled by men using heart-shaped paddles. Some had very strange names, *Bup, Bup I'm a Jup, Green Garden*, and so on. The houseboats, too, had names. *The Silver Bell* was moored along side us, HMS *Pinafore*, *The Viceroy*, *The Moghul Gardens* and *The Merryfield* were further along the serried ranks of boats. One soon got to know one's neighbours. On a nearby boat was an officer of the Black Watch. We knew what kind of a night he had had, for next morning his kilt would be hanging out to dry on the roof of his boat. I'm sure the cold night waters of the Dal soon made him sober!

The *Dar es Salaam* was moored on the Dal Lake, a beautiful clear spring-fed lake overlooked by a 1000-feet hill, Takht-i-Suliman, the Throne of Solomon, on which stands an ancient Hindu temple and by a 500-feet hill crowned by Hari Parbat, a fort build by Akbar the Great. Everyone should climb Takht-i-Suliman at least once, preferably before breakfast. Below lies the Dal Lake, covering some 12 square miles, the river Jhelum, whose twists and turns are said to have inspired the famous Paisley pattern, the city of Srinagar with its earthen, flower-covered roofs and beyond, the mountains and snows of the Pir Punjal.

Most of the merchants had their emporiums down by Third Bridge, there then being seven bridges across the Jhelum. From the Dal Lake we had to go through a lock to reach the Jhelum. We always seemed to be stuck next to a boat piled high with every kind of vegetable. Once on the river we passed many boats where the ordinary Kashmiri boatmen lived with their families. These looked very stuffy and uncomfortable, wooden boats with matting as roofing. The home and shops of the richer people were picturesque but vulnerable in a

above The Prince of Wales, the taxi shikara hired for three months in 1945 by the Vickers family.

below A travelling shop in Kashmir, 1945. (Betsy Vickers)

country where earthquakes are fairly common. The wooden upper-storeys with carved balconies and pretty windows jutted out over the river at crazy angles, as if a mad builder had been at work. Being in a minor earthquake whilst asleep on a houseboat is an interesting experience. I shot out of bed saying, 'It's an earthquake,' for the boat was slapping on the water. Not unexpectedly, a few houses did fall down, as they are often much wider at the top than at the bottom.

Near Third Bridge is the graceful wooden Shah Hamadan Mosque, with its stepped roof and pointed spire. Earth and grass covered the roof, which in spring was ablaze with hundreds of scarlet Kashmiri tulips. It was so photogenic, but alas, on our return in 1965, the tulips had gone and a silvery roof was there instead. Maybe like the spires of some of the Hindu temples the silvery roof was only a covering of beaten, yet gleaming old kerosene oil tins! Third Bridge was always busy, for along its length newly washed *numdahs* were hung to dry. Not the puny ones seen in our shops today, but thicker ones made from wool from Yarkand.

Usually, my father had only three weeks' holiday a year, but as he had been in India since before the War and had missed his furlough in England, to which he was entitled after three years service, he was taking a longer holiday in Kashmir instead, and was able to stay in Srinagar until the middle of June, when he left for a conference in Calcutta. My mother and I stayed until the end of June.

My father loved to fish, whether it was in the big, wide wells in the rice fields, by a small river surrounded by granite boulders on the Deccan, where we used to hear panthers calling at dusk, or on the Dal Lake. Shortly after arriving, we bought fishing licences. Every now and then a man came round in his skiff to check the licences. There would then be a scurrying of illegal rods being hidden. Where mulberry trees overhung the lake, the fish had acquired a taste for the fruit. Such a difficult bait to keep on a hook when casting. The fish were not wasted, for we ate them.

Two of the most beautiful gardens in town were those of the Church of England and the Residency. There was usually a Visitors

Book kept by the sentry on duty at the gate of a Government House or Residency for British people to sign. This formed the basis of one being invited to a garden party or to tea. We attended several functions at the Residency; at one I was detailed to teach some people how to play croquet, a game I had never played before. Two of our very beautiful Hyderabad princesses were present at the garden party, and that marvellous character, Tyndale Biscoe. When he arrived in Srinagar in 1890 to be the headmaster of the Mission School, he was dismayed to find the pupils looking like dirty bundles, unable to swim and unable to do much for fear of breaking their caste. In a town where water, and the danger of drowning, was ever-present, he decided that swim they must, so he introduced a sliding scale of school fees. If the boys had not learned to swim by the age of 16, the fees were doubled, quadrupled at 17 and so on. No doubt many lives were saved, including their own.

I shall never forget the two beautiful springs we spent in Kashmir. The clouds of pink and white fruit-blossom. The unfurling of the *chenar* and willow leaves, the beauty of the spring flowers, Muslim graveyards with stately purple irises, some tall, some miniature and golden fields of mustard – for the Kashmiris did not cook with *ghee*, but with mustard oil. We had a wide choice of fruit; luscious black cherries, warm, ripe apricots and paper-shell walnuts, so called because one could crack them open by crumbling two together in one's hand. I once ate so many apricots that I could not look at another for years.

Nor shall I ever forget the exquisite gardens created by the Moghul Emperors, Nasim Bagh, Nishat Bagh and the Shalimar Bagh. As the weather was getting hot, we decided to have the *Dar es Salaam* poled to Nasim Bagh. It took about two-and-a-half hours, passing many floating gardens. These were created by a wickerwork base with soil on top, on which cucumbers, tomatoes and other water-loving vegetables grew. When the owner wished to move his garden he merely tied bits of grass from two gardens together and then paddled off with them following behind.

Views of Kashmir taken in
1932 and 1940.
(Sheila Wright-Neville)

left Street scene in Srinagar.

below The Fifth Bridge,
Srinagar.

right Shalimar Gardens.

below Dal Lake scene, probably a travelling merchant selling his wares to the holiday people on the moored houseboats.

bottom Sailing on a Kashmir lake.

My favourite garden was Nishat Bagh, set on rising ground overlooking the Dal Lake, with a backdrop of mountains. Fountains played and water tinkled down the central water-course. Clouds of pink and white blossom covered the fruit trees, such a contrast to the dried-up plains. Beautiful spring flowers graced the beds, whilst hoopoes with their long beaks prodded the grass for insects. There are some beautiful birds in Kashmir. My favourites were the bulbuls with their perky crests and yellow patches under their tails, whilst in the south of India, the bulbuls have red patches. The flash of diving, blue kingfishers was fascinating to watch.

The Shalimar Bagh is well-known for its beauty. Reached by a canal almost a mile long, the garden was built on the orders of the Emperor Jehangir. It is backed by Mount Mahadeo. Pansies everywhere, the scent and sight of these flowers always takes me back to the Shalimar. The green lawns were studded with English-type daisies. Playing fountains and cascades, the *chenar* and willows bursting their buds and colourful, sweet-scented flowers all made the garden a welcome escape from the heat of the plains. How the Emperor loved his garden. Sitting in his black-marble pavilion looking on so much freshness and beauty, he is reputed to have said, 'If there be Paradise on earth, it is this, it is this.' How I agree with him!

DESMOND KELLY

In the dark days of May 1942, the British forces had been defeated by the Japanese Army, who had swept through Burma and were now poised to invade my father, Norman Kelly's, territory in the Chin Hills. He had joined the Burma Frontier Service in 1927, and had worked there ever since. Although the enemy seemed unstoppable, against all the odds my father persuaded the Chins to fight with the British. He armed and personally led a group of partisans, the Chin Levies, in a guerrilla campaign. They held the Chin Hills from May 1942 until the Spring of 1943, with the help of the 17th Indian

Division. My father wrote to my mother in India (7.11.42), 'My only object in remaining here is to keep my honour among the Chins you knew and to be able to let Desmond know hereafter the importance of sticking to a task once you have put your hand to the plough.'

My parents were remarkable people. My father could not have done what he did without my mother's inspiration. My father owed his life to the Chin people. They fought alongside him because they knew that he was prepared to risk his life for them. He was awarded the OBE pre-war for his services in Burma. After the War in 1946 he returned to Rangoon to be Additional Secretary to the last Governor of Burma, Sir Reginald Hugh Dorman-Smith.

Vum Khaw Hau, who worked with our father as a stenographer in 1945, was later to become the Burmese Ambassador to Czechoslovakia. While in Prague in 1947 he was awarded a Doctor of Philosophy Degree for his thesis *Profile of a Burma Frontier Man*. His gratitude

A unique occasion. The Kelly family re-united on the steps of Brookhill House, Naini Tal, in 1944. Maeve and Desmond were pupils at The Hallett War School, where their mother was teaching. Their father was on one of his rare short leaves from his very successful subversive activities behind the Japanese lines in Burma.

to my father was immense. This epitomised the relationship my father had with the Chin people. The qualities of integrity, loyalty and duty had served the British Raj well.

We, the last children of the Raj, have been the lucky ones.

JOHN LANGLEY

Upper Haflong was a small community of English, Asians and educated Indians clustered around the southern end of a man-made lake. At the north end was a village composed mainly of plains Indians who provided the staff for the railway offices and workshops. There was a bazaar, the local market place to which the local tribes of Nagas, Cacharis and Kukis gravitated, using it for selling their produce and buying items transported up from the plains.

Haflong also had a convent that catered for Eurasian and young orphaned girls and, since the War began, for refugees from Burma. This required a fairly large staff, and was run by Mother Superior Desmond. But Haflong was also the seat of the Roman Catholic bishop of Chittagong, Monseigneur LePailleur, who had his main residence on the south-east side of the lake.

The lake at Haflong was formed by a dam at its mid-point, and provided a reservoir to serve the community in the dry season, and our bungalow was situated at the south-west tip of the lake.

It was from the verandah that many of us watched a spectacular series of dances performed over and around huge bonfires on the tennis courts to celebrate VJ Day. The dances were performed by some of the head-hunting clans of the Naga tribes, who lived about 80 miles from us. They had been brought in by train by an English lady, Ursula Violet Graham Bower, MBE, known as the 'Queen of the Nagas'. She had lived in a rough *basha* (wood and thatched-roof open-sided dwelling) during 1943 and 1944, two days' march from the nearest township, and organised the Naga tribesmen against the Japs, establishing a chain of observation posts which gave the 14th Army a valuable intelligence service. She was largely responsible for their fighting on our side against the Japanese. Father told us that when the Nagas arrived at the station to catch the special train that had been arranged for them, and found it was crowded, as usual, with Indians from the plains, the Nagas let out a few of their rather terrifying war whoops, and the train suddenly emptied. The Nagas crowded aboard, no doubt feeling very pleased with themselves, as they did not like the lowlanders at all, and travelled in style to Haflong.

We heard the war whoops that incredible evening, and we were glad to have Ursula to explain what was going on. The Nagas were all dressed in their ceremonial clothes, and complete with war-paint. The bonfires created flickering shadows on the dancers as they stamped and jumped around the fire to the rhythm of their drums, and every so often the dancing was interspersed with warriors leaping high into the air, yelling like fiends and brandishing their spears, whose tips looked blood-red from the fire's glow. It was an exciting spectacle, and much more interesting that the Red Indian dances we had seen at the movies. We were glad that they were performing peacefully for us.

The Naga men were as vain as peacocks. They were the brightly dressed ones; the women were quite drab by contrast. Part of the reward they had received for helping the British was one or more scarlet blankets, and the men used these as cloaks and skirts, as well as for wrapping around themselves to sleep. The blankets were of extremely good quality, and Mother was given one which she had made up into a very bright suit. The men also wore bands of rope or hair, tied just below the knee and working their way down the leg muscles. This accentuated the muscles, and the more bands one had, the stronger it was thought the warrior was. Not all the Nagas were head-hunters: those who were close to the railway settlements had become 'civilised' by the teaching of missionaries, and possibly the supply of goods and liquor that civilisation brings with it.

The group that was performing the victory dances were genuine head-hunters, and as part of their decoration they wore earrings that had layers of hair braided in a horizontal pattern. Mother was invited to feel one of these earrings, and the owner took great pleasure in telling her that several layers denoted Japanese soldiers that he had scalped. The Japanese were terrified of both the Nagas and those other marvellous hill-men, the Gurkhas. The first liked to collect scalps and the second testicles, which meant intimate contact and much more terrifying than rifle fire. As both could move very quietly in the jungles and mountain terrain, the Japs never knew when or from which direction they would attack next. I suspect that night sentry duty was not a job much sought after in their Army, and they much preferred dealing with British and American troops.

The Nagas were a short, stocky people, light brown in colour and very well muscled. Like all hill people they tended to be somewhat bowlegged, and had a rolling gait. Although they seemed sombre and taciturn in appearance, they always had a cheerful greeting. Their language also seemed to belie this, as it was somewhat staccato. For example, the greeting, which could mean hello, good day, the gods be with you, was contained in the word 'Gerlum' (phonetic).

The other tribe we sometimes came into contact with were the Cacharis, who were somewhat taller and more slender than the Nagas. The Cacharis, in my opinion, were the more handsome of the two, and they also liked bright clothes. I seem to recall that their women were more colourfully clothed, and liked brightly coloured glass necklaces and lots of bracelets. Their language sounded much more musical than the Nagas', and we used to like to hear their greeting, 'Ku-be-lay' (phonetic), which we were told meant 'The gods be with you.'

The Naga hills are one of the world's finest areas for butterfly-catching, and Ursula Graham Bower met her future husband, Lieutenant Colonel Frederick Nicholson Betts, 2nd Punjab Regiment, who had a passionate interest in collecting, while he was racing up and down the hills with a butterfly-net in hand. They were married in Shillong on 26 August 1945, with Ursula accompanied by her Naga bodyguard.

MAEVE KELLY

School holidays we spent in Gonda, Benares and Bareilly in the United Provinces of India with the family of dear friends whose head, John Haskins, was Superintendent Engineer with the 'old and tired' railway (Oudh and Tirhut). His wife Joan was a born mother – attentive, humorous, never intrusive. Here, memories are always of heat: cool-sprinkled lawns, huge, flowering trees and vivid-scarlet blossoms, reading Dickens during noontide siestas (hyperactive, I could seldom sleep). And of climbing, hidden, among cool, green leaves of trees and writing poems; drinking, under duress, buffalo milk – hideous stuff – and of playing mah jong before bedtime with Des and Brian, the Haskins's son, who had a wicked sense of humour too and was the same age as us.

After Naini Tal came Simla, and muddled teaching from a 'dame' school – children of all ages sitting round a long table, struggling to make something of disjointed knowledge.

Another old chap played the violin all morning, gave us each a book and told us to 'get on with it'. He was charming; my book was French, but it might as well have been Greek. The son and daughter of General Bill Slim, who commanded the 14th Army at one point, were also there.

And then the troopship 'home'. Being seasick, the navy-blue ocean after the muddy waters of Bombay, the Suez Canal and wonderful sunsets, *gully-gully* men at Port Said, the looming Rock of Gibraltar. And arriving in a cold, distant land, alien culture, freezing winters, rationing, English boarding schools, loneliness, isolation. The War in the Far East was not much regarded by a nation bombed by Hitler just over the water – so one locked up experience and silently mourned the loss. The radio spoke a few hours a day, and here again were the chimes of Big Ben at nine o'clock as we'd heard them years before in the Tiddim bungalow, our radio run off a generator powered by Father or our gardener pedalling a stationary bicycle on the verandah.

But no hurricane lamp, smoking and guttering in the wind, no pet monkey on my arm, no Siamese cat on my bed, no imaginary tiger under Desmond's, no Wendy house in the grassy garden, or mud village built and peopled with clay around puddles beneath the pines. No vistas over range after range of distant green-blue mountains, no cosmos flowers in birdsong clearings, no – well, who wanted to know?

Here was instead the British boarding school, toughly outfacing the brown North Sea. And here was hockey, at which surprisingly I proved quite good. But not taught by the dreaded Mrs Armstrong of the Hallett, a good-looking but fearsome Irish international. Terrified though we had been of her, she totally disarmed me once by remarking, 'You'll never be pretty – but you may be attractive.' When I blushed and fumbled, she snapped, 'For heaven's sake, don't be so wet – learn to accept a compliment.' With this I still have difficulty – but that was early training for you. Be meek and gentle: this was female survival in the pre-war era of childhood. And besides, Mother had brought me up by the book fashionable in the 1930s, by Dr Truby King. 'Feed the child every four hours', 'No picking up in between, no matter how much it cries' and 'No cuddles; or getting into the parents' bed, certainly not!'

That man has much to answer for – but with hindsight, along with emotional crippling came an adult ability to endure and keep the stiff upper-lip. I've certainly had cause in life since to thank our parents for such upbringing. They were in fact naturally generous, warm-hearted, fiery but loving Irish people. As role models they were magnificent; and, as always, most appreciated when they're dead and gone. For an Oriental childhood was no passport to the easy life – though we had servants and learned Burmese from our gentle *ayah*, along with English. Never, our parents told Des and me, speak roughly to people who work for us: they work with us – and you treat everyone with respect.

As children of the Raj, we have indeed been fortunate.

NANCY LLOYD

My husband was sent on one of the staff college courses in Quetta in 1943, and we had five months together there. Quetta is bitterly cold in the winter and scorchingly hot in the summer, and my memory of it is dry, rocky and sandy country but with marvellous blossom-trees, peaches and apricots and so on, in the spring. After that he was sent to Bombay, where we were again able to be together, while he trained with the Indian Expeditionary Force for the sea-invasion of Burma. This in fact never took place, and he was sent with 33 Corps to the Assam frontier, where the Japs were attacking, and then transferred to 19th Division, as Assistant Quarter-Master General, and fought all the way down through Burma. He was awarded the OBE and was Mentioned in Despatches. Meanwhile, I lived with an uncle and aunt in Delhi. My uncle was a brother of my father, and was also in the Indian Civil Service. My aunt was a great expert on Indian history, and she also worked tirelessly for the SPCA, and founded animal hospitals all over India. She took me on a memorable little trip to Agra and Fatehpur Sikri, and the exquisite beauty of the Taj Mahal was enhanced by her knowledge of Moghul history. They lived in a comfortable low-build stone house out in Old Delhi. I took a secretarial job with the American forces in New Delhi. As I was working for their Intelligence agency, I was able to follow my husband's progress with the Army, considerably helped by my knowledge of the terrain, having trekked over it, in the opposite direction, two years previously.

I went with my uncle and aunt to Simla, the Government hill station, and also to the much smaller and more countrified Dalhousie. From both these hill stations there were breathtaking views of the distant snow-covered Himalayas. In Simla, we refugees from Burma did not feel we could live up to the very high sartorial standard of the British – and indeed the Indian – ladies, particularly that first summer, when we had just arrived from Burma with very few clothes.

above David Thom on VE Day at Quetta Station.

below VE Day Parade, May 1945, led by the Sheikh Bagh School band, in the Church Missionary Society's grounds at Srinagar. (Jonathan Lawley)

above Sheikh Bagh's Racing Team on the Dal Lake in the summer of 1945. The steersman, Mardan Mehta, later became Head Boy. (Jonathan Lawley)

below Sheikh Bagh Cub Pack in 1945. The left-hand adult was a Miss Woods, the name of the right-hand figure sadly forgotten. Jonathan Lawley half-kneeling on the left.

The Japanese War came to an end at last, after Hiroshima, in August 1945. Burma was now under British military administration, and my husband was posted to Army headquarters in Rangoon, as Deputy Director in the Civil Affairs Service Burma (CASB), with the rank of colonel. The country was destitute, and CASB had been set up to supply the basic needs of the population (sugar, dhal, salt, cloth etc.), and to help Burma get economically back on its feet. Rangoon was in a very dilapidated state, and would remain so for many months. Wives were not allowed back there at that early stage, but my husband fixed a ciphering job for me so I was able to join him. I was billeted in the YWCA Service Women's Club, and my husband was permitted to share my room, provided he went back to his own Mess when there was an influx of servicewomen passing through Rangoon. We enjoyed some excellent paper-chasing in the scrub-jungle countryside outside the town, on horses provided by the Remount Department.

In March 1946 we sailed for England and a few months' leave. It was my first sight of home for six years – and seven for my husband. He was de-mobbed on our arrival in England. He joined the Bombay Burmah Trading Corporation, and we returned to Burma in October 1946, where he worked in the Rangoon office. Burma was in political unrest at this time, with the Burmese politicians demanding immediate independence and stirring up anti-British feelings, and at one time, in January 1947, the situation became so tense that plans for evacuating had to be prepared. Things quietened down when London gave in to these demands, but then in July their leader, Aung San, was murdered together with seven of his ministers. For a while there was suspicion that the British had been involved. There was no truth in this, but it made things awkward at the time.

JOAN GRIMLEY

I was born in 1930 and, at the age of three months, went to India with my mother and brother. My father was born in India and was in the Army. Apart from a visit to England for home leave in 1938, we lived in various places in the Punjab until 1945, just before Partition.

My father was in Burma for the duration of the War and my mother, brother, sister and I spent four years in Simla. I recall once seeing Gandhi, a tiny figure in a white *dhoti* sitting in a rickshaw, and my father telling me that he was the cause of the Indians wanting us out.

I never had any sense of being 'the Raj'. India was where we lived and had always done so, England was a cold, unfriendly small country to which I had no desire ever to return.

One night we went to a 'Quit India' rally on the Mall, and I had no sense that it was us that were to quit. It was like being at a big, noisy party, and I remember being surprised when some young men glared at us! The situation grew uglier before we left, and there were cases of acid being thrown at white women. I remember one Indian friend saying, 'Go home now, and in a few years you will be able to come back again.'

I hung on to that when we finally did come 'home'. I think my mother was hugely relieved to be back with a lifestyle she understood. She had never really settled in India, despite the years she had spent there, but I took years to even begin to feel I belonged in this country. In 1956 I returned for a year to work in Lahore. I spent a month in Simla, and that still felt like home.

LYNETTE GURNER

In the latter half of 1945 I attended a troop concert on the Maidan given by Gracie Fields. Temporary seating was arranged in a circle, completed by the stage. The seats rose in tiers, many hundreds were there. Her voice must have carried a long way over the Maidan, and she sang all the favourites, 'Sally', 'Biggest Aspidistra' etc. It was dark long before she finished, and only the stage was lit. As a finale she asked everyone to get out a lighter or matches, and when she gave the signal to simultaneously light up. It worked perfectly.

For about twenty seconds the audience were united in a circle of hundreds of tiny flickering lights, that dimly lit up their faces. A wonderful ending.

With the War over, ships with women and children from Japanese prisoner-of-war camps put in briefly. Again, the Calcutta women helped where they could. I did not experience any of this, but tales regarding their general condition were grim. We were very fortunate indeed in India. The Japanese did get a toe into India at Imphal and Kohima. A month's furious fighting there turned the tide.

In September 1945 I married a subaltern in the Highland Light Infantry. I was then 19. A month's honeymoon followed in a house-boat in Srinagar, and this was to be a final sample of life in India. Then we sailed for England on a troopship. My husband's next posting was in the Army of Occupation in Italy. I joined him, and it was a very interesting time to be there.

My sister and I enjoyed everything about life in India. We knew it was artificial because of the previous ten years at school in England. This possibly stopped us from being completely ruined. It widened our outlook enormously. On returning to England, apart from learning to cook, food rationing and general scarcities, I think what struck me as a bit of problem was having to go out and look for clothes and shoes, instead of having them made to choice of style and colour and all fitting exactly. Choosing from a shop seemed difficult – ridiculous, but certainly not at the time!

PAMELA ALBERT

I think Multan sits on the edge of the Sind Desert – sand, sand and more sand! To me it felt as though it was a village at the end of the world. It was certainly isolated from the world, and I wondered why the Army would have an outpost in this God-forsaken place.

Driving through the bazaar to get to the cantonment looked no better. I had been in many Indian villages and towns, but never saw one like this. Camels and goats blocked the roads, there were flies and dust everywhere, and I did wonder what I had got myself into. As we approached the European area, the change was sudden, and much more encouraging: it seemed we had come to an oasis. There were lovely homes with lush, green lawns, date palms and tidy streets. Amongst the buildings was a small but impressive Anglican church, a beautiful Club house with tennis courts, and I breathed a sigh of relief, for it seemed that at least we were going to be comfortable whilst waiting for repatriation.

I asked my father to tell me about this place, and why he held this position as Commandant of a Holding and Enquiry Camp in the middle of nowhere. It transpired that it was a major prison camp that held members of the Indian National Army. Their crimes included atrocities against the Indian people, and also many of the prisoners were awaiting trial accused of collaborating with the Japanese for the overthrow of British India. Each case was being prepared for the courts. It was no wonder they were held in this desolate place and that its existence had to be hush-hush. My father was living in the Officers' Mess, so he made arrangements for me to stay in a flat attached to the Vicarage. It is possible he thought the vicar's wife would keep an eye on me!

The weather in Multan was something to be desired – near-freezing at night but 116 degrees Fahrenheit in the shade at midday. My meals were taken at the Vicarage unless my father invited me to the Multan Club, or occasionally as a guest at the Officers' Mess. There were no restaurants, but it was possible to go down to the bazaar for a mutton pilau.

I got back into the habit of riding twice a day at six o'clock in the morning and again after four o'clock. One could not do anything strenuous during the day for fear of heat stroke. I took up sewing with the vicar's wife to keep myself busy during the afternoons. I was strictly forbidden to go anywhere near the armed camp. This way of life began to pall on me, and I begged my father to let me work in his office. I soon had complete order with his filing – naval style – and he could not believe that everything could run so well. 'Thank heavens for the Navy!' he would often say. I also volunteered to work three days a week at a Government veterinary hospital. After all, I felt, if I was eventually going into this field, here was a splendid opportunity for me to try my skills. This quiet life went by for five months.

The camp was being readied for the Indian Government and the courts to proceed with the forthcoming trials.

My father received orders for us to return home to England. We were to sail from Bombay on 23 April 1946 on the SS *Highland Princess*. We left Multan bound for a couple of weeks' stay in Simla before proceeding on to Bombay. I donned my naval uniform for the last time for the voyage home. The ship was a troopship, with the upper decks reserved for officers and their families. Nobody cared much where they bunked – we were going home at last. It was a happy ship, and, as we sailed by the Gateway of India, tears came to my eyes. Would I ever see India again, with all its good times? I went on deck to watch the ship pull away from the dock and then walked aft, where I stayed until I could see the Gateway of India no longer.

PETER BROADBENT

Although this paragraph is about my experiences on passing through Deolali Transit Camp, a little background information is necessary to set it in context.

My father served in the Bombay Pioneers and then the Rajputana Rifles in India for a total of 26 years. He had been home on leave in England in 1938 and on completion, my mother and I went back out to India in November 1938, on the SS *City of Canterbury*. My elder sister was left with my grandparents, to avoid interrupting her schooling. The idea was that my mother and I would return in less than a year. As it turned out, we were unable to get back until 1945, and so my mother was keen to return in the very first ship possible.

We applied for a passage home when I was at The New School in Darjeeling, but nothing materialised. We therefore moved to Bombay, thinking that if we were closer to the port of embarkation, we might be able to influence the movements staff. As it turned out, all we achieved was six months living in the Juhu Hotel at Juhu, near Bombay. Hotel it might have been, but only just! We all lived in tents, and the dining room was a shack roofed with palm fronds. We kept our water in old gin-bottles, and our gin in new gin-bottles. My three-year-old sister, of course, managed to take a swig from the wrong bottle, and her mouth was blistered quite badly inside. We seemed to have a local fish called a pomphret for almost every meal, and I amused myself by counting the enormous jellyfish, up to three feet across, which were stranded on the beach, and by making the occasional trip into Bombay for the afternoon. There was no school, and so my mother taught me as best she could.

At last, we were called in to Deolali to await the final date for our voyage home. We had heard quite a lot about the place, but it was even worse than we had anticipated. The rooms were small, minimally furnished and very hot. The food was dreadful, and the HP Sauce on every table was the only saving grace. At the end of each meal the bearers put the cutlery in their pockets to prevent it being stolen like the washing, which used to disappear from the lines outside our rooms overnight. There was nothing to do, but I do remember a mound towards the back of the camp, with a white stone on the top. On the other side of the mound was a railway line, on which we would place coins and then wait patiently for a train to pass, which it hardly ever did!

I have often wondered whether Deolali led to the expression 'going Doolally'. It has been suggested that there was a mental hospital nearby, but I am unable to verify this. I have also often wondered whether the BBC series *It Ain't Half Hot Mum* was based on Deolali but I don't think I remember any concert parties while we were there.

Every day, my mother would scan the noticeboard to find our names on the list. At last, presumably in about early July 1945, we boarded a ship in Bombay for the passage home. Sadly I am unable to recall its name. We were in convoy as far as Aden, and from there the ship was allowed to proceed on its own. We arrived in Liverpool on VJ Day, to celebrations everywhere and to a joyful reunion with my elder sister. My father remained in India until after Independence, returning to Britain in late 1947.

BETSY VICKERS

During the War Kotagiri was a leave station for British soldiers, and at weekends we often entertained a group of them at our house. They were so pleased to get into a private home and I am still in touch with two soldiers from those days. There was also a Church of England and a Missionary Club where plays were put on and shows staged. Many of the local people were Budagars, a tribe which dressed in white and cultivated their crops on terraces. Belly was a popular name. We had a water carrier of that name, and one felt rather silly shouting out 'Belly'. When in Kotagiri after I left school I helped the canteen set up for the soldiers on leave. Alas, when we revisited in 1965 much of the *shola* had been cut down to make room for more tea bushes, and we did not see a single monkey.

Camped in the teak forests on the Akanapet Road about 14 miles from Medak were thousands of soldiers, part of the 14th Army. They had been destined for Burma but the War had ended. Of course, parties of other ranks and officers were very welcome at our bungalow and I had a marvellous time. When I went to the cinema or to a dance we would drive the 60 miles in a Jeep, all dressed up, and then the 60 miles home.

I would sometimes go into Secunderabad on the local bus and though vigorous efforts were made to seat me in the *purdah* section I would always refuse. Going to the cinema was always rather amusing. I never went alone, yet at the interval and at the end of the performance notes would be handed to me: 'Please miss will you meet me by...', scrawled by hopeful soldiers.

There was no bank in Medak so my father and I had to go into Secunderabad to draw money for wages. We would drive into town by the Nasapur road, which was very pretty with many trees. The money collected would take up a small suitcase, for there were many people to be paid in the compound, hospital staff, the training college etc. One of us was always with the money. We would return home a different route, via Wadiaram, for there were less trees that could be felled across the road to stage a hold-up. On reaching home very late at night, we had to record the numbers of all the big notes before they were locked up in a huge safe.

My parents were anxious for me to see as much of India as I could before we left. We started by visiting Ellora and Ajanta, those impressive temples hewn from solid rock, Ellora with its many carvings and Ajanta with its paintings. My parents had spent their honeymoon at the Nizam's Guest House nearby. On this visit we always stayed in Aurangabad with Parsee friends who lived in Apsley House, so called because the Duke of Wellington had lived there whilst on Army service. And so to Kashmir by way of Agra, Delhi and Amritsar.

In June 1946 we sailed for England. I was saddened to leave India. She had been good to me. Even during the agitation for Independence I was never rudely treated. My first memory of India was painful, for I was stung by a bee, but ever since I have been bitten by the India bug and think back on those days with pleasure and affection. It was a privilege to have been raised there.

8

1946 and After

1946

23 January	Clashes between Police and rioters in Bombay; 10 killed, 300 injured
22 March	Military authorities in Delhi arrest 93 policemen
5 May	Conference of British Cabinet Mission, the Viceroy and Congress (Hindu) and Muslim leaders opens at Simla
12 May	Conference breaks down
6 June	Muslim League Council agrees to work with British Cabinet Mission's plan, but re-affirms its demand for Pakistan, an independent Muslim state
14 June	Congress rejects British Cabinet's plans for an Interim Indian Government
16 June	Muslim's 'Direct Action' in Calcutta involves looting and the burning of shops; 90 killed, 1000 injured
2 September	New Interim Government sworn in at Delhi
15 October	Muslim League decides to form Interim Indian Government
19 October	Casualties in Eastern Bengal rioting estimated at 6000 killed, 20,000 injured

20 October	Pandit Nehru, the Congress Leader, stoned by Afridis at the Khyber Pass and, next day, at Malakand
1947	
20 February	Mr Attlee, the British Prime Minister, announces that his Government intends to transfer power in India into 'responsible Indian hands' by June 1948
24 March	Lord Louis Mountbatten becomes Viceroy of India; Lord Wavell becomes an Earl
18 July	Royal Assent is given to the Indian Independence Act; India becomes a Dominion
1948	
4 January	Burma becomes independent
30 January	Mahatma Gandhi is assassinated
11 September	Mohammed Ali Jinnah, Governor-General of Pakistan, dies of heart failure in Karachi

JOAN TOFT

Patricia and I left India on the SS *Manipur* from Calcutta just before the terrible riots which preceded Independence. My mother told me how one day, walking to a bazaar in Ballygunge, she felt someone following her. She turned to find Multan, our dear *masalchi*, on her heels carrying a large knife. 'Must keep Memsahib safe,' he said.

I had my two dogs, Hendy and Ferdi, with me on the SS *Manipur* – they were happy enough on the poop deck, though poor Hendy was ill as a result of the puppies she had recently had. The sale of the puppies paid the dogs' fare home and their six months in quarantine. I spent a lot of time on the poop deck with the dogs. We stuck at Vizag for ten days, and enjoyed the sand and seabathing – dogs too. Otherwise I didn't enjoy the voyage much, as I seemed to be looked on as something of an oddity.

England seemed cold and grey on arrival, though I think the month was August. I had a confusing journey from Tilbury, but we were welcomed in Bournemouth by dear friends who had been tea-planters in Assam.

India imbued me with a very deep love of it – its people, its countryside. And it gave me seven years of home life and love, making up a little for what I had lost in England.

HAZEL SQUIRE

When I left school, my parents wanted to make up for some of the lost years of family life, and took me out to Afghanistan for three fascinating months. During this time my father was knighted, and later his post was elevated to that of Ambassador. When he took me to Delhi to see me off by plane to England, we stayed with Lord Wavell at the Viceroy's House. It was during the hot season, and most people were away in the hill stations. There was only the Viceroy, his ADC, my father and myself. The ADC was delegated to show me the sights of Delhi. I remember climbing all the way up the Qutb Minar. At dinner in the evening there were just the four of us. Lord Wavell seemed as shy as I was, and he told this rather delightful story against himself, I am sure, to try to set me at my ease. He was hosting a big official dinner. Shortly before it, his chief guest rang up to say his wife was unwell, could he bring his daughter in her place? So he found himself sitting next to this 18-year-old girl. At the beginning of the meal, he turned and asked her how her mother was, to which she replied suitably. Having sat most of the meal in silence, he turned to her again during the dessert course and asked her how her mother was. She replied, 'Well, I think she's probably about the same as she was at the beginning of the first course'.

The dubbing of my father took place in a fairly small room, as I remember. Probably the formal rooms were shut for the hot season. My father knelt on a stool with a velvet cushion. The ADC produced a sword, and Lord Wavell touched him on each shoulder and said, 'Rise, Sir Giles.' He was then presented with a beautiful insignia of the Knight of the British Empire, which I still have in my possession. It meant a great deal to me to be present at this ceremony, and I know it was a moving moment in his life.

I retain a deep love of India. It holds my treasured memories of family life and the friends we made there. I remember with great affection my father's personal bearer, Rahim Buksh, who stuck with him and came to each new place and posting that my father had. He was wonderful to us children. It was only when he was getting old and was finding the winters in Afghanistan too cold, that he went to my father with great sadness and asked to be retired. He was too homesick. My father settled on him a pension and sent him back to his own home in Gujarat. It was like losing a member of the family.

Alongside this love of India has been the trauma of separation, which has taken me all of my adult life to unravel and resolve. Parents made good practical arrangements for their children, but there was little planning of how to cope with their feelings. Indeed, did they have feelings? The separations must have been equally agonising for the parents. There were no airfares built into the salaries to bring children out for the holidays – or, for that matter, flights available. It took the whole holiday to go one way by ship.

JOHN LANGLEY

With the War over for almost six months, and the horrors of the atomic bomb gradually receding, the mood was towards regaining the type of life that had existed before the War. Of course, this did not happen, and with the change of government in England we were already seeing the effects of the process of turning the country back to the Indian people.

It was then that we met Mr and Mrs Skene. He had recently been liberated from a Japanese prisoner-of-war camp in Burma, and was still recuperating from his ordeal. Judging by his gaunt, emaciated appearance, he still had a long way to go to regain his normal stature. He had been in one of the camps that provided the labour for building the infamous Burma railway, which killed a very large number of allied prisoners – through malnutrition, disease, heat exhaustion and untreated accidents.

On one occasion, we had a turkey for dinner. When it was served our hostess looked at it in horror. 'How am I to serve ten of us from this tiny bird?' she asked. Bob Skene (who had been a well-known polo player before the War) replied, 'That bird is plenty big enough to serve all of us, let me carve it for you.' He proceeded to carve the bird into the thinnest slices I had ever seen. It certainly appeared from his handiwork that there would be more than enough for all of us. Much to our surprise, we all felt we had received sufficient. 'One of the things you learn in a Jap POW camp is how to make food go a long way,' said Bob, with a grin. 'If you didn't, you would not survive very long.'

Soon after our return to Haflong, the news came that we had berths on the MV *Brittanic* leaving Bombay for England at the end of March. Father had been given leave, but also informed that he would not be returning to Haflong on his return. He would be stationed at Kanchrapara again. I don't think this was very welcome news, as the situation in the Calcutta area was deteriorating fast. Riots were commonplace between the Hindu and Muslim factions, each striving to be dominant, as it became common knowledge the British were preparing to pull out of India.

Our departure was marked by a series of farewell parties, both from the residents of Haflong as well as from the engineering and Workshop staff. The three of us were formally invited to attend this party, and Father received a neatly designed blueprint with a fancy-edged scrolled border, to simulate a diploma. This had been prepared by the engineering staff, and was presented with due pomp and ceremony. It read:

H.V. Langley, Esq
Executive Engineer, Bengal Assam Railway, Haflong

Sir,

We have gathered here today to pay our highest tribute to you and memsahib on the eve of your departure from our midst on long leave.

Your presence in our midst, we felt not as a master amongst his servants, but as an affectionate teacher amidst his pupils, ever mindful to rectify what is wrong.

Your kind, sympathetic and impartial treatment to your staff, your fatherly solicitude for our intellectual and moral progress, your never failing assistance to all who have been in need of your fatherly advice in all matters of office and outdoor works and hearty co-operation in enjoyment everywhere in and outside the office endeared you to the staff and contractors of this district.

Your untiring zeal for our welfare and upgrading will always leave its impression on our mind. We shall never forget your enthusiasm for everything good and noble to give an adequate expression of what you have done for us our meagre words will fail, but though this address is poor, it will be very acceptable to you as it does come from the very heart of your beloved staff and contractors.

The institute members will never forget your personal interest in the welfare of the institute and all its functions. In a nutshell we are losing you, a master, a teacher, a friend and a guardian.

Sir, it is with heavy hearts that we bid you farewell. We pray to God Almighty to be pleased to shower his choicest blessings on you and your family.

Remember Sir,
Your most loving and faithful
The Engineering staff of Haflong
Bengal Assam Railway, Haflong District
Dated Haflong, the 15th March 1946

We left Haflong on 16 March with great regret. It had been a wonderful place to be stationed, and we would always have happy memories of the house, the town, our neighbours and the Nagas and Cacharis.

The journey was uneventful, with the usual interlude of crossing the Brahmaputra by steamer from Jaggernautganj to Sirajgani where, about halfway across, we hit a log which delayed us for about half an hour and gave added interest to the trip.

We also made a trip into Calcutta for some last-minute shopping, and to see the Ortners. We had been advised that this could be a dangerous outing, as there had been numerous riots, and bombs had exploded in buildings and streets.

On our way to the station on our return journey, we had only just started when we were stopped by a military detachment, who warned us that there were riots in progress between us and Sealdah Station, and advised that we join a military convoy that was taking a number of people through. We naturally agreed, and were instructed to lie on the floor and be prepared to cover ourselves with rugs. This was to provide protection against flying bottles and brickbats. We had also been warned of the danger of landmines in the road, but it was felt that we would be unlikely to encounter those, as we would be keeping to the main routes. Our escort was armed with machine guns, rifles and revolvers, and we felt reasonably secure. Generally, the riots were not directed against the British, but if we got in the way, too bad! In spite of the carefully chosen route, we did encounter one small pocket of rioters, and were advised to seek the protection of the rugs. We had just cleared the area when there was an explosion in one of the side streets, and we were told that someone had driven over a landmine. *The Statesman,* the local newspaper, always reported the number of casualties as much lower that the actual – the reverse of normal newspaper sensationalism – at one stage we used to add a zero to the figures reported. It may have been exaggerating some-what, but was closer to the truth.

After several hold-ups we finally got through to the station with no further mishaps or adventures: but this trip had been scary enough, although I thought at the time it was exciting, as I had no concept of the danger we had been in. It was a relief to find Sealdah Station as crowded as ever but with no sign of violence.

BETTY PAKENHAM-WALSH

In 1946 my father returned to Burma as a High Court Judge in Rangoon. My mother and I followed when I was demobbed from the Wrens. At the end of 1946 we travelled out on the *Monarch of Bermuda*, a troopship, where I met my future husband, then in the Royal Signals. My father's Government housing was in Windermere Park. We were there only a few months before handover, and Burma became Myanmar. Awful potholes in the roads – only military telephones, and very few cars. Nevertheless, I was glad to return to Burma – for the last time! My uncle by marriage also returned to Rangoon as General Manager of the Burmah Oil Company – his wife, my aunt, travelled out with us. She was accidentally shot and was killed by dacoity crossfire.

ROY DE VANDRE

By 1946 I was stationed at Secunderabad. I was a captain in a Gurkha regiment then. I got friendly with this girl, Dorothy. She was the daughter of a warrant officer in the Ordnance Corps. She was Anglo-Indian. There was this 'do' at Christmas, a dance at the Officers' Club, one of the oldest in India. I took Dorothy. While I was there, the Club Secretary comes up and says, 'That lady you're with, is she Anglo-Indian?' I said, 'Yes, why?' 'She's not allowed here,' he replied, 'so she'll have to leave.' I couldn't believe this. The other officers all liked her and would take her to the pictures for me when I was on duty. I said, 'I'm sorry, she's not bloody leaving.' 'She'll have to leave. Those are the rules.' I said, 'If she leaves, I leave.' He said, 'That's up to you. She can't stay.'

I went up to my Colonel and said, 'I'm sorry, Sir, I've got to leave'. He said, 'Why?' I explained. He said, 'If she goes, we're all going.' He made all us six officers leave. He wrote a letter to the Secretary saying what he thought: it was damn bad form, damn bad show. Damn well insulting to one of his officers. It was the first time it struck home to me. I felt very sorry for the girl, because she was well-educated, a convent girl, a strict Roman Catholic. Her father had served in the British Army.

There was also the case of a friend, whose father was Corsican and who had a sister who married a Scotsman during the War. He was in the Ordnance Corps. When the War was over he came to England with her. They arrived at Waterloo from Southampton. He said, 'Hang on a second, while I get a taxi'. He picked up his bags, and that was the last she saw of him. She stayed on the station till eleven o'clock. A policeman kept going past her and she was crying. She'd never been outside blooming Lahore in all her life. Anyway, I was coming over for the Victory Parade with the Gurkha Brigade. Ken and his mother gave me some money and said, 'Can you make sure that Audrey comes back to us?' and gave me an address. When I came she was working for an import company at Tilbury Docks. I went to see her. She started crying, 'I don't like this country.' She had been after him, but he didn't want to have anything to do with her. She was Anglo-Indian, and the family wouldn't accept her. Anyway, I fixed everything up and she got back. A lot of that happened. Englishmen brought our girls here and dumped them, or dumped them over there, pretending they were being posted, and then never came back, having gone to England. The Army wouldn't lift a finger.

A lot didn't let this happen. My sister married an Englishman, but she was a real tomboy, and could swear like a trooper. He adored her. She's head of a comprehensive in Devon now.

PHILIP BANHAM

Some time in 1946, when I was clearing up some of the mess from the Second World War, I remember driving by Jeep along a very rough, dusty road in north east Assam, when suddenly the dust stopped. It was tarmac; and houses, schools, shops, playing fields. I couldn't believe it. I asked a boy, carrying his books to school, where I was. He was surprised I didn't know, and said, 'Digboi.' I'd never heard of it. I asked him how to spell it. I asked him why it was there. 'Oil,' he said. Oil? Here, in north-east India? My geography master was very thorough – out from Cambridge – but he'd never mentioned it. Perhaps he'd never heard about oil in Assam – or coal – which I discovered was dug out of hillsides at Ledo. That, too, was a surprise.

I was a captain at this time, in the Indian Army Ordnance Corps, searching out and destroying all the weapons of war you can think of – small arms, shells, mortar bombs, anti-tank mines, grenades, Bangalore Torpedoes, not to forget the Japanese stuff as well. But the greatest proportion of it was blocks of TNT, each about the size of a pint beer-can, packed in wooden crates (the TNT had been used to blast the road to Chungking). It all had to be got rid of.

It was a little while after the Jap capitulation that I was posted to Assam, to report to HQ at Panitola. I got there by train, and the Brigadier in command lent me a Jeep and sent me to Makum. The depot there was run by a Major Casabon, who had been at boarding school, in Dehra Dun, I think. But like the Indian lads who were boarders in my school, he could listen to ITMA and see the funny side of it, and roll around with laughter.

Casabon sent me off on my first lot of demolition work – mostly those TNT crates which hadn't been scattered in the jungle. As we were surrounded by tea gardens, I went to Sadiya and consulted the Political Officer there. He suggested a site 10 miles downriver – called the Luhit, I think – and I went on with it day after day, week in, week out, occasionally taking a Sunday off.

Towards the end of 1946 I moved to Lekhapani. I must have come across Digboi when going there. I got to know a man called Walter Littler, from Manchester, who was the boss of the coal mining. As it was easier for me to get 'liberty petrol' I used to collect him, and we'd Jeep to the nearest Planters' Club. I don't need to tell you we had a memorable Christmas Eve out at one – and I'd still be there if Mountbatten hadn't handed India over.

ELIZABETH LEIGH

One of the saddest times in my early years in India was when my baby sister died at just one year old, when I was four years and eight months old. Every night I would say my prayers and these were always finished off by blessing everyone individually, including Ayah, and when on the night of the 23rd of June, 1944, I said '… and God bless Jane,' my mother said something like 'You don't need to bless Jane now as she is up in Heaven,' and I remember crying for a long time.

Another memory I have is the excitement of clambering up the front leg of an elephant, at Madura Temples I think, and being deposited on its back. Another strong memory is – when there were floods in Madras. We were near a river and I can remember the water being in the house and the fear of snakes that might be floating in – and seeing bodies and flotsam being swept at great speed down the river which was nearby. I have a vision of someone on a bicycle trying to cycle up our driveway and getting stuck in the mud.

Everywhere we lived we had a dog of some sort. They must have been hand-over or inherited dogs because there was such a variety, from Dachshund to Spaniel or Heinz 57 type, and all enormous fun to play with. Leave always consisted of at least six months, so I expect we minded other people's dogs at times when we moved into their homes; I don't even remember taking them for a walk. In one house we had a mongoose that lived under the verandah. My mother hated snakes, and when the snake man came to find snakes in the garden my mother always said he'd put them there in the first place so that he would get his rupee per snake. We were only allowed to have curry once a week – Government order – because of the shortage of food for the Indians. Our curry was usually eaten on a Sunday, and I loved it so much I can remember rolling around on the floor afterwards because I'd eaten too much! Over the dining-room table there was a wonderful lampshade and light that you could pull up, or down – over the centre of the table. My parents went to a lot of parties, including fancy-dress parties. In England we had a trunk full of fancy-dress costumes for years afterwards. My favourite of my Mother's was the Gypsy dress – which had little coins all round the hem and headdress. They also played a lot of tennis and golf, and won endless trophies and cups (which we only sold in 1995 when my mother died, as her bequest to the Animal Welfare charity).

The most heartrending time was saying goodbye to Ayah in April 1946 when we finally left India. I cried and cried then too; I have a feeling she came with us as far as Bombay, and so we said our goodbyes there. There were riots in Bombay when we left; I can remember being very frightened by all the noise and the banging of drums outside in the streets all night. I can remember being driven off to the ship in the back of a Land Rover and waving until I could no longer see Ayah. We did write to each other for a few years though, and I still have her letters and a postcard. My mother had found her a position with another family.

All these memories, and yet I cannot always pinpoint where they belong. Having started my life in Madura, I can only say that we then alternated from time to time in Madras and Bangalore, frequently went up to Ootacamund in the hills (one bungalow we stayed in was called 'Firgrove') or to the temperate climate of Trichinopoly from October 1943 until departure in April 1946. Both my late sister and

Bungalow at Kodaikanal, either 'Stirling' or 'Franklin'. 1945. (Elizabeth Leigh)

my brother were born in the Van Allen Nursing Home in Kodaikanal. William, my brother, was born on the 13th of April 1945, and so was only 18 months when we came home. It must have been ironic for my mother, to have gone out to India with a baby and come back with another one – having lost one in between. The journey home was remembered only for throwing my *topee* overboard and having my long plaits pulled all the time! I can remember the excitement of running up and down the ship on arrival at Liverpool and looking down on to the quayside having unfamiliar grandparents pointed out to me. I was six-and-a-half years old – and about to find out what living in Ration Book England was like!

GILLIAN OWERS

When the Indian nation turned on itself with such appalling sava-gery. I was in England, reading with sheer unbelief of the horrors of Partition. For my parents, it was a nightmare from which they never recovered. Living outside Calcutta, they had Muslim, Hindu, Buddhist and Christians in the compound and lived in terror of the mobs coming over the wall to kill, burn and loot. Not afraid for themselves, for they were not threatened, but for the people who were part of the household. Often the village creek would be choked with bodies, run with blood from the slaughter, but somehow, miraculously, those living with them were spared. My parents, leaving, never wanted to return, and I am sure that what they had seen and known changed their view of India forever. They left without a backward glance or thought of return.

For me this is not true. For years, I longed to return. Now I am not sure. A childhood in India is as near as anyone can have to a perfect childhood, but I am not sure that I have ever truly adapted. It took me years to believe that I would not return to live in India, and I suffered and caused pain when I could not settle in my new circumstances because of that belief. As I have grown older, I have accepted that one cannot enter the same river twice; the India I knew does not exist. And certainly, my children reaped the benefit of our move: they grew up without the wrenching separations all Raj families knew, even if they also grew up without the magic and expansion of another culture – and that was why we left.

ERNEST CAMPBELL

When my wife and I returned to India in 1946 – after an absence of 11 years – the British were still in India. We got to know Brigadier Bristow, the Deputy Commissioner and various people who 'stayed on' – among them the Cambridge Brotherhood, who worked – and still work – in the slums of Delhi. Many of the Indian Civil Servants who succeeded the Englishmen were themselves educated in England, and cherished their English education. Some of these became very good friends. I have a whole treasurehouse of ICS stories that I heard about from them. They were almost as eccentric as the missionaries!

Soon after we arrived (my wife had never been in India), Mahatma Gandhi and Mohammed Ali Jinnah partitioned India. We were (or I was, my wife was in the mountains) in Jullundur when the boundary line between India and Pakistan was announced, and all hell broke loose. I was very much a part of the events of August and early September 1947. At the request of the new Indian Government, we formed a team of three doctors and I, as an 'India hand', met Pandit Nehru, who gave us a *rohdari* (*laissez-passer*) to go into Pakistan and try to nip in the bud a cholera epidemic that had broken out among the India-bound refugees in Pakistan. This we did for several months, until most of the refugees had crossed over. We did some hundred thousand inoculations.

The early years of Independence were very eventful. Everything was changing. We got to do things we would never have been able to do before, or were able to do after India 'settled down'. We have innumerable pictures of the older India, in which there is not much interest or curiosity.

There is no way of measuring the extent to which we (non-English Europeans) benefited from the system that the British put in place in their several hundred years in India. It will be generations – and perhaps never – before the effects of English language, laws, institutions, manners and attitudes are not pervasive in India.

Our family, and several others who returned in succeeding generations to India, love it of course. It is home to us now as America can never be. The sounds, the smells, the birds, the trees, the weather, the mountains. We sometimes seem more Indian than the Indians. At least, we often know more about its history, culture and differences, than a majority of Indians.

THELMA SMART

I was born in Jhansi on 6 March 1929 at the British Military Hospital. The house where we lived was 1 Garden Road. A typical bungalow of the time, with wide verandahs and high skylights. Pull *punkahs* and cusscuss *tatties* were the methods used to cool the house during the summer months. I can still recall the scent of the fragrant root that was the make-up of the *tattie* (or screen), and the cool breezes that blew through them. My mother took great pride in her garden, and it was always a riot of colour. Tea on the *chabutra* was always a treat.

No 1 Garden Road, Jhansi, home to the Smart family, 1929. A later photograph. (Thelma Smart)

My father, John William Smart, came to India in 1921 as a soldier in the British Army – the RAOC (Royal Army Ordinance Corps). In 1927 he married Leah Mary Carvalho. She was the youngest of 13 children, and was born in Jubbulpore in 1905. Her father, Alfred Emanuel Carvalho, was born in Karachi. He married Florence Violet Skinner, who was also born in Karachi. Florence's father was Benjamin Frederick Skinner from London, England, and her mother was Mary Ann Elizabeth, née Chamberlain, from Ireland. They married in Karachi in 1866. What brought Benjamin to India is not known.

Jhansi was a military and railway centre. By the time I was born, my father was already a Warrant Officer. He was frequently away on active service on the North West Frontier. As my grandfather worked for the GIP (Great Indian Peninsula) railway, we had many ties to the railway community, and therefore spent time at the Railway Institute, which was the hub of social life. There we played games and attended functions, dances and Christmas parties. Jhansi is, of course, famous for the exploits of Lakshmi Bai, the Queen of Jhansi. She fought bravely against the British at the time of the mutiny of 1857, and was first knocked off her horse and then shot by a trooper of the 8th Hussars during a skirmish.

By the time my brother Gerald was born we were stationed at Rawalpindi – the year was 1932. In 1943 I was at school in Rawalpindi, at the Presentation Convent. The following year was my first year at boarding school, at the Convent of Jesus and Mary at the hill station of Murree. Later schools were in Jhansi and Bangalore, but most of my schooldays were spent as a boarder at St Mary's Convent, Naini Tal.

Our holidays were during the cooler winter months, December to March. On returning home in time for Christmas we enjoyed the rounds of parties prior to Christmas, and the excitements of Burra Din – Christmas Day. As children, we never saw the Christmas tree till Christmas morning – the sitting room was off limits. I always remember my father playing the part of Father Christmas – in full regalia, although he did not fool his two children for long! Our days were fun-filled, and we roamed the jungle around the house, free as the wind. My brother Gerald became a crack shot with his 'catty', shooting down birds and lizards. How little we considered our cruel behaviour! We had a pet mongoose, a monkey, numerous parrots and other birds and always a dog or two.

Frequently there would be entertainments in the compound by jugglers, fire eaters, sword swallowers and snake charmers. Then there were the puppeteers with their makeshift theatre and colourful puppets, the 'monkey man' with his monkeys dressed to play their parts and the *balloowallah* with his trained dancing bears. All these *tamashas* we took in our stride – never giving a thought, in our childish minds, to what was suffered by these animals. It was all part of the life we led.

Garden Road was near the local cinema. In those days there was an interval between the 'shorts' and the main film. Gerald and I would run home during the interval, shout to the cook for 'chips' and Heinz Ketchup – served on the *chabutra* with speed – and we'd eat and then run back to see the movie. The late show was attended by adults and was the occasion for them to dress more formally, with the ladies in evening dress.

At the onset of the Second World War in September 1939, it was not long before my father, by now having attained the rank of

St Mary's Convent, Naini Tal, where Thelma Smart went to school.

major, was gone. Once again on active service, he was captured when Singapore fell to the Japanese in 1942, and interned at the infamous Changi Jail, where he remained until repatriation at the end of 1945. On his return, he was posted to Quetta in Baluchistan. I remember still, the long, hot train-ride from Bombay to Quetta through the Bolan Pass. By now, the writing was on the wall – the promise to give India its independence was soon to be honoured. My father felt it was time to return to England, after a working lifetime spent in India. So it was that, in February 1947, we waved goodbye to India. I was 18 years old, and was not to return to the land of my birth until November 2000.

KRISTIN SQUIRE

I returned briefly in 1947, arriving in Karachi on the day India and Pakistan got their independence. I was on my way to Afghanistan, and was lucky to get through before all the riots started. I only remember walking the streets of Karachi amongst all the happy jostling crowds who, maybe, took a delight in pushing me, an Englishwoman, off the pavements. But all in good spirits. It was a delightful occasion, and what followed was so heartbreaking. Only a few days after I had arrived in Afghanistan, a French nurse, also on her way, got stabbed several times during a raid on her train.

I went to six different schools, in the East and Britain. The contemplation of a coming parting (usually for at least a year, which seemed a long time) was far worse than when it actually happened. I also have a dreadfully confused knowledge of history, knowing probably more about Moghul emperors than about the kings of England, though I did study the Tudor period three times over, I think. But I have had more experience in other ways. I found it easy to make friends with people or to meet strangers, but perhaps not easy to make permanent relationships. I don't want to travel any more, perhaps because I never had the security of a permanent home, though at the time I suppose I took it all for granted. I think it was far harder for my mother, who was constantly torn between our needs and my father's need for a wife and hostess. Now with my husband I have put down roots, and am part of a village and its life. I can watch its children growing up, and have a sense of belonging.

When I was 20, I heard an Indian speak at a conference – he was relaxed and confident – a kind I had never met. I was shaken by the thought of the kind of Indians we had created – I only knew the bowing, sometimes obsequious 'yes men' of ruled to rulers. Is that what our superiority and arrogance, often unconscious, had done? I was ashamed.

I have since been back to Bombay and Maharashtra, but never to the areas I knew. But India does not seem to have changed a lot. The marvellous railway network with its crowded trains and stations, and even the thermos, brought, at least, to first-class passengers! The roads lined with trees, planted by the British for the marching troops. Many houses that were probably originally built for the British are still in use, though a little shabby, but their gardens have disappeared. We stayed with an Indian doctor and his family in Sangli. He had trained in England, and now has his own hospital. His colleague, Arun Chavan, who is the main reason for our visits, has launched a society for helping to develop the villages around. He was inspired by his Communist uncle, an admirer of Mahatma Gandhi, loves Shakespeare and has a wonderful command of the English language. Arun watched with gentle amusement my feelings of unease with those who are proud of India and glad to be free of the 'Raj', and then one day took us to meet a proud princeling and his family. 'You will like these people,' he said with a smile. He told us we were going to visit a 'ranch', and we bumped along dusty roads for several hours, until he took out a comb and started to comb his hair. I luckily took the hint, and tried to bring some order into my wind-tangled locks, which was just as well, because in the next few minutes we arrived at a small fort where we were welcomed by the village band and the princeling and his whole family, including his mother and grandmother! They received us royally, and later expressed regrets at the passing of the British Raj, and his mother nostalgically reminisced about the old days. Yes, we have left our mark, but we too were only a passing phase.

YOMA CROSFIELD

My parents were not, I believe, typical of some of the British people who found themselves living and working in the various countries of the British Empire. When *The Jewel in the Crown* was shown on television in England years later, with its depiction of narrow-minded Englishwomen in India, my mother refused to watch it, saying, 'I've spent quite enough time with women like that.' She liked to tell the story of how she had secured a decent flat in Karachi, when accommodation was very scarce after the Partition of India, into Pakistan and India, in 1947. A Pakistani official came to the flat they were living in temporarily to see how much space they had and determine what kind of flat she should move into. It was a hot day, and my mother offered him a soft drink with ice in it. This simple gesture so touched the man that he persuaded the relevant committee to allot her a better flat than she could have hoped for otherwise.

At the time of Partition, my father was stationed in Karachi as General Manager for his firm. My mother, then very high in the Guiding hierarchy in India as Provincial Commissioner for Sind, India, became one of only two European members of the committee called by Miss Jinnah – sister of Mohammed Ali Jinnah, founder of Pakistan – to set up the Pakistani Girl Guide movement. In the new organisation, my mother was Provincial Commissioner for Sind, Pakistan.

My father tried to get Indians into good jobs and, indeed, into Clubs restricted to Europeans. Towards the end of his years in the East, he had to meet with a Collector of Customs to discuss some releases he needed. He went along with several experts, anticipating a tough negotiation. He need not have worried. When he walked into the office, the man behind the desk stood up and declared to his staff that Leonard Crosfield was the man who had secured his election to his first Club, in Chittagong.

PATRICK HUGH STEVENAGE

On 15 August 1947 the Labour Government in Britain gave India its independence and Pakistan its beginning. With the surrender of the 'jewel in the crown', the British Empire began to crumble. Lord Louis Mountbatten, the cousin of King George VI, had been appointed Viceroy of India, and took up this post with the firm intention of carrying out the Government's mandate and bringing the job to a speedy conclusion.

The Anglo-Indian population of India had never believed that they would ever witness the end of British rule in India. To them it was something so far in the future that nobody seemed to clearly face up to such a future. To any suggestion that they should become fully Indianised, the answer was an indignant 'never'. They were Christians, not Hindus or Muslims, Jains, or Buddhists. English was their mother tongue, they dressed in European fashion, they went to superior schools and served the Government in many reserved occupations in the post and telegraph departments and on the railways and their ancestors had formed the backbone of the regiments, both British and Indian, which had conquered India and fought in so many of the wars of the Empire with more than a little distinction. They could never become just another Indian community.

I was at this time working as assistant stationmaster of the joint Madras and Southern Mahratta Railway and the Nizam's railway station at Bezwada, where the broad-gauge and metre-gauge services met. One morning, in the control office; I was surprised by the arrival of a bullock cart, from which a young man was carried unconscious and laid on the ground outside the office. He had been bitten by a cobra. Distraught relatives dashed in the office and demanded that a message be passed over the control telephone line to 'Pambu' Narasiah, one of our stationmasters down the line. In a few minutes he answered the phone and asked only two questions. When had the man been bitten, and was he conscious or unconscious? There was a short pause and then he reassured the anxious people that they were not to worry and that the lad would live. About 20 minutes later the victim of the snakebite, which often proved to be fatal, got up, asked for a drink of water, climbed back into the cart and set off for home. This experience would have been absolutely astonishing, had I not heard about 'Pambu' Narasiah and his strange powers from a friend many years earlier. 'Pambu' in Tamil means snake, and Narasiah was a railway employee who had the 'power' to cure snakebite from a distance, as I had indeed witnessed. He had refused promotion many times, asking only to remain on the main line where he could be reached by the quick railway telephone system.

As Independence Day, 15 August approached, the troubles that some of us had expected began. Hindus massacred Muslims, and in turn were massacred by their Muslim neighbours, who had lived peacefully beside them for so many years.

In Bezwada I witnessed a small part of the madness that had taken over a hitherto peaceful country. The Grand Trunk Express was perhaps the most important train in India. It ran from Delhi to Madras, taking about 52 hours to travel some 1300 miles. Rumours began to spread that on many occasions *en route* it was being attacked, and the passengers slaughtered. At Bezwada, where the train moved from Muslim Hyderabad State into India, I found proof of this. On several occasions when it arrived the only people left alive on the train were European or Indian Christians. As the train passed through Hindu areas the Muslims were killed, and as it progressed into Muslim areas the Hindus passengers suffered the same fate. The terrified remnants of what had been fully loaded trains were taken off at Bezwada and treated to hot meals and drinks of tea or coffee in the refreshment rooms. The train itself was pushed into the traffic yard, and the sweepers were put in to wash away the blood which caked the floors of the compartments, inches deep. This happened on several occasions while I was on duty at Bezwada.

LYNETTE GURNER

A friend of my parents dined with a mutual friend in Calcutta in 1947, shortly after my father had left India for good. During the meal his host mentioned that my father had a grandchild, as I had had a baby son recently. Our friend became aware of intense excitement in the previously totally impassive servant serving him. For a moment he wondered if the food would land on him, rather than on his plate. He looked up at the man and realised that he was Kancha, my father's bearer for 25–30 years. He spoke directly to Kancha regarding this event and some order was restored, but Kancha's delight was still obvious.

None of my family would ever return to India, but I believe that the children who arrived in 1940 were not forgotten when they left. Nor would we ever forget those unexpected years in India where we then grew up, within our family and in privileged surroundings, which contrasted so sharply with our previous lives in this country.

GRETA THOM

When I left school, I had a couple of years in Lahore before coming to England. In that time I worked for an electrical engineering firm (having done a full secretarial course in school which included shorthand, typing, and book-keeping). I used to cycle to work with friends (mostly boys) down the wide mall. We worked from about seven o'clock in the morning till two then came home for the afternoon sleep. We swam a lot and had a lot of fun. I can remember one New Year's Eve going to the Gymkhana for the dance and then having breakfast by the Ravi (a tributary of the Indus) – all very innocent I can assure you. I learned to drive before I left India, in a Morris Minor – I remember knocking a policeman off his stand in the middle of the road where he was directing traffic. He took his pencil from the back of his ear and said he would have to – I think the word was *challan* – which meant report me. So I quite innocently said I was the daughter of the then Head of Police, who was the father of a friend of mine, and was let off. No wonder when I came to sit my test here I nearly drove my driving instructor mad – in India the only thing was avoiding the bulls, who sat in the middle of the road and as they are sacred you could not harm them. In those days, and I expect it still applies, you had to have a car horn and you used it a lot.

I had wanted to go to music college, but Dad had two boys to train, and in those days music was a hobby not a vocation, so I came to England and worked in the bank. I can remember the bank looking at my School Certificate, of which I was very proud, being First Class, and saying they were sending it to Cambridge for verification – talk about feeling a second-class citizen. I can remember coming away from Karachi and seeing my parents and my brothers receding into the distance, and wondering what on earth I was coming to. When we arrived at Liverpool I looked down and saw the dockers, and could not believe white men were labouring: they never did that in India. My aunt and uncle came to meet me, and when we drove through the English countryside I could not believe how green it was, a truly green and pleasant land. When I took the train to London I found it hard to believe that the stations were so close together: in India it would be two to three hours between stations.

When I came to live in Cheam I was fortunate to have a very loving uncle and aunty to look after me, because I was a handful. I was homesick, and there were so many changes. My aunty desperately tried to make me a good cook; she desperately failed. She asked me to put the kettle on, as I looked at the gas cooker and thought it was like an Indian range. I put the kettle on the hob and lit the oven. She also asked me to go to get some fish and chips. I happily cycled to the shop and went straight to the counter in front of the queue – I was informed there was a queue, and I told them in no uncertain terms where I came from I was always served first!

Despite the fact that we were brought up in Spartan conditions, no central heating in school, tin baths which had water in them carried up by the servants, poor sods – what a life they must have led – I consider myself to be privileged, not because we lorded it over others – that I regret – but because we were given sound education, saw a different world and were therefore not insular. During the War we saw soldiers coming from the Burma front and the Japanese POW camps, young men looking like 80-year-olds: we did concerts for them. I was privileged to play at Viceregal Lodge in front of Lady Wavell for troop concerts because I had won a music prize. I was taken there by rickshaw and felt like a queen: not being very old at the time I had no nerves – today I would be a jellyfish in the circumstances. I think we are a tough generation.

ROBERT C. ALTER

As an American missionary family – my parents, my three older brothers and I – we were always conscious of living within and under the British Raj, but it was always as though we were on the outside looking in. My parents were friendly with a few British families, both civil and military. This was especially true in Abbotabad. But most of their friends and contacts were with Indians or other members of the missionary community. I have no memory of playing with British children – except the few who attended Woodstock School. Most were 'away' in England. Our playmates, until we started school at Woodstock, were all Indian, and our orientation to India was more Indian than British.

Though we never knew any of them personally, British soldiers, 'tommies', became very much a part of my earliest memories in places like Abbotabad, Rawalpindi and Mussoorie. The clip of marching boots, starched khaki shorts and shirts, polished leather, drill and precision dominate those memories. Kipling stories, which we avidly read, and were as avidly read to us by my father, rounded out an image (exaggerated I am sure!) of jaunty, good-natured, disciplined rogues!

As I attended Woodstock School, and completed high school there in November 1943, my most vivid memories of the Raj were of its last days, which coincided with the Second World War. Pearl Harbour, the fall of Singapore and Burma, refugees who trekked overland from Burma into India – some who even attended Woodstock – air-raids over Calcutta, the stopping of the Japanese advance into India at the battle of Kohima, Italian prisoners of war (10,000 camped in Dehra Dun), flights over the 'hump' into China, the arrival of Australian troops and US Army Air Force units and Jim Corbett training soldiers in jungle survival in the nearby Shivalik forests were the kind of things we heard and talked about. During this time (for some reason I never understood) Woodstock hosted, on several occasions, bandsmen of the Yorks and Lancs Regimental Band. After-school 'jam sessions', held several times a week, were a special treat, and helped 'humanise' my earlier images of the British soldier.

Though my parents accepted it as an ideal, and saw it as inevitable, I do not remember their ever being enthusiastic supporters of Indian Independence. For them it was always a matter of 'Yes, but they're not ready for it yet'. I have to confess that my own feelings at the time, along with those of most of my classmates, were coloured by the War. In our minds Subhas Chander Bhose was a traitor who hobnobbed with the enemy, not the martial hero of independence revered by later generations of Indians. The 'Quit India' movement of 1942 was somehow a betrayal of the very things 'our side' was fighting for. Looking back, I am ashamed of the way we treated some of our Indian schoolmates, who clearly, and quite rightly, had other loyalties.

After completing college in the United States (I escaped military service for health reasons) I returned as a very young teacher to Woodstock School in July 1947. By now the die was cast. India was to be independent, and I had become an enthusiastic convert and supporter of the idea. Those were exciting days, but they were also days marred by the tragedy and anguish of events that accompanied Partition. August 15 1947, India's first Independence Day, was celebrated at Woodstock with due pomp and enthusiasm. The new flag was raised for the first time. Staff and students presented a pageant that traced the history of Indian independence. This was followed by a suitably appropriate all-school banquet. I remember hearing that morning a recording of Nehru's 'midnight speech', and of being moved by his superbly articulated dreams for a new, modern and progressive India. Sadly, the euphoria of that day was followed by months of violence and brutality, some of which we experienced first-hand in Mussoorie.

Independent India, of course, has been much more a part of my life than India under the Raj. It is good, however, to be able to look back and trace some of India's strengths, which grew out of its years of subjugation. The Independence Movement under the leadership of people like Gandhi, Nehru, Sardar Patel, Ambedkar and others has left India with a heritage of idealism that has stood it well, one that emerged perversely, as it were, out of the confrontation between the ruled and those who ruled.

Civil administration, the judicial system, the Indian Army, India's irrigation and transportation systems, and, of course, India's parliament, all bear a distinctly British mark. The use of English (the standard being English as the English use and speak it!) as widespread today as it ever was, and an amazingly rich body of 'Indian-English' literature has been added to India's cultural heritage, much written since Independence.

But India is still uniquely Indian. I have a deep appreciation for what I am convinced is the inherent liberalism of its ancient culture – its tolerance, its acceptance of immense diversities, and its capacity to absorb the best of what comes to it. I say this despite the current spate of communal tension, religious fanaticism, and militancy. These things have happened before and undoubtedly will happen again. But India has survived and, more than survived, it has flourished, due in large part to a resilience born of those ideals.

THEON WILKINSON

One of my most treasured possessions is the Farewell Address, painted on silk, which my father received on his retirement.

To H. Wilkinson, Esqr, CBE

We, the old workers and pensioners of Elgin Mills, Co., Ltd and Cawnpore Textiles Ltd, Cawnpore, beg to express our feelings of sorrow at your going away from Cawnpore and regret that we could not present a Farewell Address before your departure. We are however, proud of you and of your meritorious services rendered not only as a Senior Director of Messrs. Begg, Sutherland & Co, Ltd, but as a greatly respected citizen of Cawnpore, taking active interest in many worthy affairs of the city.

In fact during the War you gave effective assistance in raising money for war purposes in the United Provinces, with the result that the honour of CBE was conferred upon you. In our opinion this was not an adequate recognition of your great contribution, as a Knighthood would have been a more fitting honour, which would also have been a further recognition of the fact that Mrs Wilkinson is a Lady in every sense of the word. For in her own quiet way she too served in the War Effort, with the Girl Guides and in several other ways.

Although you have left Cawnpore we still think of you. In fact those of us who are pensioners cherish the fragrance of your memory because you were always generous towards the workers and did not forsake them in their old age. We owe you a deep debt of gratitude for all that you did for us through the Welfare Department, the foundation of which was originally laid by you and which is still there carrying on the good work that you intended it to do.

We are happy to know that you are now back in your homeland, enjoying good health and engaged in the simple enjoyment of tending the garden of your new house. We think of you as a true gentleman, generous and honourable in all your dealings, kind and courteous even unto the least of us.

We pray that you and your family may live long and enjoy all the blessings of this life.

We are,

Sir,

Your obedient servants, OLD WORKERS AND PENSIONERS, Elgin Mills Co., Ltd., Cawnpore Textiles Ltd, Cawnpore

Dated Cawnpore

January 1948

NANCY LLOYD

Independence was granted to Burma in January 1948. It was a sorrowful day on 4 January when the British governor, Sir Hubert Rance, sailed away down the Rangoon River, leaving Independent Burma behind him, and we ourselves were suddenly in a foreign country, no longer part of the British Empire. The Burmese, who had been united in their determination to achieve independence from Britain, quickly fragmented into warring factions, and the whole country was in turmoil, with insurgency rife. The Karens attacked Rangoon in January 1949. They did not succeed in taking the town but their forces were close to the outskirts of the town, and we could hear the firing uncomfortably near to our home.

All the teak forests were nationalised soon after Independence, and so the Bombay Burmah Trading Corporation as a timber extracting and milling company ceased to exist. My husband was left in Rangoon as the only European member of the firm to clear everything, but quite soon he was sanctioned by the powers-that-were in London to start other projects, and soon he had a boat-repair and boat-building yard working, and an asbestos-cement factory and a cement-pipe factory. The firm still retained the little tea factory up in the hills of the Shan States, and we greatly enjoyed visiting up there in the glorious, cool climate which refreshed us after months in the enervating heat of Rangoon.

We lived in a comfortable house, provided by the firm, with good servants to look after us. As we became more senior we had to do a lot of entertaining, and housekeeping was still quite difficult; but there was great excitement, and frozen food was sent up from Singapore, and we acquired a deep-freeze. Rangoon, as a foreign city, had many embassies, and we had to attend endless official parties. These were pleasant enough in the dry season, as they were usually held outdoors with the gardens all attractively lit up by fairy lights. But we much preferred the cheerful informal parties given by our Burmese friends. My husband worked extremely hard at his job and was also, for two separate years, Chairman of the Chamber of Commerce, which entailed much extra work. Nevertheless, we still led a very active life, with lots of sailing, tennis and golf. In the cold weather we used to go out shooting in the jungle at weekends. This made a nice break, as we always stayed overnight, ready for a dawn start, in a Burmese village, or in camp. The shooting was mostly for jungle-fowl, which is the ancestor of the farmyard fowl and makes excellent eating, as well as good sport. There was also duck-shooting and my husband used to go out after snipe as well, accompanied only by a bearer, which he particularly enjoyed.

I took a little job working for the SPCA, which was somewhat heart-rending as the Oriental is, on the whole, very cruel to animals. Otherwise I played lots of music and organised several charity concerts with the local talent, taking part. A group of us ladies took painting lessons. Our teacher was a Burmese artist, whose style was mostly Burmese – a very stylised form of composition – but he had trained in Paris and so was able to help us with our Western form of painting.

BEULAH STIDSTON

By the time I was seven the Second World War had started, and we had left northern India and moved down to Poona.

After being a day scholar at St Mary's for a while until we left for Ahmednagar, I then became a boarder for a very short time. We were all allowed to have a sweets ration supplied by our parents and the dreadful day came when we, the juniors, had our sweets temporarily confiscated as punishment for making too much noise early and waking the senior boarders. Horror of horrors! When the day at last came when we were to get our sweets back, it was announced that we should donate them to a charity instead!

Then Ahmednagar in the presidency of Bombay was to be my home, until finally leaving India for New Zealand in 1948. My education in India continued, initially, at a very small private school run by an officer's wife, and later, at home from books and supervised by my mother. My first algebra lessons were from a lovely Parsee lady teacher – my recollection has always been that I was rather horrid to her, as I hated algebra. I stayed with her extended family in 1995 and apologised, but she gallantly insisted she didn't remember my bad behaviour.

During much of the time in Ahmednagar I kept a diary and again, most of the important things in my life seem to have involved animals, with friends also being very important. The diary constantly records going to watch polo, held on a ground near where I lived, visiting friends, going swimming at the cantonment pool. Ahmednagar has always been an important Army post and a big attraction for me and my best friend, Carola, was the Army Remount Depot, where horses and mules were trained for work in the jungles of Burma. The residence of the colonel in charge of the Remount Depot was very close to Carola's house, and we got in the habit of going there to visit the horses in the stables.

When a new colonel, Colonel McLaughlin, came to the Remount Depot we were in heaven, as he took us under his wing and gave us formal riding lessons. Carola's parents did have horses but mine did not, so it was particularly wonderful for me. When we weren't mooning around the stables or having riding lessons, we most often played horses, and galloped endlessly around the grounds of Carola's home on foot. During the heat of the afternoon we had to play inside. I well remember being over-exuberant one day bouncing on one of the beds and breaking the wooden side-strut. Carola's dear mother allowed me to swear her to secrecy and not tell my own mother. It was Army furniture so, hopefully, didn't incur her in any personal expense.

Prior to Carola's arrival in Ahmednagar there had been no girls for me to play with in our area, and my main playmate had been a boy named Billy. Billy was a great attraction because he had a pony named Araby, a fair bicycle (quarter size), a football and a Meccano set. I learned to ride a bicycle on Billy's bike, but when later friends had a full-size bike I wasn't able to manage it. Once again, Colonel

McLaughlin came to the rescue. Finding I had quite a long walk to and from home, he lent me his sister's bicycle until she came to Ahmednagar. There was a circular gravel drive in front of his house and he simply commanded me to get on and ride, and I did! After making sure I was reasonably competent he let me wobble off home. The colonel was a widower, and prior to his sister's arrival he used to have afternoon tea alone, served on the porch. Occasionally Carola and I would be invited to join him and, because I was older than Carola, he would make me be 'mother' and pour the tea for all of us.

The other most important friends of my time in Ahmednagar were a Parsee family, including my algebra teacher. Initially, we lived opposite to them and later, when my father, who was a doctor, was

Beulah Stidston, with the *chowkidar*, outside Salabat Khan's tomb, Ahmednagar, 1941.

away in Burma where he set up the first base-hospital in Kohima after the Japanese were driven from there, Mum and I rented part of a bungalow from them, which was set in the same grounds as their own home. When appendicitis with various complications beset me in 1948, I spent two months in the Salvation Army hospital. Because of the many different religions being cared for, with their varying dietary customs, the hospital regime was for relations to supply patients' meals. Our Parsee friends took on the task of supplying all my meals. Prayers were also said for me in the Parsee Fire Temple. I was truly honoured.

The Salvation Army hospital was an interesting mini United Nations. The senior surgeon, a lovely man, was Norwegian. He used to have to take my pulse several times in a row before it settled down! The matron was from Perth, Australia, the head nurse was English, while the Financial Manager was a Canadian. One of the visiting chaplains was Burmese.

Another friend of my mother and me during this time was the elderly Italian priest who officiated at the Roman Catholic Church. We were Anglicans, and I used to attend Sunday School in the garrison Anglican Church but dear old Father Alberghetti was a most welcome visitor for gentle relaxed afternoon teas, until he became a 'casualty' of war and was taken away to be interned elsewhere in India.

As the War came to an end and the need for the Remount Depot receded, horses and mules returned from Burma and had to be disposed of. Some horses were sold at auction, several of which I attended, but others, and all the mules, were put down. Sad lines of them used to pass our front gate on their way to their final resting place.

My parents never kept as many servants as was often the case, so perhaps I don't have as many memories of them as others may have. Among the most memorable were two from our time in the Punjab early in my life. My father's bearer was Matha Prasad, a Brahmin (high-caste Hindu), and on one occasion when I was ill he caught my vomit in his hands to try to save damage to the carpet. This would have been a highly undesirable thing to do in view of his caste status. Our cook during our time in the north was a Muslim, Abdul Gaffur. He was a terrific cook: he used to pamper me with titbits in the kitchen, and was greatly regarded by my parents. For some time after we left he and my father used to correspond occasionally, and we were always worried as to what may have happened to him when Partition came, with all its unfortunate bloodshed.

A memorable person in Ahmednagar, though not a servant of ours, was Gau, a woman suffering leprosy, who used to visit our Parsee doctor friend. In spite of her infirmities and poverty-stricken life, Gau had a lovely personality and I have always remembered her. Poor Gau; at night in her little hut in the village in which she lived, rats sometimes nibbled her toes because the leprosy had caused loss of feeling in them. There was also Sikander, servant of our Parsee friends. As well as cooking and various other duties, he used to hold a torch out of the open side of the old Austin Tourer to light the way on the rare occasions when a trip had to be taken after dark.

Ahmednagar was our home at Independence, and also when Mahatma Gandhi was assassinated. One of his assassins came from Ahmednagar, so there was a particular sense of involvement. I still possess the *Times of India* editions with reports of the eventual trial.

December 1948 saw our final departure from India for a future life in New Zealand.

ROBERT MATTHEWS

Shah was about my own age. Assigned to look after both me and my brother, Geoffrey, who at 17 was a year older, Shah was almost family. He was certainly my friend. With the pale skin and grey eyes of the Pathan tribesmen, Shah accompanied me everywhere when I came home in the school holidays. Beating for partridge, drumming up hare, fishing for *mahseer* in the Sohan river with me, Shah was my confidante. Highly intelligent, he spoke good English.

Out one day on a fishing expedition, he remarked that it was about time I had a woman. He claimed to have had many.

'Many, Bobby-sahib,' he boasted in English. 'Very nice,' he grinned. 'Why not try?'

'Ingrezi-*sahibs* don't do that sort of thing. Well, at least not till they are older,' I blustered, going red.

The whole subject was very embarrassing. Not that I didn't like girls, I did, very much indeed. But going the whole hog? That was entirely out of the question. Petting was as far as I'd ever got. Even so, opportunities for that had been few and far-between. In school, contact with girls was *verboten*. One only saw them in church on Sundays, and then it was a case of 'lookee lookee, no touchee'. Holidays were different. But so gauche were we school boarders that, plucking up the courage to hold a girl's hand, let alone deliver a kiss, required huge resolve. Yet, I did not wish Shah to know exactly how inexperienced I was.

'Then you can never be a man,' said Shah. 'Tell you what, Bobby-sahib, what if I can fix it up for you?'

'How?'

'At Chakla, Bobby-sahib.'

An Attock Oil Company house at Morgah, lived in by Robert Matthews between 1942 and 1948.

'Where's Chakla? What's Chakla?'

Shah roared with laughter. 'Chakla is near the Raja Bazaar in Rawalpindi. It is where you can jiggy jig, Sahib, with prostitutes. It is a famous place, Sahib.' I was now intrigued, in spite of myself.

'But you have to pay them, don't you?' I said. 'I could never afford it, even if I wanted to, which I don't. I've got no rupees. By the way,' I said, trying not to show much interest, 'how much is it?'

'60 rupees. I will pay for you, Bobby-sahib,' said Shah, thumping his chest.

'That's ridiculous, Shah, that's your whole month's pay. I could never allow it.'

In the end, because Shah was so insistent, I did allow it. Two days later, disguised in one of Shah's spare *shalwar kameez*, I cycled into 'Pindi with him at night. He was laughing the whole way. I, on the other hand, was wondering what I'd got myself into. Armed with spermicidal creams and antiseptics, stolen from my brother's supply of American 'K' rations he had acquired from a US soldier, I followed Shah down an alleyway leading to a row of small, unedifying, mud structures on the outskirts of 'Pindi.

'This is the place,' said Shah, dismounting. 'Wait here for me.'

I watched as he went from hut to hut trying to settle on a price he could afford. To my surprise, I saw women shouting abuse at him as he proceeded down the line. Emerging from the doorway of the very last house, he gave me a thumbs-up signal, and shouted in English, 'Sahib, this one will do us both for 60 rupees! I go first, okay?' I stood there trembling with apprehension, wishing Shah to never reappear. But he did, and it was now my turn. He grinned, took my bike, and said, 'She good, you will like.'

Reluctantly, I drew aside the curtain of the small dwelling and found myself facing a wizened, bare-breasted woman wearing a long skirt. She might have been about 30, but to me she looked ancient. She smiled in welcome, showing gaps in her beetlejuice-stained teeth. The room, lit by an oil lamp, was surprisingly clean. It had a clay *lotha* full of water standing in a shallow recess in one corner, presumably for washing, a calendar on the wall illustrated with a picture of King George V and Queen Mary, and under the tiny window a *charpoy* bed, whose coverlet was disturbed. The woman spoke to me in Pushtu, which I did not understand. Her words were followed by a lewd gesture whose meaning was inescapable. She then lay down on the bed and drew her legs up. At this point, I fled. Shah was waiting outside for me.

'How was it, Bobby-sahib?' he exclaimed excitedly. 'Didn't I tell you it was good?'

'Brilliant, Shah, brilliant,' I lied, unable to admit the truth.

'Then, Sahib, you are now a man at last!' Shah's glee was so infectious, I laughed with him.

(The postscript to this story is that, in 1986, I discovered Shah's whereabouts from old servants still at Morgah. Wounded in one of the Indo–Pak wars, whilst serving as a *havildar* in the Pakistan Army, Shah had retired to his village near Peshawar. Living on a small Army pension, he seemed contented enough with his wife and four grown-up sons. Flabbergasted to see me again, he recognised me instantly. Overcome with emotion, we fell into bearhugging and later, talked for hours over a mutton curry and pilau prepared by his wife. Shah's amusement at my story turned to tears when I pressed on him the 60 rupees he'd spent on me, plus compound interest at 10 percent calculated over 37 years. This amounted to the grand total of 3456 rupees. I added 1500 rupees to take into account inflation(!). Shah died in 1987.)

PATRICK HUGH STEVENAGE

At first, the residual authorities of the British Government in India tried to help the Anglo-Indians to leave. They were given assisted passages and temporary documentation, and in many cases where British descent could be proved, however slightly, British passports were readily handed out. But in due course the rules were tightened. It became harder, if not impossible, for savings, pensions and personal fortunes to be taken out of India. British passports were harder to obtain, and the Anglo-Indians had to turn to other Commonwealth countries, such as Australia, which still operated an 'open-door' policy.

The Anglo-Indian population in India was never under any illusion as to how the new governments would treat them. Certainly, Anglo-Indians were never physically attacked. As long as they could not be replaced overnight by suitably trained Indians they would be tolerated, but promotion was quite another matter. Some Anglo-Indians were retained to serve in the armed forces, particularly the Army and the Navy. They also had a continuing role to play on the railways and in the telegraph offices. But clerical and administrative jobs were for the Indians and the Pakistanis. The Police and the judiciary were sensitive positions, and they were readily recognised as the perks of the political parties and politicians. As the years passed, the better elements of the community vanished from the scene. Those who remained, mostly those who could not afford to get out or who left it too late, found that they had become a 'depressed class', in every sense.

But the Stevenages did not wait to be pushed out or depressed. We were among the first to quit the shores of the country where they had lived happily, prosperously and usefully for more than four generations, nearly two hundred years. After the death of my father in 1941, my mother seemed to surrender the battle against her own failing health. She had long suffered from chronic, cardiac asthma, but till now had resisted its impact upon her life and many activities. She retired into her shell and spent more and more of her time in bed. All her children, except the youngest son, had married and left home, and it was her family doctor's considered verdict that she would only get well when one of her children became sick or in some other way demanded her active help and intervention. It was not illness in the family that finally aroused her spirits, but the more vital impact of Indian independence upon them and their future lives.

As her doctor had correctly diagnosed, her will was always stronger than any ailment. She arranged her affairs in India and determinedly marched up the gangway of the ship which was to bring her from Bombay to the England she had never seen, but which she confidently expected would offer the best future for her children. Her eldest son and his family had preceded her, her second son accompanied her, and one by one all the other children followed. She argued, pleaded with and bullied each one in turn, and where she, a frail old lady could lead, how could they resist following her?

I set about getting my papers together and proving my right to British citizenship and a British passport. My wife, Babs, was in Bangalore with her mother, and a complication had arisen to bedevil our plans. She was pregnant. I was delighted at the prospect of another child (we already had a daughter) – maybe a son – but that could upset the delicate timing of our plans to leave India and join the growing family in Britain. But I pushed ahead. Citizenship papers and passports were secured for me, for Babs and for Patricia, our daughter. I tried unsuccessfully to get a redundancy package from the railways, but failing that put in my resignation with effect from 14 November 1950. The customary month's notice was given and I set about trying to fix a cheap and early passage to Britain.

Thomas Cook offered me just that, a passage on the *Chusan* leaving Colombo on 20 December. Babs was very upset at the thought of my going on ahead and having to follow later with the children. But we agreed that it was the only course open to us, and I wrote accepting the offered passage. I posted it in the postbox at the office, but when I got home Babs was in such a state that I asked my office superintendent to stand by the box and recover my letter when the postman came to clear the box. Such things were possible in India, and in due course the letter came back to me. I handed it to Babs to be destroyed, saying I would write another the next day. Then I went for my bath and when I came out I discovered that Babs had steeled herself and come to a decision. She took the letter and posted it herself at the main post-office box.

A letter to the High Commissioner asking for my next child's name, a blank at present, to be inserted on Babs' passport was drafted, and Thomas Cook were asked to try for another passage for my wife and children after a suitable interval. I hardly had time to reflect on the gravity of the step I was taking. I was giving up a good position, going to a new country to try and find another job, leaving my wife and children to follow; and all this with hardly any money, and no contacts other than my mother and my brothers in Britain. Looked at in retrospect, it was an awesome decision.

We spent the last week in Bangalore, with Babs's mother and stepfather trying not to face the inevitable fact that the date for my departure was coming ever nearer. It arrived, and I steeled myself into a dry-eyed goodbye but dissolved into tears as the train steamed out of Bangalore cantonment. In Madras I found time to visit Dad's grave, and was surprised to find that somehow our old servants – the *ayah*, the chauffeur and the cook – had discovered my plans, and were already there to bid me farewell. Our servants were more than just that, they were truly our friends.

And so, on 20 December 1950, Dad's birthday – it would have been his seventy-third – the *Chusan* steamed out of Colombo, taking me to a new and very different life.

CARL HIGGINSON

In 1944 we were transferred to Dhanbad in Bihar. There was a large transit camp less than a hundred yards from us, and we spent hours watching the troops training.

We returned to Asansol in 1946. August 15 1947 was Independence Day, and we all know of the violence and bloodshed that led up to it. I didn't see any myself, but stories came back through the running staff of terrible atrocities.

In 1948 my father received his final promotion to mail driver, and we were transferred to Cawnpore (Kanpur) in the United Provinces (Uttar Pradesh). My three brothers and I were attending the local school (St Patrick's High School) while we were in Asansol. We now returned to the school as boarders. I enjoyed boarding school; it's a pity schoolwork got in the way. Being transferred wasn't a problem either; it was a way of life. The railway supplied the family with a freight wagon for their furniture, and a team of labourers to load the wagon. The wagon was attached to the train that took them to their destination and another team of labourers unloaded the wagon and delivered the furniture to their new quarters. All free of charge.

Railway staff also got a certain amount of free travel. As a mail driver he got three first-class passes a year to anywhere he wanted to go. But as we were going to boarding school and had to travel over 500 miles, he got as many first-class school passes as were needed. A first-class compartment was also reserved for us. We were very comfortable, we could sleep comfortably and there was a washbasin, toilet and shower.

A catering company ran a catering service throughout the whole railway that I knew. They had restaurants on all the main stations. We ordered food through the conductor guard, and the food was delivered to our compartment. We would eat in comfort, and the crockery was collected at the next main station. Top-class service. Railway stations at some of the larger towns, like Cawnpore, Lucknow, Delhi and Howrah were vast places. The main building had several floors. The waiting rooms were large and airy, with very comfortable seating. There were small rooms with clean beds for rent. Toilets, washing and bathing facilities. All very clean and well looked after. There were also several restaurants.

Some railway language: going from Calcutta towards Delhi was Up Country; Delhi towards Calcutta was Down Country; railway people did not live in towns, they lived at Stations; the people who worked the trains (drivers and their crews, guards) were Running Staff; when the driver and his crew were on the locomotive, they were On the Footplate.

The public knew trains by different names: the Delhi Mail, the Toofah Express, etc. Railway people knew them by numbers.

The odd numbers travelled up towards Delhi, the even numbers travelled down towards Calcutta. 1 Up, 2 down, 3 up and 4 Down were the mail trains, and 4, 6, 7 and 8 were express trains, which were not quite as fast as the mails. The mail drivers drove the mail trains and the express trains. The other drivers on the grade below drove only express trains. When world leaders visited India, special trains were laid on for them. These trains were driven by the mail drivers. My father met most of these people, because most of them came up to the locomotive and thanked him and his crew.

In about 1949, India's railways were divided into zones. The East Indian Railway was divided into two. From Delhi to Moghal Sarai became the Northern Railway, and from Moghal Sarai to Howrah (Calcutta) became the Eastern Railway. As we lived in Cawnpore, we were now on the Northern Railway.

Cawnpore was the mail station on our section of the main line. A driver would take a train to Delhi, a journey of about 300 miles, a day's work. After leaving his engine in the shed, he would go to the Running Room where he could have a bath and a meal, relax and sleep. A Running Room was a place for the running staff to rest while away from home. It had all the facilities: bathrooms, a dining room and a kitchen complete with a cook so you had freshly cooked food, and clean beds. The driver would then bring another train back to his home base, a round trip taking about 24 hours. The following day he would take another trip in the opposite direction and so on. During the 1950s, certain foods were still rationed. One of them was wheat. The wheat had to be cleaned, and foreign bodies like grit etc. removed. It was my job to take small amounts, as required, to the market and get it ground into flour. It was an interesting journey and process. The main shopping for items like rice, lentils, spices and cooking oil, etc., was done once a month. One cook we had didn't like it. He told my parents that if he couldn't go to the market to do the shopping and make a few annas for himself the job was no good. He said goodbye and left. All the stores were kept in large containers in a large store box.

Kulfi is an ice-cream which is unique. No recipe was ever written. The recipe was passed down from generation to generation. The *kulfiwallah* was a poor man who made his living making and selling this ice cream. He made it in cone-shaped moulds and packed them in ice in a large, clay pot. The taste of the *kulfi* was unique. No one has ever managed to reproduce it. Throughout Britain, in the best Indian restaurants, with the finest equipment, no one has succeeded. The *kulfiwallah* made it using very poor equipment.

When I was in Bengal and Bihar I was a young boy doing what was important to young boys. We played games like Tip Cat, Kick the Can and Jack the Monkey. These games had been around for a long time. No one knows how they started, or how the rules developed, and they were very popular. Jack the Monkey was played in a tree, and was dangerous. It was a game of Catch. If you were 'it', you had to chase and catch the others. It all took place up a tree, and there were a lot of nasty tumbles. But young boys never learn. It was very difficult keeping your injuries from your parents. There were also miles of wild, open spaces, and during the school holidays we ran wild out there.

We also spent a lot of time in the shed, in the yard watching the shunters working, helping to turn engines on the turntable. Sometimes we even managed to get the shunters to give us a ride on their engines. We knew our way around and we didn't take liberties or get up to mischief.

Over the years we had several servants. I did not appreciate the jobs they did until I was in my teens. We were all brought up to treat them with respect. One that stood out above all the others was Mabhoob, our sweeper. He was an 'untouchable'. But Mabhoob was a Muslim, not a Hindu. He married a Hindu who was 'untouchable' and so became 'untouchable'. He was a wonderful man. He never had to be asked to do anything, he would just appear when needed.

When I was about 18 years old, my two older brothers and I were practically the same size. So very often our summer clothes, mainly cotton, would get mixed up. Mabhoob would step in and decide which article belonged to which brother, and we would accept his judgement. When we were going to any functions, such as dances at the institute or some Club, he took it on himself to lay out our clothes, polish our shoes and have everything ready. He always knew what was on and where. He would even give me a once-over before I left. Mabhoob was not just a servant. He was a friend.

Because my father had over 30 years' service on the railway, he could take early retirement with full privileges. So he retired aged 50 years. He decided to come to Britain. We left India in October 1956. It was a painful time saying goodbye to our servants and friends. It must have been a difficult time for my parents taking such a step. The journey from Bombay to Tilbury was supposed to take 19 days. Our journey took 42 days. Due to the Suez Crisis the Canal was blocked, we were ordered back to Aden, and the next day we were told to proceed via the Cape of Good Hope. It was a most enjoyable experience. We had good entertainment, good food, and we got to know a lot of different kinds of people. I was lucky; I didn't get seasick, so I was able to enjoy everything. The food was a new experience for me. I also celebrated my twenty-first birthday and had my first taste of British beer.

We arrived at Tilbury on 3 December 1956. It was a bright and sunny day, but I was freezing. I had never been so cold: I stood against a building with the sun shining directly on me and I couldn't feel any warmth. I thought, this is it, I'm going to be cold for the rest of my life. I wasn't happy. For the next 18 months I never went out without wearing an overcoat, scarf and gloves.

We were a large family, so my father bought a large house. We soon settled in, got jobs and got on with our lives. Even though I was happy I was terribly homesick. I eventually got married, had a family and a home of my own, but within was this yearning that would not go away. It went on for over twelve years.

VALERIE THURLEY

My two brothers, my sister and I grew up in Ghora Gali. When I meet people at school reunions, they always refer to the place as 'the school', or 'the Lawrence College', but for me both the estate and surrounding forest were never just school, but home. My parents were both on the staff, and we lived there summer and winter, sunshine and snowfall, so it was only natural we knew every inch of the estate, every servant and woodcutter. I grew up speaking Urdu as fluently as I spoke English, though later I was often told my grammar was inherited from the servants, not the text-books!

From the start, my father thought of Ghora Gali as an enchanted place. He arrived from England in 1931 to teach Latin and English to the senior boys. Later, after Partition, he was asked to take over as Principal, which he did. My mother, also a teacher, used to deal with children in the junior school until she married and had her own children. After Partition she taught poetry and drama to the new Pakistani boys, and read them books like *Winnie the Pooh* and

The Chapel at Lawrence College, Ghora Gali. (Robert Matthews)

Wind in the Willows to broaden their outlook. The Pakistani boys remember both my parents with great affection, and they gave my mother a warm welcome back there. I am particularly touched that the new hospital has been named after my father. It is certainly a memorial he would have been proud of claiming.

In 1947 my youngest brother died very suddenly of pneumonia. He was only three and a half, and the death shook my father badly. Later, he wrote that Timmy's death ended a particular period of his life in India, and that afterwards he became involved in an increasingly troubled world. This reference was to the Partition of India, and how badly he felt it had been thought through. Certainly, by the middle of July, our remote area in the hills was involved in the general bleakness of what was happening all over the country. As my father once said: Paradise was being ruined in front of our very eyes.

Two members of the staff at college were badly affected during 1947. We were now in Pakistan. Abdul Hamid was an old friend of the family, and loved walking the hills with my father. He would not believe anyone would harm his family in Jullundur, but returned to find out. The experience changed him completely, and left him very embittered. Person after person in his family had been taken out and slaughtered by friends they had known all their lives.

The other staff member who suffered used to live in the house adjoining ours. Every evening we would hear him barricade himself and his Sikh family into one bedroom, and place a mattress up against the door. The twin houses were built close to the edge of the forest which led up to the Murree Hills, and on several occasions that early summer we would hear hooligans from outside arrive and throw things against the house. For some reason the *chowkidar* was always absent, and it must have come as a great relief to my parents when the family left the estate late one night in the early part of August. According to the *chowkidar* they all left wearing *burkhas*, but this was never confirmed.

Other incidents of violence impinged on us. Two miles from the college was Hays Farm, which bred pigs and employed Hindu butchers. One night some Muslims went to the farm, slaughtered the pigs, and hung the Hindu butchers up on meat hooks. Earlier that same year the Murree Brewery, half a mile down from the college, was burnt down, and the smoke from it hung all over the school buildings. Fires began to burn in Murree, less than two miles away up the mountain road. The smell of smoke would greet us when we woke, and I vividly remember standing with my father one evening on the crest of the hill, and hearing the noise of people screaming. In the valley below us fire burnt building after building.

Nobody on the estate or at the college suffered while the school remained open. The advice given to us was to remain aloof from the political situation and not take sides. This came easily to the adults, but to me, a child, it just didn't make sense. I had grown up with the servants and their children. The bearer, *ayah* and cook were my friends. Some were Muslims, others Hindu. I had shared their festivals, just as they shared our Christmas. Now, suddenly, things had changed. They were they, and we were we, and if big trouble came, we would be saved, while they were left to roast in their own juices.

The adults became suddenly very serious, even the very young teachers. In the evenings, the senior masters would meet in one of the houses, and most often it was our house, which was not too close to the school. They would discuss things they had read in the newspapers, and not any worrying news. The college had an AFI (Auxiliary Force India) division, and via this, access to guns and ammunition. Every night a different member of staff was chosen to sleep with the key to this armoury under his pillow. The college servants were on tenterhooks, and the fear was that one of them could get hold of the guns and make off with them to protect their own families. Or even, as some claimed, to protect us, their *memsahibs* and *sahibs*.

Of course, things passed me by. I've no idea just how it was arranged for most of the children to get back to their homes. What I do remember is that many did not return at the normal time or year, but remained on, along with those who were going to take their senior and junior Cambridge Examinations in November, early December. At about this time my father was contacted by the DPI (Director of Public Instruction), who asked him whether he would take charge of 144 people and see that they arrived safely in places which ranged variously, and ended in Madras. It was explained to him that these people would include more than the usual Cambridge pupils and the few children whose parents lived in what had now become 'India' as opposed to 'Pakistan'. And also that among the people would be some Hindu and Sikh teachers, and some students who were in a position of having to leave Pakistan. Since we, as a family, had already signalled we were making our way to Bangalore, my father agreed. In normal circumstances, the journey from Rawalpindi to Bangalore took four days. He did not know then it would take ten days before we reached the end of this particular trip.

I always feel my childhood ended during that terrible journey. It was a fiery baptism into adulthood, and started (for me!) when we reached Lahore Station, and not a single member of my family remembered to wish me happy thirteenth birthday, let alone give me a present. We had travelled third-class from Rawalpindi, squashed into the huge bogey, the adults standing so the children could sit. Our new brother, Martin, had been born since Timmy died, and the only way he could survive the journey was in a hard cot, pushed beneath out feet. I knew that as an English girl I was safe on the station platform and no one would touch me, but this was a stigma in itself. I remember running up the platform towards the engine driver, holding a bottle filled with two spoonfuls of condensed milk. The driver poured hot water into the bottle, providing me with the next meal for four-month-old Martin. All I had to do was to return to the bogey with it. I'm sure it was not such a huge journey, but it felt so to me. There was something frightening to run through such hordes of people and their quiet desperation.

When we finally reached Lahore we faced confusion. The bogey of the train we should have been put on to lay in a siding, quite unfit for use. The dead and dying had been ladled on to it, and it stank. Meanwhile, there were 144 people to feed. Fortunately the Army helped out, though the food they provided was a very hot curry, which greatly upset the stomachs of the smallest children. My father and a group of college boys and Senior Cambridge students helped to scrub down two of the bogeys, and some of the more vulnerable people were able to sleep there for that night. Meanwhile a group of us, me included, slept in the station master's office. I remember being tired, cross and missing Ghora Gali very much.

Next day a change of plan was announced. My father told us we must face a truck journey across what was known as 'no-man's land'. This would be in armoured trucks, with the Army in charge. Vehicles were meant to keep within a short distance of each other, but unfortunately a sandstorm blew up, which delayed the last of the trucks keeping up with the first ones. Because of this we returned to Lahore, and what I recall of the station still haunts me. During that day a train must have arrived from India, and everywhere you looked there were dead, piled like old sandbags against the railings. One other train went through the station at top speed. It was so crowded that the roof was sagging with people, and people clung to the windows and doors outside. There was not a spare inch of space anywhere, and it was evident that people were dying and nobody cared. I was 13 and had lived in what my father called 'Paradise', and now everything was hell. But we weren't allowed to cry. Nobody was allowed to cry on that journey, because ours was such a small share of the suffering.

As the journey went on, so my father handed over the children to parents. Or took leave of the adult who had come in his care. For part of the rest of our journey by train he was given the title Major Thurley, which was stuck on our two large compartments. I remember being told over and over again that on no account were any of us to open the window or door to anyone at all or allow anyone to enter the compartment. Though on one station my father was so upset by the noise of a woman crying in the compartment next door, he brought the young woman through to travel the rest of the journey with us. She had not been hurt herself, but she told my father that when the train stopped at a station, the Sikh sitting opposite her would get out, kill a few people, and return wiping the blade of his knife.

Nobody could protect us from seeing things from the window of the train. It was like a nightmare. I lost track of time and dates, and what was amazing was that my father kept his cool. Despite having no doctor on hand, and despite the length of the journey, every passenger on that journey was brought safely to their destination. All that could be accounted for as suffering was that by the time we reached Bangalore, my father had completely lost his voice. Also he, as well as several others among us, suffered from scabies.

Years later, my father was awarded the OBE. It was almost certainly the most rewarding moment of his quiet life, and by his own reckoning it was given him for undertaking the journey in 1947 with the 144 people and no complications.

ROBERT BAKER

In mid-July 1945 I went down with jaundice. I was hospitalised in Abbotabad, spent three weeks in bed and was then given 21 days' sick leave, so was at last free to go home to Kumarakom, in the far south of India, in Travancore.

My journey to Kumarakom from Abbotabad took a week by train as far as Cochin Harbour terminus.

I was awaited by my mother, but the absence of my father made me realise just how sick he must be. I had known he was ill, but had not realised until then just how ill. On reaching home I found him resting on a bed on the west verandah. I am sure my return was a huge relief to him, and he showed some animation despite his emaciated condition. He was still completely dominant over all his family – my mother and myself – and of course the staff and labourers on the estate.

I returned from my sick leave to Rawalpindi, where my one thought was to get out of the Army. My demob category was 26. My father had applied to the Army authorities for me to be demobbed immediately on the grounds of his ill-health, and the need for him to hand over to me the responsibility of running the large family business. Perhaps his letter carried some weight, as my demob did come through, though no more than a few days before my demob group came up anyway.

There were very few British officers wanting to be demobbed in India, and certainly none in Rawalpindi. I therefore, to a large extent, demobbed myself, with the very valuable help of an Indian clerk in the office. Together, we looked up the regulations in the appropriate manual, and, after a couple of days, I was free to go. I missed out on some of the items I was entitled to – a civvy suit with shoes for instance – but I did not much care. After five years and eight months I was free.

My mother and I were now alone with my dying father, for whom some days were worse than others. On very bad days an Indian doctor would be brought in, but each time we knew, and the doctor knew, that my father's illness was terminal. On one occasion, one of our overseers told my father that, for stomach trouble, he personally used a daily portion of opium, and recommended it as highly efficacious. My father did in fact for some days take opium. It was in the form of a small, round ball the size of a pea, black and sticky, akin to tar. It was easily available in the bazaar. But neither this, nor any other medicament, prevented my father from getting weaker every day.

Finally, I quietly and diffidently asked him to consider a move to the hospital in Neyyoor. He hated the idea, knowing, I am sure, that if he left Kumarakom, he would never return: 'I want to die here at home.' But eventually he agreed. With my mother and myself in attendance, he went by boat to Olesha and then by car 140 miles to Nagercoil hospital, then presided over by a Dr Noble, my father having refused to go to Neyyoor.

Both Neyyoor and Nagercoil were mission hospitals. Neyyoor was sponsored by the non-conformists, and supported by the London Missionary Society. Nagercoil was run by the American Salvation Army. His illness was sprue, caused by eating all the wrong things, highly spiced and fried foods, even fish that was no longer fresh. The symptoms were a complete inability of the digestive system to function. All food consumed came away in a yellow liquid froth and, as the body received no sustenance, it became more emaciated every day. It was the most distressing experience to watch him dying by the smallest margin each day. He was starving to death.

In the end, my father agreed to go back to Neyyoor, where he had received excellent treatment before. My mother went to stay at the Savoy Hotel in Ootacamund and Dora, my father's sister, went home to Kodaikanal. I was left alone at Kumarakom, but visited my father in both hospitals. The round trip was very nearly 300 miles, and despite using my small Ford (10 hp) I owned from before the War, I found it extremely difficult to get enough coupons to buy petrol for this weekly journey.

I applied for coupons in Trivandrum and experienced a small glimpse of the new India on occasion when I was not given preferential treatment by the Government official doling out the coupons. I learned I would be given immediate attention if I gave a tin of cigarettes. I did so once, but I was reluctant to make it a drill. It was foolish of me not to have done so, for Indians do not queue, but jostle, push and shove on all occasions when queuing would be the better way. Thus I found myself in a melee of humanity, and in India this is to be avoided.

Towards the end, my father was so emaciated that his bones would have protruded through his skin had it not been that he was so frequently moved by his personal servants, who remained with him. When his distress, and ours at his bedside, was beyond bearing, Sister Margaret English came in and gave my father a huge injection of some very strong sedative. Shortly afterwards he lost consciousness, and about eight hours later he died. I have never had any doubt that

Sister English did the right thing. My only criticism was that the decision to give my father a painless last few hours was too long delayed. In similar circumstances I would hope that someone would do the same for me.

My father's funeral service was held in Christ Church, Trivandrum, and he was buried in the churchyard there. The funeral oration was given by Bishop Jacob, the first Indian Bishop of the Church of South India. I had, a couple of weeks previously and in anticipation of my father's death, made arrangements for the construction of a suitable coffin. There were no undertakers to help one bury the dead in India, and no sources of ready-made coffins. I felt that perhaps it was ethically wrong to anticipate my father's death in this way, but I am glad I did.

ROBERT MATTHEWS

Early in 1947, on my school vacation, vicious rioting broke out between Muslims, Hindus and Sikhs, in the vicinity of our house in Morgah. Muslim workers at the refinery, who had lived for years in harmony with their Hindu and Sikh colleagues, took it upon themselves to turf them out. Joined by black-shirted peasants from surrounding villages, wielding pitchforks and spades whose edges had been razor-sharpened, they set upon the defenceless Hindus and Sikhs. Although some escaped massacre, several men, women and children were despatched with little mercy. The Attock Oil Company doctor, himself a Hindu, tried to take cover in the main office, directly opposite where my family was safely holed up in our bungalow. From there, we witnessed the flight of the poor doctor who, just before he made the main door, had his hand taken off at the wrist by a spade. Mercifully, he got away, but the vision of his severed hand lying in the dust afflicts me to this day.

Bored, after a week's enforced confinement, I decided to get out of the place into the surrounding countryside. Without telling anyone, I rode my bicycle to a point where the Grand Trunk Road from

Rawalpindi is bridged at the Sohan river. There I sat smoking an illicit cigarette. As I looked down on the ribbon of road below, several buses filled with women and children passed by on their way to Lahore. Since all the buses had armed guards on board, I assumed that the occupants would safely reach their destination.

After about half an hour, I decided I'd had enough. It was hot, there was the sound of distant gunfire, and I was nervous. As I made my way down to the road, a busload of women, wearing the all-enveloping black *burkhas* of Muslims, approached at speed. The bus travelled so close to me that I was nearly brushed by its sides. I noticed that there were perhaps 30 people crammed on the bus, all with their faces covered. Of more than passing interest to me was the sight of a large woman perched precariously on the running board near to the driver. The woman's *burkha* flew up in the wind just as the vehicle passed, to expose the wearer's large, shiny, black boots. Understandably, I rode away from the scene feeling most confused. Obviously, the bus contained not women, but men, disguised as women.

A couple of hundred yards further down the road, I encountered a group of seven blackshirts, who climbed out of the Hindu doctor's purloined Buick car and waved me down. All carried rifles. Amongst them, I recognised my stepfather's foreman at the refinery. Fortunately for me, he realised who I was. He told his colleagues that I was the son of his boss and that I should be allowed to pass. As I was about to leave, he asked me in Urdu, which I understood well, whether I had seen some Sikhs they were after.

'My friends tell me that they saw a bus full of Sikhs coming this way, Sahib,' he said, eyeing me closely. 'Did you not see them go by here going towards Lahore? The *bhadmashes* [bad men] were all dressed in *burkhas*, Sahib.'

'No,' I replied nervously. 'No, nothing.'

'Are you sure, Sahib?' The man's tone of voice suggested he did not believe me.

His colleagues crowded round to hear my answer. The only thought in my head was how I could thwart the Sikhs' pursuers.

Maybe I could put them off track by admitting I'd seen a passing bus, but tell them it had been travelling in the opposite direction to Lahore. I hoped the ploy would send the men the wrong way.

'I'm not sure,' I said, 'but I think I did see a bus a while back. I was too far away to see if there were any women on board it. But this bus was not going on the Lahore road, it was heading towards Topi Park, where there's a short cut to the Murree Road. It could not have been the one you are looking for.'

The men became extremely agitated and started talking loudly among themselves, some abusively. Again, the foreman asked, 'Sahib, are you certain? Surely the bus was going the other way?'

'No, no,' I protested, 'Topi Park, I'm absolutely certain now, Topi Park.'

'All right, Sahib,' the man said, 'if you say so, Sahib. Now please go home and give my salaams to your father. We will go to Topi Park and look.'

The men squeezed back into the Buick and roared off down the road. Not in the direction of Topi Park, as they'd said, but headed for Lahore. Obviously I had not convinced the blackshirts. However, my only consolation was that the bus was now so distant that the Buick would never catch it up. That the Buick could travel much faster than the bus never entered my calculation.

Three days later, I left the house once more. Things had quietened in the vicinity of the refinery. Down to the river I went again, over the bridge and beyond. Riding off the road, through scrub and bush, over the hard, high ground, my eyes caught sight of a burned-out bus lying upturned on the dried-out riverbed. Pushing my bike by hand, I came closer in. There, strewn beside the torched vehicle, were scattered bodies, barely covered with flame-blackened *burkhas*. The saving grace for me was that the corpses were so hideously gas-inflated, they bore no resemblance to humans. But for that, I could never have faced that terrible abomination, without forever experiencing feelings of remorse and guilt. As it is, I have asked myself the same question a thousand times over.

Had I told the blackshirts the truth about the way in which the bus was heading: might not then the Muslims have gone after the Sikhs in the wrong direction?

DAVID MICHAEL THOM

My father continued to work for the North Western Railway – now Pakistan Railways – after Partition, and Mother and I went back, first to Rawalpindi and afterwards to Karachi, in 1947. We sailed from Tilbury on the *Empire Windrush*, just missing that terrible winter, and docked at Karachi.

The Presentation Convent in Rawalpindi was run by Catholic nuns. Being Church of England, there were certain lessons I had to miss – I can't think what my reports were like. I went home on the bus to Westridge – a railway house again. I can't remember having any friends away from school. I built brick houses in the garden with fireplaces in, and climbed and swung on a huge banyan tree in the garden. Evening walks were the norm, to the church where my grandparents were buried, St Mary's. The house had very high ceilings to keep it cool, and the beds always had their legs kept in tins filled with water to keep the scorpions and centipedes away. Evenings were spent in the garden. Mother and Father liked a whisky, and I do remember the Johnny Walker bottles. I played ships in the fountain and paddled around in a tin bath.

The school bus came at 5.30 a.m., and we got back home just after midday, to avoid the heat. Sundays usually consisted of a cycle ride to the railway sheds – Father was very conscientious with his work.

Partition must have been terrible. Parents would talk about it, but when I came into earshot the conversation changed. All I was able to find out was that every night the killings went on around the compound – how Father kept on working we shall never know. The railways obviously kept going, but now with more Pakistanis taking control. In Rawalpindi he was Divisional Mechanical Engineer No 3, but his promotion now meant that we had to go to Karachi.

Here, we lived in a railway bungalow in Hoshang Road. We cycled around, though father had a car as well, an Austin this time. We cycled to the sheds and, much later, to where the Jinnah Monument was being built. I went to open-air cinemas with Mother, and round the bazaars and to Kemari in the evenings to see the boats.

I was a chorister at Holy Trinity Church. I used to walk to the Sind Club, where I had tea with a Captain Young, a pilot with BOAC, then on to Church. I can only think of evensong – I can't remember morning services. I loved the anthems, in particular, 'Crossing the Bar'. I read one of the lessons at Christmas, 'Adam and Eve'. We went back to Quetta only once in this period. The railways were still mainly steam – still coal from Wales: the Welsh anthracite couldn't be beaten. Experiments in oil firing were underway, but I imagine diesel power was approaching fast for mainline work.

I was now at Karachi Grammar School, just then celebrating its centenary. There were still lots of Europeans, Army, railway, RAF, business children. We had sandwiches for lunch, and had to watch out for the kites, who would swoop down and snatch them out of your hands. The teaching was entirely in English, although we did Indian history: Akbar the Great, the Moghul Emperors, etc. The sports were run on traditional lines, and we had houses, which competed for cups and shields – Frere, Streeton and Napier. The examinations were still for the Cambridge School Certificate. I remember being bussed over to the radio station to broadcast a programme of Christmas carols, sung in English. I wonder for how many more years that continued – probably not many. But the flavour of that school is preserved most marvellously in the pages of its magazine, *The Grammarian*. In this we find the principal's speech on centenary day, 4 November 1947:

> Mr. Justice Tyabji, ladies and gentlemen, girls and boys, on this very proud day in the history of our school, we extend a very warm welcome indeed to you, Sir, for so very kindly to preside this evening. We can imagine something of the enormous problems that must be confronting you in these days, and are therefore all the more thankful to you for so generously sparing the time to be present today. Your presence is indeed

a signal honour which the school will always remember, and we hope it will be the first of many occasions when the school will have the privilege of welcoming you to its portals.

The school was founded by the Rev. H.H. Brereton in 1847, but we do not know the exact date, and the classes were held in a temporary building on the site of the present Methodist Church. On 1 November 1845, the school moved to its present site, but the girls, who in those days were taught in a separate school, continued to have their classes on the old site. The school has seen many vicissitudes of fortune, has experienced much joy and some sorrow, has shared in the varying fortunes of Sind, and we hope has contributed something to the progress and prosperity of the city of Karachi, and the province of Sind.

It is surely of great significance that the Centenary of the School almost coincides with the birth of the Dominion of Pakistan. The school has always offered unquestionable loyalty to established authority. From the moment that the new Dominion was born, it pledged its unhesitating support to it. We may truthfully claim that the school has always sought in the past to assist the government in every possible way, and it will certainly be no less eager to assist in the future.

We now offer instruction in commercial subjects to those boys and girls who wish to avail themselves of it, in addition to that in the usual academic subjects; but to keep pace with the times we need to provide facilities for technical classes. We are hoping that the Government of Sind would be able to help us by providing some financial assistance for these classes, but as the government has its own plans for a technical institution, financial assistance from the government is not forthcoming.

The Centenary Concert included a recitation of the speech by Queen Elizabeth of England to her troops before the *Armada*, by Georgina Thomas of Frere House, and of Mark Antony's *Funeral Oration*, by R. Ragman Khan of Streeton House. There was a play called *Prayer*, performed by Standards IA&B, and the proceedings ended with everyone singing the School Song. At Speech Day, on 19 December 1947, the recitation was of Abraham Lincoln's speech at Gettysburg, by Mujibur Rahman Khan. The senior boys performed a play called *The Death Trap*, the girls' choir sang 'Jesu, Joy of Man's desiring' (J.S. Bach, arranged by W.G. Whittaker), and, once again, the school song closed the concert.

From the Principal's Report for 1947:

The outstanding event of the year has, of course, been the celebration of the school's centenary in the first five days of November.

The public meeting and concert was well attended… The school building was illuminated, and the school crest, in coloured lights, was greatly admired, and was visible from afar… The Art Exhibition was the largest ever held… The gymnastic display was excellent, and delighted a very large crowd of spectators… The elocution competition again revealed a very high standard… The celebration of the centenary gave us an opportunity to renew contact with a large number of old Grammarians, and… we regret that disturbed conditions in many parts prevented numerous Old Grammarians from being present at various functions.

In the Cambridge School Certificate Examination, out of 17 candidates, 15 passed, and of these no less than eight received a First-Class Pass. This was probably the highest proportion of First-Class Passes in any school in India. Both the Government Senior Scholarships were won by the school. In the Junior Cambridge Exam we did not fare quite so well. The Guides and Bluebirds are flourishing, and we are most grateful to the ladies who run them so zealously, but we regret that owing to the departure of military personnel who rendered invaluable service to the Scouts and Cubs, these groups are not at the moment satisfactory. We hope to reorganise then in the new year.

In August the two lower floors of the school had to be vacated to provide accommodation for the Pakistan Government officials, so school work was carried on with great difficulty, and we regret that some children had no instruction for a month.

The wedding of HRH Princess Elizabeth to the Duke of Edinburgh was celebrated with great joy, largely because of a most generous gift from the UK High Commissioner which enabled us to entertain the children with ice-cream, sweets, etc., and to purchase Rs 1000-worth of books for the library.

The school log for 1947 records that on 4 November the centenary meeting was convened,

but it was deprived of some importance by the unavoidable absence of the Quaid-I-Azam (Mohammed Ali Jinnah), who could not do us the signal honour of presiding on account of very urgent matters of state demanding his presence elsewhere. Sind's chief judge very gallantly stepped into the breach. The concert that followed the speeches was well received.

Mujeeb Khan's interpretation of Mark Antony's [Christianised in the programme] speech, the play by Standards IA&B, and the singing of 'Worship' by Massed Voices were the titbits of the evening's fare.

In 1948 the school re-opened on 19 January. Sports Day was on 20 March, and Streeton became 'cock' House! The Easter holidays were from 25 to 29 March, but from 9 to 16 April the entire school received jabs to 'ward off typhoid'. The summer holidays were from 15 May to 20 June. Independence Day celebrations were on 14 August, but 15 August was Pakistan Day. On 11 September, however:

The Father of the Nation, His Excellency Quaid-I-Azam Mohammed Ali Jinnah, passed away at about 10.20 p.m.

12 September: funeral of the Quaid-i-Azam. Interred at 6.20 p.m.

13 and 14 September: school closed to mourn the death of the Quaid-i-Azam. The principal sent on our behalf letters of sympathy to Miss Fatima Jinnah and the Hon. The Premier.

These last three entries are surrounded by a thick black border.

September 15th: at morning assembly the principle in a few words extolled the greatness and the goodness of the Quaid-i-Azam, and appealed to all to go ahead with the work he had started.

But perhaps the most interesting things in this magazine were two accounts of journeys from Simla and Bombay, in India, to Karachi, in Pakistan. The author of the first one became a classmate of mine, and would have been approximately nine-and-a-half years old. The second was a year younger, perhaps eight and a half.

Evacuee from Simla:

The evacuation was done in Simla on Tuesday morning at about six o'clock. Lord Louis Mountbatten came to our school and said that 'all Mohammedan boys should be evacuated because there will be trouble soon'. So the next morning we were packing up. From the school we were given a tin of cheese, a packet of biscuits, and a bottle of lemonade. About half-past six in the morning we went in trucks to Kalka first, under the protection of the 49th Gurkha Regiment, from there we were taken straight to Ambala. We stayed at Ambala for a night at a Sikh Hospital, where we were quite safe because Gurkhas were all night going round the hospital on duty.

The next morning the doctor came and said, 'There might not be a plane at half-past eight,' and everybody was very unhappy. After about ten minutes he came again and said, 'There will be a plane at 9.30a.m.' After half an hour, the CO of the Gurkha Regiment came with his men, and told his men to put our luggage in the trucks: we were taken off to the aerodrome, and at nine o'clock we were flying.

We reached Lahore in an hour's time: we had our lunch with the pilots, and at half-past two we were off again to Karachi. It took us exactly four hours to get to Karachi. When we got to Karachi I didn't know where to go, but I had the address of my parents, so I showed the address and I went to the address, which was the Baluch Mess. I went there, but the policeman said that my mother was at the intelligence school. I found the house with the help of Colonel Afridi. I stood at the door. My mother thought it was a dream to see me back from Bishop Cotton School after a whole year.

N. Haq, VB.

My Trip from Bombay to Karachi:

In November 1947 we commenced our packing in readiness to leave Bombay. After much confusion and hammering of cases we were finally ready to leave on 1 December. We took with us Joe, the parrot, in his cage, and our brindled bull-terrier, Pop, very, very unhappy because he had to travel in a crate. On leaving the apartment, the servants garlanded us with flowers; they were sorry to see us go.

We travelled by car to Santa Cruz Aerodrome, and after an hour's delay we boarded the Dakota that was to transport us to Karachi. We found Pop in his crate whining because he was frightened, and wondered what was happening, but Joe, the parrot, was having a grand time perched high on the top of our luggage. He was screaming, 'Wakey! Wakey! What's the matter, Eh? Pretty Polly! Hello Joe!' This greatly amused the RAF boys who were travelling on the same plane.

We fixed our safety belts, and with a roar of the engine our plane set off at 1.00p.m. It circled the airfield and then gently rose in the air; we were on our way. The noise of the engines drowned Joe's chatter, but his beak could be seen moving up and down, and nothing seemed to daunt him. We flew over the Ghats and high over the sea, passing very few clouds, and at 4.30p.m. we landed at Maripur. An old 'tonner' was waiting to convey us from the airport to our new home in Drigh Road.

Victor Keary, IIIA.

Begum Liaquat Ali Khan congratulates Old Grammarian team. From David Thom's old school magazine.

I finally left Karachi in 1948, on the *Circassia*, an Anchor Line ship. Worldly goods were taken to the docks on a camel-drawn cart. We had to have our dog Lassie put down, as we really couldn't leave her to anyone else. I do remember digging a hole at the back of the garage and saying goodbye.

I started at Hardyes School in Dorchester, becoming a boarder when Mother rejoined Father, but this time by air, flying with BOAC in an Argonaut. They were to remain in Pakistan until 1951, when Father took early retirement, reluctantly I think, as more and more Pakistanis were replacing the Europeans. My mother was probably pleased, as she found the humidity in Karachi most oppressive.

STAR STAUNTON

The War was over. My husband Don was back from Burma, and it was indeed time to go home. Home! Home was now 72 degrees longitude to the west. Don would be posted somewhere or other and the rest of us would be found, by courtesy of his father, a *pied-à-terre* in Yorkshire. So off we set from Bombay in the P&O liner *Britannia*, Father, Mother, Christopher – aged one year and four months – and Andrew, four months only.

At sea it was discovered that the water was over-chlorinated, and some babies were dying as a result. Over the tannoy came a request for breast-feeding mothers to share their milk, and along with two others I volunteered. One of the others was rejected on medical grounds, so there were only a pair of us to meet a large demand. In those days breast-feeding was unfashionable, and all the other mothers were milkless. So four times a day milk was pumped from me. But what about Andrew? 'Oh,' they said, 'the more you draw, the more there will be. There will be plenty for him.' There was not plenty for him. By the time we reached Liverpool, Andrew was visibly suffering from under-nourishment and looking pinched and thin, a fact which added a nuance of distress to my introduction to Don's father. This formidable gentleman met us on the quay, shook hands briefly with Don, and then turned to me, looked me over, and said, 'So, you are the mother of my grandsons.' He turned to the children and continued, 'The older one looks all right. I'll have him. But what's this thing?' This thing was poor, wizened and yellow little Andrew. All my mother-love sprang at once to the defence of my baby, whom I loved more fiercely at that moment than I had ever done before, while a black hatred for his grandfather sprang up inside me. Yorkshire bluntness, with the very first ball, had knocked over my self-composure, diplomat that I was. Our further converse was glum and unfriendly, and I made no effort to impress. The journey that followed across the black and sunless Pennines did little to raise my spirits.

Don had received a summons to attend a course at Aldershot and departed immediately, leaving the three of us as the temporary guests of his father and grandmother. I put a 'black' at our very first breakfast. With typical Yorkshire hospitality, and in spite of the stringent rationing then prevalent in England, I was given a plate of eggs and bacon, of which, watched hungrily by my father-in-law, I ate the eggs and left the bacon. Having been brought up among Indians, pigs' flesh was revolting to me. I was told, 'Eat your bacon,' and when I explained that I never ate it, was asked, 'What! Are you a bloody Jew or something?'

'No but swine's flesh houses worms, and I do not eat it.'

'Bloody nonsense!' returned my father-in-law, correctly as I now understand, but in words that fell short of the finest standards of politeness to a guest. I was furious.

A week after Don's departure my host and hostess found me a cottage in Castleton, a remote Yorkshire village where dwelled Don's maternal grandmother and her daughter, 15 years my senior, who was to be called Aunt Sylvia. Ugh! That cottage was appalling. It was what remained of an old farmhouse. A downstairs kitchen-cum-living room, three bedrooms, a bath, and a washbasin upstairs; a paraffin-burner and a black-leaded kitchen range for all heating and cooking purposes, an outside loo in a yard where someone kept geese and turkeys. There was a double bed, a wardrobe and dressing table in one of the bedrooms. The children's room had Christopher's bed and Andrew's carry-cot. Downstairs, two chairs and a table, and that was that.

Here I was deposited, and in all haste left to fend for myself. It is hard to believe how incompetent my upbringing in India had left me. Never a hands-turn of work to do until I joined the Army, and thereafter servants galore to provide the load on one's plate, wash up, make beds and do all the chores. Servants to coddle me even during that short period between Andrew's birth and our homecoming. I blush to say that I could not light that awful black stove – I couldn't even boil an egg, let alone cook on that contraption. All I could do for the first few days was to sit and weep and feed the three of us on milk and cornflakes from the village shop.

I was utterly out of my element, and I felt that the people knew it who passed me as I walked to the village. With the babies in the pram I crept out to find the butcher's shop.

Fortunately, the proprietor was there in person, smiling benevolently at me over his greying whiskers, as I pushed the pram through the door. 'Can you please sell me something that will cook easily. I'm afraid I don't know how to cook.'

'Are you Don Mitchinson's wife?' he said.

'Yes,' I said.

'And related to my niece Sylvia Watson?'

'Yes.'

'Well I'm Charlie Watson. How do you do?' We shook hands. 'And you can't cook?'

'I've never cooked in my life. I've always had servants to cook for me'.

'Oh Princess,' he said, 'we must do something about that. I know where you live. I'll be there at six o'clock and I'll show you how.' I was so overcome with gratitude that I burst into tears. This was my first experience of the kindliness that so often goes with the bluntness in Yorkshire, though I have often met with it since.

I went home to my wilderness and sat down. I told myself he would never come, but oh, I hoped he would, and in that hope I set about getting the paraffin stove to light, leaving the big black-leaded stove for him. True to his word, the kind Charlie turned up at six o'clock and put some chops down on the table.

'Where are the vegetables?' he says.

'Vegetables?'

'Princess, you don't think you're going to eat the meat all by itself? Hold on. I'll be back in half an hour.' And back he came with potatoes, carrots and onions all beautifully prepared, I suppose by his wife. When the meat was sizzling in the pan, he turned his attention to the stove and showed me how to deal with it, and soon the vegetables were cooking too.

That night I slept like a top, and woke up in the morning feeling a different woman. The worst was over.

Charlie Watson's name for me stuck. No one seemed to bother what I was really called. I was 'Princess' to my face, to all the villagers.

Another good thing Charlie did for me was to go to Aunty Sylvia and tell her of my plight. Dear soul, she had had no idea, and quickly came running round to see what she could do to help. As it happened, she had been very kind to Don as a child, when, like myself, he had been left motherless, and she at once became a tower of strength to me, my friend and instructress. I owe her a lot.

It rejoices me to remember that eighteen months later, on our departure to join Don in Egypt, our village friends, quite a crowd of them, gathered to wave us goodbye. 'Good-bye, Princess, come back again,' was their farewell.

ANONYMOUS

I was born in 1934, on the Kolar Gold Fields in Mysore, where my father was a hard-rock mining engineer. He was the first member of his family, which came from Cornwall, to work in India, but my mother's family had been there for generations. There was a legend in that family that one of their forebears had come from Pondicherry able to speak French, and that she had been invited into the *zenanas* to write letters for the Muslim ladies.

Father had a real passion for hard-rock mining, and he was very good at his job. In his capacity as underground manager he was devoted to the efficiency, smooth-running and safety of the area within his charge. In his off-duty hours he would sometimes pop down underground to see how things were going, and to iron out any potential difficulties. Indeed, quite often we would all be taken for what we thought was to be a nice drive, only to find him stopping at some mine shaft on the way home. He would go underground and we would be left sitting in the car for what felt like *hours*! But his enthusiasm was much appreciated by the company, who named one of their new shafts after him.

Until I was 11, I went to the local convent school with my sisters. The standard of education was very high, as I was to find to my great satisfaction when I first attended an English school in 1948.

I remember especially the lunchtime ritual. We would all assemble in the lunch hall, which had one half-wall but was otherwise open to verandahs, and the Sister in charge would lead us in saying Grace. Then the servants would come in, bringing the locked lunchboxes with them. I had a key, and my mother had a key. They would wait until we had finished and then walk home with the empty lunchboxes, three miles in our case! There were no fridges, and it was very important to eat freshly prepared food to avoid food poisoning and so on. But we had an ice box, which we used sometimes. One of the servants would go to the ice factory and collect a block of ice to carry home, wrapped in sacking on his head. My mother often employed more servants than she actually needed, because it was a charity to do so, and my father was indulgent of her wishes. Our school was run on conventional British lines, so we had a Boy Scout troop. What was not so conventional, though I didn't realise this at the time, was our Boy Scout Promise, which was: 'I promise to do my best, to do my duty to God, the King-Emperor and the Maharajah of Mysore.'

I don't remember any adventures during the Second World War, although there was the threat of a Japanese invasion. I remember once that a man called at our bungalow offering to make model likenesses of people's heads. He made a beautiful one of my younger sister, out of rice-flour, but very soon afterwards we heard that he was Japanese, and had been arrested as a spy! There were quite a lot of Italians working in the mines before the War started, but I'm not sure what happened to them. Probably they just went on working.

One of our great treats was to go to Bangalore by train. On the way there was a certain station where there were hordes of monkeys. The monkeys used to board the train when it came into the railway station and steal anything that took their fancy. Once, my younger sister was sitting eating a banana when a little, black hand reached down from the roof and took it from her. There was a big, old monkey with only one hand – maybe he had lost it in an accident with the train. He used to keep watch and, as the train was about to move, he would call out a warning, and all the monkeys would scamper off the train and into the trees.

I remember, too, seeing a contest between two magic men, one Muslim and one Hindu. One of them broke a pot, and a large wound appeared on the other man's head. I remember, too, seeing a fire in the house for the first time. It was of eucalyptus logs, in Ootacamund where I had gone with Father, who was recovering from an operation. Ooty is 8000 feet high, and I had never really been cold before. We bought an alsatian dog there and ate the most luscious vegetables.

We did see something of the troubles around the time of Independence. We had had Muslim and Hindu neighbours for many years, and had always got on well with them all, but at the end of January in 1948, when my mother was in the maternity hospital after the birth of my youngest sister, she sent a message that she needed some things from home. I was 13 at the time and set out, after school, to take them to her. My route lay through the market square and, on my way back, I realised that everything was ominously silent. From a distance I could see Muslims and Hindus facing each other on each side of the street, but before I could even duck into a side street heads had started to roll. I walked as fast as I could – to have run would have made me very conspicuous – but I hadn't gone far before I heard a Land Rover coming. It was my father, looking for me, and I was very glad to climb into that Land Rover!

We were all very sad to leave India, particularly parting with the servants, whom we could no longer help or protect. Father brought me to Cornwall in 1948 and left me there in the care of his mother. He retired from the goldfields two years later, and so by 1950 the whole family was reunited in England.

DAN FERRIS

Calcutta during the War. 'Don't be a jungly,' they used to tease when I came to the big city from the village of Bandel where my father worked for the East India Railway Company. Calcutta was the place for family visits, treats and parties.

The highlight of the year was my birthday picnic at Calcutta Zoo for over fifty children. There were tea parties and games in the grounds of the Victoria Memorial. I remember being in awe of the white marble monument, and seldom went inside. My mother used to train me to do poetry recitations for the Saturday children's talent shows at the Metro Cinema. One of my prizes was a large tin of Glaxo powdered milk – a great disappointment.

Being just five years old when the War ended, I only had a slight inkling of its dangers on the few occasions when a visit to Calcutta coincided with an air-raid by one or two Japanese planes on the docks. When the siren sounded, we went indoors and listened for explosions. I only once heard the distant sounds of bombs going off. Then there were large, silver barrage balloons above Howrah Bridge. Otherwise it seemed like fun, entertaining by the troops and being introduced to candy, chewing gum and Hershey bars by the Americans.

I returned to Calcutta with my family in 1990, and received a very different impression. The city was choked with traffic. At midday, the one-way system on Park Street was reversed, and chaos ensured. Pollution and crime saw to it that the open verandahs where we spent so much of our time were walled-in. Many of the large gardens, with their tennis and badminton courts bordered by bright beds of flowers, were built on. The pavements were in disrepair and were home to the destitute. The elegance and openness of the areas I knew in my childhood had gone.

Despite the dramatic increase in car traffic, there were still the bullock and hand-drawn carts, cycle rickshaws and horse cabs. I keep a lasting image of a crowd gathering round a horse cab which had been hit by a car. The thin, white horse, rear legs bespattered with red, stood trembling with shock while the driver stood beside it all day waiting for help.

A memory of Foss Westcott, Archbishop of India, Burma and Ceylon. Soon after arriving at St Paul's, Darjeeling in a cold and windy March in 1948 for a nine-month stretch at boarding school, I contracted measles, soon to be followed by chickenpox, and spent a couple of months in a quarantined area of the dormitory.

The monotony was alleviated by regular visits from the Archbishop, who would read us bedtime stories. These were read with the aid of a large magnifying glass, as his eyes were weak. We were greatly impressed, as he translated the adventures of Hercules directly from the Latin reader *Fabulae Faciles*.

He was a kind, gentle man with white hair, a short beard and thick, rimless glasses. He had returned to his old school to spend his last days, and stayed with the rector, Trevor Goddard.

On sports day he took part in the Old Boys' Race, tripped on his cassock and fell over, losing his glasses but remaining unharmed. As a result, he was regarded as a good sport, and his occasional sermons on Sundays received more attention from the boys than those of any other preacher. He died the following year, and had chosen a lovely spot for his grave. It was on a mound below the chapel with a magnificent view of the Himalayas.

> See the eternal snows
> Pure be thy soul as those.

These were lines of the school song that he particularly liked. I was a treble in the choir and walked in procession behind the coffin, carried by prefects from the chapel to the graveside on a sparkling-blue sunny day, with the cloudless range of snows in the distance. A photograph of it appeared in the *Statesman*. 'Where were his family?' I wondered, and 'How was it possible to be the Archbishop of so vast and populous an area as India, Burma and Ceylon?'

ELIZABETH LEIGH

On the 19th of March 1949, Ayah sent a typewritten letter to my mother. She was now employed at 'Lanka' Racecourse, Trichinopoly, South India, by the Lindon family.

> Dear Madam,
>
> This is my Good Wishes 1949 on all your families. Thank you so much for your letter received in December. I hope Madam and Master and children are quite well, in England, same like myself and my mother Edward all quite safe in Trich. Now I am working under Mrs. Lindon. She looks same as you. No trouble. She gave birth to a child in January 1948. Child name is Ian Stone Lindon. Now child is 13th month.
>
> It is very good and quiet child. Like little Elizabeth. I am very glad on this child.
>
> Madam wrote in a letter very great trouble in England. Therefore I am very sorry on your matters. Trichy too great trouble to get food. Things very dear too. Mrs. Lindon going to England middle of August 1949...whether she will recommend me I don't know. Later I will inform

Elizabeth Leigh with her *ayah*. Sixth birthday, 1945.

Madam, otherwise. My wrist giving great trouble now. I can't carry heavy things. Mrs. Duff is thickest friend to Mrs. Lindon. Therefore she brought [me] to Kodai last year... when Master coming to India. Please let me know he coming or not. I am very proud when I saw your letter. And Mrs. Lindon read that letter and translated to me. Now India is upset. Same like your country. But I don't know what will happen in India. Poor families very ruining in India. No job so great trouble.

Finishing the letter. Thanks very much.

Your kindness Ayah.

On the back – it was a standard Air Letter, still with King George VI on it, the postage was six annas – she wrote:

Dear Elizabeth,

I am very glad now you are being quite a girl with your mother and William too. Elizabeth please kindly write one letter for me. I very like to see your handwriting. Don't forget me Elizabeth. And give Happy Birthday for William.

I am waiting for your letter. Therefore send your letter soon as possible.

Your kindness and lovely Ayah

R. PUSPAM (in her own hand)

MALCOLM MURPHY

My leaving school coincided with the outbreak of the Second World War and in no time at all, India was awash with troops. Recruiting offices opened and the Anglo-Indian community answered the call with characteristic spontaneity. I myself joined an Infantry Regiment (1st Wilts.) with a view to transferring later to the British wing of the Indian Army Corps of Clerks (IACC). Service took me initially to the North West Frontier, Baluchistan, central India, the United Provinces and finally to Burma on the heels of the retreating Japanese in 1944.

It was to be another four years before I would return to India and 'civvy street'. I found India independent, and most of my community gone. My own family (parents, brother and sisters) were on edge and waiting for me. We had to leave too, but it would take time. My parents had built a house in Pakala after Dad's retirement. They sold it to William Wheeler, a retired locomotion foreman who said he was staying on.

We could leave for England at last, but I'd missed out on something: I was still horribly single. I married the lovely Merle, from Fort Cochin ('British Cochin', she reminded me with an elbow in my ribs). While living out our last Indian days in Bombay our son, Ged, was born. It was time to pull up sticks and follow our natural instincts, our culture, our language, our way of life.

It was 1962 when we arrived in England. It was hard to take in the fact that the adventure was over. We were 'home', if not dry.

It was raining.

Appendix of Authors

PAMELA ALBERT: Born London 1927, only child of Lt. Col. Edward Francis Albert, 7th Rajput Regiment, and his wife Lydian Gladys Ross Perri. Hallett War School, Naini Tal. Married. 2s 1d.

MARION ALEXANDER: Born Kerkeria, Assam 1929, only child of Gordon and Margaret Alexander, Corramore Tea Estate. The New School, Calcutta and Darjeeling. Whincroft Girls' School, Crowborough, Sussex. Women's Royal Naval Service. Nursing 1978–83. Married. 2d.

ANGELA ALLEN: Born Mussoorie 1918, younger daughter of Guy Oldfield Allen, ICS, and his wife Barbara Egerton. Corran School, Watford. Kinnaird Park School, Watford. Saint Anne's College, Oxford. Teacher of German and French. Full-time with Moral Re-Armament Movement, now known as Initiatives of Change. Married. 2s.

DOROTHY ALLEN: Born Mirzapur UP 1911, elder sister of above. Studied piano at Howard-Jones School of Music, London. Worked as a photographer throughout Second World War. Private piano teacher. Married.

ROBERT C. ALTER: Born Srinagar, Kashmir 1926, Son of Reverend D. Emmet Alter, and his wife Martha Payne Alter, Missionaries under United Presbyterian Church. Woodstock School, Mussoorie, both as pupil and as Principal, 1968–78. Church Administrator and Social Worker. Married.

BEATRICE BAKER: Born Kodaikanal 1916, daughter of George Alexander Baker, Owner/Planter Travancore, and his wife Maud Jessie Hooper. Malvern Girls' College. Royal Academy of Dramatic Art. Women's Auxiliary Air Force. Married. 3s.

ROBERT BAKER: Born Kodaikanal 1913, brother of above. King's School, Canterbury. War service in Army. Married.

DOROTHY MARGARET BAKER: Born Ootacamund 1928, elder daughter of Frederick Charles Baker, Customs and Excise, Madras, and his second wife Phyllis May Holton. Bishop Cotton's Girls' High School, Bangalore. London School of Economics BSc (Econ). University of London Institute of Education Graduate Teacher's Certificate 1968 and Diploma in Sociology 1970. Teacher, Secretary and Civil Servant. Married. 1s 1d.

JESSICA MAY BAKER: Born Madras 1930, younger sister of above, Bishop Cotton's Girls' High School, Bangalore. BA (Open University) 1975. Worked for Shell for nearly forty years. Now does voluntary work with Citizens' Advice Bureau and Mediation. Single.

PHILIP BANHAM: Born Poona 1922, son of William John Banham, Indian Police, and his wife Winifred Roberta Waller. Cathedral School, Bombay. Chelmsford College, Ghora Gali. Emergency Commission Indian Army Ordinance Corps. School Master. Married. 2s 1d.

PATRICIA BANHAM: Born Poona 1923, sister of above. St Mary's High School, Poona. Barnes High School, Deolali. VAD Nursing Sister 8th Army North Africa and Palestine. Married. 4ch.

JAMES BENTHALL: Born Calcutta 1933, younger twin son of Sir Paul Benthall KBE, The Bird/Heilgers Group, Calcutta, and his wife Mary Lucy. The New School, Darjeeling. Eton College, Berkshire. Magdalene College, Cambridge. Bird/Heilgers Group, Calcutta. Prep. School Teacher. Married. 1s 1d.

HENRY BERRIFF: Born Simla 1927, elder son of Arthur Berriff, of Alan Henry & Co. The Mall, Simla, later Stores Manager at the Gun Carriage Factory in Jubbulpore and the Railway Repair Shops, and his second wife Elfriede Davison. Christ Church School, Jubbulpore. Bishop Cotton's School, Simla. Apprenticed to The British Thompson-Houston Company, Rugby. Director Cameraman with the Central African Film Unit, Salisbury, Rhodesia. Southern Rhodesian Engineers. Owner of Bridge Film Productions, Salisbury, Rhodesia. Single.

JENNIFER BETTEN: Born Darjeeling 1934, third daughter of Malcolm Betten, tea planter with Williamson and Magor, and his wife Eva. Singamari School, Darjeeling. Author of *In the Shade of Kanchenjunga* (BACSA). Married. 5ch.

JANE BIRKMYRE: Born Calcutta 1929, daughter of Sir Henry Birkmyre, Bart., Chairman and Managing Director, Birkmyre Brothers, Calcutta, Member Bengal Legislative Assembly 1935–44, and his wife, Doris Gertrude Austen Smith (daughter of Colonel Austen Smith, CIE), Assistant Red Cross Commissioner for Military Hospital Welfare, India and Burma, Kaisar-I-Hind Silver Medal. St David's School, Englefield Green. The New School, Calcutta. Singamari, Darjeeling. Evendine Court Domestic Science College, Malvern. Secretary at War Office, London. Married life in Kenya. Married. 2d.

JOHN BLANDY: Professor, CBE, MA, DM, MCh, FRCS, FACS, Hon. FRCSI, born Calcutta 1927, son of Sir Nicolas Blandy, KCIE, CSI, ICS, Governor-elect of Assam, and his wife Dorothy Kathleen Marshall. The New School, Darjeeling. Clifton College, Bristol. Balliol College, Oxford. Consultant Surgeon. Emeritus Professor of Urology, University of London. Hon. Fellow, Royal College of Surgeons, Ireland. Past Vice-President, Royal College of Surgeons. Past President British Association of Urological Surgeons, and much more. Married. 4d.

NANETTE BOYCE: Born Mussoorie 1928, eldest daughter of Brigadier Thomas Walker Boyce, OBE, MC, MM, 14th Punjabi Regiment, and his wife

Heather Baxter. The New School, Darjeeling. MI5 in London and Singapore. Married. 1s 1d.

LORNA BRADBURY: Born Nagpur 1924, daughter of Herbert Edgar Bradbury (born Bellary 1886), Superintendent, Post & Telegraphs, and his wife Daisy Beryl Harvey Johnson. Bishop Cotton School, Nagpur. St Mary's Training College, Poona. School Teacher at Baldwin Girls' School, Bangalore. Married. 1s 2d.

JOAN BRAGG: Born Rawalpindi 1927, elder daughter of Lt. Col. H.V. Bragg, 3rd/9th Jat Regiment, and his wife Bessie Pinkerton. Sheikh Bagh School, Srinagar. Presentation Convent, Srinagar. Teacher of Art and Languages. Married. 2ch.

BOB BRAGG: Born Norwood 1930, brother of above. Sheikh Bagh School, Srinagar. Bedford School. Birkbeck College, London, BSC, MA. RAF pilot. Married twice. 4ch.

HEDI BRAUN: Born Vienna 1936, daughter of Rudolph M. Braun, Engineer, and his wife Elise (Lisl) Herbratschek, Concert Pianist. The New School, Darjeeling. Barnard College and Columbia University, New York. Teacher of Musical Theory at Hunter and Mannes Colleges, US. Married. 1s.

PETER BROADBENT: Born Bournemouth 1933, son of Col. R.B. Broadbent, Bombay Pioneers and Rajputana Rifles, and his wife Jean Thorburn. The New School, Darjeeling and eight others. Royal Naval College, Dartmouth. Captain Royal Navy. OBE 1982. Registrar Institute of Landscape Architects. Married. 1s 1d.

H.C.G. BROWN CBE DSC: Born Rangoon 1918, son of H.C.G. Brown, Deputy Conservator of Port of Rangoon, and his wife Matilda Mann. Hammond's School, Swaffham, Norfolk. Choral Scholar, King's College, Cambridge (Boxing Blue). Director, Burmah Oil Trading Ltd. DSC 1945, CBE 1966. Married.

MICHAEL BRUCE: Born Laheraserai, Dharbanga District, North Bihar 1927, son of Harold Easton Bruce, MC, Deputy Inspector General, Indian Police, and his wife Aileen Fitzgerald. Oratory School, Woodcote. Hallett War School, Naini Tal. Exeter College, Oxford. Lieut. Royal Artillery 1948–50. Director Reinsurance Brokers, London and Vice President, New York. Underwriting Member of Lloyds. Now Freelance Translator, Member of Institute of Translators and Interpreting. Married. 3s 1d.

BARRY BRYSON: Born Weymouth 1929, younger son of Andrew Bryson and his wife Kathleen. Stepson of Reginald Wallace Thom MBE, Divisional Mechanical Engineer North Western Railway, Quetta, Baluchistan. Bishop Cotton's School, Simla. National Service in RASC. Company Secretary. Married. 3d 2s.

SUSAN BURDER: Born Calcutta 1931, elder daughter of Lt. Col. Sir John Burder, Member of Council of State 1943, President Bengal and Associated Chambers of Commerce, India 1943, President Imperial Bank of India 1947, and his wife Betty Bailey. The New School, Calcutta and Darjeeling. PNEU course at Dr Graham's Homes, Kalimpong. St James's, West Malvern. Married. 1s 3d.

CAROLINE BURDER: Born Calcutta 1933, younger daughter of Sir John and Lady Burder, Jardine Skinner & Co. PNEU course at Dr Graham's Homes, Kalimpong. St James's, West Malvern. Married. 1s 1d.

ANN BURKINSHAW: Born Calcutta 1928, only child of Dick Burkinshaw, Jessop & Co., and his wife Kathleen Grimley. The New School, Calcutta and Darjeeling. St Anne's College, Oxford. Her Majesty's Overseas Civil Service, Tanganyika. Foreign and Colonial Office, London. British Oxygen Company Group, London. Married.

ERNEST YOUNG CAMPBELL: Born Sialkot 1917, second son of James Garfield Campbell, and his wife Mabel Young, Missionaries under United Presbyterian Church. Woodstock School, Mussoorie. Wooster College, Ohio. Representative in India of United Presbyterian Church of America. Director of Relief and Rehabilitation in Vietnam. International Church in Bangkok, Thailand. Flood Relief Organisation, Punjab. Conducted Study of Bengal Refugees. Church of North India. Married. 2s 1d.

DONALD CATTO: Born Quetta 1921, son of Major Herbert Catto, Royal Indian Army Service Corps, and his wife. Infants Boarding School, Murree. Bishop Cotton's Day School, Bangalore. Lawrence Schools at Lovedale and Ghora Gali. Commissioned into Indian Army. Served in Burma, Captain 17th Indian Division, later as Major, 23rd Indian Division. Transferred to British Army in 1947, serving mostly overseas. Retired Major. Married. 1s.

BILL CHARLES: Born Poona 1928, son of James Meadows Charles, Sergeant in British Army, 1914–18, later Planter, fruit and dairy Farmer, and his wife, Ethel Gladys Smith. Breeks Memorial School, Ootacamund. Took over father's plantation until 1948. Thomas Cook Financial Services. Married. 2s.

YOMA CROSFIELD: Born Broadstairs 1936, only child of Leonard Crosfield, Burmah and Assam Oil Companies, and his wife Margaret Daniell, Chair of Training, Girl Guides, All-India. The New School, Darjeeling. Effingham House, Sussex. Lady Margaret Hall, Oxford. Editor, Academic Research Assistant, Writer. Divorced. 2d.

ISABEL DAVIDSON: Born Glasgow 1936, only child of John Davidson, Drilling Engineer with Burmah and Assam Oil Companies, and his wife Agnes Calder. Ida Villa, Darjeeling. Laurel Bank School, Glasgow. Glasgow and West of Scotland College of Domestic Science. Institutional Management Association

Course in hotel management and catering. Assistant Caterer Royal Victoria Hospital for Children, London. Part-time Fashion Consultant. Married. 2s 1d.

GEORGE DUNBAR: Born India 1915.

SHEILA FERGUSON: Born Darjeeling 1926, daughter of Lt. Col. Robert Ferguson, Northern Bengal Mounted Rifles, Tea Planter in Dooars 1909–1944, and his wife. Battle Abbey, Sussex. The New School, Darjeeling. Married. 1s 1d.

DAN FERRIS: Born Calcutta 1940, son of Edward Ferris, East India Railway Company, and his wife Iris, Commissioner for Training in Bengal, Bharat Scouts and Guides. St Paul's School, Darjeeling. Highgate School, London. Trinity College, Cambridge. Principal of Language School. Married.

JANE FLEMING: Born Chabua, Assam 1935, daughter of William Fleming CIE, General Manager, The Assam Oil Company Limited, and his wife Jean Lennox Hastings. The New School, Darjeeling. Headington School, Oxford. Royal Academy of Dramatic Art. BBC Production Assistant. Children's Television Recruitment Assistant, BBC. Office Manager, Janssen Pharmaceutical Company Ltd. Divorced. 1s 1d.

LAURENCE FLEMING: Born Shillong 1929, brother of above. The New School, Calcutta and Darjeeling. Repton School, Derbyshire. National Service RAF. St Catharine's College, Cambridge. Author, Artist, Garden Designer. Single.

FAY FOUCAR: Born Moulmein, Burma 1923, daughter of E. C.V Foucar, Barrister-at-law, author of several books on Burma and of the official history of the First Burma Campaign in 1942. Father and two brothers started a timber business in Burma in the 1880s. Private school in Rottingdean. Roedean. Married. 2d.

ADRIAN FRITH: Born Wellington, Coonoor 1928, son of Lt. Col. John Frith, Indian Army, The Baluch Regiment, and his wife Erica Bovey. Winchester College, Hampshire. National Service in Military Police. Queens' College, Cambridge. Bombay Burmah Trading Co., Singapore. Craigmyle Company Ltd, London. Married. 1d.

PATRICK GIBSON: Born Walton-on-Thames 1928, son of Edward Leslie Gibson, The Bombay Burmah Trading Co., and his wife Charlotte Noreen Fuller-Good. Uplands School, Heathfield, Sussex. Highlands School, Kaban Djahe, Sumatra. Hallett War School, Naini Tal. Highgate School, London. 47 years in the Chemical Industry. Author of *Childhood Lost*. Married. 2s 2d.

ELSPET GRAY: Born Inverness 1929, daughter of James MacGregor-Gray, Lloyds Bank, and his wife Elspet Eleanor Morrison. Actress. Married. 2d 2s.

JANE GRICE: Born Calcutta 1935, daughter of William Henry Grice, Managing Director ICI (India) Ltd, Commanding Officer Calcutta Light Horse, and his wife Doris May Walsh. The New School, Darjeeling. St Felix School, Southwold. Ordrey Fleming School of Speech Therapy. Speech Therapist. Married twice. 2s 2d.

JOAN GRIMLEY: Born London 1930, elder daughter of Lt. Col. Harry Bridgeman Grimley MBE (Military), Royal Indian Army Service Corps, and his wife Margaret Elsie Grimley, Pianist. Loreto Convent, Simla. Secretarial Course at Brighton Technical College. Diocesan Office, Lahore. Peabody Trust, Secretary to Director, then Admin Officer. Single.

AURIOL GURNER: Born Calcutta 1927, third daughter of Sir Walter Gurner CSI ICS and his wife Phyllis Mills Carver. Southall, Surrey. Westonbirt, Gloucestershire. The New School, Calcutta and Darjeeling. Garnell College of Education, Roehampton. Lecturer, Further Education, Open University (BA Hons), Teacher of Secretarial Subjects in Technical Colleges. Married. 2d.

LYNETTE GURNER: Born London 1925, elder sister of above. St Monica's, Surrey. Westonbirt, Gloucestershire. The New School, Calcutta and Darjeeling. Garnell College of Education, Roehampton. Lecturer, Further Education, Open University (BA Hons). Married. 2s.

EVELYN ROSE HADLEY: Born Edinburgh 1934, second daughter of Owen Hadley, Chief Accountant Burmah Oil Company, and his wife Effie Richardson. Married.

RUBY HADLEY: Born Rangoon 1921, eldest daughter of Owen Hadley, sister of above. Married. 3d.

BRIAN PETER HASKINS: Born Lewisham 1933, only child of John Begley Haskins, Chief Engineer Oudh & Tirhout and Bengal Nagpur Railways, and his wife Joan Mary Lilley, a professional nurse. Woodstock School, Landour. Portora, Northern Ireland. Loughborough College. Chief Engineer for British Waterways. Married. 1s 1d.

CLARE HAYNES: Born Cork 1921, third daughter of Major Edward John Haynes, IEME (Indian Electrical and Mechanical Engineers) Indian Army, and his wife Marjorie Denning. Convent of Jesus and Mary, Murree. Red Cross VAD 1944–46. Married. 1d.

ANN HENRY: Born Bushey Heath 1925, eldest child of Brigadier T.R. Henry CBE, 8th Punjab Regiment, and his wife Dora Dalton. Uplands School, St Leonard's-on-Sea. Presentation Convent, Srinagar. Hallett War School, Naini Tal. Radio Mechanic in Woman's Auxiliary Corps (India). Trained as Nurse at St Thomas's Hospital, London. Married. 3d.

ROBIN HERBERT CBE: Born London 1934, son of Sir John Herbert GCIE Governor of Bengal, and his wife Lady Mary Fox-Strangways. Singamari,

Darjeeling. Eton College, Berkshire. Royal Horse Guards. Christ Church, Oxford. Chairman, Leopold Joseph Holdings PLC. President and Chairman of Council, Royal Horticultural Society. Divorced. 2s 2d.

CARL HIGGINSON: Born Andal, Bengal 1935, third son of Charles Higginson, Mail Driver on East India and Northern Railways, and his wife Dorothy McCready. Railway Schools at Asansol, Bengal, and Dhanbad, Bihar. St Patrick's High School, Asansol. Girls' High School, Cawnpore. Storeman at Energen Food Limited. Fitter/Machinist (Engineering) at Babcock Wire Equipment Limited. Married twice. 2s 1d.

DICK HINDMARSH: Born Lyme Regis, 1931, son of Lt. Col. J.H.L. Hindmarsh and his wife Phyllis Palmer, National Service in Royal Artillery. University of London. Teacher of English and Physical Education. Examiner in English for University of Cambridge Board. Married.

FRANK HIPPMAN: Born Aldershot 1923, son of Sergeant W. Hippman MM, Royal Fusiliers, and his wife Chrissie Leedham. Lawrence School, Mount Abu. Apprentice RAF Cranwell 1939. Fleet Air Arm 1942–44. Commissioning Course 1956. Flight Lieutenant 1959. Retired from RAF 1978. Technical writer, retired. Married. 3s.

GLORIA HOLLINS: Born Jubbulpore 1927, daughter of Albert G. Hollins, The Great Indian Peninsular Railway, and his wife, Agnes Kenny (born Rangoon 1894). Hebron High School, Coonoor. Lawrence School, Lovedale. Hebron again. Nurse. General Training, St Mary's Paddington. Midwifery at Shoreham-by-Sea and Epsom. Norfolk General Hospital, Ontario. St John's Hospital, Lewisham. Single.

PAMELA HOPKINS: Born Jubbulpore 1932, daughter of Alan Hopkins, Indian Forestry Service, and his wife. St Hilda's, Ootacamund. After marriage, lived mostly in Ghana. Married. 3s.

DONALD FERGUSON HOWIE: Born Meerut 1918, younger son of Staff Sergeant Charles Thomas Howie, the Bedfordshire Regiment, later Regimental Instructor to the Auxiliary Forces, India for the North Western Railway, and his wife Ethel Muriel. Lawrence Royal Military School, Sanawar, Simla Hills. Chelmsford Training College for European Teachers, Ghora Gali, Murree. War Service in Indian Army Ordinance Corps. Royal Army Educational Corps until 1964. Retired Major, later School Teacher. Married. 1s 1d.

HAZEL INNES: Born Ickenham 1930, daughter of Norman Innes, The Gramophone Company, India and London, Lt. Col. Indian Engineers (Emergency Commissioned Officer) and his wife, Daisy Phillips. Mount Hermon School, Darjeeling. Author of *Under the Old School Topee* (BACSA 1990 and 1995). Married.

ELIZABETH IRELAND: Born Scone, Perthshire 1914, only child of John Ireland, Manager, Confectionery Department, East India Distilleries and Sugar Factories, Nellikuppam, Madras, and his wife Bell McGibbon McCormick. Prep School at Coonoor. St Hilda's, Ootacamund. Adcote School, Shrewsbury. Secretarial Training in Glasgow. Finally Secretary to General Manager, Director of Redpath, Dorman, Long Limited, Glasgow. Single.

LAVENDER JAMIESON: Born Edinburgh 1914, younger daughter of Henry William Jamieson, Chief Auditor, Great Indian Peninsular Railway, and his wife Lorna Grieve. School Matron. Red Cross in Belgium. Single.

BARBARA ANN JARDINE: Born Peshawar NWFP 1925, eldest daughter of Lionel Jardine ICS, serving in Lucknow, Peshawar, Dik, Kashmir, Central Provinces and Baroda, and his wife Marjorie. Sherfield School, Simla. Sophia College, Bombay. Married. 2d.

JOHN JUDGE: Born Sydney 1928, eldest son of 'Mick' Judge CIE, MD of Govan Bros Ltd., Delhi & Rampur UP. Sheikh Bagh School, Srinagar. Aitchison College, Lahore. Bradfield College, Berkshire. Royal Navy 1946-83, followed by several civilian jobs. Married. 1d 2s.

DESMOND KELLY MD FRCP FRCPsych: Born Loilem, Shan States 1934. Son of Lt. Col. Norman Kelly OBE, Burma Frontier Service and his wife Betty Megarry. Hallett War School, Naini Tal. King's School, Canterbury. Visiting Professor University College, London. Medical Director, The Priory Hospital, Roehampton. Married. 2s.

MAEVE KELLY: Born Loilem, Shan States, 1933, sister of above. Hallett War School, Naini Tal. Felixstowe College, Suffolk. Journalist and Registered Nurse. Divorced. 4s 2d.

NETTIE LAMONT: Born Glasgow 1926, eldest daughter of Donald Lamont MBE, Shipping Engineer with Simons & Co. Clydeside, and his wife Jane Beattie Wilson. Hebron High School, Coonoor, Women's Auxiliary Corps (India). Domestic Science at Orchard Road College, Edinburgh. Married. 2d.

JOHN LANGLEY: Born Calcutta 1931, only child of Horace Vernon Langley, Eastern Bengal and Assam Bengal Railways, and his wife Mary Audrey Clark. The New School, Calcutta and Darjeeling. Convent, Haflong. Gresham's School, Holt, Norfolk. Royal Naval Air Service. Bournemouth School of Art. School of Architecture, Oxford. Architect. Fellow of Royal Architectural Institute of Canada. Received an Award for his restoration of the Old Masters Galleries in Ontario Art Gallery, Toronto. In Canada since 1957. Married 1s 1d.

JONATHAN LAWLEY: Born Murree 1936, eldest son of Wilfred Lawley OBE, Indian Service of Engineers and his wife Elizabeth Lowis. Sheikh Bagh,

Srinagar. Whitestone School, Bulawayo. Rhodes University, Grahamstown. St John's College, Cambridge. Colonial Service in Africa 1960–69, in business in Africa 1969–94. Africa Director of British Executive Service Overseas 1994–2000. PhD City University 1996. Director The Royal African Society 2000–2003. Married 1s 2d.

ELIZABETH LEIGH: Born Preston 1939, eldest child of Cecil Leigh, Agent, Imperial Bank of India and his wife Eve Ashcroft. Acton Reynold School, Shropshire. Women's Royal Naval Service, Admiralty and Gibraltar. Communications/Secretary, Foreign and Commonwealth Office, Delhi, Budapest, Lagos and Washington D.C. Lived in Canada for six years after marriage. Married.

JEREMY LEMMON: Born Calcutta 1935, third child of Richard Dennis Lemmon, Merchant, and his wife Dorothy Constance Harris. Hilltop School, Kalimpong. Northaw, Kent. Harrow School, Middlesex. Christ Church, Oxford. Head of English at Harrow School for 25 years, Author of several books on the Shakespearian Theatre. Single.

JOHN LETHBRIDGE: Born Leeds 1926, eldest son of Montagu Lethbridge ICS, and his wife Ann Christian. Hebron School, Coonoor. The New School, Calcutta and Darjeeling. Royal Military College, Dehra Dun. Commissioned into Royal Engineers, attached Bengal Sappers and Miners. Trinity College, Cambridge. Chartered Accountant. Married. 1s 1d.

NANCY LLOYD: Born 1918, youngest daughter of Sir Idwal Lloyd ICS and his wife. Teaching Diploma ARCM, teacher of the violin for over twenty years. Married.

RUTH LUCAS: Born Bolton 1917, daughter of Frederick Lucas, Captain Indian Army Royal Engineers and Chief Engineer, Carnatic Mill, Perhambur, Madras, and his wife Sarah Anne Caldwell. St Hilda's, Ootacamund. Adcote School, near Shrewsbury. Skerry's College, Liverpool. Secretary, Ministry of Transport. Teacher of Shorthand, Post Office, London. Village Sub-Post Master. Married. 1s 1d.

JONQUIL MALLINSON: Born Jubbulpore 1930, elder daughter of Lt. Col. Ernest (Simon) Mallinson, 17th Dogra Regiment, Indian Army, and his wife Flora (Pat) Carson. St Joan's School, Srinagar. Rosemead, Littlehampton. Married into Colonial Police Service, living in Kenya, Uganda and Sarawak. Married. 3d.

ORIOLE MALLINSON: Born Srinagar, 1932, younger sister of above and niece of Miss Muriel Mallinson MBE CMS, Principal Sheikh Bagh School for Girls, Srinagar. St Joan's School, Srinagar. Hereford House, Ilfracombe. Limura Girls School, Nairobi. Married life in Bihar, Tanzania and Kenya. Married. 1s.

ROBIN MALLINSON: Born Srinagar (on a houseboat) 1928, elder brother of above and nephew of Sir Charles Carson KCIE OBE ICS, Finance Minister in Gwalior. Breeks Memorial School, Ootacamund. Fettes College, Edinburgh. University College, Oxford (Hockey Blue). National Service in Royal Artillery, 2nd Lieut. serving in Kenya. Chartered Accountant and Finance Director, Alcan Aluminium (Latin America). Married. 4s.

ANN MARINDIN: Born London 1934, elder daughter of F.J. Marindin, Burmah-Shell, and his wife Marcia Gordon Firebrace. St Hilda's, Ootacamund. Married. 1s 1d.

ROBERT MATTHEWS: Born Delhi 1931, second son of Arnold Monteath Matthews, Professor of English at Forman Christian College, Lahore, and his wife Alys Belletti. Lawrence College, Ghora Gali. Managing Director, Deutsche Extrakt Kaffee UK Ltd. Married twice. 3d.

PATRICIA McCOY: Born Bangalore 1928, only child of Captain William James McCoy, Queen Victoria's Own Madras Sappers and Miners, and his wife Florence Brake. Bishop Cotton's Girls' High School, Bangalore. Secretary to Builders Merchant. Married. 1d 1s.

HELEN McLAREN: Born Rangoon 1926, only daughter of Alexander McLaren, Head of A.F. Ferguson & Company, Lahore, and his wife Catherine Mitchell. McLaren High, Callander, Scotland. Mrs Ancrum's School for Young Ladies, Gulmarg, Kashmir and Lahore. Married. 2s 1d.

MOLLY MILNE: Born Rangoon 1927, eldest child of Eric Ivan Milne, Traffic Manager, Burma Railways, and his wife Doris Ransford. Pinewood, Crowborough, Sussex. BBA School, Rangoon. Hallett War School, Naini Tal. Eastbourne School of Domestic Science. Married twice. 2s 2d.

ANN MITCHELL: Born Saharanpur UP 1928, daughter of Harold Mitchell CIE, Indian Police, Deputy Inspector General, Allahabad, and his wife Edna Evadne Bion. Woodstock School, Landour. Council of Europe, Strasbourg. Married. 2s 1d.

MICHAEL MULLER: Born Murree 1930, son of Colonel Hugo Muller, Indian Army, and his wife Veronica Buck. Sheikh Bagh Preparatory School, Srinagar. Wellington College, Berkshire. Jesus College, Cambridge. Consulting Engineer. MA FR Eng FICE. Married. 2d 1s.

MALCOLM MURPHY: Born Madras 1920, son of Joe Murphy, Senior Chargeman, Madras and Southern Mahratta Railway, and Company Sergeant Major Auxiliary Force (India), and his wife Louise Magee. St Mary's European High School, Madras. War Service in Wiltshire Regiment and Indian Army Corps of Clerks. Served on North West Frontier and with Chindits, Burma. International Computers Limited (India), Bombay. Married. 1s.

SHIRLEY ODLING: Born Kalimpong 1926, third daughter of Norman Odling, Architect, and his wife Bunty Graham, daughter of Dr Graham of the Homes. Educated at the Homes, Battle Abbey, Sussex and Sherborne School for Girls, Dorset. Joined Field Artillery Nursing Yeomanry 1944 in UK and returned to India. Married. 2s 1d.

TIMOTHY O'BRIEN: Born Shillong 1929, elder son of Captain Brian Palliser Tighe O'Brien, 2nd Battalion 8th Gurkha Rifles, and his wife Elinor Laura Mackenzie. Wellington College, Berkshire. Corpus Christi, Cambridge. Stage Designer. Married.

IAN O'LEARY: Born Oxford 1927, son of Michael George O'Leary MBE, Lieut. Colonel 8/2 Punjab Regiment, and his wife Daphne Sylvia Osmaston. Hallett War School, Naini Tal. Royal Indian Military College, Dehra Dun. Commissioned into Royal Indian Engineers. Service in Burma and Singapore. Managed a trading company in Nigeria. Pilot's licence in UK. Various employment in USA. Married.

TONY ORCHARD: Born Mombasa, Kenya 1926, elder son of G.L. Orchard, Burmah-Shell Oil Company, and his wife Dorothy Watkins. The New School, Calcutta and Darjeeling. Hilton College, Natal, South Africa. University of London. Director, European New Products Development, Quaker-Europe Oats Company. Married. 2s.

GILLIAN OWERS: Born London 1927, only child of Bernard Charles Owers, Sinclair, Murray of Calcutta, and his wife Millicent Ellacott Pethick. The New School, Calcutta and Darjeeling. School of Art, Calcutta. Ruskin School of Drawing and Fine Art, Oxford. Sculptor and Arts Instructor. Divorced. 4ch.

DESMOND PAILTHORPE: Born at Sea 1922. Retired Major. Lives Lancashire.

BLAKE PINNELL: Born St Leonard's-on-Sea 1925, elder son of L.G. Pinnell CIE ICS, District Commissioner for Chittagong, and his wife Margaret Coxwell. Hurst Court School, Ore, Sussex. The New School, Calcutta and Darjeeling. University of Cape Town, South Africa. Balliol College, Oxford. Economist with Finance Corporation IBM (United Kingdom) and Pilkington Brothers. Married. 1s 1d.

MARTIN PINNELL: Born Darjeeling 1928, younger brother of above. The New School, Calcutta and Darjeeling. Balliol College, Oxford. Computer Systems Engineer. Married. 3d.

SHIRLEY POCOCK: Born Cawnpore 1925, younger daughter of Major S.R. Pocock CBE MC, The Leinster Regiment, The Machine Gun Corps and The Welch Regiment, and his wife Florence Albin. Hallet War School, Naini Tal. Sophia College, Bombay. Associated Advertising Agencies, Simla. Married.

DENNIS POWELL: Born Toungoo 1931, son of Valentine Murray Powell, Chief Operating Superintendent, Burma Railways, and his wife Kathleen Kendall. Bishop Cotton's School, Simla. Felsted School, Essex. Royal Engineers. Data Analyst with Welding Institute.

ANNE PROWSE: Born Ootacamund 1935, elder daughter of Dr Arthur Skardon (Keith) Prowse, Medical Director, The Assam Oil Company, and his wife Joan Willoughby Grant. The New School, Darjeeling. St Hilda's, Ootacamund. Effingham Hall School, Bexhill. Uplyme Domestic Science College. Nursing training Middlesex Hospital, London. Ward Sister to 1961. Married. 1s.

BETTY PAKENHAM-WALSH: Born Rangoon 1926, daughter of Wilfrid Pakenham-Walsh, ICS, and his wife Gwen Elliott. Uplands, Heathfield, Sussex. Tormead, Guildford, Surrey. Mrs Ancrum's Class in Lahore and Gulmarg. Women's Royal Naval Service 1944–46 at Bletchley Park, decoding. Motor Transport Section, Royal Naval Air Direction Centre, Haverfordwest. Married. 2s.

JOHN PAKENHAM-WALSH CB QC: Born Rangoon 1928, younger brother of above. Bradfield College, Berkshire. University College, Oxford. Barrister. Crown Counsel, Hong Kong 1953–57. Parliamentary Counsel, Nigeria 1958–61. Home Office 1961–87. Standing Counsel to General Synod of Church of England 1988–2000. Married. 1s 4d.

PATRICIA RAYNES: Born Rangoon 1932, elder daughter of Charles Raynes, MC King's Police Medal, Deputy Inspector General, Burma Police, and his wife Doreen Heenan. Hallett War School, Naini Tal. Uganda Electricity Board, Kampala. Part-time Secretary at Bracknell College. Married. 2s.

PETER ROBB: Born Ceylon 1927, son of James Alexander Robb, General Manager of ESSO, Ceylon and Bengal, and his wife Dorothy Louisa Bicknell. The New School, Calcutta and Darjeeling. King William College, Isle of Man. National Benzole, Shell and BP. Married. 2s 2d.

RONALD RULE: Born Singapore 1918, son of Malcolm Rule, Operator and Accountant with the Eastern Extension Telegraph Company in Batavia, Singapore and Penang, and his wife Margaret Fitzpatrick. Bishop Cotton's School, Bangalore. Breeks Memorial School, Ootacamund. Deal School, Kent. War Service with the Buffs. British Malayan Administration, Singapore Magistrate. Shell Group from 1949. Married. 3ch.

THELMA SMART: Born Jhansi 1929, daughter of Major J.W. Smart, Royal Army Ordinance Corps, and his wife Leah Mary Carvalho. Convent of Jesus and Mary, Murree. St Mary's Convent, Naini Tal. Married twice, 2d 5s.

LYNETTE SMITH: Born Madura 1931, daughter of Charles Harry Smith (High School, Baldwin's, Bangalore), Special Grade Driver, South Indian Railway, Madura, and his wife Hilda May Cuxton, Steno-Typist at A.&F. Harvey Mills, Madura. St John's Vestry High School, Trichinopoly. London Chamber of Commerce, Madras. Diploma of Short Stories and Creative Writing, Melbourne, Australia. IBM Data Processing, Australia. Private Secretary, Australian Federal Government, Perth, Western Australia. Married twice. 1s 1d.

PADDY SMITH: Born Calcutta 1931, son of Francis Arthur Smith MBE CEng FIMechE, Chief Mechanical Engineer, Bengal and Assam Railway, and his wife Lilian Evelyn. Loreto Convent, Darjeeling. St Paul's School, Darjeeling. Campbell College, Northern Ireland. Naval Architect. Married.

HAZEL SQUIRE: Born Lahore 1928, eldest daughter of Sir Giles Squire, Indian Political Service and future Ambassador to Afghanistan, and his wife Irene Arnold, teacher at a Muslim Girls' School in Hyderabad. Headington School, Oxford. Royal College of Music. Worked with Moral Re-Armament Movement. Married. 2s.

KRISTIN SQUIRE: Born Mount Abu 1930, second daughter of Sir Giles Squire, younger sister of above. Auckland House School, Simla. Badminton School, Bristol. King's College of Household and Social Science, London. Degree in Social Science. Worked in many countries with Moral Re-Armament Movement. Bred and showed Haflinger Ponies. Married.

STAR STAUNTON: Born Assam Jungle, 1922, only child of Major Staunton and his first wife. Convent in Belgium. Married. ch.

BEULAH STIDSTON: Born Lahore 1933, only child of Dr Dudley Stidston, North Western Railway and Major Indian Army, and his wife Elizabeth Violet Brown-James. St Mary's School, Poona. Moved to New Zealand 1948. Chartered Accountant, New Zealand. Company Accountant, Australia. Judged Australian Cattle Dogs at Crufts, 2002. Married twice.

PATRICK HUGH STEVENAGE: Born Bangalore 1922, younger son of Emanuel Anthony Stevenage, Captain, Senior Assistant Surgeon, Indian Medical Department, and his wife Helena Augusta Rylands. Loyola College, Madras. MA (Econ). Fellow of Association of Certified and Corporate Accountants. Senior Finance Officer, British Railways Board. Author of *A Railway Family in India* (BACSA). Married twice. 2s 2d.

DAVID MICHAEL THOM: Born Quetta 1938, son of Reginald Wallace Thom MBE, Divisional Mechanical Engineer, North Western Railway, and his second wife Kathleen. Half-brother to Barry Bryson. Presentation Convent, Rawalpindi. Karachi Grammar School. Hardeys School, Dorchester. Heles School, Exeter. National Service RAF. Architectural Consultant. Married. 4s 1d.

GRETA THOM: Born Rawalpindi 1930, daughter of Francis Thom, Assistant Mechanical Engineer, North Western Railway, and his wife Audrey Grassby. Auckland House School, Simla. Property Negotiator. Church Organist. Musical Director of a Gilbert and Sullivan Society. Divorced. 2s 1d.

VALERIE THURLEY: Born Bangalore 1934, daughter of S.J. Thurley OBE, Principal of Lawrence College, Ghora Gali, and his wife Doreen McLeish Game. Lawrence College, Ghora Gali. Married. 1s 5d.

LAVENDER TODD: Born Quetta 1926, younger daughter of Sir Herbert Todd KCIE ICS, Resident for the Madras States 1943, Resident for the Eastern States 1944 (later Chief Representative, Iraq Petroleum Company, Baghdad), and his wife Nancy, second daughter of Col. A.F. Pullen, Commanding Officer, Royal Artillery, Rangoon (awarded the Kaisar-i-Hind Gold Medal and the Red Crescent for her work in the Second World War). Godolphin School, Salisbury. 'Sherfield', Delhi and Simla. Women's Auxiliary Service (Burma) 1943. Married. 1s 1d.

JOAN TOFT: Born Eastbourne 1926, eldest daughter of Walter Toft, Senior Partner, Price, Waterhouse, Peat & Company, Calcutta, and his wife Kathleen Kearney. Chartwell, Westgate-on-Sea. St Bridget's, Bexhill. The New School, Calcutta and Darjeeling. Teacher's Training Course at Bishop Sutton School, Alresford, Hampshire. Later ran her own Riding School, first at Alresford, then at Fordingbridge. Single.

PATRICIA TOFT: Born Cowley, Middlesex 1930, second daughter of Walter Toft, sister of above. The New School, Darjeeling. Nazareth Convent, Ootacamund. Wessex School of Dancing, Bournemouth. International Ballet School, London. Ballet Teacher. Aromatherapist. Married. 1s 3d.

SALLY TOFT: Born Cowley, Middlesex 1934, youngest daughter of Walter Toft, sister of above. The New School, Darjeeling. Lowther College, Abergele. London College of Secretaries. Secretary to Bishop Trevor Huddlestone. Married. 1s 1d.

MARK TULLY: Born Calcutta 1935, eldest son of William Tully, CBE, Gillanders, Arbuthnot, Calcutta, and his wife Patience Betts. The New School, Darjeeling. Marlborough College, Wiltshire. The Royal Dragoon Guards. Trinity Hall, Cambridge. Joined BBC in 1964 and became their Chief of Bureau in New Delhi. Author, Journalist and Broadcaster. Knighted 2002. Married. 2s 2d.

ROY ELMO DE VANDRE: Born Sibi, Baluchistan 1926, son of Frederick Charles Valentine Downes, Loco-Foreman North Western Railway, and his wife Janet Maude Stringer. Lawrence College, Ghora Gali. St Anthony's High School, Lahore. Chelmsford College. Commissioned into Indian Army, 10th Gurkha Rifles. Transferred to British Army Sherwood Forresters. Wounded in

Korea. Colonial Police, Kenya and Uganda. Later Dunlop and British Leyland. Married. 2s 8d.

BETSY VICKERS: Born Windsor 1927, daughter of O. Lionel Vickers, Methodist Missionary Society, and his wife Bertha Isabella Aitken. Hebron High School, Coonoor. Edgehill College, Bideford. Hebron again. Worked as a Secretary in The Gambia, then for the World Wildlife Fund as a volunteer for 15 years. Married.

HILARY VIRGO: Born Calcutta 1927, only child of Sidney Virgo, Bank Manager with Imperial Bank of India, and his wife Rita Hay. High Trees School, Horley. The New School, Calcutta and Darjeeling. Bournemouth School of Art. Central School of Art, London. Painter, Theatre Costume Designer. Fellow of Guild of Glass Engravers. Single.

NICOLE WALBY: Born Antwerp 1926, elder daughter of Herbert Walby DSO MC Croix-de-Guerre, Manager of Jenson & Nicholson Ltd (paints, varnishes etc) Calcutta, and his wife Marie Magdeleine Ville. The New School, Darjeeling. Slade School of Art, London. Ecole des Beaux Arts, Paris. Worked in a textile studio in Paris. Art Teacher in London. Married. 2s 1d.

THEON WILKINSON MBE: Born Cawnpore 1924, son of Harold Arthur Wilkinson CBE, Managing Director of Begg, Sutherland & Company Ltd (Agents for Cotton, Electricity, Sugar etc) and his wife Ruby Georgina Butterworth. Radley College, Abingdon. St Paul's School, Darjeeling. Captain, 3rd Gurkhas. Worcester College, Oxford. District Commissioner, Kenya. Personnel Management, various organisations. Founder of BACSA 1976. MBE 1986. Married. 1s.

ZOE WILKINSON MBE: Born Cawnpore 1922, sister of above. Wycombe Abbey, Bucks. MBE 1958 for work in India at the United Kingdom Citizens Association School (now Shieling House), a community enterprise. Author of *Traders and Nabobs: The British in Cawnpore 1765–1857* and *Boxwallahs: The British in Cawnpore 1857–1901*. Married. 2s 1d.

FRANCES WINDRAM: Born Holywood, Co. Down 1929, Daughter of Major William Windram, Royal Inniskillings, and his wife Jessie Hadland. Hebron School, Coonoor. Wellesley School, Naini Tal. Hallet War School, Naini Tal. Women's Royal Naval Service 1949–66. Married. 1s.

SHEILA WRIGHT-NEVILLE: Born London 1927, elder daughter of Col. V.R. Wright-Neville, 5th/2nd Punjab Regiment, and his wife, Gwenneth Northe. The Old Vicarage School, Richmond, Surrey. The New School, Calcutta and Darjeeling. Secretarial College, London. Managed an antiquarian bookshop with international mailing list. Human Resources Officer with Provincial Government. Married. 1s 1d.